THE INNOVATORS

The 100 Most Influential
Entrepreneurs of All Time

Piers M. Wolf

The Business House

Copyright © 2023 Piers M. Wolf

All rights reserved

No part of this book may be reproduced, or stored in a retrieval system, or transmitted in any form or by any means, electronic, mechanical, photocopying, recording, or otherwise, without express written permission of the publisher.

ISBN-13: 9798390625446

Cover design by: Art Painter
Library of Congress Control Number: 2018675309
Printed in the United States of America

To those who suffered so the rest would prosper

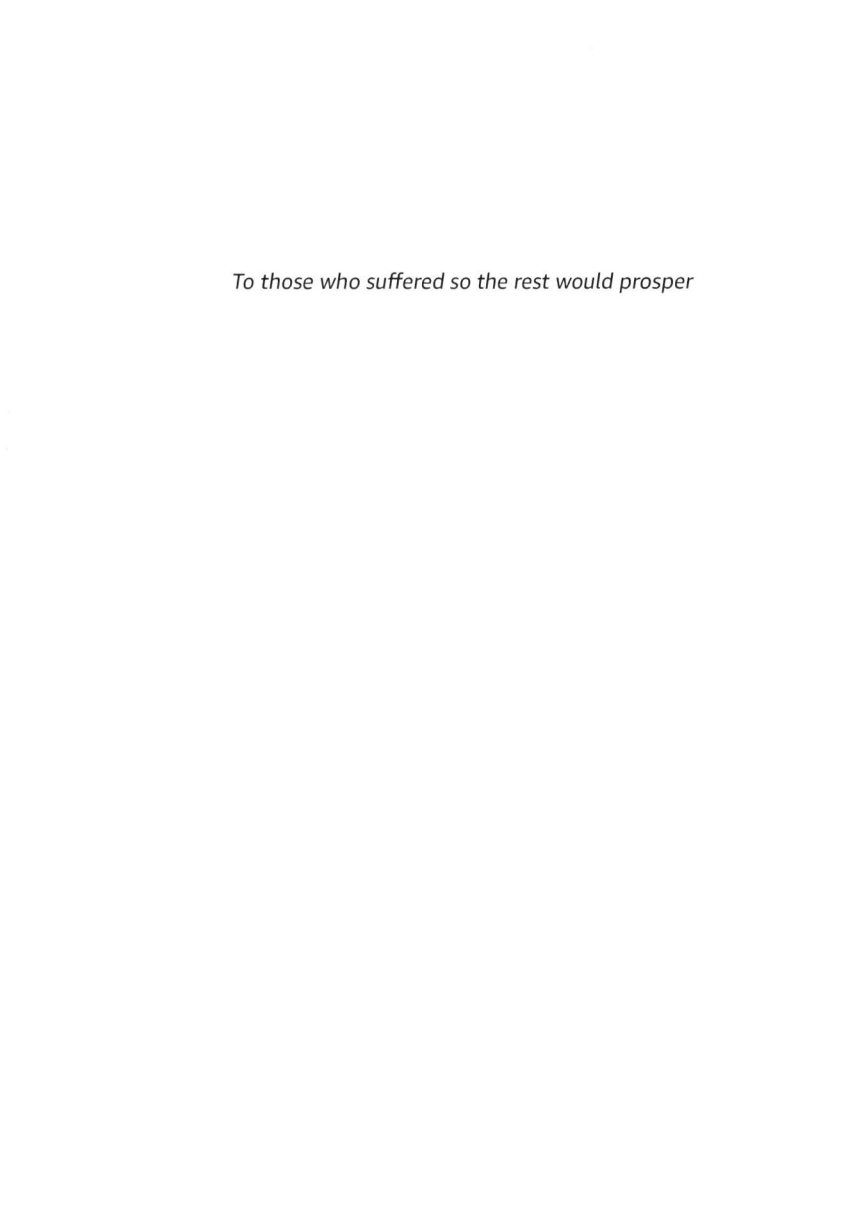

"In your actions, don't procrastinate. In your conversations, don't confuse. In your thoughts, don't wander. In your soul, don't be passive or aggressive. In your life, don't be all about business."

MARCUS AURELIUS

CONTENTS

Title Page
Copyright
Dedication
Epigraph
Introduction
The Innovators   1
Mohamed Al Fayed   6
Mary Kay Ash   12
Bernard Arnault   20
P.T. Barnum   26
Marc Benioff   32
Linda Bennett   38
Silvio Berlusconi   43
Jeff Bezos   49
Michael Bloomberg   55
Richard Branson   61
Sergey Brin   67
Matthew Boulton   73
Asa Griggs Candler   79
Andrew Carnegie   85
Shawn "Jay-z" Carter   91

Steve Case	97
Coco Chanel	103
Brian Chesky	109
Tim Cook	115
King Croesus	121
Mark Cuban	127
Adam D'Angelo	133
Walt Disney	139
Jack Dorsey	145
George Eastman	151
Thomas Alva Edison	157
Daniel Ek	163
Larry Ellison	170
Henry Ford	176
Simon Fuller	182
Bill Gates	188
David Geffen	194
Katharine Graham	200
Edward H. Harriman	207
Reed Hastings	213
William Randolph Hearst	220
Hugh Hefner	226
Conrad Hilton	232
Ryan Hoover	238
Tony Hsieh	244
Ma Huateng	250
Ariana Huffington	256
Howard Hughes	262

Lee Iacocca	269
Steve Jobs	275
Peter Jones	281
Lyn Jurich	287
Henry J. Kaiser	293
Travis Kalanick	300
Ingvar Kamprad	306
Herb Kelleher	311
Adnan Khashoggi	318
Dara Khosrowshahi	324
Phil Knight	330
Ray Kroc	336
Estée Lauder	343
William Lever	349
Henry Luce	355
Jack Ma	360
John Mackey	366
Andrew W. Mellon	372
J.P. Morgan	377
Elon Musk	384
Xavier Niel	390
Simon Nixon	396
Alfred Nobel	402
Aristotle Onassis	408
Larry Page	414
Sean Parker	421
Kevin Plank	427
Francois Henri Pinault	434

Marjorie Merriweather Post	441
Sumner Redstone	447
John D. Rockefeller	453
Anita Roddick	460
Meyer Amschel Rothschild	466
Charles Saatchi	472
Howard Schultz	478
James Sinegal	484
Carlos Slim Helu	490
Alfred P. Sloan	496
George Soros	502
Martha Stewart	508
Penny Streeter	513
Gerard Swope	519
Sakichi Toyoda	526
Donald Trump	532
Ted Turner	538
Cornelius Vanderbilt	544
Gary Vaynerchuk,	550
Madam CJ Walker	556
Sam Walton	563
Aaron Montgomery Ward	569
Jack Warner	575
Thomas Watson Jr.	581
James Watt	586
Josiah Wedgwood	593
Charles Kemmons Wilson	599
Oprah Winfrey	606

Mark Zuckerberg	613
Epilogue	621
good luck	623

INTRODUCTION

Entrepreneurship and business have been fundamental to the growth and prosperity of human societies since the dawn of civilization. From the earliest traders and merchants who exchanged goods and services across great distances, to the titans of modern industry who have transformed entire sectors and reshaped the global economy, entrepreneurs and businessmen have been among the most important drivers of innovation, wealth creation, and social progress.

In this book, we will explore the lives and legacies of 100 of the most influential entrepreneurs and businessmen of all time. These individuals represent a diverse array of backgrounds, industries, and eras, but they all share a common thread: a remarkable ability to identify opportunities, mobilize resources, and create value where none existed before.

Some of the entrepreneurs and businessmen profiled in this book are household names, instantly recognizable for their iconic products, services, or brands. Others are lesser-known figures whose contributions to business and society have been equally significant, but perhaps less widely celebrated. Together, they form a tapestry of innovation and achievement that spans centuries and continents, and that has shaped the world we live in today.

The stories of these 100 entrepreneurs and businessmen are as varied as they are inspiring. Some overcame incredible obstacles and adversity to achieve success, while others were born into privilege and leveraged their advantages to great effect. Some were visionary pioneers who saw opportunities where others saw only challenges, while others were shrewd tacticians who outmaneuvered their competitors with cunning strategy and decisive action.

But despite their differences, all of these entrepreneurs and businessmen share a common set of traits and skills that have made them successful. They are all risk-takers, willing to put their own resources and reputations on the line to pursue their goals. They are all driven by a passion for their work, a belief in their own abilities, and a desire to make a difference in the world. And they are all masters of innovation, constantly seeking new and better ways to meet the needs of customers, improve efficiency, and stay ahead of the curve in a rapidly changing business landscape.

In the pages that follow, you will encounter entrepreneurs and businessmen from every corner of the globe and from every era of human history. From the ancient Egyptians who built an empire on trade and commerce, to the modern-day tech giants who are reshaping the world with their revolutionary products and services. You will meet entrepreneurs and businessmen who have built empires out of nothing, who have revolutionized entire industries, and who have left an indelible mark on the world.

But beyond the individual stories of these 100 entrepreneurs and businessmen, this book also offers a broader perspective on the history and evolution of business itself. Through the lens of these remarkable figures, we can see how business has evolved over time, adapting to changing technologies, markets, and social norms. We can see how the challenges and opportunities of different eras have shaped the strategies and tactics of entrepreneurs and businessmen, and how their innovations have in turn shaped the world around us.

In short, this book is both a celebration of the achievements of 100 remarkable individuals, and a journey through the history of business and entrepreneurship. Whether you are a student of history, a budding entrepreneur, or simply someone who is interested in the stories of extraordinary people, I hope that you will find this book informative, engaging, and inspiring.

As we explore the lives and legacies of these entrepreneurs and businessmen, it is important to note that their impact extends far beyond the realm of business. In many cases, their innovations and contributions have transformed entire societies and have had a profound influence on human progress and development.

For example, the industrial revolution, which was fueled by the innovations of entrepreneurs such as James Watt and Andrew Carnegie, brought about a transformation in the way goods were produced and distributed, paving the way for the modern consumer economy. Similarly, the rise of the internet and the digital age, which was spearheaded by entrepreneurs like Steve Jobs and Jeff Bezos, has had a profound impact on the way we communicate, work, and live our lives.

But the impact of these entrepreneurs and businessmen goes beyond just economic and technological progress. Many of them have also been philanthropists, using their wealth and influence to give back to their communities and to promote social causes. Andrew Carnegie, for example, donated much of his vast fortune to establish libraries, universities, and other institutions that have had a lasting impact on education and culture. Bill Gates, the founder of Microsoft, has dedicated his post-business career to philanthropy, using his wealth to tackle global health and development challenges through his foundation.

In writing this book, it is important to acknowledge that entrepreneurship and business are not without their challenges and controversies. Many of the entrepreneurs and businessmen we will be discussing have faced criticism for their business practices, their treatment of workers, or their impact on the environment. These are important issues that deserve serious consideration and discussion, and we will not shy away from them.

At the same time, it is important to recognize the immense positive impact that entrepreneurship and business have had on human society. From creating jobs and wealth, to driving technological and social progress, to promoting innovation and competition, entrepreneurs and businessmen have played a vital role in shaping the world we live in today.

In the pages that follow, we will explore the stories of 100 remarkable individuals who have left an indelible mark on the world of business and beyond. Through their stories, we will gain a deeper understanding of the history and evolution of entrepreneurship, and we will be inspired by their achievements and contributions to human progress.

Whether you are a student of business, a budding entrepreneur, or simply someone who is interested in the stories of remarkable individuals, I hope that this book will inform, inspire, and entertain you.

THE INNOVATORS

1. Mohamed Al-Fayed   1929-
2. Mary Kay Ash   1918-2001
3. Bernard Arnault   1949-
4. P.T. Barnum   1810-1891
5. Marc Benioff   1964-
6. Linda Bennett   1942-
7. Silvio Berlusconi   1936-
8. Jeff Bezos   1964-
9. Michael Bloomberg   1942-
10. Richard Branson   1950-
11. Sergey Brin   1973-
12. Matthew Boulton   1728-1809
13. Shasa Griggs Candler   1851-1929
14. Andrew Carnegie   1835-1919
15. Shawn Carter - Jay Z   1969-
16. Steve Case   1958-
17. Coco Chanel   1883-1971
18. Brian Chesky   1981-
19. Tim Cook   1960-
20. King Croesus   585-546 bC

21. Mark Cuban — 1958-
22. Adam D' Angelo — 1984-
23. Walt Disney — 1901-1966
24. Jack Dorsey — 1976-
25. George Eastman — 1854-1932
26. Thomas Alva Edison — 1847-1931
27. Daniel Ek — 1983-
28. Larry Ellison — 1944-
29. Henry Ford — 1863-1947
30. Simon Fuller — 1960-
31. William "Bill" Gates III — 1955-
32. David Geffen — 1943-
33. Katharine Graham — 1917-2001
34. Edward H. Harriman — 1849-1909
35. Reed Hastings — 1960-
36. William Randolph Hearst — 1863-1951
37. Hugh Hefner — 1926-2017
38. Conrad Hilton — 1887-1979
39. Ryan Hoover — 1987-
40. Tony Hsieh — 1973-2020
41. Ma Huateng — 1971-
42. Ariana Huffington — 1950-
43. Howard Hughes — 1905-1976
44. Lido Anthony "Lee" Iacocca — 1924-2019
45. Steve Jobs — 1955-2011

46. Peter Jones   1961-
47. Lynn Jurich   1979-
48. Henry J. Kaiser   1882-1967
49. Travis Kalanick   1976-
50. Ingvar Kamprad   1926-2014
51. Herb Kelleher   1931-2019
52. Adnan Khashoggi   1935-2017
53. Dara Khosrowshahi   1969-
54. Phil Knight   1938-
55. Ray Kroc   1902-1984
56. Estee Lauder   1908-2004
57. William Lever   1851-1925
58. Henry Luce   1898-1967
59. Jack Ma   1964-
60. John Mackey   1953-
61. Andrew W. Mellon   1855-1937
62. J.P. Morgan   1837-1913
63. Elon Musk   1971-
64. Xavier Niel   1967-
65. Simon Nixon   1967-
66. Alfred Nobel   1833-1896
67. Aristoteles Onassis   1906-1975
68. Larry Page   1973-
69. Sean Parker   1979-
70. Kevin Plank   1972-

71. Francois-Henri Pinault 1962-
72. Marjorie Merriweather Post 1887-1973
73. Sumner Redstone 1923-2020
74. John D. Rockefeller 1839-1937
75. Anita Roddick 1942-2007
76. Meyer Amschel Rothschild 1744-1812
77. Charles Saatchi 1943-
78. Howard Schultz 1953-
79. James Sinegal 1936-
80. Carlos Slim Helu 1940-
81. Alfred Sloan 1875-1966
82. George Soros 1930-
83. Martha Stewart 1941-
84. Penny Streeter 1967-
85. Gerard Swope 1872-1957
86. Sakichi Toyoda 1867-1930
87. Donald Trump 1946-
88. Ted Turner 1938-
89. Cornelius Vanderbilt 1794-1877
90. Gary Vaynerchuk 1975-
91. Madam CJ Walker 1867-1919
92. Sam Walton 1918-1992
93. Aaron Montgomery Ward 1843-1913
94. Jack Warner 1892-1978
95. Thomas Watson Jr 1914-1993

96. James Watt   1736-1819
97. Josiah Wedgwood   1730-1795
98. Charles Kemmons Wilson   1913-2003
99. Oprah Gail Winfrey   1954-
100. Mark Zuckerberg   1984-

Epilogue

MOHAMED AL FAYED

is a name that has become synonymous with business innovation and entrepreneurship. Born on January 27, 1929, in Alexandria, Egypt, Al Fayed has made a name for himself as one of the most successful businessmen in the world. He is known for his incredible work ethic, innovative mind, and unconventional tactics that have helped him to build a multi-billion dollar empire.

Al Fayed's business career began in the 1950s when he started working for his uncle's import-export business in Egypt. He quickly rose through the ranks and eventually became the company's managing director. However, his ambitions went beyond just managing someone else's business, and he eventually struck out on his own.

In the 1960s, Al Fayed moved to London and started a chain of successful department stores. He used his innovative mind to transform the traditional shopping experience and make it more accessible to a wider range of people. He introduced the concept of discount pricing, which was unheard of at the time, and created a shopping environment that was more appealing to younger consumers.

In the 1970s, Al Fayed made his biggest business move when he purchased Harrods, the iconic London department store. Under his leadership, Harrods underwent a massive transformation, becoming a true luxury shopping destination. He introduced a range of new products and services, such as gourmet food halls, personal shopping services, and exclusive designer boutiques. He also invested heavily in marketing and advertising, which helped to increase the store's visibility and attract even more customers.

Al Fayed's business success has not been without controversy. He has been involved in several high-profile legal battles, including a long-running dispute with the British government over his citizenship status. He has also been accused of using his wealth and influence to gain favors and manipulate the political system.

Despite these challenges, Al Fayed's legacy as a businessman and entrepreneur is undeniable. His innovative mind, hard work, and unconventional tactics have helped him to build a multi-billion dollar empire that has had a significant impact on the global business landscape. His success at Harrods has made him a true icon in the luxury retail industry, and his impact on the world of business is sure to be felt for many years to come.

In conclusion, Mohamed Al Fayed is one of the most influential business minds of all time. His innovative approach to business, his hard work, and his unconventional tactics have helped him to build a multi-billion dollar empire that has had a significant impact on the global business landscape. Despite the controversy that has surrounded him, his legacy as a businessman and entrepreneur is undeniable, and he will always be remembered as a true icon in the world of business.

Mohamed Al Fayed is known for his exceptional work ethic, innovative mind, and unconventional tactics. Here are some more details about his business practices and tactics:

Attention to detail: Al Fayed is known for his attention to detail and his insistence on perfection. He is said to be very hands-on when it comes to running his businesses, and he pays close attention to every aspect of the business. This attention to detail has helped him to create successful businesses that are known for their quality and excellence.

Innovation: Al Fayed is a true innovator and is not afraid to try new things. He has been known to introduce new products and services, as well as new business models, that have disrupted the industry and created new opportunities. For example, his introduction of discount pricing and personal shopping services at his department stores was considered groundbreaking at the time.

Risk-taking: Al Fayed is not afraid to take risks, and he has made some bold moves over the course of his career. For example, his purchase of Harrods was considered a risky move at the time, as the store was struggling financially. However, Al Fayed saw potential in the brand and was able to turn it around, making it one of the most successful luxury retailers in the world.

Customer focus: Al Fayed is known for his customer-focused approach to business. He has always put the needs and wants of his customers first and has gone to great lengths to ensure that they are satisfied. For example, his introduction of personal shopping services at Harrods was designed to make the shopping experience more personalized and enjoyable for customers.

Marketing and branding: Al Fayed is a master of marketing and branding. He has always been very savvy when it comes to promoting his businesses and creating strong brand identities. For example, his investment in advertising and marketing at Harrods helped to increase the store's visibility and attract even more customers.

Overall, Mohamed Al Fayed's business practices and tactics have been characterized by his attention to detail, innovation, risk-taking, customer focus, and marketing and branding savvy. These traits have helped him to build successful businesses that have had a significant impact on the global business landscape.

> *The one thing that he did, that an entrepreneur should follow to be great today*

It's difficult to point to just one thing that Mohamed Al Fayed did that entrepreneurs should follow to be great today, as his success was the result of a combination of factors, including his innovative approach to business, his exceptional work ethic, and his customer-focused mindset. However, if I had to choose one thing that entrepreneurs could learn from Al Fayed's example, it would be his willingness to take risks.

Throughout his career, Al Fayed was not afraid to take risks and make bold moves that others might have shied away from. For example, his purchase of Harrods was considered a risky move at the time, but he saw potential in the brand and was able to turn it around. Similarly, his introduction of discount pricing and personal shopping services at his department stores was considered groundbreaking at the time.

In today's fast-paced and constantly changing business environment, taking calculated risks is often necessary to stay ahead of the competition and create new opportunities. However, it's important to note that taking risks without careful consideration can also lead to failure. Therefore, it's essential for entrepreneurs to be strategic and thoughtful when it comes to taking risks, and to weigh the potential benefits against the potential drawbacks before making any major moves.

In summary, Mohamed Al Fayed's willingness to take risks, combined with his innovative approach to business and customer-focused mindset, were key factors in his success. Entrepreneurs looking to follow in his footsteps should consider taking calculated risks that are based on careful consideration and strategic thinking, and that have the potential to disrupt the industry and create new opportunities.

A few more things about Mohamed Al Fayed:

Humble beginnings: Al Fayed was born into a humble family in Alexandria, Egypt, and his family was not wealthy. He started his career in retail as a low-level employee at a department store in London, where he worked his way up the ranks over the years.

Entrepreneurial spirit: Al Fayed's entrepreneurial spirit was evident from a young age. Even as a child, he was always looking for ways to make money, and he sold ice cream on the streets of Alexandria to earn extra cash.

Harrods purchase: One of Al Fayed's most notable business moves was his purchase of Harrods, the luxury department store in London, in 1985. He bought the store for £615 million, and under his ownership, Harrods became one of the most profitable retail businesses in the world.

Controversy: Al Fayed has been involved in several high-profile controversies over the years, including his long-standing dispute with the British royal family over the death of his son Dodi Al Fayed and Princess Diana in a car accident in 1997. He has also been accused of corruption and bribery in his business dealings, although he has denied these allegations.

Philanthropy: Despite his controversial reputation, Al Fayed is also known for his philanthropic efforts. He has donated millions of pounds to various charitable causes over the years, including the building of a children's hospital in Egypt.

Retirement: In 2010, Al Fayed sold Harrods to the Qatari royal family for a reported £1.5 billion. He has since retired from business and now spends much of his time on his estate in Scotland.

Overall, Mohamed Al Fayed's life and career have been marked by his entrepreneurial spirit, his willingness to take risks, and his reputation for controversy. Despite these challenges, he has also been a notable philanthropist and has made a significant impact on the global business landscape.

MARY KAY ASH

Was a trailblazing businesswoman who founded Mary Kay Cosmetics, one of the most successful direct selling companies in the world. Born in Hot Wells, Texas in 1918, Mary Kay Ash was the daughter of a self-made entrepreneur who owned a successful restaurant. She developed a strong work ethic at a young age and learned the importance of hard work, determination, and perseverance.

Mary Kay Ash started her career in sales as a young woman, working for Stanley Home Products. She quickly rose through the ranks and became one of the company's top salespeople. However, despite her success, she faced discrimination and was passed over for a promotion in favor of a man she had trained. Frustrated and disillusioned, Mary Kay Ash left Stanley Home Products and started her own business.

In 1963, Mary Kay Ash founded Mary Kay Cosmetics with her son, Richard Rogers. The company's unique business model, which relied on independent sales consultants who sold products directly to customers, was revolutionary at the time. Mary Kay Cosmetics quickly became a huge success, thanks in large part to Mary Kay Ash's innovative leadership and marketing tactics.

One of Mary Kay Ash's greatest strengths as a

businesswoman was her ability to motivate and inspire her sales force. She understood that the key to success was not just in selling products, but in building relationships with customers and creating a sense of community among the sales team. To that end, she created a culture of empowerment and recognition, offering bonuses, trips, and other incentives to top performers.

Mary Kay Ash was also a pioneer in the use of technology in business. In the early 1980s, she introduced a computerized inventory system that streamlined the ordering process for sales consultants. This system, which was ahead of its time, allowed Mary Kay Cosmetics to keep track of inventory in real-time, ensuring that products were always in stock and ready to be shipped to customers.

Despite her success, Mary Kay Ash remained humble and grounded. She was known for her down-to-earth personality and her commitment to giving back to the community. She was a philanthropist who supported a wide range of causes, including cancer research, education, and women's empowerment.

Mary Kay Ash's legacy as a businesswoman is remarkable. She not only built a highly successful company from scratch, but she also inspired and empowered thousands of women to become entrepreneurs themselves. Her innovative leadership and marketing tactics helped to revolutionize the direct selling industry, and her commitment to giving back to the community set an example for others to follow.

In conclusion, Mary Kay Ash was a visionary entrepreneur who built a highly successful business through hard work, determination, and innovation. Her focus on empowering and recognizing her sales force, as well as her use of technology, helped to make Mary Kay Cosmetics one of the most successful direct selling companies in the world. Her legacy as a philanthropist and advocate for women's empowerment is equally impressive. Mary Kay Ash's life and work serve as an inspiration to entrepreneurs and business leaders everywhere, and her place among the most influential business minds of all time is well-deserved.

Mary Kay Ash was known for her innovative business tactics and her strong work ethic. Here are some additional details about her approach to business:

Empowerment and Recognition: Mary Kay Ash believed in empowering her sales force and recognizing their achievements. She understood that people are motivated by more than just money, and that recognition and a sense of accomplishment were just as important. To that end, she offered bonuses, trips, and other incentives to top performers, and created a culture of recognition within the company.

Building Relationships: Mary Kay Ash believed that building relationships with customers was essential to success in business. She encouraged her sales force to create personal connections with customers and to build a sense of community within their sales teams. She also emphasized the importance of listening to customer feedback and incorporating it into the company's product offerings and marketing strategies.

Focus on Quality: Mary Kay Ash believed that quality should be the top priority in any business. She insisted on using only the highest quality ingredients in her products and put a great deal of emphasis on research and development. She also encouraged her sales force to focus on selling quality products, rather than just pushing sales.

Use of Technology: Mary Kay Ash was a pioneer in the use of technology in business. She recognized early on the potential of computerized systems to streamline operations and improve efficiency. In the early 1980s, she introduced a computerized inventory system that allowed Mary Kay

Cosmetics to keep track of inventory in real-time, ensuring that products were always in stock and ready to be shipped to customers.

Philanthropy and Community Involvement: Mary Kay Ash was committed to giving back to the community and supporting charitable causes. She established the Mary Kay Foundation, which supports cancer research, domestic violence prevention, and other charitable causes. She also encouraged her sales force to get involved in community service and volunteer work.

Overall, Mary Kay Ash's business tactics were focused on empowerment, recognition, quality, and innovation. She believed in building strong relationships with customers and within her sales force, using technology to streamline operations, and giving back to the community. Her commitment to these principles helped her to build one of the most successful direct selling companies in the world, and her legacy as an innovative and compassionate business leader continues to inspire entrepreneurs and businesspeople today.

> *The one thing that she did, that an entrepreneur should follow to be great today*

One thing that entrepreneurs can learn from Mary Kay Ash is the importance of building relationships with customers and employees. Mary Kay Ash believed that strong relationships were the foundation of a successful business, and she worked tirelessly to create a culture of empowerment, recognition, and community within her company.

In today's highly competitive business environment, it's easy to get caught up in the day-to-day operations and lose sight of the importance of building relationships. However, taking the time to connect with customers and employees on a personal level can have a significant impact on the success of a business.

Entrepreneurs who follow Mary Kay Ash's example can benefit from:

Building a strong brand identity that resonates with customers

Creating a culture of recognition and empowerment that motivates employees to excel

Fostering a sense of community within the company that encourages collaboration and teamwork

Using technology to streamline operations and improve efficiency, while still maintaining a personal touch

Giving back to the community and supporting charitable causes, which can help build goodwill and enhance the company's reputation.

In summary, entrepreneurs who prioritize building relationships with customers and employees can create a strong foundation for long-term success, just as Mary Kay Ash did with her direct selling company. By following her example, entrepreneurs can build a loyal customer base, attract top talent, and create a culture of innovation and excellence that sets them apart from the competition.

Some additional facts about Mary Kay Ash:

Mary Kay Ash started her company, Mary Kay Cosmetics, in 1963 after working for a direct sales company for many years. She was frustrated by the gender discrimination and lack of opportunities for women in the company, and decided to start her own company that would provide more opportunities for women to succeed.

Mary Kay Ash was a pioneer in the direct sales industry, and her company became one of the largest and most successful direct selling companies in the world. She believed in the power of word-of-mouth marketing and the importance of personal relationships in building a successful sales organization.

Mary Kay Ash was known for her innovative business practices, including offering bonuses, trips, and other incentives to top performers, creating a culture of recognition within the company, and introducing a computerized inventory system to streamline operations.

Mary Kay Ash was a strong advocate for women's rights and believed that women could be successful in business if given the opportunity. She created a company culture that valued and recognized the contributions of women, and her company became a model for other businesses seeking to empower women in the workplace.

Mary Kay Ash was also committed to philanthropy and gave generously to charitable causes throughout her life. She established the Mary Kay Foundation, which supports cancer research, domestic violence prevention, and other charitable causes, and encouraged her sales force to get involved in community service and volunteer work.

Overall, Mary Kay Ash was a trailblazer in the business world, and her innovative business practices, commitment to women's rights, and dedication to philanthropy continue to inspire entrepreneurs and businesspeople today.

Back cover

From the earliest days of human civilization to the present day, entrepreneurs and businessmen have been at the forefront of driving innovation, progress, and change. In this book, we explore the stories of 100 of the most influential and groundbreaking entrepreneurs and businessmen of all time, from ancient merchants and traders to modern-day tech giants and innovators.

Through their stories, we gain a deeper understanding of the history and evolution of entrepreneurship, and we see firsthand how these individuals have transformed entire industries, economies, and societies. We learn about the challenges they faced, the risks they took, and the legacies they left behind.

From the visionary leadership of Henry Ford and Walt Disney, to the technological innovations of Bill Gates and Steve Jobs, to the social impact of Andrew Carnegie and Oprah Winfrey, this book covers the full spectrum of entrepreneurship and business success.

But it is not just a celebration of business success. It is also an honest and nuanced exploration of the controversies and criticisms that have surrounded many of these individuals and their companies. We examine the impact of their business practices, their treatment of workers, and their environmental impact, giving readers a well-rounded understanding of their contributions and limitations.

Written in an accessible and engaging style, this book is perfect for anyone who is interested in the stories of remarkable individuals, the evolution of business and entrepreneurship, or the ways in which business has shaped our world. Whether you are a student, a professional, or simply someone who is curious about the history of business, this book will inform, inspire, and entertain you.

BERNARD ARNAULT

is one of the most prominent business leaders of our time, and his story is a testament to his exceptional innovation mind and entrepreneurial spirit. His success can be attributed to his unique business tactics and strategies that have enabled him to become a dominant force in the luxury goods industry.

Arnault was born in Roubaix, France, in 1949, to a family of industrialists who owned a construction company. He studied engineering at the École Polytechnique in Paris and the École des Ponts et Chaussées. After completing his education, Arnault joined his father's construction business, but he quickly realized that his interests lay elsewhere.

In 1984, Arnault purchased Christian Dior, a struggling fashion house, and transformed it into one of the world's most successful luxury brands. He then went on to acquire other prestigious brands, including Louis Vuitton, Givenchy, and Fendi, and created the world's largest luxury goods conglomerate, LVMH.

Arnault's business tactics are centered around innovation and strategic thinking. He has a keen eye for identifying undervalued companies and transforming them into profitable ventures. He has also been known to take calculated risks, such as his acquisition of the ailing Christian Dior in the 1980s.

Arnault is also known for his shrewd management style, which is focused on creating a culture of excellence and innovation within his companies. He encourages his employees to take risks and be creative, and he values diversity and inclusivity within his organizations.

Another key aspect of Arnault's success is his commitment to quality. He believes that luxury goods should be made with the highest standards of craftsmanship and materials, and he has invested heavily in research and development to ensure that his brands continue to lead the industry in innovation and quality.

Arnault's success has not gone unnoticed, and he has been recognized as one of the most influential businessmen of all time. His contributions to the luxury goods industry have been immense, and his impact on the fashion world has been significant.

His influence can also be seen in the way that other luxury brands have modeled themselves after his innovative business practices. Many of the techniques and strategies that Arnault has developed over the years have become standard practices in the luxury goods industry, and his success has inspired countless entrepreneurs and businessmen around the world.

In conclusion, Bernard Arnault is one of the most influential business minds of our time. His innovative thinking, strategic planning, and commitment to excellence have enabled him to become a dominant force in the luxury goods industry. His impact can be seen not only in the success of his own companies but also in the way that his strategies and tactics have influenced the wider business community. Arnault's legacy will undoubtedly continue to inspire future generations of entrepreneurs and businessmen for years to come.

Bernard Arnault is known for his innovative work tactics

and business ethics, which have contributed greatly to his success in the luxury goods industry.

One of Arnault's key work tactics is his ability to identify undervalued companies and transform them into successful ventures. He has a talent for recognizing the potential of struggling businesses and using his resources and expertise to turn them around. This was evident in his acquisition of Christian Dior, which was a struggling fashion house when he bought it in 1984. Arnault transformed the brand into a global luxury powerhouse, and it now generates billions of dollars in revenue each year.

Another important aspect of Arnault's work tactics is his focus on quality and innovation. He believes that luxury goods should be made with the highest standards of craftsmanship and materials, and he has invested heavily in research and development to ensure that his brands continue to lead the industry in innovation and quality. This commitment to excellence has helped his companies maintain their status as some of the most prestigious and sought-after luxury brands in the world.

Arnault is also known for his shrewd management style, which emphasizes creating a culture of excellence and innovation within his companies. He encourages his employees to take risks and be creative, and he values diversity and inclusivity within his organizations. This has resulted in a work environment that fosters innovation and collaboration, and has helped his companies stay at the forefront of the luxury goods industry.

In terms of business ethics, Arnault has been known to take a long-term view in his decision-making. He is willing to make investments and take risks that may not pay off immediately, but that he believes will be beneficial in the long run. This approach has allowed him to build a portfolio of successful luxury brands that have stood the test of time.

Arnault is also known for his commitment to social responsibility and sustainability. He has implemented numerous initiatives across his companies to reduce their environmental impact, and he has donated millions of dollars to various charitable causes. This focus on social responsibility has helped him build a positive reputation in the business world and among consumers.

In summary, Bernard Arnault's work tactics and business ethics have been critical to his success in the luxury goods industry. His ability to identify undervalued companies, his focus on quality and innovation, his shrewd management style, and his commitment to social responsibility have all contributed to his success. Arnault's legacy serves as an inspiration to entrepreneurs and businessmen around the world, and his innovative approach to business will continue to influence the industry for years to come.

The one thing that he did, that an entrepreneur should follow to be great today

One thing that Bernard Arnault did exceptionally well, and that entrepreneurs today can follow to be great, is his relentless pursuit of innovation.

Arnault's success in the luxury goods industry can be attributed in large part to his ability to continually innovate and stay ahead of the curve. He was always looking for new ways to push the boundaries of what was possible in the industry, whether it was through the use of cutting-edge materials, innovative design techniques, or groundbreaking marketing strategies.

Entrepreneurs today can learn a lot from Arnault's focus on innovation. In order to succeed in today's fast-paced business environment, it's essential to be constantly exploring new ideas and pushing the limits of what's possible. This means taking risks, experimenting with new approaches, and being willing to fail in order to learn and grow.

In addition to innovation, another key lesson that entrepreneurs can learn from Arnault is the importance of building a strong team and fostering a culture of excellence. Arnault surrounded himself with talented individuals who shared his vision and were passionate about their work. He also created a work environment that encouraged creativity, collaboration, and risk-taking. By building a strong team and fostering a culture of excellence, entrepreneurs can create a foundation for long-term success and growth.

In summary, the one thing that entrepreneurs can learn from Bernard Arnault is the importance of relentless innovation. By continually pushing the boundaries of what's possible, and by building a strong team and culture of excellence, entrepreneurs can follow in Arnault's footsteps and achieve great things in the business world.

Some additional facts about Bernard Arnault:

Net worth: As of 2023, Bernard Arnault is the richest person in Europe and the third-richest person in the world, with a net worth estimated at over $150 billion USD.

Early life: Arnault was born in 1949 in Roubaix, France. His father owned a construction company, and Arnault initially studied engineering in college before switching to business.

Career beginnings: Arnault began his career in business working for his father's construction company. He then moved on to work for the luxury goods company Ferret-Savinel, where he learned the ins and outs of the industry.

Early business success: In the 1980s, Arnault made a series of strategic acquisitions, including Boussac, a bankrupt textile company that owned the struggling fashion house Christian

Dior. He used Dior as a platform to build a global luxury goods empire, acquiring brands like Louis Vuitton, Fendi, and Celine.

LVMH: In 1987, Arnault merged his fashion brands with Moët Hennessy, a leading producer of champagne and cognac, to create LVMH, the world's largest luxury goods conglomerate. Today, LVMH is home to over 70 brands, including some of the most iconic names in fashion and luxury, such as Bulgari, Givenchy, and Marc Jacobs.

Art collector: Arnault is a passionate art collector and is known for his love of contemporary art. He has a private collection that includes works by some of the world's most famous artists, including Pablo Picasso, Andy Warhol, and Jeff Koons.

Philanthropy: Arnault is also known for his philanthropic efforts. He has donated millions of dollars to various charitable causes, including the restoration of the Palace of Versailles and the creation of the Louis Vuitton Foundation, a contemporary art museum in Paris.

Honors and awards: Arnault has received numerous honors and awards throughout his career, including being named a Commander of the French Legion of Honor and receiving the Woodrow Wilson Award for Corporate Citizenship. He has also been recognized for his contributions to the arts, including being awarded the Royal Academy of Arts' first Lifetime Achievement Award in 2011.

Overall, Bernard Arnault's life and career are a testament to the power of innovation, hard work, and strategic thinking. His influence on the luxury goods industry is undeniable, and his impact on the world of business and philanthropy will be felt for generations to come.

P.T. BARNUM

born on July 5, 1810, in Bethel, Connecticut, was a well-known American showman, businessman, and entertainer. He is most famously known for founding Barnum & Bailey Circus, which became the "Greatest Show on Earth" and ran for over a century. However, his life as a businessman was not limited to the circus, as he had many other ventures and contributions to the world of business.

One of the main reasons why P.T. Barnum is considered one of the most influential business minds of all time is his innovative ideas and approaches. He was a master of promotion, marketing, and salesmanship, always looking for ways to attract the public's attention and make a profit. For instance, in the early 1840s, he started a small lottery that offered cash prizes and rare books as the main prize. The lottery was a great success, and it helped him acquire the funds to start his first museum, which became very popular in New York City.

Another example of his innovative mind was his use of advertising. Barnum was one of the first to use large-scale advertising to promote his shows and attractions. He understood the importance of getting his message in front of as many people as possible, and he did so by placing ads in newspapers and magazines, as well as printing posters and distributing handbills. He also used the power of the press to his advantage by giving interviews, staging publicity stunts, and creating controversy.

In addition to his marketing and advertising tactics, Barnum was also a great salesman. He knew how to persuade people to buy his products and attend his shows. One of his famous quotes was, "Without promotion, something terrible happens... nothing!" He also understood the importance of creating a unique and memorable experience for his customers. He constantly added new and exciting exhibits to his museums and circuses, making sure that people always had something to talk about and come back for.

Barnum's business ventures were not without controversy. He was often criticized for his methods, which sometimes involved deception and manipulation. For example, he famously exhibited a woman named Joice Heth, who he claimed was 161 years old and had been George Washington's nursemaid. It was later revealed that Heth was not as old as Barnum had claimed, and she may not have even been the same woman that Washington knew. Nonetheless, Barnum's ability to generate controversy and capture people's attention through his exhibits was a key part of his success.

Barnum's business ventures also included real estate, politics, and publishing. He owned several hotels and apartment buildings, and he was involved in politics, serving as a mayor and a member of the Connecticut legislature. He also published several books, including his autobiography, "The Life of P.T. Barnum," which was a best-seller in its time.

Overall, P.T. Barnum was an innovative and influential business mind who revolutionized the world of marketing and entertainment. He was a master of promotion, advertising, and salesmanship, and he understood the importance of creating a unique and memorable experience for his customers. Although his methods were sometimes controversial, his legacy as a businessman and showman continues to inspire entrepreneurs and marketers today.

One of the key tactics that Barnum used in his business was his ability to identify and capitalize on trends. For example, he recognized the growing interest in exotic animals and the world beyond America's borders, and he brought these interests to life through his museums and circuses. He also recognized the power of celebrity, and he often hired famous performers to draw crowds to his shows.

Barnum was also a master at creating hype and buzz around his exhibits and shows. He would often create elaborate promotions and publicity stunts to generate excitement and curiosity in the public. For example, he once staged a fake lecture on the "discovery of a mermaid" and even produced a fake mermaid for people to see, which drew large crowds.

In terms of business ethics, Barnum was known for his honesty and transparency in his dealings. He believed that it was important to deliver on the promises he made to his customers and to treat them fairly. He once said, "The foundation of success in life is good health: that is the substratum fortune; it is also the basis of happiness. A person cannot accumulate a fortune very well when he is sick."

However, Barnum was also known for his willingness to push the boundaries of truth and honesty in order to generate attention and interest in his exhibits. For example, he was involved in the "Feejee Mermaid" hoax, where he presented a fake mermaid skeleton as a real creature. He later admitted to the hoax and explained that it was a way to create interest and excitement in his shows.

Despite these controversial tactics, Barnum's business ethics were ultimately shaped by his belief that the customer was always right. He believed that the key to success was providing his customers with an enjoyable and memorable experience. This philosophy led him to constantly innovate and improve his shows and exhibits, ensuring that his customers always had something new and exciting to see.

In conclusion, P.T. Barnum was a savvy businessman who employed innovative tactics to generate interest and excitement in his exhibits and shows. He was known for his honesty and transparency in his dealings, but he was also willing to push the boundaries of truth and honesty to capture people's attention. His ultimate business ethic was centered around providing his customers with an enjoyable and memorable experience, which he believed was the key to success.

The one thing that he did, that an entrepreneur should follow to be great

One of the key things that entrepreneurs can learn from P.T. Barnum is the importance of being willing to take risks and try new things. Barnum was always looking for new and innovative ways to capture people's attention and generate excitement for his exhibits and shows. He was willing to try things that others thought were too risky or too unconventional, and he was always looking for ways to stand out from the competition.

Today, in a rapidly changing business environment, entrepreneurs need to be willing to take risks and try new things in order to stay competitive and keep up with the latest trends. They need to be willing to experiment with new technologies, business models, and marketing strategies, and to pivot quickly when things don't work out as planned.

In addition to taking risks, entrepreneurs can also learn from Barnum's ability to create buzz and generate excitement around his products and services. In today's crowded marketplace, it's not enough to simply have a great product or service. Entrepreneurs need to be able to effectively market and promote their offerings, and to create a sense of urgency and excitement around what they're selling.

Overall, the key lesson that entrepreneurs can learn from P.T. Barnum is the importance of being willing to take risks and try new things, while also being able to effectively market and promote their offerings. By doing so, entrepreneurs can stay competitive and keep up with the latest trends, while also standing out from the competition and building a loyal customer base.

Some additional facts and insights about P.T. Barnum:

Barnum was a skilled marketer and promoter, and he understood the power of advertising and publicity. He often used bold and attention-grabbing headlines in his advertisements, and he was not afraid to exaggerate or stretch the truth in order to generate interest in his exhibits.

Barnum was also a master of showmanship and spectacle, and he was always looking for ways to make his exhibits and shows more engaging and entertaining. He was known for his ability to create elaborate sets, costumes, and props, and for his use of special effects and illusions to create a sense of wonder and excitement among his audiences.

In addition to his work in entertainment, Barnum was also involved in politics and social activism. He served as a member of the Connecticut legislature and the mayor of Bridgeport, Connecticut, and he was a vocal advocate for causes such as temperance, women's suffrage, and the abolition of slavery.

Despite his successes as a businessman, Barnum also experienced setbacks and failures. He was once bankrupted by a fire that destroyed his museum, and he lost a fortune investing in a failed railroad venture. However, he was always willing to bounce back from these setbacks and continue pursuing his passions.

Barnum's legacy as a businessman and showman has had a lasting impact on American culture and entertainment. His influence can be seen in everything from modern-day circuses and amusement parks to reality TV shows and social media influencers.

In summary, P.T. Barnum was a skilled marketer and showman who understood the power of advertising and spectacle. He was also a political activist and advocate for social causes, and his legacy as a businessman and entertainer has had a lasting impact on American culture and entertainment.

MARC BENIOFF

is widely recognized as one of the most influential entrepreneurs of our time, having revolutionized the world of business through his innovative ideas and strategic tactics. As the founder and CEO of Salesforce, a cloud-based software company, Benioff has left an indelible mark on the technology industry and beyond.

Benioff was born in San Francisco in 1964 and grew up in the city's affluent Pacific Heights neighborhood. He attended the University of Southern California, where he studied business, before starting his career at Oracle Corporation in the late 1970s. It was at Oracle that Benioff honed his skills as a salesman and became inspired to start his own company.

In 1999, Benioff founded Salesforce, a cloud-based software company that provides customer relationship management (CRM) solutions to businesses of all sizes. From the beginning, Benioff's vision was to create a company that would revolutionize the way businesses use technology to interact with their customers. He envisioned a future where businesses could connect with their customers in a more meaningful way, using real-time data to deliver personalized experiences and build long-lasting relationships.

To achieve his vision, Benioff focused on innovation, both in terms of technology and business strategy. He created a culture of innovation within Salesforce, encouraging his employees to think outside the box and come up with new ideas that would disrupt the status quo. This led to the development of several groundbreaking products, including Salesforce's flagship CRM software, which has been praised for its user-friendly interface and powerful features.

In addition to his focus on innovation, Benioff is also known for his philanthropic efforts. He has pledged to donate 1% of Salesforce's equity, 1% of its employees' time, and 1% of its products to charitable causes. He has also been a vocal advocate for social justice issues, using his platform as a business leader to push for change on issues such as LGBTQ rights and climate change.

One of Benioff's most famous business tactics is the use of the "1-1-1" model, which he developed to help businesses give back to their communities. The model calls for companies to donate 1% of their equity, 1% of their employees' time, and 1% of their products to charitable causes. This model has been adopted by thousands of businesses around the world, and has helped to create a culture of corporate social responsibility.

Another key tactic employed by Benioff is his focus on customer success. He believes that businesses should be laser-focused on their customers, and should do everything in their power to ensure that their customers are happy and successful. This philosophy has been instrumental in the success of Salesforce, which has a reputation for providing excellent customer service and support.

Overall, Marc Benioff's life as a businessman is characterized by his innovative mind, his focus on customer success, and his commitment to social responsibility. He has revolutionized the world of business through his visionary ideas and strategic tactics, and has left an indelible mark on the technology industry and beyond. For these reasons, he is considered one of the most influential business minds of our time, and his legacy is sure to endure for generations to come.

Marc Benioff is known for his unique approach to business, which is focused on innovation, customer success, and social responsibility. Here are some specific examples of his work tactics and business ethics:

Innovation: Benioff is a strong believer in the power of innovation to drive business success. He has created a culture of innovation within Salesforce, encouraging his employees to think outside the box and come up with new ideas that can disrupt the status quo. One example of this is the company's "hackathons," where employees are given time to work on passion projects and come up with new ideas that can benefit the company and its customers.

Customer Success: Benioff is a big believer in the idea that businesses should be laser-focused on their customers. He has built Salesforce around this philosophy, and the company is known for providing excellent customer service and support. One way that Benioff ensures customer success is by regularly communicating with customers to understand their needs and pain points. He then uses this feedback to improve Salesforce's products and services.

Social Responsibility: Benioff has a strong commitment to social responsibility and has made it a core part of Salesforce's business model. One example of this is the company's 1-1-1 model, which calls for companies to donate 1% of their equity, 1% of their employees' time, and 1% of their products to charitable causes. Benioff also uses his platform as a business leader to advocate for social justice issues, such as LGBTQ rights and climate change.

Collaborative Leadership: Benioff is known for his collaborative leadership style. He encourages open communication and transparency within the company, and is not afraid to make tough decisions when necessary. He also values the input of his employees and is known for seeking out diverse perspectives to inform his decision-making.

Strategic Partnerships: Benioff understands the importance of strategic partnerships in driving business success. He has formed partnerships with other companies, such as Google and Apple, to integrate Salesforce's products and services with their platforms. These partnerships have helped Salesforce to expand its reach and offer even more value to its customers.

Overall, Marc Benioff's work tactics and business ethics are characterized by his focus on innovation, customer success, and social responsibility. He has built Salesforce around these core values, and his unique approach to business has helped to make the company one of the most successful and respected in the tech industry.

The one thing that he did, that an entrepreneur should follow to be great today

It's difficult to pinpoint just one thing that Marc Benioff did that entrepreneurs should follow to be great today, as his success is the result of a combination of factors. However, one key lesson that entrepreneurs can learn from Benioff is the importance of being customer-focused.

Benioff has built Salesforce around the idea that businesses should be laser-focused on their customers, and this has been a major factor in the company's success. By constantly listening to his customers and understanding their needs, Benioff has been able to build a company that provides products and services that truly add value.

Entrepreneurs today can follow Benioff's lead by adopting a customer-centric approach to their business. This means not only listening to customer feedback, but actively seeking it out and using it to inform product development and business strategy. By truly understanding their customers and meeting their needs, entrepreneurs can build businesses that are not only successful, but also have a positive impact on the world.

A few more interesting things about Marc Benioff:

Philanthropy: As I mentioned earlier, Benioff is committed to social responsibility and philanthropy. In addition to Salesforce's 1-1-1 model, he has also personally donated millions of dollars to charitable causes, including San Francisco General Hospital and UCSF Children's Hospital.

Mentorship: Benioff is known for his mentorship of young entrepreneurs and business leaders. He is a frequent speaker at business schools and conferences, and has mentored numerous entrepreneurs throughout his career.

Personal Development: Benioff is also a proponent of personal development, and encourages his employees to prioritize their own growth and development. He has spoken publicly about the importance of mindfulness and meditation, and has even built meditation rooms in Salesforce's offices.

Environmentalism: In addition to his philanthropic work, Benioff is also committed to environmentalism. Salesforce has set ambitious sustainability goals, such as achieving net-zero greenhouse gas emissions by 2050, and Benioff has been a vocal advocate for climate action.

Tech Industry Influence: Benioff is widely respected within the tech industry, and has been recognized as one of the most influential people in tech by Forbes and other publications. He has also been a vocal critic of issues such as income inequality and the gender pay gap in the tech industry, and has used his platform to advocate for change.

Overall, Marc Benioff is a multifaceted entrepreneur and business leader who is known for his commitment to innovation, customer success, and social responsibility. His influence extends beyond just the tech industry, and he is widely regarded as one of the most influential business leaders of our time.

LINDA BENNETT

is a British entrepreneur and fashion designer, best known for founding the LK Bennett brand, a high-end women's fashion and footwear company that became one of the most successful British retail companies of the 21st century. Bennett's success in the fashion industry, her innovative business tactics, and her leadership skills have made her one of the most influential businesswomen of her generation.

Linda Bennett was born in Shefford, Bedfordshire, in 1962, and grew up in rural England. From an early age, Bennett had an interest in fashion, and after studying design at the Cordwainers College in London, she began her career in the footwear industry. In 1990, Bennett founded LK Bennett with a small loan from a bank and a vision to create a luxury footwear brand that was both stylish and affordable.

Bennett's innovative business tactics were evident from the beginning of her career. She recognized the gap in the market for high-quality shoes that were not only fashionable but also comfortable, and she set out to create a brand that could cater to the needs of the modern, working woman. Bennett's shoes were designed to be worn all day, and she used high-quality materials and skilled craftsmanship to ensure that they were both durable and stylish.

One of Bennett's key strategies for building the LK Bennett

brand was to focus on customer service. She believed that creating a personal connection with her customers was essential for building loyalty, and she made sure that her stores provided a warm and welcoming atmosphere where customers could browse and shop in comfort. Bennett also listened to her customers' feedback and used it to inform her product design and marketing strategies, ensuring that the brand remained relevant and desirable to its target audience.

As the LK Bennett brand grew in popularity, Bennett continued to innovate and expand her business. In addition to shoes, the brand began to offer clothing, bags, and accessories, and Bennett also launched a successful e-commerce platform, allowing customers to shop online from anywhere in the world. She also expanded the brand internationally, opening stores in the US and Europe, and secured a number of high-profile collaborations and partnerships with celebrities and influencers.

Despite the success of her business, Bennett faced challenges along the way. In 2019, the company went into administration and was eventually bought out by a Chinese partner. However, Bennett's innovative approach to business and her focus on customer service and quality continue to inspire entrepreneurs and business leaders around the world.

Bennett's legacy as an influential businesswoman is due in large part to her ability to combine innovation with a personal touch. By prioritizing customer service and feedback, and by staying ahead of the curve in terms of design and marketing, she was able to create a successful brand that resonated with women around the world. Bennett's leadership skills, business acumen, and determination have cemented her place as one of the most influential business minds of her generation.

Linda Bennett's work tactics and business ethics were critical factors in the success of her brand, LK Bennett. Here are some of the key elements of her approach:

Focus on quality: From the beginning, Bennett was committed to using high-quality materials and skilled craftsmanship in her footwear and fashion designs. She believed that quality was essential to building a loyal customer base and creating a brand that would stand the test of time.

Innovation: Bennett was constantly looking for new ways to innovate and improve her business. She recognized the need for stylish, comfortable shoes that women could wear all day, and she worked to design products that would meet this need. She also expanded into new product categories, such as clothing and accessories, and launched an e-commerce platform to reach customers around the world.

Customer service: Bennett understood the importance of building strong relationships with her customers. She created a warm and welcoming atmosphere in her stores and encouraged her employees to engage with customers and provide personalized service. She also listened to customer feedback and used it to inform her product design and marketing strategies.

Attention to detail: Bennett was known for her meticulous attention to detail, both in her product design and in her business operations. She was involved in every aspect of the business, from product design to marketing to store layout, and she was known for her perfectionism and high standards.

Ethical business practices: Bennett was committed to operating her business ethically and with integrity. She treated her employees with respect and fairness, and she was a strong advocate for social and environmental responsibility. For example, she launched a sustainable fashion initiative that aimed to reduce waste and promote ethical manufacturing practices.

Overall, Linda Bennett's work tactics and business ethic were characterized by a commitment to quality, innovation, customer service, attention to detail, and ethical practices. These values helped her to create a successful and influential brand that has left a lasting impact on the fashion industry.

The one thing that she did, that an entrepreneur should follow to be great today

One key lesson that entrepreneurs can learn from Linda Bennett's success is the importance of customer focus. Bennett understood that building strong relationships with customers was essential to creating a successful brand, and she worked tirelessly to ensure that her customers were satisfied with the products and services her company provided.

To be a great entrepreneur today, it's essential to focus on the needs and desires of your target customers. This means understanding their pain points and challenges, as well as their preferences and aspirations. By listening to your customers and incorporating their feedback into your product development, marketing, and customer service strategies, you can build a loyal following and create a brand that resonates with your audience.

Additionally, Bennett's commitment to quality, innovation, attention to detail, and ethical business practices are also important factors for entrepreneurs to consider. By prioritizing these values in your own business operations, you can create a strong foundation for long-term success and growth.

A few more interesting facts about Linda Bennett and her career as a businesswoman:

Bennett founded LK Bennett in 1990 with a £13,000 loan from her parents. She began by designing and selling just a few styles of shoes, but over time the brand grew to include clothing, accessories, and more.

Bennett is known for her classic, feminine designs, which are often inspired by vintage styles. She has described her aesthetic as "modern nostalgia" and has cited Audrey Hepburn and Princess Diana as style icons.

In 2008, Bennett received an OBE (Order of the British Empire) for her services to the fashion industry.

Bennett sold a majority stake in LK Bennett to private equity firm Phoenix Equity Partners in 2008, but she remained involved in the business as a creative director until 2011.

After leaving LK Bennett, Bennett went on to found a new footwear brand, called LINDA BENNETT. The brand focuses on luxury footwear with a sustainable and ethical ethos.

In 2019, LK Bennett went into administration (bankruptcy) due to financial difficulties. However, the brand was later acquired by Byland UK and has since been relaunched with a renewed focus on sustainability and ethical business practices.

Overall, Linda Bennett's career as a businesswoman is a testament to the power of creativity, innovation, and hard work. Despite facing numerous challenges and setbacks along the way, she remained committed to her vision of creating high-quality, stylish products that women would love. Today, her legacy lives on through her brand LK Bennett and her continued work in the fashion industry.

SILVIO BERLUSCONI

is a name that is synonymous with business and entrepreneurship in Italy. Born on September 29, 1936, in Milan, Italy, Berlusconi is widely regarded as one of the most influential businessmen in the world. He has been a media mogul, a politician, and a cultural icon in Italy. Berlusconi's story is one of innovation, hard work, and relentless ambition, and his rise to the top of the business world is a testament to his unwavering determination.

Berlusconi's entrepreneurial journey began in the late 1960s when he founded a construction company called Edilnord. The company focused on building low-cost housing in Milan, which was in high demand at the time. Berlusconi's innovative approach to construction, which included using prefabricated materials and streamlining the building process, allowed Edilnord to become one of the largest construction companies in Italy. Berlusconi's success with Edilnord would pave the way for his entry into the media industry.

In 1973, Berlusconi founded the television company Telemilano, which would later become Mediaset. Berlusconi's vision for Mediaset was to create a media empire that would rival the state-owned broadcaster, RAI. He accomplished this by acquiring local television stations across Italy and creating a national network. Berlusconi's innovative approach to programming, which included producing soap operas and game shows, quickly made Mediaset a household name in Italy. Today, Mediaset is one of the largest media companies in Europe, with interests in television, cinema, and advertising.

Berlusconi's success in the media industry allowed him to branch out into other areas of business, including real estate, banking, and insurance. His investment in the football club AC Milan is also well-known. Berlusconi's ownership of AC Milan saw the club win numerous titles, including five Champions League trophies. Berlusconi's innovative approach to football management, which included investing in youth development and using data analytics to scout players, helped AC Milan become one of the most successful football clubs in the world.

Despite his success in business, Berlusconi's political career has been fraught with controversy. He served as the Prime Minister of Italy on three separate occasions, and his tenure was marked by allegations of corruption and abuse of power. Berlusconi's legal troubles, which included multiple trials and convictions, would ultimately force him to resign from politics in 2011.

Despite his controversies, Berlusconi's legacy as a businessman and entrepreneur remains intact. He is widely regarded as one of the most innovative and influential business minds of his generation. Berlusconi's vision for Mediaset revolutionized the Italian media industry, and his investments in real estate, banking, and insurance have had a lasting impact on the Italian economy. Berlusconi's contributions to football management have also been significant, with his innovative approach to scouting and player development changing the way that football clubs operate.

In conclusion, Silvio Berlusconi is a name that

is synonymous with innovation, hard work, and entrepreneurial spirit. His success in the media industry, as well as his investments in real estate, banking, and insurance, have had a significant impact on the Italian economy. Berlusconi's contributions to football management have also been significant, with his innovative approach to scouting and player development changing the way that football clubs operate. Despite his controversies in politics, Berlusconi's legacy as a businessman and entrepreneur remains intact, and he is widely regarded as one of the most influential business minds of his generation.

Silvio Berlusconi's work tactics and business ethic have been the subject of much scrutiny and debate over the years. Some view him as a shrewd and successful businessman, while others see him as an opportunistic and controversial figure. Here are some details about his work tactics and business ethic:

Risk-taking: Berlusconi was known for taking big risks in business. For example, his decision to invest in the media industry was considered risky at the time, as the industry was dominated by the state-owned broadcaster, RAI. However, Berlusconi saw an opportunity to create a national network of local television stations, and he went all-in on that vision. This risk paid off, as Mediaset became one of the largest media companies in Europe.

Innovation: Berlusconi was an innovator in the media industry. He introduced new programming concepts, such as soap operas and game shows, which quickly became popular with Italian audiences. Berlusconi also invested in cutting-edge technology, such as satellite broadcasting, which allowed him to expand his media empire across Europe.

Business Acumen: Berlusconi was a skilled negotiator and businessman. He was known for his ability to close deals and get what he wanted. For example, he was able to acquire local television stations across Italy by offering generous compensation packages to the owners. He also used his political connections to secure favorable deals for his businesses.

Controversial business practices: Berlusconi's business practices were not always above board. He has been accused of tax evasion, corruption, and other forms of financial impropriety. He has also been criticized for using his media outlets to advance his political interests.

Unconventional leadership style: Berlusconi was known for his unconventional leadership style. He was hands-on in his management of his businesses, often making decisions on the fly and relying on his instincts. He was also known for being a charismatic and persuasive communicator, using his charm and wit to win over supporters.

In conclusion, Silvio Berlusconi's work tactics and business ethic were a mix of risk-taking, innovation, business acumen, controversial practices, and unconventional leadership. While he had many successes in business, he also had his fair share of controversies and legal troubles. Despite this, Berlusconi's legacy as a businessman and entrepreneur remains significant, and he is widely regarded as one of the most influential business minds of his generation.

The one thing that he did, that an entrepreneur should follow to be great today

One of the key things that an entrepreneur could learn from Silvio Berlusconi is his ability to innovate and take risks. Berlusconi was not afraid to invest in new ideas and concepts, even if they were considered risky or unconventional at the time.

In today's fast-paced business environment, innovation

and risk-taking are critical to success. Entrepreneurs who are able to identify emerging trends, disrupt traditional markets, and pioneer new business models are often the ones who achieve the greatest success.

However, it is important to note that taking risks does not mean being reckless or unethical. Entrepreneurs should always conduct their business with integrity and transparency, and be mindful of the impact their decisions have on their stakeholders.

In addition to innovation and risk-taking, another lesson that entrepreneurs can learn from Berlusconi is the importance of building strong relationships and networks. Berlusconi was known for his ability to cultivate personal and professional relationships, which helped him to gain access to resources, funding, and other opportunities.

Entrepreneurs who are able to build strong networks and establish meaningful relationships with customers, investors, suppliers, and other stakeholders are often able to create more opportunities for growth and success.

Overall, by following Berlusconi's example of innovation, risk-taking, and relationship building, entrepreneurs can increase their chances of achieving their goals and making a meaningful impact in their industries.

Some additional details about Silvio Berlusconi:

Political career: In addition to his business ventures, Berlusconi was also involved in politics. He founded the Forza Italia party in 1994 and served as Prime Minister of Italy for a total of three terms, from 1994 to 1995, 2001 to 2006, and 2008 to 2011. His political career was controversial and marked by allegations of corruption and conflicts of interest due to his ownership of media companies.

Sports ownership: Berlusconi was also involved in sports

ownership. He owned the Italian football club A.C. Milan for over 30 years, from 1986 to 2017. During his ownership, the team won numerous titles, including five UEFA Champions League titles.

Philanthropy: Berlusconi was also involved in philanthropic activities. He founded the Silvio Berlusconi Foundation, which aimed to promote cultural and social initiatives in Italy and abroad. The foundation supported a variety of causes, including education, healthcare, and disaster relief.

Legal troubles: Berlusconi's business and political career was marred by numerous legal troubles. He faced numerous allegations of corruption, tax evasion, and other financial crimes throughout his career. He was also accused of having sex with an underage prostitute and abusing his power to cover it up. In 2013, he was convicted of tax fraud and sentenced to four years in prison, although the sentence was later reduced to one year due to an amnesty law.

Personal life: Berlusconi's personal life was often the subject of media attention. He has been married twice and has five children. He was known for his lavish lifestyle, which included expensive yachts, homes, and parties. In addition to his legal troubles, he was also accused of having affairs with numerous women, and was once quoted as saying, "I am the best political leader in Europe and the world... the best lover, too."

Overall, Silvio Berlusconi was a complex figure with a diverse range of interests and activities. While he achieved significant success in business, politics, and sports ownership, his career was also marked by controversy, legal troubles, and scandal.

JEFF BEZOS

I is a well-known figure in the business world and is widely recognized as one of the most influential business minds of all time. He is the founder and former CEO of Amazon, the world's largest online retailer. In this article, we will explore his life as a businessman, focusing on his innovative mind, work and tactics, and why he is considered to be amongst the most influential business minds.

Jeff Bezos was born in Albuquerque, New Mexico, in 1964. He graduated from Princeton University with degrees in electrical engineering and computer science. After graduation, he worked for several companies, including Fitel, Bankers Trust, and D. E. Shaw & Co.

In 1994, Bezos founded Amazon in his garage in Seattle, Washington. He initially started the company as an online bookstore but quickly expanded into other product categories, such as electronics, clothing, and home goods. Today, Amazon has become one of the most successful companies in the world, with a market capitalization of over $1 trillion.

One of the key reasons why Jeff Bezos has been so successful as a businessman is his innovative mind. He is constantly looking for new ways to improve and disrupt existing industries. For example, in 2007, he introduced the Kindle e-reader, which revolutionized the book publishing industry by making it possible to buy and read books digitally. Bezos also pioneered the use of drones for delivery, a technology that is now being adopted by many other companies.

Another reason for Bezos's success is his relentless work ethic. He has famously said that he works at least 12 hours a day, seven days a week, and he expects his employees to do the same. He is also known for his intense focus on customer satisfaction. He once said, "If there's one reason we have done better than any of our peers in the Internet space over the last six years, it is because we have focused like a laser on customer experience, and that really does matter, I think, in any business."

Bezos is also known for his business tactics, which have been both praised and criticized. For example, he is famous for his "two-pizza rule," which states that no team should be larger than can be fed with two pizzas. This rule is meant to encourage small, focused teams that can move quickly and be more agile.

Another tactic that Bezos has employed is the use of data to make decisions. He is a firm believer in the power of data-driven decision-making and has built Amazon's culture around it. This approach has helped Amazon to become one of the most successful companies in the world, but it has also raised concerns about privacy and the use of customer data.

Despite these criticisms, it is clear that Jeff Bezos's influence on the business world has been immense. He has disrupted numerous industries, including book publishing, retail, and cloud computing. He has also created thousands of jobs and helped to drive innovation and economic growth. And while he has recently stepped down as CEO of Amazon, his legacy will continue to inspire entrepreneurs and business leaders for years to come.

In conclusion, Jeff Bezos is undoubtedly one of the most influential business minds of all time. His innovative mind, relentless work ethic, and data-driven decision-making have helped to transform the business world and create some of the most successful companies in history. Despite his controversial tactics, his impact on the world of business cannot be denied, and he will undoubtedly be remembered as one of the most important figures in the history of entrepreneurship.

Jeff Bezos is known for his unique work tactics and business ethics, which have helped to shape Amazon's corporate culture and drive its success. Here are some additional details about his approach:

Customer-centric focus: Jeff Bezos is known for his relentless focus on customer satisfaction. He once said, "We're not competitor obsessed, we're customer obsessed. We start with what the customer needs and we work backwards." This approach has led Amazon to prioritize things like fast delivery, easy returns, and personalized recommendations, all of which help to enhance the customer experience.

Data-driven decision-making: Bezos is a strong believer in the power of data. He has famously said, "In business, what's dangerous is not to evolve." He has built Amazon's corporate culture around the use of data, which is used to inform everything from product development to marketing strategies.

Long-term thinking: Bezos has always taken a long-term view of Amazon's success. He has said, "If everything you do needs to work on a three-year time horizon, then you're competing against a lot of people." He is willing to invest heavily in new technologies and products, even if they may not pay off for several years.

Experimental mindset: Bezos encourages experimentation and risk-taking within Amazon. He once said, "If you're not failing, you're not innovating enough." This approach has led to the creation of new products and services, such as Amazon

Web Services, that have become major revenue streams for the company.

Small teams: Bezos believes in the power of small, focused teams. He has instituted a "two-pizza rule" that states that teams should be small enough to be fed with two pizzas. This approach encourages agility and allows teams to move quickly and make decisions without bureaucratic delays.

Frugality: Bezos has always emphasized the importance of frugality within Amazon. He has said, "Frugality drives innovation, just like other constraints do. One of the only ways to get out of a tight box is to invent your way out." This approach has led to Amazon's reputation for being a lean, efficient company that is focused on minimizing waste.

Overall, Jeff Bezos's work tactics and business ethics have helped to create a unique corporate culture at Amazon that is focused on customer satisfaction, data-driven decision-making, long-term thinking, experimentation, small teams, and frugality. These approaches have allowed Amazon to innovate and disrupt numerous industries, and have helped to establish Bezos as one of the most influential business minds of all time.

The one thing that he did, that an entrepreneur should follow to be great

One key thing that entrepreneurs can learn from Jeff Bezos is the importance of putting the customer first. Bezos has always been a strong advocate of customer-centric thinking, and this approach has been a major factor in Amazon's success. By focusing on the needs and preferences of their customers, entrepreneurs can create products and services that truly resonate with their target market, which can lead to increased loyalty, word-of-mouth marketing, and ultimately, revenue growth.

Another important lesson that entrepreneurs can learn from Bezos is the value of experimentation and risk-taking. Bezos has always encouraged his teams to try new things, even if they might fail. This approach has allowed Amazon to innovate and create new products and services that have disrupted multiple industries. By embracing an experimental mindset, entrepreneurs can also test new ideas and iterate quickly, which can help them to identify what works and what doesn't, and ultimately, find new opportunities for growth.

Finally, Bezos has also demonstrated the importance of thinking long-term. Rather than focusing on short-term gains or quick wins, he has always taken a broader view of Amazon's potential, and has been willing to invest heavily in new technologies and initiatives that may not pay off for several years. This long-term approach has allowed Amazon to grow and evolve over time, and has helped to establish the company as a major player in multiple industries. By thinking beyond immediate goals and taking a strategic, long-term approach to their business, entrepreneurs can also position themselves for success over the long haul.

Some additional details about Jeff Bezos:

Early life and education: Bezos was born in Albuquerque, New Mexico, in 1964. He attended Princeton University, where he studied electrical engineering and computer science.

Early career: After graduating from Princeton, Bezos worked for several companies in the technology and finance industries, including Fitel, Bankers Trust, and D.E. Shaw & Co.

Creation of Amazon: In 1994, Bezos founded Amazon.com, an online bookstore that would eventually become one of the largest retailers in the world. He chose Seattle as the company's headquarters due to the city's talented pool of software engineers.

Innovative business model: Bezos revolutionized the retail industry with Amazon's business model, which involved offering a vast selection of products, low prices, and fast, reliable shipping. He also pioneered the use of customer reviews and recommendations, which helped to drive sales and build customer loyalty.

Diversification and expansion: Under Bezos's leadership, Amazon has diversified into a wide range of businesses, including cloud computing, streaming media, and artificial intelligence. The company has also expanded globally, operating in dozens of countries around the world.

Personal life: Bezos is known for his philanthropy and has donated billions of dollars to causes such as education and climate change. He also owns The Washington Post and has invested in other companies such as Blue Origin, a space exploration company.

Leadership style: Bezos is known for his hands-on leadership style and his willingness to take risks. He is also known for being highly demanding of his employees and for setting ambitious goals for the company.

Overall, Jeff Bezos's career has been marked by innovation, risk-taking, and a relentless focus on customer satisfaction. His leadership style and business strategies have helped to shape the modern retail industry and have made him one of the most influential business minds of all time.

MICHAEL BLOOMBERG

Is undoubtedly one of the most influential business minds of our time. He is a self-made billionaire who built his fortune from scratch through sheer hard work, dedication, and innovative thinking. Born in Boston in 1942, Bloomberg graduated from Harvard Business School in 1966 and went on to build a media and financial empire that has made him one of the wealthiest people on the planet.

Bloomberg's entrepreneurial journey began when he was working at Salomon Brothers, a Wall Street investment bank. He became a partner at the firm in 1972 and was eventually put in charge of the equity trading desk. However, he was fired in 1981, and he decided to use his severance package to start his own company, which he named Bloomberg LP.

Bloomberg's business model was based on providing financial information and analytics to the financial industry. His company's flagship product, the Bloomberg Terminal, was a revolutionary tool that allowed traders and investors to access real-time financial data and news. This product was a game-changer for the financial industry, as it gave traders and investors a competitive edge by providing them with up-to-the-minute information.

Bloomberg's success was not solely due to his innovative

products. He was also a savvy businessman who knew how to navigate the complex world of finance and politics. For example, in the late 1990s, he used his wealth and influence to run for mayor of New York City. Although he had no political experience, he was able to win the race by using his business acumen and innovative thinking to solve the city's problems.

During his time as mayor, Bloomberg implemented a number of controversial policies, including a smoking ban and a soda tax. He also championed education reform and public health initiatives. Despite facing criticism from some quarters, he was generally seen as an effective leader who was able to get things done.

In addition to his political career, Bloomberg has continued to innovate and invest in new technologies. For example, his philanthropic foundation, Bloomberg Philanthropies, has invested heavily in renewable energy and other environmental initiatives. He has also been an advocate for gun control and has invested in companies that are developing new technologies to combat climate change.

Bloomberg's success as an entrepreneur and businessman can be attributed to several key factors. Firstly, he is an innovative thinker who is always looking for new ways to solve problems and improve processes. Secondly, he is a risk-taker who is not afraid to invest in new ideas and technologies. Finally, he is a savvy businessman who knows how to build and grow successful companies.

In conclusion, Michael Bloomberg is undoubtedly one of the most influential business minds of our time. He has built a media and financial empire that has revolutionized the way that traders and investors access financial information. He has also been a successful politician and philanthropist, using his wealth and influence to champion causes that are important to him. His success can be attributed to his innovative thinking, his willingness to take risks, and his savvy business skills. He is a role model for aspiring entrepreneurs and businessmen who want to make a difference in the world.

Michael Bloomberg is known for his strong work ethic and business tactics, which have played a significant role in his success as an entrepreneur and businessman.

One of Bloomberg's key business tactics is his focus on innovation and disruptive thinking. Throughout his career, he has always been on the lookout for new technologies and ideas that could transform industries and create new opportunities. This focus on innovation has led to the development of numerous groundbreaking products and services, including the Bloomberg Terminal, which has transformed the financial industry.

Bloomberg is also known for his data-driven approach to decision-making. His company, Bloomberg LP, is built on the foundation of providing accurate and up-to-date financial data to its clients. This data-driven approach has enabled him to make informed business decisions and stay ahead of the competition.

Another aspect of Bloomberg's work tactics is his attention to detail. He is known for his meticulous approach to business operations and is involved in every aspect of his companies' operations. This attention to detail has allowed him to identify and address potential problems before they become major issues.

In addition, Bloomberg is also known for his willingness to take risks. He has invested in a wide range of ventures, from media and finance to renewable energy and gun control. This willingness to take risks has enabled him to identify and capitalize on emerging trends and opportunities.

Bloomberg is also known for his philanthropy and commitment to social causes. He has donated billions of dollars to charitable causes, including education, the environment, and public health. This commitment to social causes has not only helped to improve the lives of countless people, but it has also helped to burnish his reputation as a socially responsible business leader.

Overall, Michael Bloomberg's work tactics and business ethics are characterized by a focus on innovation, attention to detail, data-driven decision-making, and a willingness to take risks. His commitment to social causes and philanthropy has also helped to set him apart as a business leader who is not solely focused on making money but also on making a positive impact on the world.

The one thing that he did, that an entrepreneur should follow to be great today

There are many things that entrepreneurs can learn from Michael Bloomberg's success. However, one key thing that stands out is his relentless focus on innovation.

Bloomberg has always been on the lookout for new technologies and ideas that could transform industries and create new opportunities. He is constantly pushing the boundaries of what is possible and is always looking for ways to improve his products and services.

For entrepreneurs, this means that it is important to be open to new ideas and technologies. It is not enough to simply follow the status quo or to do things the way they have always been done. To truly succeed in business, entrepreneurs need to be innovative and disruptive in their thinking. They need to be willing to take risks and to try new things, even if they are not sure if they will work.

In addition, entrepreneurs can also learn from Bloomberg's attention to detail and his data-driven approach to decision-making. By carefully analyzing data and paying attention to the details of their business operations, entrepreneurs can identify potential problems and opportunities before they become major issues.

Overall, the key lesson that entrepreneurs can learn from Michael Bloomberg is to focus on innovation and to always be on the lookout for new ways to transform industries and create value for their customers. By adopting this mindset, entrepreneurs can set themselves apart from their competition and position themselves for long-term success.

Some more interesting facts about Michael Bloomberg:

Bloomberg is a self-made billionaire: He started his career at Salomon Brothers, an investment bank, where he worked his way up to become a partner. He founded Bloomberg LP in 1981, which initially focused on providing financial data through its Bloomberg Terminal. Today, Bloomberg LP is a global media and financial data company that generates billions of dollars in revenue each year.

He was the mayor of New York City: In 2001, Bloomberg was elected mayor of New York City, where he served for three terms. During his tenure, he implemented a number of innovative policies, including a smoking ban in public places, a bike-sharing program, and an ambitious sustainability plan.

He is a major philanthropist: Bloomberg has donated billions of dollars to charitable causes over the years, including education, public health, and the environment. In 2018, he pledged to donate $1.8 billion to Johns Hopkins University to fund financial aid for low- and middle-income students.

He is a proponent of gun control: Bloomberg is a vocal advocate for gun control and has donated millions of dollars to support gun control measures. He founded Everytown for Gun Safety, a nonprofit organization that advocates for stronger gun laws in the United States.

He is an author: Bloomberg has written several books over the years, including "Bloomberg by Bloomberg," a memoir about his life and career, and "Climate of Hope," which he co-authored with former Sierra Club executive director Carl Pope.

He is a fitness enthusiast: Bloomberg is known for his dedication to fitness and has been an avid runner for many years. He has completed numerous marathons and triathlons, and in 2011, he founded the Bloomberg Square Mile Relay, a race that takes place in cities around the world.

RICHARD BRANSON

is a well-known British entrepreneur who has had a significant impact on the business world. His innovative mind, unique work style, and strategic tactics have made him one of the most successful and influential businessmen of all time. In this essay, we will discuss Richard Branson's life as a businessman, his innovative mind, and why he is considered one of the most influential business minds.

Richard Branson was born on July 18, 1950, in Blackheath, London. As a child, he struggled in school due to dyslexia, but he was able to find success through entrepreneurship. He started his first business, a student magazine called "Student," when he was just 16 years old. Later on, he started a mail-order record business, which eventually grew into the Virgin Group, a conglomerate of over 400 companies.

Branson is known for his innovative mind, which has helped him develop unique business ideas and products. He has always been willing to take risks and try new things, which has allowed him to stay ahead of his competitors. For example, in 1984, Branson launched Virgin Atlantic Airways, which revolutionized the airline industry by offering better service and lower prices than its competitors. He also introduced Virgin Mobile, a mobile phone service provider that offered affordable rates and innovative features.

Another aspect of Branson's innovative mind is his ability to identify gaps in the market and create new products to fill them. For example, when he noticed that there was a lack of quality hotels in the world, he created the Virgin Hotels brand. He also recognized the potential of the internet early on and started Virgin Net, an internet service provider, in 1996.

Branson is also known for his unique work style, which sets him apart from other businessmen. He believes in creating a fun and relaxed work environment, where employees can be themselves and have fun while working. He encourages his employees to be creative and come up with new ideas, and he is known for rewarding his employees with unusual perks like unlimited vacation time.

One of the tactics that Branson uses to grow his businesses is to partner with other companies. He believes that partnerships can help businesses grow faster and reach new markets. For example, he partnered with Singapore Airlines to expand Virgin Atlantic's reach in Asia, and he partnered with Pepsi to create Virgin Cola, a soft drink that competed with Coca-Cola and Pepsi.

Branson is also known for his strategic thinking and his ability to make bold decisions. He has made some risky moves in his career, like launching Virgin Galactic, a space tourism company that aims to take paying customers to space. He has also made some controversial decisions, like selling Virgin Records to EMI in 1992, which was a difficult decision for him, as he had founded the company and was passionate about music.

In conclusion, Richard Branson is one of the most influential business minds of all time. His innovative mind, unique work style, and strategic tactics have allowed him to create successful businesses in a variety of industries. He has always been willing to take risks and try new things, and he has been able to identify gaps in the market and create new products to fill them. His partnerships and strategic thinking have helped him grow his businesses, and he has made bold decisions that have paid off in the long run. Richard Branson is truly a visionary entrepreneur, and his influence on the business world will continue to be felt for many years to come.

One of Branson's most well-known tactics is his emphasis on the importance of his employees. He believes that happy and motivated employees are the key to a successful business. He treats his employees like family and creates a fun and relaxed work environment where they can be creative and have fun while working. He also gives his employees a sense of ownership in the company, allowing them to contribute their ideas and feel invested in the success of the business.

Another key tactic that Branson uses is his willingness to take risks. He believes that taking risks is necessary to succeed in business, and he is not afraid to try new things, even if they seem unconventional. For example, when he launched Virgin Atlantic, he took a big risk by starting a new airline in a market dominated by established players. However, his innovative approach, which included features like in-flight entertainment and comfortable seats, allowed him to successfully compete with larger airlines and disrupt the industry.

Branson is also known for his emphasis on customer service. He believes that providing excellent customer service is critical to the success of any business. He understands that customers are the lifeblood of any business and is committed to providing them with high-quality products and services. For example, when he started Virgin Atlantic, he made sure that the airline offered better service and more amenities than its competitors, which helped it stand out in a crowded market.

In addition to his work tactics, Branson is known for his

strong business ethics. He believes in doing the right thing, even if it is not the most profitable option. He is committed to environmental sustainability and social responsibility, and he has made efforts to reduce the carbon footprint of his businesses and support charitable causes. For example, he pledged to donate all profits from his airline and train companies to combat climate change, and he has donated millions of dollars to various charities and causes.

Branson's business ethics also extend to his relationships with his partners and competitors. He believes in treating everyone with respect and honesty, and he has built strong relationships with many business leaders around the world. He is not afraid to compete, but he does so in a fair and ethical manner, and he is always looking for opportunities to collaborate with other businesses to achieve common goals.

Overall, Richard Branson's work tactics and business ethics are characterized by his emphasis on employees, willingness to take risks, commitment to customer service, and strong sense of ethics and social responsibility. These tactics and values have allowed him to build successful businesses and make a positive impact on the world, and they serve as a model for aspiring entrepreneurs who want to build businesses that are both profitable and socially responsible.

The one thing that he did, that an entrepreneur should follow to be great

It's difficult to point to just one thing that Richard Branson did that all entrepreneurs should follow to be great today, as his success is the result of a combination of many factors. However, one key lesson that can be drawn from his career is the importance of being willing to take risks and try new things.

Branson has often emphasized the importance of taking calculated risks in business. He believes that entrepreneurs should not be afraid to try new things, even if they seem risky or unconventional. This willingness to take risks has been a key factor in many of his business successes, including the launch of Virgin Records and the creation of Virgin Atlantic.

Of course, taking risks is not the same as being reckless. Branson is known for carefully evaluating the risks and benefits of each new venture, and he has a track record of making calculated decisions that have paid off. This approach requires a combination of boldness and prudence, and it's not always easy to strike the right balance.

Ultimately, the lesson that entrepreneurs can learn from Branson is that success often requires taking risks and trying new things. By being willing to step outside of your comfort zone and take calculated risks, you can create opportunities for yourself and your business that might not have been possible otherwise. Of course, this approach also requires careful planning, evaluation, and execution, but the willingness to take risks is an essential ingredient in any successful entrepreneurial journey.

Here are some additional interesting facts and achievements of Richard Branson:

In addition to his business ventures, Branson is also known for his philanthropic work. He has established several charities, including Virgin Unite, which focuses on supporting social and environmental causes, and The Branson Centre of Entrepreneurship, which provides support and resources for aspiring entrepreneurs in developing countries.

Branson is an advocate for environmental sustainability and has taken a number of steps to reduce the carbon footprint of his businesses. For example, he has invested in renewable energy sources and launched the Virgin Earth Challenge, a $25 million prize for anyone who can develop a commercially viable way to remove greenhouse gases from the atmosphere.

Branson has also been involved in several record-breaking adventures and stunts. In 1986, he set a record for the fastest crossing of the Atlantic Ocean in a powerboat, and in 1991, he crossed the Pacific Ocean in a hot air balloon, becoming the first person to do so.

Branson has been knighted by both the Queen of England and the Emperor of Japan for his contributions to business and entrepreneurship.

Branson has written several books, including "Losing My Virginity: How I've Survived, Had Fun, and Made a Fortune Doing Business My Way," which is a memoir of his life and career, and "Screw Business as Usual," which advocates for a more socially and environmentally responsible approach to business.

Branson has been recognized as one of the most influential people in business and entrepreneurship. He has received numerous awards and accolades, including being named one of Time magazine's 100 most influential people in the world and being inducted into the Junior Achievement U.S. Business Hall of Fame.

These are just a few examples of the many interesting and noteworthy achievements of Richard Branson. He is truly a remarkable individual who has had a significant impact on the world of business and entrepreneurship.

SERGEY BRIN

is widely regarded as one of the most influential businessmen and entrepreneurs of all time. Co-founder of the world's most popular search engine, Google, Brin's innovative mind, tireless work ethic, and strategic thinking have been critical to the success of one of the most important companies of the digital age. In this article, we will delve into Brin's life as a businessman, exploring his entrepreneurial journey and how he revolutionized the tech industry.

Early Life and Education

Sergey Brin was born on August 21, 1973, in Moscow, Russia. His parents were both mathematicians, and the family moved to the United States when Sergey was just six years old. Brin grew up in Maryland and developed an early interest in computers and technology. He attended Stanford University, where he studied computer science, and it was there that he met Larry Page, his future business partner.

The Birth of Google

In 1995, Brin and Page began working on a project called Backrub, which was aimed at improving search results using a new algorithm. They soon realized that their idea had significant potential, and in 1998, they launched Google, a new search engine that quickly gained a following. The company was incorporated in September of that year, and the rest is history.

Brin's Role in Google's Success

As Google grew, Brin played a critical role in the company's success. He focused on the technical side of the business, developing and improving the search algorithm that made Google so popular. He was also responsible for the company's infrastructure and played a key role in developing the company's advertising platform.

However, Brin's most significant contribution to Google's success was his willingness to challenge the status quo. He believed in pushing boundaries and was not afraid to take risks. This approach led to some of Google's most innovative products, including Google Maps, Google Earth, and Gmail.

Innovative Mind

Brin's innovative mind has been one of his most significant strengths throughout his career. He is known for his ability to think outside the box and come up with new and exciting ideas. He has always been passionate about technology and is continually looking for ways to push the limits of what is possible.

One of Brin's most notable contributions to the tech industry was his development of the PageRank algorithm, which is still used by Google today. This algorithm revolutionized the search industry by ranking pages based on their relevance to the user's query rather than just the number of times a keyword appeared on a page.

Work and Tactics

Another key factor in Brin's success has been his tireless work ethic. He is known for working long hours and pushing himself to achieve his goals. Brin has also been very strategic in his approach to business. He has always been willing to take risks, but he does so in a calculated and thoughtful way. He is always thinking about the big picture and how his decisions will impact the company's future.

Brin's approach to management has also been critical to Google's success. He has always been focused on creating a culture of innovation and collaboration within the company. He is known for his hands-on approach, regularly meeting with employees to discuss new ideas and ways to improve the company's products and services.

Why Brin is Considered Amongst the Most Influential Business Minds

There are several reasons why Brin is considered one of the most influential business minds of all time. First and foremost, he revolutionized the search industry and created one of the most successful companies in history. Google has changed the way we access information and has had a profound impact on the world.

Secondly, Brin's innovative mind and willingness to take risks have been critical to his success. He has always been willing to push the boundaries.

One of the defining characteristics of Brin's work tactics is his approach to innovation. He is known for his willingness to take risks and experiment with new ideas, even if they seem unconventional or unpopular at first. For example, when Google was first founded, the company's decision to make its search engine ad-free and its commitment to providing users with the most relevant search results, rather than the most profitable ones, was seen as a risky move. However, Brin and his co-founder Larry Page believed that this was the right approach, and their bet paid off in the long run.

Brin is also known for his analytical approach to problem-solving. He is a data-driven thinker who relies on quantitative analysis to inform his decisions. He has a reputation for being detail-oriented and meticulous in his work, which has helped him to identify and solve complex problems in innovative ways.

Another key aspect of Brin's work tactics is his dedication to his company. He has a hands-on approach to management and is deeply involved in all aspects of the business. He is known for his long hours and his willingness to put in the work necessary to achieve success. This dedication to his company has helped to build a strong sense of team spirit and camaraderie among Google employees.

Brin's business ethics are also worth noting. He has a reputation for being honest and straightforward in his dealings with others, and for valuing integrity above all else. He has been outspoken about his belief that businesses should be transparent in their operations and should strive to do what is right, even if it is not always the most profitable option.

Another aspect of Brin's business ethics is his commitment to diversity and inclusion. He has been a vocal advocate for increasing the representation of women and minorities in the tech industry and has taken concrete steps to promote diversity within Google. For example, he has established programs to support underrepresented groups in tech and has made diversity and inclusion a core value of the company.

In conclusion, Sergey Brin's work tactics and business ethics are characterized by innovation, dedication, and integrity. He has a hands-on approach to management and is deeply involved in all aspects of his company. He is a data-driven thinker who is willing to take risks and experiment with new ideas, and he places a high value on transparency and honesty in business. Additionally, he is committed to promoting diversity and inclusion in the tech industry and has taken concrete steps to support underrepresented groups. These qualities have helped to make him one of the most influential business minds of all time.

The one thing that he did, that an entrepreneur should follow to be great

One thing that entrepreneurs can learn from Sergey Brin is the importance of taking risks and being willing to experiment with new ideas.

Brin and his co-founder Larry Page famously took a risk when they decided to make Google's search engine ad-free and focus on providing users with the most relevant search results, rather than the most profitable ones. This approach was unconventional at the time, and many people were skeptical that it would succeed.

However, Brin and Page believed in their vision, and their willingness to take a risk paid off in the long run. Google's ad-free search engine quickly gained a loyal following, and the company's commitment to providing high-quality search results helped it to become one of the most successful businesses in history.

Entrepreneurs can learn from Brin's example by embracing risk and being willing to experiment with new ideas, even if they seem unconventional or risky at first. By doing so, entrepreneurs can differentiate themselves from their competitors and create innovative solutions that meet the needs of their customers in new and exciting ways.

Of course, taking risks is not always easy, and it requires a willingness to fail and learn from mistakes. But by following Brin's example and embracing risk, entrepreneurs can set themselves up for success and create businesses that have a lasting impact on the world.

Some additional things about Sergey Brin that may be of interest:

He was born in Russia: Sergey Brin was born in Moscow,

Russia in 1973. His family emigrated to the United States when he was six years old to escape anti-Semitism in Russia.

He has a strong academic background: Brin earned a Bachelor of Science degree in mathematics and computer science from the University of Maryland, College Park, and went on to earn a Master of Science degree in computer science from Stanford University.

He co-founded Google with Larry Page: In 1998, Brin and Larry Page co-founded Google, which quickly became one of the most successful and influential companies in history.

He played a key role in developing Google's search algorithm: Brin was instrumental in developing the algorithm that powers Google's search engine. His work helped to make Google's search results more relevant and accurate than those of its competitors.

He is a philanthropist: In addition to his work at Google, Brin is also a philanthropist who has donated millions of dollars to support scientific research and technology education. He has also established the Brin Wojcicki Foundation with his ex-wife, Anne Wojcicki, to support a variety of charitable causes.

He is a private person: Despite his high profile as one of the co-founders of Google, Brin is known for being a private person who avoids the spotlight. He rarely gives interviews and is notoriously media-shy.

He is interested in space exploration: Brin has a keen interest in space exploration and has invested in several space-related companies, including SpaceX and Planetary Resources. He has said that he believes that space exploration has the potential to solve some of the world's biggest problems, such as climate change and resource depletion.

MATTHEW BOULTON

Was a British entrepreneur and industrialist who lived from 1728 to 1809. He was a highly innovative businessman who played a significant role in the Industrial Revolution, and his contributions to the fields of engineering, manufacturing, and metallurgy made him one of the most influential business minds of his time.

Boulton was born in Birmingham, England, in 1728. He was the son of a successful button maker, and he inherited his father's business when he was just 31 years old. However, Boulton was not content to simply run his father's button-making business. He was always looking for new opportunities to innovate and improve his products.

In 1761, Boulton began a partnership with Scottish engineer James Watt. Watt had developed a new type of steam engine that was more efficient than previous designs, and Boulton recognized the potential of this invention. Together, Boulton and Watt formed the partnership of Boulton and Watt, which would become one of the most successful and innovative engineering firms of the Industrial Revolution.

One of the keys to Boulton's success was his ability to recognize and invest in new technologies. He was an early adopter of the steam engine, which allowed him to automate his button-making business and increase his production output. He also invested heavily in the development of new metallurgical processes, which allowed him to produce higher-quality products at a lower cost.

Boulton was also a shrewd businessman who was known for his marketing and sales tactics. He understood the importance of branding and advertising, and he was one of the first entrepreneurs to use advertising to promote his products. He also developed a strong network of business contacts and suppliers, which helped him to secure the resources and raw materials he needed to run his business.

Perhaps one of Boulton's most important contributions to the world of business was his role in the development of the factory system. Boulton's factory in Birmingham was one of the first modern factories, and it served as a model for the factories that would become the backbone of the Industrial Revolution. Boulton was a strong advocate for the use of specialized machinery and division of labor, which allowed for greater efficiency and productivity.

Overall, Matthew Boulton was an innovative and influential businessman who played a significant role in the Industrial Revolution. His ability to recognize and invest in new technologies, his marketing and sales tactics, and his role in the development of the factory system all contributed to his success as a businessman. Today, Boulton is remembered as one of the most important figures of the Industrial Revolution, and his legacy continues to inspire entrepreneurs and business leaders around the world.

Matthew Boulton was known for his meticulous attention to detail and his focus on quality. He believed that the key to success in business was to produce high-quality products that customers would be willing to pay a premium for.

One of the ways that Boulton ensured the quality of his products was by investing heavily in research and development. He employed a team of skilled engineers and craftsmen who were dedicated to improving his products and developing new technologies. Boulton was also known for his willingness to take risks and experiment with new ideas, even if they were unproven or unconventional.

Boulton was also a master of marketing and sales. He recognized the importance of branding and advertising, and he was one of the first entrepreneurs to use advertising to promote his products. He created a strong brand identity for his business and used a variety of marketing tactics, including print advertisements and trade shows, to build awareness and generate sales.

In addition to his focus on quality and marketing, Boulton was also a strong advocate for employee welfare. He recognized that his success was due in large part to the hard work and dedication of his employees, and he believed in treating them fairly and providing them with opportunities for professional development. Boulton was also a strong advocate for workplace safety and was known for his efforts to improve working conditions for his employees.

One of the most significant contributions that Boulton made to the world of business was his role in the development of the factory system. Boulton's factory in Birmingham was one of the first modern factories, and it served as a model for the factories that would become the backbone of the Industrial Revolution. Boulton was a strong advocate for the use of specialized machinery and division of labor, which allowed for greater efficiency and productivity.

Boulton was also a master of financial management. He understood the importance of financial planning and was known for his ability to manage his business finances effectively. He used a variety of financial tools, including cost accounting and cash flow forecasting, to manage his business operations and make strategic investments.

In summary, Matthew Boulton was a highly innovative and influential businessman who was known for his meticulous attention to detail, his focus on quality, his marketing and sales tactics, his advocacy for employee welfare, his role in the development of the factory system, and his mastery of financial management. His work tactics and business ethic set a standard for future generations of entrepreneurs and continue to inspire business leaders around the world.

The one thing that he did, that an entrepreneur should follow to be great

There are many things that Matthew Boulton did that modern entrepreneurs can learn from, but one of the most important lessons is his relentless pursuit of innovation.

Boulton was constantly looking for new ways to improve his products, increase his production output, and reduce his costs. He was an early adopter of new technologies, such as the steam engine, and he invested heavily in research and development to create new products and processes.

In today's rapidly evolving business landscape, innovation is more important than ever. Entrepreneurs who are able to innovate and adapt to changing market conditions are the ones who are most likely to succeed. This requires a willingness to take risks, experiment with new ideas, and constantly iterate and improve.

One of the keys to Boulton's success as an innovator was his ability to assemble a team of talented engineers and craftsmen who shared his passion for innovation. Today's entrepreneurs can follow his example by building a strong team of like-minded individuals who are dedicated to pushing the boundaries of what is possible.

Another important lesson that entrepreneurs can learn from Boulton is the importance of financial management. Boulton was a master of financial planning and used a variety of tools and strategies to manage his business finances effectively. In today's competitive business environment, financial management is essential for success, and entrepreneurs who are able to manage their finances effectively are more likely to survive and thrive.

Overall, the lesson that modern entrepreneurs can learn from Matthew Boulton is to never stop innovating. By constantly pushing the boundaries of what is possible and investing in research and development, entrepreneurs can create products and processes that are truly transformative and set them apart from the competition.

A few more interesting facts about Matthew Boulton:

Boulton was born in Birmingham, England, in 1728. He came from a family of craftsmen and inherited his father's business, which produced small metal goods like buttons and buckles.

Boulton's breakthrough came when he met James Watt, a Scottish inventor who had developed a steam engine that was far more efficient than any previous design. Boulton recognized the potential of Watt's invention and partnered with him to develop and market it.

Boulton's partnership with Watt was a huge success. They formed the firm Boulton & Watt, which produced steam engines that were used in a wide range of applications, from powering factories and mills to propelling ships. Boulton was also a prolific coin designer and produced some of the most beautiful and intricate coins of his time. He was appointed as the official manufacturer of coins for the British government and produced a wide range of coins, including the famous "Cartwheel" penny.

Boulton was a member of the Lunar Society, a group of prominent intellectuals and scientists who met regularly in Birmingham to discuss scientific and technological advances. The group included other luminaries like James

Watt, Josiah Wedgwood, and Erasmus Darwin.

Boulton was a philanthropist who supported a range of charitable causes, including hospitals, schools, and churches. He was also a strong supporter of the arts and sciences and founded the Birmingham Philosophical Society to promote scientific inquiry and education.

Boulton's legacy continues to be felt today. The Boulton & Watt steam engine played a key role in the Industrial Revolution and helped to transform the world economy. Boulton's dedication to innovation, quality, and financial management set a standard for future generations of entrepreneurs and continue to inspire business leaders around the world.

ASA GRIGGS CANDLER

Was an American entrepreneur and businessman who is best known for his pivotal role in the development and success of the Coca-Cola Company. Candler's innovative ideas, tireless work ethic, and strategic business tactics helped to turn Coca-Cola into one of the world's most recognizable brands, and cemented his place in history as one of the most influential business minds of all time.

Candler was born on December 30, 1851, in Villa Rica, Georgia, and grew up in a family that valued hard work and entrepreneurship. His father was a successful farmer and merchant, and his mother was a skilled seamstress and homemaker. Candler showed an early interest in business and sales, and after completing his education, he started working for his older brother, who owned a drugstore in Atlanta.

In 1887, Candler purchased the recipe for Coca-Cola from its inventor, John Pemberton, for $2,300. At the time, Coca-Cola was a relatively unknown beverage, and Candler recognized its potential as a popular and profitable drink. He began aggressively marketing Coca-Cola, using innovative advertising techniques such as coupons, free samples, and product placements to increase its visibility and popularity.

Candler's efforts paid off, and Coca-Cola quickly became one of the most popular beverages in America. He expanded the company's reach by franchising its production and distribution to independent bottlers, and by introducing new flavors and packaging options to appeal to different consumer preferences. He also helped to establish Coca-Cola as a household name by sponsoring popular events such as the Olympics and the World's Fair.

Candler was known for his shrewd business tactics, and he was not afraid to use his wealth and influence to get what he wanted. He used his political connections to secure favorable tax breaks and regulations for Coca-Cola, and he was not above using intimidation and bribery to silence his critics and competitors. Despite these controversial tactics, Candler's leadership helped to turn Coca-Cola into a global brand that remains one of the most successful and profitable companies in history.

One of Candler's most significant contributions to the Coca-Cola Company was his focus on innovation and experimentation. He was constantly looking for ways to improve the taste, quality, and marketability of Coca-Cola, and he invested heavily in research and development to achieve these goals. He also encouraged his employees to be creative and innovative, and he fostered a culture of experimentation and risk-taking within the company.

Candler's legacy as an influential business mind is evident in the lasting impact that Coca-Cola has had on the world. His innovative ideas, tireless work ethic, and strategic business tactics helped to turn a relatively unknown beverage into a global brand that is recognized and enjoyed by billions of people. His focus on innovation and experimentation has influenced countless other entrepreneurs and business leaders, and his legacy as one of the most influential business minds of all time is secure.

In conclusion, Asa Griggs Candler was an innovative, tireless, and strategic business leader who played a pivotal role in the success of the Coca-Cola Company. His focus on innovation, experimentation, and strategic business tactics helped to turn Coca-Cola into a global brand that remains one of the most successful and profitable companies in history. Candler's legacy as one of the most influential business minds of all time is evident in the lasting impact that Coca-Cola has had on the world, and his innovative ideas and tactics continue to inspire entrepreneurs and business leaders today.

Asa Griggs Candler was known for his shrewd business tactics and work ethic, and there are several key elements of his approach that contributed to his success.

First, Candler was a master of advertising and marketing. He recognized early on that in order to build a successful business, he needed to create a strong brand and cultivate a loyal customer base. To do this, he invested heavily in advertising, using a range of innovative techniques to promote Coca-Cola and build its reputation.

One of Candler's most effective marketing strategies was his use of free samples and product placements. He would distribute samples of Coca-Cola at public events, such as fairs and festivals, to give people a taste of the beverage and create buzz around the brand. He also worked to secure product placements in movies, TV shows, and other forms of popular culture, helping to make Coca-Cola a household name.

Candler was also known for his aggressive business tactics. He was not afraid to use his wealth and influence to get what he wanted, and he was willing to take risks and make bold moves in order to grow his business. For example, he aggressively expanded the Coca-Cola brand by franchising its production and distribution to independent bottlers, which helped to increase its reach and popularity.

At the same time, Candler was also highly focused on quality and innovation. He believed that in order to succeed in the competitive world of business, he needed to constantly improve and innovate. He invested heavily in research and development to improve the taste, quality, and marketability of Coca-Cola, and he encouraged his employees to be creative and innovative in their work.

Finally, Candler was known for his strong work ethic and dedication to his business. He was willing to work long hours and make personal sacrifices in order to achieve his goals, and he expected the same level of commitment from his employees. He fostered a culture of hard work and dedication within the Coca-Cola company, which helped to build a strong and loyal team that was committed to the success of the brand.

In summary, Asa Griggs Candler was a shrewd businessman who used innovative advertising and marketing tactics, aggressive business strategies, and a focus on quality and innovation to build one of the most successful brands in history. He was known for his strong work ethic and dedication to his business, and he fostered a culture of innovation and hard work within the Coca-Cola company. These qualities and tactics helped to make him one of the most influential business minds of all time, and his legacy continues to inspire entrepreneurs and business leaders today.

The one thing that he did, that an entrepreneur should follow to be great today

One of the most important things that Asa Griggs Candler did that modern-day entrepreneurs can learn from is his focus on branding and marketing.

Candler recognized the importance of building a strong brand and cultivating a loyal customer base, and he invested heavily in advertising and marketing to achieve this goal. He used a range of innovative techniques, such as free samples and product placements, to promote Coca-Cola and build its reputation.

In today's highly competitive business environment, building a strong brand and developing effective marketing strategies is more important than ever. Entrepreneurs who want to be successful need to focus on creating a unique and compelling brand identity that resonates with their target audience. They need to invest in effective marketing strategies, such as social media advertising, influencer marketing, and content marketing, to reach their audience and build their reputation.

In addition, entrepreneurs can also learn from Candler's willingness to take risks and make bold moves in order to grow his business. While it's important to be cautious and strategic in decision-making, entrepreneurs who are willing to take calculated risks and make bold moves can often achieve great success and drive innovation in their industries.

Overall, by focusing on branding and marketing, taking calculated risks, and continually investing in innovation and quality, modern-day entrepreneurs can follow in the footsteps of Asa Griggs Candler and achieve great success in their businesses.

Some additional details about Asa Griggs Candler and his life as a businessman:

Candler was born in 1851 in Villa Rica, Georgia, and grew up on a farm. He attended Emory College and later went into the drugstore business with his brother.

Candler first became involved with Coca-Cola in 1888 when he purchased the formula and brand from its inventor, John Pemberton, for $2,300. He quickly recognized the potential of the brand and set about building it into a major business.

One of the keys to Candler's success with Coca-Cola was his ability to scale the business through franchising. He allowed independent bottlers to produce and distribute the drink, which helped to expand its reach and popularity.

Candler was also involved in philanthropy and civic life. He donated significant sums of money to Emory University, where he served on the board of trustees, and he was involved in various civic organizations and charitable causes.

In addition to Coca-Cola, Candler also owned a range of other businesses, including real estate holdings, banks, and newspapers.

Despite his success, Candler was known for his modest lifestyle and unassuming manner. He lived in a simple home and was known to dress plainly and drive a modest car.

Candler retired from active management of Coca-Cola in 1919 and sold his remaining stake in the company in 1923 for $25 million. He died in 1929 at the age of 77.

Overall, Asa Griggs Candler was a savvy businessman who recognized the potential of the Coca-Cola brand and worked tirelessly to build it into a major success. He was known for his innovative marketing and franchising strategies, as well as his focus on quality and innovation. His legacy continues to inspire entrepreneurs and business leaders today.

ANDREW CARNEGIE

Was a Scottish-American industrialist and philanthropist who rose to prominence during the late 19th century. He was born in Dunfermline, Scotland, on November 25, 1835, and immigrated to the United States with his family in 1848, settling in Allegheny, Pennsylvania. Although he came from humble beginnings, Carnegie became one of the wealthiest men in American history through his innovations, hard work, and business tactics.

Carnegie's rise to wealth began when he secured a job as a telegraph operator for the Pennsylvania Railroad at the age of 16. He quickly rose through the ranks, becoming the personal assistant to the president of the railroad company. He used this position to learn about the steel industry and eventually left the railroad to start his own steel business, the Carnegie Steel Company, in 1873.

Carnegie's innovation and vision were key to the success of his company. He was one of the first industrialists to implement the Bessemer process, a technique for mass-producing steel that made it more affordable and accessible. This allowed Carnegie to produce large quantities of steel at a lower cost than his competitors, giving him a significant advantage in the market.

Another key innovation of Carnegie's was his vertical

integration of the steel industry. He believed that controlling every aspect of the steel-making process, from mining the raw materials to shipping the finished product, would allow him to reduce costs and increase efficiency. This approach was highly successful, and by the early 20th century, Carnegie Steel was the largest steel company in the world.

Carnegie's business tactics were also highly influential. He was known for his aggressive approach to competition, using his wealth and influence to buy out his rivals or force them out of the market. He was also a master of negotiation, using his persuasive skills to secure favorable deals with suppliers and customers.

Despite his reputation as a ruthless businessman, Carnegie was also known for his philanthropy. He believed that the wealthy had a moral obligation to use their wealth for the greater good and donated millions of dollars to support causes such as education, scientific research, and the arts. His most famous philanthropic endeavor was the establishment of Carnegie libraries, which provided free access to books and knowledge for people of all ages and backgrounds.

Overall, Andrew Carnegie's life as a businessman was marked by innovation, hard work, and strategic thinking. His use of the Bessemer process and vertical integration helped him build a steel empire, while his aggressive tactics and negotiating skills allowed him to dominate the market. He also demonstrated a strong commitment to philanthropy, using his wealth to support causes that he believed would benefit society as a whole. For these reasons, Carnegie is considered one of the most influential business minds of all time.

Andrew Carnegie was a shrewd businessman who used a variety of tactics to build his empire. One of his most notable tactics was his focus on efficiency and cost-cutting.

He believed that by reducing costs, he could undercut his competitors and gain a larger share of the market. To this end, he implemented a number of cost-saving measures at his steel mills, including reducing the number of skilled workers in favor of more automation and using the latest technology to improve production processes.

Another key aspect of Carnegie's business ethic was his emphasis on vertical integration. He believed that by controlling every aspect of the steel-making process, he could reduce costs and improve efficiency. To this end, he purchased mines and railroad companies to secure a reliable supply of raw materials and transportation. He also invested heavily in research and development to improve the quality of his products and find new ways to reduce costs.

Carnegie was also known for his aggressive approach to competition. He was not afraid to use his wealth and influence to buy out his competitors or force them out of the market. He was also a skilled negotiator who used his persuasive skills to secure favorable deals with suppliers and customers. He was a strong believer in the power of networking and building relationships, and he worked tirelessly to cultivate connections that would benefit his business.

Despite his reputation as a ruthless businessman, Carnegie was also deeply committed to philanthropy. He believed that the wealthy had a moral obligation to use their wealth to improve society, and he donated millions of dollars to support causes such as education, scientific research, and the arts. He also established the Carnegie Foundation, which focused on promoting world peace and social progress.

In terms of how he did things, Carnegie was a hands-on manager who was deeply involved in every aspect of his business. He was known for his attention to detail and his ability to identify potential problems before they became major issues. He also placed a high value on teamwork and collaboration, and he worked closely with his employees to find ways to improve processes and increase efficiency.

Overall, Andrew Carnegie's work tactics and business ethic were characterized by a focus on efficiency, cost-cutting, and vertical integration. He was a skilled negotiator who was not afraid to use his wealth and influence to gain an advantage in the market. He was deeply committed to philanthropy and believed that the wealthy had a moral obligation to use their resources to benefit society. Through his innovations, hard work, and strategic thinking, Carnegie became one of the most successful businessmen in American history.

The one thing that Carnegie did, that an entrepreneur should follow to be great

There are several things that an entrepreneur could learn from Andrew Carnegie's business strategies and ethics. However, if I were to identify one thing that entrepreneurs could follow to be great today, it would be Carnegie's emphasis on continuous learning and innovation.

Carnegie was constantly seeking to improve his business and find new ways to reduce costs, increase efficiency, and improve the quality of his products. He was an early adopter of new technologies and production methods and was not afraid to invest heavily in research and development.

This emphasis on continuous learning and innovation is just as relevant today as it was during Carnegie's time. In today's rapidly changing business landscape, entrepreneurs need to be agile and adaptable, constantly seeking out new opportunities and ways to improve their operations.

Entrepreneurs can follow Carnegie's example by staying up to date with the latest trends and technologies in their industry, investing in research and development, and fostering a culture of innovation within their organization. They should also be willing to take calculated risks and try new approaches to stay ahead of the competition.

By adopting Carnegie's approach to continuous learning and innovation, entrepreneurs can position themselves for success and build businesses that are sustainable and resilient in the face of change.

Here are some additional details about Andrew Carnegie and his business career:

Early Life: Andrew Carnegie was born in Scotland in 1835 and emigrated to the United States with his family when he was 13 years old. He began working in a textile mill but soon moved on to other jobs, including telegraph messenger, railroad worker, and telegraph operator.

Rise to Prominence: Carnegie's breakthrough came when he was hired as the personal secretary to Thomas A. Scott, the president of the Pennsylvania Railroad. Scott recognized Carnegie's talents and helped him get involved in the railroad industry, where he made his first fortune.

Steel Industry: Carnegie's most significant business venture was in the steel industry. In the late 19th century, he founded the Carnegie Steel Company, which quickly became the largest and most profitable steel company in the world. He used a variety of strategies, including vertical integration and cost-cutting measures, to maintain his dominance in the market.

Philanthropy: Despite his enormous wealth, Carnegie was a strong believer in the power of philanthropy. He donated millions of dollars to charitable causes, including libraries, universities, and scientific research. He also established the Carnegie Foundation, which focused on promoting world peace and social progress.

Legacy: Andrew Carnegie's legacy as a businessman and philanthropist continues to this day. His innovative business strategies and emphasis on efficiency and cost-cutting have had a lasting impact on the business world, and his philanthropic efforts have helped to improve society in countless ways.

Writings: Carnegie was also a prolific writer and authored several books on business and personal development. His most famous book, "The Gospel of Wealth," argued that the wealthy had a moral obligation to use their wealth to benefit society.

Overall, Andrew Carnegie was a complex and multifaceted individual who left a significant mark on the business world and society as a whole. His innovative business strategies, commitment to philanthropy, and emphasis on continuous learning and improvement continue to inspire entrepreneurs and business leaders today.

SHAWN "JAY-Z" CARTER

also known as Shawn Corey Carter, is a musician, rapper, and entrepreneur, who has made significant contributions to the world of business. He is widely recognized for his innovative approach, unique style, and his ability to create and sustain successful businesses. In this article, we will take a closer look at his life as a businessman, his work and tactics, and explore why he is considered amongst the most influential business minds.

Early Life and Career:

Jay Z was born in Brooklyn, New York, in 1969. He grew up in a rough neighborhood and started selling drugs at a young age to make money. However, his love for music led him to pursue a career in the industry. He released his first album, "Reasonable Doubt," in 1996, which was a critical and commercial success. Since then, he has released numerous albums and has become one of the most successful musicians of all time.

Innovation Mind:

Jay Z's innovation mind is one of the key reasons why he has been so successful as a businessman. He has always been willing to take risks and try new things. For example, he was one of the first musicians to embrace digital music, and he launched his own streaming service, Tidal, in 2015. Tidal was designed to offer high-quality music and exclusive content to its subscribers, and it has since become a popular platform for music lovers around the world.

Work and Tactics:

Jay Z's work ethic and business tactics are also noteworthy. He is known for his attention to detail and his focus on creating high-quality products and services. He has also shown an ability to adapt to changing market conditions and to stay ahead of the competition. For example, he acquired the luxury champagne brand Ace of Spades in 2014 and has since transformed it into a major player in the industry.

Jay Z is also known for his collaborative approach to business. He has partnered with a variety of companies and individuals over the years, including Samsung, Live Nation, and his wife, Beyoncé. These partnerships have allowed him to expand his reach and to create new opportunities for his businesses.

Why Jay Z is Considered Amongst the Most Influential Business Minds:

Jay Z's impact on the business world cannot be overstated. He has built a diverse portfolio of businesses, including record labels, clothing lines, sports teams, and more. He has also demonstrated a keen understanding of marketing and branding, and his businesses have become known for their high-quality products and innovative marketing strategies.

Moreover, Jay Z has used his platform to advocate for social justice and to support causes that he believes in. He has been a vocal supporter of criminal justice reform and has used his music and businesses to raise awareness of issues affecting communities of color.

In conclusion, Jay Z's life as a businessman is a

testament to his innovation mind, work ethic, and business tactics. He has built an impressive portfolio of businesses and has demonstrated a unique ability to stay ahead of the competition and to adapt to changing market conditions. Moreover, his advocacy for social justice and his commitment to using his platform for positive change have made him a role model for aspiring entrepreneurs and business leaders around the world. It is for these reasons that he is considered amongst the most influential business minds of all time.

Jay Z has always been known for his attention to detail and his focus on creating high-quality products and services. He has consistently demonstrated a willingness to put in the time and effort required to achieve his goals, and he has never been afraid to take risks.

One of his key tactics has been to leverage his personal brand to build successful businesses. He has been able to create a strong brand identity that resonates with consumers and has used this identity to build a diverse portfolio of businesses.

For example, Jay Z launched his clothing line, Rocawear, in 1999. The line quickly became popular and was eventually sold to Iconix Brand Group for $204 million in 2007. Similarly, he launched his record label, Roc-A-Fella Records, in 1995 and used his personal brand to help promote the label and its artists.

Jay Z has also shown an ability to adapt to changing market conditions and to stay ahead of the competition. For example, he was one of the first musicians to embrace digital music, and he launched his own streaming service, Tidal, in 2015. Tidal was designed to offer high-quality music and exclusive content to its subscribers, and it has since become a popular platform for music lovers around the world.

Another important aspect of Jay Z's business ethic is his commitment to collaboration. He has formed partnerships with a variety of companies and individuals over the years, including Samsung, Live Nation, and his wife, Beyoncé. These partnerships have allowed him to expand his reach and to create new opportunities for his businesses.

Jay Z has also been vocal about the importance of giving back to the community. He has used his businesses and personal brand to support causes that he believes in, including criminal justice reform, education, and youth development.

In conclusion, Jay Z's work tactics and business ethic are characterized by his attention to detail, his willingness to take risks, his ability to adapt to changing market conditions, and his commitment to collaboration and giving back to the community. These qualities have helped him to build a successful and diverse portfolio of businesses and have made him a role model for aspiring entrepreneurs and business leaders.

The one thing that he did, that an entrepreneur should follow to be great today

There are many things that Jay Z did throughout his career that an entrepreneur could learn from, but if I had to pick just one, it would be his ability to identify and capitalize on emerging trends in the marketplace.

Throughout his career, Jay Z has consistently demonstrated an ability to stay ahead of the curve and to anticipate the changing needs and preferences of consumers. He was one of the first musicians to embrace digital music and to launch his own streaming service, Tidal, in response to the growing popularity of online music streaming.

In order to be successful as an entrepreneur today, it is

essential to be able to identify emerging trends and to adapt quickly to changing market conditions. This requires a combination of creativity, foresight, and a willingness to take calculated risks.

One way to develop this skill is to stay informed about the latest developments in your industry and to keep a close eye on emerging technologies and changing consumer behaviors. You can also seek out mentorship and guidance from experienced entrepreneurs who have a track record of success in your field.

Ultimately, the key to following in Jay Z's footsteps and becoming a great entrepreneur today is to be proactive, adaptable, and forward-thinking in your approach to business. By staying ahead of the curve and anticipating the needs of your customers, you can create innovative products and services that will set you apart from the competition and help you to achieve your goals.

Some more things about Jay Z that you may find interesting:

He started out as a drug dealer: Before pursuing a career in music, Jay Z was involved in selling drugs on the streets of Brooklyn. He has spoken openly about his past experiences with drugs and violence and has used his platform to advocate for criminal justice reform and social change.

He is a self-made billionaire: According to Forbes, Jay Z's net worth is estimated at $1.4 billion, making him one of the wealthiest musicians in the world. He achieved this level of success through a combination of his music career, his business ventures, and his investments.

He has won multiple Grammy Awards: Jay Z has won 22 Grammy Awards over the course of his career, including awards for Best Rap Performance, Best Rap Song, and Best Rap Album. He is tied with Kanye West for the most Grammy wins by a rapper.

He is a philanthropist: Jay Z has used his wealth and influence to support a variety of charitable causes over the years, including education, criminal justice reform, and social justice initiatives. He has donated millions of dollars to organizations like the Shawn Carter Foundation, which provides scholarships and mentorship to young people in need.

He is married to Beyoncé: Jay Z has been married to singer and actress Beyoncé since 2008. The couple has three children together and are widely regarded as one of the most influential and powerful couples in the entertainment industry.

STEVE CASE

is a name that is synonymous with innovation, entrepreneurship, and business acumen. He is one of the most influential business leaders of our time, having played a significant role in shaping the way we live, work, and interact with technology. From co-founding America Online (AOL) to his current role as CEO of Revolution LLC, Steve Case has proven himself to be a force to be reckoned with in the world of business.

Early Life and Career:

Born in Honolulu, Hawaii, in 1958, Steve Case was the son of a lawyer and a teacher. He attended Williams College, where he earned a degree in political science. After graduation, he landed a job at Procter & Gamble, but his passion for technology led him to join a startup called Control Video Corporation (CVC). It was at CVC that he met Jim Kimsey, who would later become his business partner at AOL.

Founding America Online:

In 1985, Case and Kimsey founded Quantum Computer Services, which was later renamed America Online (AOL). Initially, the company offered an online service for the Commodore 64 computer, but it wasn't until the mid-1990s that AOL became a household name. Case and Kimsey saw the potential of the internet and transformed AOL into a major internet service provider (ISP) and content provider.

They were instrumental in making the internet accessible to the masses, by offering easy-to-use dial-up services and a user-friendly interface.

Innovation and Strategy:

One of Steve Case's biggest strengths is his ability to think outside the box and come up with innovative ideas. He was one of the first business leaders to recognize the potential of the internet, and he played a major role in popularizing it. Case was also instrumental in developing AOL's business model, which relied on offering content and services to users rather than just providing internet access. This strategy helped AOL grow rapidly and become one of the most successful companies of the dot-com era.

Another key strategy that Case employed was mergers and acquisitions. AOL acquired several companies, including CompuServe and Netscape, which helped it expand its user base and diversify its offerings. Case was also an early investor in companies like Zipcar and LivingSocial, which showed his foresight in recognizing the potential of emerging industries.

Challenges and Legacy:

However, AOL faced several challenges during Case's tenure as CEO. The company struggled to keep up with the rapid pace of technological change and failed to adapt to the rise of broadband internet. AOL's merger with Time Warner in 2001 was also a failure, and the company's stock price plummeted, leading to Case's resignation as CEO.

Despite these setbacks, Steve Case's legacy as a business leader is indisputable. He was a pioneer in the internet industry and played a major role in popularizing the internet and making it accessible to the masses. His innovative thinking and strategic approach helped AOL grow into a multi-billion dollar company, and his foresight in recognizing emerging industries and technologies helped him become one of the most successful venture capitalists in the world.

In conclusion, Steve Case is a true icon of the business world. His innovative thinking, strategic approach, and foresight in recognizing emerging industries have made him one of the most influential business leaders of our time. While AOL faced challenges during his tenure as CEO, his legacy as a pioneer in the internet industry and as a successful venture capitalist is undeniable. Steve Case's story serves as an inspiration to aspiring entrepreneurs and business leaders, showing that with hard work, determination, and a willingness to take risks, anything is possible.

Steve Case was known for his unique work tactics and business ethic, which set him apart from other business leaders of his time. Here are some details about his work tactics and business ethic:

Long-term thinking: Steve Case was a visionary leader who always thought long-term. He recognized early on that the internet was going to be a game-changer and focused on building AOL into a company that could adapt to the changing landscape of the internet.

Customer-centric approach: Case was a firm believer in putting the customer first. He understood that the success of AOL depended on its ability to meet the needs of its users, and he worked tirelessly to ensure that AOL's products and services were user-friendly and met the needs of its customers.

Risk-taking: Steve Case was not afraid to take risks. He recognized that in order to succeed in the highly competitive world of technology, he had to be willing to take risks and make bold moves. For example, he invested heavily in emerging industries like car-sharing and social media, which paid off in the long run.

Strategic partnerships: Case was a master of strategic

partnerships. He recognized the value of partnering with other companies and organizations to achieve his goals. For example, he formed a partnership with Time Warner to merge AOL and Time Warner, which at the time was the largest corporate merger in history.

Innovation: Steve Case was a true innovator. He was constantly looking for new and better ways to do things, and he was not afraid to try out new ideas. For example, he pioneered the concept of offering online content and services to users, which was a game-changer in the internet industry.

Ethical business practices: Case was known for his strong ethical values and his commitment to doing business the right way. He believed in treating his employees, partners, and customers with respect and honesty, and he always conducted himself in a professional and ethical manner.

Overall, Steve Case's work tactics and business ethic were characterized by a focus on the long-term, a customer-centric approach, risk-taking, strategic partnerships, innovation, and ethical business practices. These values and strategies helped him build AOL into a highly successful company and made him one of the most influential business leaders of our time.

The one thing that he did, that an entrepreneur should follow to be great today

There are many things that Steve Case did throughout his career that entrepreneurs today can learn from and emulate, but if I had to highlight just one thing, it would be his ability to think long-term and anticipate future trends.

Steve Case was a visionary leader who recognized early on that the internet was going to be a game-changer and that it would transform the way we live and do business. He saw the potential of the internet before most people did and worked tirelessly to build AOL into a company that could adapt to the changing landscape of the internet.

In today's rapidly evolving business environment, it's more important than ever for entrepreneurs to be able to think long-term and anticipate future trends. This requires staying on top of emerging technologies and market trends, and being willing to take risks and make bold moves in order to stay ahead of the curve.

By following Steve Case's example and focusing on long-term thinking and anticipating future trends, entrepreneurs can position themselves for success in today's competitive business environment. This means investing in emerging technologies, building strong partnerships, and constantly innovating to stay ahead of the competition.

More details about Steve Case's life and career:

Early life and education: Steve Case was born in Honolulu, Hawaii in 1958. He attended Williams College in Massachusetts and graduated with a degree in political science.

Founding of AOL: In 1985, Case co-founded America Online (AOL), an online service provider that would go on to become one of the most successful internet companies of its time. Case played a key role in building AOL's brand and growing its user base, and under his leadership, the company became a dominant player in the industry.

Mergers and acquisitions: In addition to growing AOL's business organically, Case was also involved in a number of high-profile mergers and acquisitions during his time at the company. Perhaps the most notable of these was the merger of AOL and Time Warner in 2000, which was valued at $165 billion and was the largest corporate merger in history at the time.

Philanthropy and advocacy: In addition to his work in the business world, Steve Case has also been involved in a number of philanthropic and advocacy efforts throughout his career. He is a strong advocate for entrepreneurship and innovation, and he has used his wealth and influence to support a number of causes related to education, healthcare, and economic development.

Current projects: After stepping down as CEO of AOL in 2003, Case has continued to be active in the business world and in philanthropy. He is the chairman and CEO of Revolution LLC, a venture capital firm that invests in startups in a variety of industries. He is also the co-founder and chairman of the Case Foundation, a philanthropic organization that supports entrepreneurship and social impact initiatives.

COCO CHANEL

Also known as Gabrielle Bonheur Chanel, was a French businesswoman who revolutionized the fashion industry in the 20th century. Born in 1883 in Saumur, France, Chanel's childhood was marked by poverty and tragedy. Her mother passed away when she was young, and her father left her and her siblings in an orphanage. It was during her time at the orphanage that Chanel learned how to sew, a skill that would later become the foundation of her fashion empire.

Chanel began her career as a singer in cafes and clubs, where she earned the nickname "Coco." She eventually met and became involved with wealthy men who helped to finance her fashion endeavors. Chanel's first foray into fashion was designing hats, which quickly gained popularity among the elite in Paris. In 1910, she opened her first boutique, selling hats and later expanding to clothing.

One of the key factors that contributed to Chanel's success was her innovative approach to fashion. At the time, women's clothing was restrictive and uncomfortable, with corsets and petticoats being the norm. Chanel rejected these styles and instead designed clothing that was comfortable and practical, with clean lines and minimal embellishments. Her designs were a breath of fresh air in an industry that was dominated by frills and flounces.

Chanel was also a savvy businesswoman who employed a number of tactics to grow her brand. She created a signature scent, Chanel No. 5, which is still popular to this day. She also made strategic partnerships with other businesses, such as the jewelry company Gripoix, which helped to expand her reach and appeal to a wider audience.

Chanel was not afraid to take risks and break with convention, which helped to set her apart from her competitors. For example, she was one of the first designers to use jersey fabric in her designs, which was considered a bold move at the time. She also popularized the "little black dress," which was a departure from the brightly colored dresses that were popular in the 1920s.

Another factor that contributed to Chanel's success was her ability to adapt to changing times. During World War II, she closed her boutiques and moved to Switzerland, but she continued to design and create fashion during this time. When she returned to Paris after the war, she found that the fashion industry had changed, and she adapted her designs to reflect the new styles and trends.

Chanel's impact on the fashion industry cannot be overstated. She was a pioneer who revolutionized the way women dressed and paved the way for future designers to experiment with new styles and fabrics. Her legacy lives on today in the form of the iconic Chanel brand, which remains one of the most recognizable and influential fashion houses in the world.

In conclusion, Coco Chanel's innovation, work ethic, and business tactics make her one of the most influential business minds of all time. Her ability to reject convention and embrace new ideas helped to set her apart from her competitors and establish her as a leader in the fashion industry. Her legacy lives on today, and her impact on the world of fashion will continue to be felt for generations to come.

Chanel was a shrewd businesswoman who employed a number of tactics to grow her brand and establish herself as a leader in the fashion industry. Here are some additional details about her work tactics and business ethics:

Attention to detail: Chanel was known for her meticulous attention to detail, which was evident in her designs as well as in the way she ran her business. She was involved in every aspect of her brand, from the design process to the manufacturing to the marketing.

Brand identity: Chanel understood the importance of building a strong brand identity, and she did so by creating a signature look that was instantly recognizable. Her use of the interlocking CC logo and the colors black and white became synonymous with the Chanel brand.

Customer experience: Chanel was committed to providing her customers with an exceptional experience, from the moment they entered her boutiques to the moment they left. She created a luxurious and elegant environment in her stores and trained her staff to provide personalized service to each customer.

Strategic partnerships: Chanel made strategic partnerships with other businesses to help grow her brand and expand her reach. For example, she partnered with the jewelry company Gripoix to create beautiful, high-quality accessories that complemented her clothing designs.

Innovation: Chanel was a true innovator who was not afraid to take risks and experiment with new ideas. She was one of the first designers to use jersey fabric in her designs, and she popularized the "little black dress" at a time when brightly colored dresses were the norm.

Adaptability: Chanel understood the importance of adapting to changing times and trends, and she was able to do so successfully throughout her career. When World War II broke out, she closed her boutiques and moved to Switzerland, but she continued to design and create fashion during this time. When she returned to Paris after the war, she adapted her designs to reflect the new styles and trends.

Work ethic: Chanel was known for her tireless work ethic and her commitment to her craft. She was often quoted as saying, "I have not slept for 20 years. I have sacrificed everything to my work."

Overall, Chanel's work tactics and business ethic were characterized by attention to detail, a focus on building a strong brand identity, a commitment to providing an exceptional customer experience, strategic partnerships, innovation, adaptability, and a tireless work ethic. These qualities helped to make her one of the most influential business minds of all time, and her legacy continues to inspire designers and entrepreneurs to this day.

The one thing that she did, that an entrepreneur should follow to be great today

One thing that entrepreneurs can learn from Chanel is the importance of innovation and taking calculated risks. Chanel was not afraid to try new things, and she often experimented with fabrics, designs, and marketing tactics that were unconventional for her time. For example, she introduced the concept of the little black dress at a time when bright colors were the norm, and she was one of the first designers to use jersey fabric in her designs.

Today, entrepreneurs can also benefit from taking calculated risks and experimenting with new ideas. In a rapidly changing business landscape, it's important to be adaptable and willing to try new things in order to stay ahead of the competition. By embracing innovation and taking calculated risks, entrepreneurs can create unique products or services that stand out in a crowded marketplace.

Chanel's legacy also underscores the importance of creating a strong brand identity and delivering an exceptional customer experience. By focusing on these aspects of her business, Chanel was able to create a loyal customer base that remains committed to the brand today. Entrepreneurs who prioritize these elements in their own businesses can also create a strong following and establish themselves as leaders in their industry.

Some additional details about Coco Chanel's life and career as a businesswoman:

Early life: Chanel was born in Saumur, France in 1883, and was raised in an orphanage after her mother's death. She learned to sew while living in the orphanage and later worked as a seamstress in a small shop in Moulins.

Early career: Chanel began her career as a singer in cafes and clubs in the early 1900s, but she soon shifted her focus to fashion design. In 1910, she opened her first hat shop in Paris, and her designs quickly gained popularity among the fashionable elite.

Breakthrough designs: Chanel is credited with introducing a number of groundbreaking designs to the fashion world. In addition to the little black dress and the use of jersey fabric, she also popularized the use of costume jewelry, created the Chanel suit (a classic tweed jacket and skirt combination), and introduced the quilted handbag.

Controversies: Chanel's life was not without controversy. During World War II, she was accused of collaborating with the Nazis and fled to Switzerland for a time. She was also involved in a number of personal scandals, including a relationship with a Nazi officer.

Legacy: Despite the controversies surrounding her life, Chanel's legacy as a fashion designer and businesswoman remains significant. Her designs continue to be influential in the fashion world, and her brand is one of the most recognized and respected in the industry. In addition, her focus on simplicity, elegance, and practicality has influenced generations of designers and entrepreneurs.

Overall, Coco Chanel's life and career were marked by innovation, creativity, and a tireless work ethic. Despite facing personal and professional challenges, she was able to create a brand and a legacy that continue to inspire designers and entrepreneurs around the world.

BRIAN CHESKY

Is an American entrepreneur and businessman who is widely regarded as one of the most influential and innovative business minds of his generation. He is the co-founder and CEO of Airbnb, a popular online platform that connects travelers with unique accommodations and experiences around the world.

Born in Niskayuna, New York, in 1981, Chesky developed an early interest in design and technology. He graduated from the Rhode Island School of Design in 2004 with a degree in industrial design and began his career working as a designer for a variety of companies, including 3DID, Inc., and Industrial Light and Magic.

In 2007, Chesky and his college roommate, Joe Gebbia, founded Airbnb in San Francisco, California. The company's initial concept was to rent out air mattresses in their apartment to attendees of a design conference who were unable to find a hotel room. From this humble beginning, the company has grown into a global phenomenon that has disrupted the hospitality industry.

One of the key factors that has made Chesky such an influential businessman is his innovative approach to solving problems. When faced with the challenge of creating a new type of lodging experience that would appeal to travelers seeking a more authentic and personalized experience, Chesky and his team came up with the idea of allowing hosts to rent out their spare rooms, apartments, or even entire homes to travelers.

This concept not only allowed Airbnb to differentiate itself from traditional hotel chains but also enabled the company to tap into a vast and previously untapped market of travelers who were looking for a more immersive and authentic travel experience.

Chesky's focus on design and user experience has also been a key factor in the success of Airbnb. From the early days of the company, Chesky recognized the importance of creating a seamless and intuitive user experience that would make it easy for hosts and guests to find each other and transact on the platform. This focus on design and user experience has enabled Airbnb to create a loyal and engaged community of users who have helped to fuel the company's growth and success.

Another important aspect of Chesky's leadership style is his willingness to take risks and try new things. Despite facing significant regulatory challenges and pushback from traditional hotel chains and landlords, Chesky and his team have continued to innovate and push the boundaries of what is possible in the hospitality industry.

For example, in 2016, Airbnb launched a new platform called Trips, which allows users to book not only accommodations but also experiences and activities led by local hosts. This move into the experience economy represented a significant expansion of Airbnb's business model and has helped to cement the company's position as a leader in the travel industry.

Chesky's commitment to social responsibility and sustainability is also worth mentioning. Under his leadership, Airbnb has taken steps to promote eco-friendly practices among its hosts and guests, and has also launched initiatives to provide support and assistance to communities affected by natural disasters and other crises.

In conclusion, Brian Chesky's innovative approach to problem-solving, focus on design and user experience, willingness to take risks, and commitment to social responsibility and sustainability have all contributed to his status as one of the most influential and innovative business minds of his generation. His leadership of Airbnb has not only disrupted the hospitality industry but also opened up new opportunities for travelers and hosts around the world. It is clear that Chesky's legacy as a businessman and entrepreneur will be felt for many years to come.

Brian Chesky is known for his unique work tactics and business ethics that have helped him lead Airbnb to great success. Here are some of the key aspects of his approach:

Focus on community: Chesky has always prioritized building a sense of community among Airbnb hosts and guests. He believes that creating a strong and engaged community is essential to the success of the platform. To this end, he has encouraged hosts to connect with one another, share their experiences, and provide feedback on how to improve the platform.

User-centered design: Chesky's background in design has influenced his approach to business, particularly in the area of user-centered design. He has always prioritized creating a seamless and intuitive user experience that makes it easy for hosts and guests to use the platform. Chesky and his team have conducted extensive user research to ensure that they understand the needs and preferences of their users and have used this knowledge to continually improve the platform.

Experimentation: Chesky is not afraid to take risks and try new things. He believes that experimentation is essential to innovation and has encouraged his team to try out new features and products. This willingness to experiment has helped Airbnb stay ahead of its competitors and has enabled the company to expand into new markets and business areas.

Data-driven decision-making: Chesky has always emphasized the importance of data in decision-making. He and his team regularly analyze data to identify trends, understand user behavior, and make informed decisions about product development and marketing. This data-driven approach has helped Airbnb make strategic decisions that have contributed to the company's success.

Social responsibility: Chesky has emphasized the importance of social responsibility in business. He has encouraged Airbnb hosts to promote sustainability and eco-friendliness by adopting practices like recycling and using energy-efficient appliances. He has also launched initiatives to support communities affected by natural disasters and other crises, demonstrating his commitment to making a positive impact on the world.

Overall, Brian Chesky's work tactics and business ethics reflect his commitment to creating a platform that provides value to users while also promoting social responsibility and sustainability. His user-centered design approach, willingness to experiment, and data-driven decision-making have helped Airbnb stay ahead of its competitors and continue to innovate in the travel industry.

The one thing that he did, that an entrepreneur should follow to be great today

One key aspect of Brian Chesky's approach that entrepreneurs can follow to be great today is his emphasis on user-centered design. Chesky's background in design has influenced his approach to business, and he has always prioritized creating a seamless and intuitive user experience that makes it easy for hosts and guests to use the Airbnb platform. Entrepreneurs today can learn from Chesky's focus on user-centered design by placing the needs and preferences of their customers at the center of their product development process. This means conducting user research to understand customer pain points, preferences, and behaviors, and using this knowledge to create products and services that meet their needs.

In addition, entrepreneurs should be willing to experiment and try new things. Chesky's willingness to take risks and try out new features and products has helped Airbnb stay ahead of its competitors and has enabled the company to expand into new markets and business areas. Entrepreneurs today can follow this example by being open to new ideas, trying out new approaches, and being willing to pivot their business strategy as needed.

Finally, social responsibility is another key aspect of Chesky's approach that entrepreneurs can learn from. Chesky has emphasized the importance of social responsibility in business and has encouraged Airbnb hosts to promote sustainability and eco-friendliness. Entrepreneurs today can follow this example by incorporating social responsibility into their business model and being mindful of the impact their business has on the world. This can help create a positive brand image and attract customers who value sustainability and social responsibility.

Some additional interesting facts about Brian Chesky:

Early life and education: Chesky was born in New York in 1981 and grew up in Albany, New York. He attended the Rhode Island School of Design, where he earned a Bachelor of Fine Arts degree in Industrial Design.

Early career: After graduating from college, Chesky moved to Los Angeles and worked as an industrial designer for several years. He also founded a design company called Redefine, which focused on creating sustainable and eco-friendly products.

Founding Airbnb: In 2007, Chesky and his roommate Joe Gebbia came up with the idea for Airbnb when they were struggling to pay their rent in San Francisco. They decided to rent out air mattresses in their apartment to attendees of a design conference who were having trouble finding accommodations. The idea proved to be popular, and Chesky and Gebbia decided to turn it into a business.

Growth of Airbnb: Under Chesky's leadership, Airbnb has grown from a small startup to a global platform with over 4 million listings in more than 220 countries and regions. The company has raised over $6 billion in funding and is valued at over $100 billion.

Philanthropy: Chesky is known for his philanthropic efforts, particularly in the areas of homelessness and education. In 2019, he pledged $25 million to support affordable housing and homelessness initiatives in San Francisco, and he has also pledged to donate the majority of his wealth to charitable causes.

Recognition and awards: Chesky has been recognized as one of Time magazine's 100 most influential people, and he has received numerous awards for his leadership and entrepreneurship, including the Bloomberg 50 and the Fortune 40 under 40.

TIM COOK

is an American business executive who currently serves as the CEO of Apple Inc. He was born on November 1, 1960, in Mobile, Alabama, and grew up in Robertsdale. Cook's father was a shipyard worker, and his mother was a homemaker.

Cook received a Bachelor of Science degree in Industrial Engineering from Auburn University in 1982 and a Master of Business Administration (MBA) from Duke University's Fuqua School of Business in 1988.

Cook started his career at IBM, where he worked for 12 years in various positions, including the Director of North American Fulfillment. In 1994, Cook joined Compaq, where he served as Vice President of Corporate Materials.

In 1998, Cook joined Apple Inc. as the Senior Vice President for Worldwide Operations. He was responsible for the company's global supply chain, sales activities, and service and support. Cook's expertise in managing supply chains made him an instrumental figure in the success of the iPod and the iPhone.

In August 2011, Cook was named the CEO of Apple Inc. following the resignation of Steve Jobs due to health reasons. Cook became the first CEO of Apple who was not a founder of the company. Since then, Cook has been credited with steering the company to continued success, making him one of the most influential business leaders of his time.

One of Cook's biggest contributions to Apple is his innovation mindset. Cook has been instrumental in the development and launch of several products, including the Apple Watch and the AirPods. He also spearheaded the development of the iPhone, which has become one of the most successful products in Apple's history.

Under Cook's leadership, Apple has continued to innovate in terms of design, technology, and user experience. Cook has also championed the company's commitment to sustainability, overseeing the implementation of clean energy initiatives across the company's operations.

Cook's work and tactics have been instrumental in Apple's continued success. He is known for his attention to detail and his ability to manage complex operations. Cook has also been praised for his leadership style, which emphasizes collaboration and teamwork.

In addition to his work at Apple, Cook has been an outspoken advocate for social and political issues. He has been a vocal supporter of LGBT rights, and in 2014, he publicly announced that he is gay. Cook has also been an advocate for environmental sustainability and has been vocal about the need for action on climate change.

Overall, Tim Cook's contribution to the success of Apple, his innovation mindset, his attention to detail, and his commitment to sustainability and social issues have made him one of the most influential business leaders of all time. His leadership and management style have been praised by many, and his dedication to innovation and progress have cemented his place in the pantheon of great business minds.

Tim Cook is known for his hands-on approach to leadership, attention to detail, and his commitment to ensuring that Apple's products and services are accessible to everyone. Here are some specific examples of Cook's work tactics and business ethic:

Attention to Detail: Cook is known for his meticulous attention to detail. He reviews every aspect of the company's operations and is actively involved in the development of new products and services. Cook is also known for his focus on data-driven decision-making, using metrics and analytics to guide his decision-making process.

Focus on Customer Experience: Cook is committed to ensuring that Apple's products and services deliver an exceptional customer experience. He has been known to personally respond to customer complaints and inquiries, and he encourages Apple employees to prioritize customer satisfaction in all aspects of their work.

Supply Chain Management: Cook's expertise in supply chain management has been a key factor in Apple's success. Cook has worked to streamline the company's manufacturing and distribution processes, ensuring that products are delivered on time and at a reasonable cost.

Ethical Business Practices: Cook is committed to running Apple in an ethical and sustainable manner. He has been a vocal advocate for environmental sustainability, human rights, and social justice issues, and he has made it a priority to ensure that Apple's suppliers operate in a responsible and ethical manner.

Innovation: Cook is known for his commitment to innovation, and he has continued to push the boundaries of what is possible in the tech industry. Under Cook's leadership, Apple has introduced numerous groundbreaking products and services, including the iPhone, iPad, and Apple Watch.

Corporate Social Responsibility: Cook has made it a priority to ensure that Apple operates in a socially responsible manner. He has led the company's efforts to reduce its carbon footprint and has been a vocal advocate for issues such as LGBT rights and immigration reform. Cook has also established programs to promote diversity and inclusion within the company.

Collaboration: Cook has been praised for his collaborative approach to leadership. He works closely with Apple's senior management team to make strategic decisions and encourages employees at all levels of the company to contribute their ideas and insights.

In summary, Tim Cook's work tactics and business ethic are characterized by attention to detail, customer focus, expertise in supply chain management, commitment to ethical business practices, a focus on innovation, corporate social responsibility, and collaboration. These qualities have helped to make Cook one of the most influential business minds of all time and have contributed to Apple's success as a company.

The one thing that he did, that an entrepreneur should follow to be great today

There are many things that Tim Cook has done that have contributed to his success as an entrepreneur and businessman, so it's difficult to single out just one thing. However, if I had to choose, I would say that one of the most important things that entrepreneurs can learn from Cook is his focus on customer experience.

Cook has always been committed to ensuring that Apple's products and services deliver an exceptional customer experience. He understands that customers are the lifeblood of any business, and he has made it a priority to prioritize their needs and expectations in all aspects of Apple's operations.

By focusing on the customer experience, Cook has been able

to build a loyal customer base and differentiate Apple from its competitors. He has also been able to drive innovation within the company, as he recognizes that customer needs and expectations are constantly evolving.

For entrepreneurs who are just starting out, this focus on customer experience is crucial. By putting the customer at the center of everything you do, you can build a strong brand, establish a loyal customer base, and differentiate yourself from your competitors. This requires a deep understanding of your target market, a willingness to listen to customer feedback, and a commitment to delivering products and services that meet their needs and exceed their expectations.

In short, if there is one thing that entrepreneurs can learn from Tim Cook, it is the importance of putting the customer first and focusing on delivering an exceptional customer experience.

Some additional things about Tim Cook:

Career at Apple: Tim Cook joined Apple in 1998 and worked his way up the ranks, eventually becoming the company's CEO in 2011 after the resignation of Steve Jobs. Prior to becoming CEO, Cook served as Apple's Chief Operating Officer, where he oversaw the company's global sales and operations.

Education and Early Career: Cook holds a Bachelor of Science degree in Industrial Engineering from Auburn University and an MBA from Duke University's Fuqua School of Business. Before joining Apple, Cook held various executive positions at companies such as Compaq and IBM.

Philanthropy: Cook is a philanthropist and has used his wealth to support various causes, including education, social justice, and environmental sustainability. In 2015, Cook launched the Apple Global Volunteer Program, which encourages Apple employees to volunteer their time and expertise to support local communities.

LGBT Rights: Cook is openly gay and has been a vocal advocate for LGBT rights. In 2014, he became the first CEO of a Fortune 500 company to publicly come out as gay. Cook has been a strong supporter of LGBT rights and has used his position at Apple to advocate for issues such as marriage equality and workplace diversity.

Board Memberships: Cook serves on the board of directors for several companies, including Nike and the National Football Foundation. He has also served on the board of directors for the Robert F. Kennedy Center for Justice and Human Rights.

Apple's Financial Performance: Under Cook's leadership, Apple has continued to be one of the most valuable and profitable companies in the world. In 2020, Apple became the first U.S. company to reach a market capitalization of $2 trillion.

In summary, Tim Cook's career at Apple, education and early career, philanthropy, advocacy for LGBT rights, board memberships, and Apple's financial performance are all notable aspects of his life and career as a businessman.

KING CROESUS

Was a ruler of the ancient kingdom of Lydia, which was located in what is now western Turkey. He is often credited with being one of the most successful businessmen and entrepreneurs of all time, due to his innovative ideas and tactics, as well as his considerable wealth and influence. In this essay, we will examine the life and business practices of King Croesus and explore why he is still considered a major influence on business today.

Early Life and Rise to Power

King Croesus was born into a wealthy family, and he inherited the throne of Lydia from his father around 560 BCE. At the time, Lydia was a prosperous kingdom that had a thriving trade network with neighboring countries, and Croesus saw an opportunity to expand that network and increase his own wealth and power.

Innovation and Business Tactics

One of Croesus' most innovative ideas was to mint his own currency, which allowed him to control the economy of Lydia and make it easier for merchants to conduct trade. He also standardized weights and measures, making it easier for merchants to conduct transactions without fear of being cheated.

In addition to these innovations, Croesus was known for his

shrewd business tactics. He would often buy up goods in advance of a shortage and then sell them at a higher price when demand increased. He also encouraged merchants to settle in Lydia and offered them protection and other incentives to do so.

Perhaps Croesus' most famous business tactic, however, was his use of spies to gather information about his competitors. He would send spies into neighboring kingdoms to gather information about their resources, trade practices, and military capabilities, which he would then use to his advantage in negotiations and trade agreements.

Wealth and Influence

Croesus' business innovations and tactics paid off handsomely, and he became one of the wealthiest and most powerful rulers of his time. He amassed a vast fortune in gold and other precious metals, which he used to build grand monuments and other public works in Lydia.

In addition to his wealth, Croesus was also known for his influence on other rulers and states. He was able to negotiate favorable trade agreements with neighboring kingdoms and even formed alliances with some of them. He was also known for his military prowess and was able to successfully defend Lydia against attacks from other kingdoms.

Legacy and Influence

Despite his eventual downfall, which came when he was defeated by the Persian king Cyrus the Great, Croesus remains a major influence on business and entrepreneurship today. His innovations in currency, trade, and espionage helped to shape the business practices of his time and laid the groundwork for many of the practices that are still used today.

Furthermore, Croesus' focus on wealth and power serves as a reminder of the potential benefits and dangers of business.

While his wealth allowed him to build grand monuments and provide for his people, it also made him a target for enemies and ultimately led to his downfall.

In conclusion, King Croesus was an innovative and successful businessman and entrepreneur whose ideas and practices continue to influence the business world today. His focus on innovation, shrewd business tactics, and wealth accumulation made him one of the most powerful rulers of his time and a major influence on the course of history.

King Croesus was known for his innovative business tactics and his focus on wealth and power. Some of his most notable work tactics and business ethics include:

Minting His Own Currency: As mentioned earlier, Croesus minted his own currency, which allowed him to control the economy of Lydia and make it easier for merchants to conduct trade. This was a revolutionary idea at the time and helped to standardize trade practices in the region.

Standardizing Weights and Measures: In addition to minting his own currency, Croesus also standardized weights and measures in Lydia. This ensured that merchants could conduct transactions without fear of being cheated and helped to build trust among traders.

Encouraging Merchants to Settle in Lydia: Croesus understood the importance of having a thriving trade network, so he encouraged merchants to settle in Lydia and offered them protection and other incentives to do so. This helped to build a strong economy and made Lydia an attractive destination for traders.

Using Spies to Gather Information: Perhaps Croesus' most famous business tactic was his use of spies to gather information about his competitors. He would send spies into neighboring kingdoms to gather information about their resources, trade practices, and military capabilities, which he would then use to his advantage in negotiations and trade agreements.

Negotiating Favorable Trade Agreements: Croesus was a skilled negotiator and was able to secure favorable trade agreements with neighboring kingdoms. He understood the importance of building strong relationships with other rulers and was able to use diplomacy to his advantage.

Building Public Works: Croesus used his wealth to build grand monuments and other public works in Lydia. This helped to build his reputation as a powerful and benevolent ruler and ensured that he had the support of his people.

Military Prowess: Finally, Croesus was known for his military prowess and was able to successfully defend Lydia against attacks from other kingdoms. This helped to secure his position as a powerful ruler and allowed him to expand his influence in the region.

Overall, King Croesus was a shrewd businessman and skilled negotiator who understood the importance of innovation, diplomacy, and military power. His business tactics and ethics continue to influence the business world today and serve as a reminder of the potential benefits and dangers of business.

The one thing that he did, that an entrepreneur should follow to be great

One thing that entrepreneurs can learn from King Croesus is the importance of gathering information and intelligence about their competitors. Croesus' use of spies to gather information about neighboring kingdoms was a revolutionary tactic at the time and gave him a significant advantage in negotiations and trade agreements.

In today's business world, gathering competitive intelligence is still critical to the success of any business. Entrepreneurs should research their competitors' products, marketing strategies, and pricing to gain a better understanding of the market landscape and identify areas where they can differentiate themselves. This can help entrepreneurs to make more informed decisions, develop better products and services, and stay ahead of the competition.

Additionally, like King Croesus, entrepreneurs should focus on building strong relationships with other businesses and industry leaders. By networking and collaborating with others, entrepreneurs can build a support system and gain valuable insights and resources that can help them grow and succeed in their businesses.

Some additional things to know about King Croesus:

Croesus was a wealthy king who lived in the ancient kingdom of Lydia, which was located in what is now modern-day Turkey. He is known for his legendary wealth and was said to have been the first ruler to mint his own coins.

Croesus is also known for his legendary wisdom, which he demonstrated when he sought advice from the Oracle of Delphi before going to war with the Persian Empire. The Oracle famously responded, "If Croesus goes to war, he will destroy a great empire." Croesus took this to mean that he would emerge victorious, but in fact, it was a warning that his own empire would be destroyed.

Despite this warning, Croesus went to war with the Persians, and his empire was eventually conquered by the Persian king Cyrus the Great. Croesus was spared from execution and was said to have lived out the rest of his life in the Persian court as an advisor to Cyrus.

In addition to his military campaigns, Croesus was also known for his contributions to the arts and sciences. He is said to have commissioned the construction of the Temple of Artemis, which was one of the Seven Wonders of the Ancient

World.

Croesus was also known for his generosity and is said to have distributed his wealth among the people of Lydia. He was known to be a kind and just ruler who cared about the welfare of his subjects.

In later years, Croesus became a symbol of wealth and prosperity, and his name became synonymous with a wealthy man. Today, the phrase "rich as Croesus" is still used to describe someone who is very wealthy.

Overall, King Croesus was a legendary figure who is remembered for his wealth, wisdom, and contributions to art and science. While his military campaigns ultimately led to his downfall, his legacy continues to inspire people to this day.

MARK CUBAN

is a well-known entrepreneur, investor, and owner of the NBA's Dallas Mavericks. He is also known for his appearances on the television show "Shark Tank," where he invests in new businesses and products. Cuban has made a name for himself in the business world with his innovative ideas, hard work, and unique tactics.

Cuban was born in Pittsburgh, Pennsylvania in 1958. He grew up in a working-class family and showed an early interest in business and entrepreneurship. He attended the University of Pittsburgh and then transferred to Indiana University, where he graduated with a degree in business administration.

After college, Cuban moved to Dallas, Texas, where he started his first business, MicroSolutions. The company provided computer software and hardware to businesses and quickly grew into a successful venture. In 1990, Cuban sold MicroSolutions for $6 million and moved on to his next venture, Broadcast.com.

Broadcast.com was a streaming audio and video website that provided live coverage of events such as the Grammy Awards and the Victoria's Secret Fashion Show. Cuban recognized the potential of streaming media and quickly built Broadcast.com into a successful business. In 1999, Yahoo! acquired Broadcast.com for $5.7 billion, making Cuban a billionaire.

After the sale of Broadcast.com, Cuban turned his attention to other ventures. He started a film production company called 2929 Entertainment, which produced movies such as "Good Night, and Good Luck" and "Akeelah and the Bee." He also invested in several startups and became a regular on the television show "Shark Tank."

Cuban's success as a businessman can be attributed to several factors. First and foremost, he is known for his innovative ideas. He recognized the potential of streaming media long before it became mainstream and was able to capitalize on this early on. He also has a knack for identifying opportunities in emerging markets and investing in startups that show promise.

Another key factor in Cuban's success is his work ethic. He is known for working long hours and putting in the time and effort necessary to make his businesses successful. He is also willing to take risks and make bold decisions, even if they go against conventional wisdom.

Cuban's unique tactics have also helped him succeed in the business world. He is known for being a hands-on manager who is not afraid to get involved in the day-to-day operations of his businesses. He is also known for being a shrewd negotiator and has been involved in several high-profile business deals over the years.

In addition to his success as a businessman, Cuban is also known for his philanthropic efforts. He has donated millions of dollars to various charities and causes, including the fight against cancer and efforts to help veterans.

In conclusion, Mark Cuban is one of the most influential business minds of all time. His innovative ideas, hard work, and unique tactics have helped him succeed in the business world and make a name for himself as a successful entrepreneur and investor. His ability to identify opportunities in emerging markets and his willingness to take risks have set him apart from other businessmen and made him a role model for aspiring entrepreneurs.more details about Mark Cuban's work tactics and business ethics.

One of the most notable aspects of Cuban's work tactics is his hands-on management style. He is known for being heavily involved in the day-to-day operations of his businesses, and he takes a very active role in decision-making processes. For example, when he bought the Dallas Mavericks, he quickly began making changes to the team's management and player personnel, which led to a significant improvement in their performance.

Cuban is also known for being very data-driven in his decision-making. He is a big believer in using analytics and metrics to evaluate performance and make strategic decisions. This has been particularly evident in his ownership of the Mavericks, where he has implemented a number of innovative statistical analysis techniques to evaluate player performance and make roster decisions.

Another key aspect of Cuban's work tactics is his willingness to take risks. He is not afraid to invest in new and unproven ideas or to make bold decisions that go against conventional wisdom. This willingness to take risks has led to some of his biggest successes, such as his early investment in streaming media with Broadcast.com.

In terms of business ethics, Cuban is known for being very honest and straightforward in his dealings. He has been very vocal about his disdain for shady business practices and has taken a strong stance against insider trading and other forms of financial fraud. He also has a reputation for being very fair and respectful to his employees and business partners, and he is known for treating people with respect and kindness.

Another key aspect of Cuban's business ethics is his

commitment to philanthropy. He has donated millions of dollars to various charities and causes over the years, and he is known for using his wealth and influence to make a positive impact in the world. He has also been very vocal about social issues, such as racial inequality and climate change, and has used his platform to advocate for change.

Overall, Mark Cuban's work tactics and business ethics are characterized by his hands-on management style, data-driven decision-making, willingness to take risks, commitment to honesty and fairness, and dedication to philanthropy. These qualities have made him one of the most successful and influential businessmen of all time, and they serve as a model for aspiring entrepreneurs and business leaders.

The one thing that he did, that an entrepreneur should follow to be great today

There are many things that Mark Cuban has done throughout his career that have contributed to his success as an entrepreneur and businessman. However, one particular thing that stands out and that other entrepreneurs could learn from is his relentless focus on innovation.

Cuban has always been a champion of new and innovative ideas, and he has been willing to take risks and invest in unproven technologies and business models. He was an early investor in the internet, recognizing its potential for disruption and growth long before many others did. He also invested in the development of streaming media and was a key player in the early days of online video.

Cuban's focus on innovation has also been evident in his ownership of the Dallas Mavericks. He has been willing to try out new approaches to player evaluation and game strategy, using cutting-edge analytics and metrics to gain a competitive advantage. He has also been an advocate for new technologies in sports, such as virtual reality and wearable technology.

In today's rapidly changing business landscape, innovation is more important than ever. Entrepreneurs who want to be successful need to be willing to take risks and try new things, even if they go against conventional wisdom. They need to be willing to invest in new technologies and business models, and to be constantly on the lookout for new opportunities for growth and expansion.

By following Mark Cuban's example and making innovation a top priority, entrepreneurs can stay ahead of the curve and position themselves for long-term success in today's dynamic and constantly evolving business environment.

Some more interesting things about Mark Cuban:

Early Career: Before he became a successful businessman, Cuban worked as a bartender, disco dancing instructor, and even started his own business selling garbage bags door-to-door.

Broadcast.com: Cuban co-founded Broadcast.com, an internet radio company that he sold to Yahoo! for almost $6 billion in 1999. This was one of the biggest tech deals of its time.

Dallas Mavericks: In 2000, Cuban bought the Dallas Mavericks NBA franchise for $285 million. Under his ownership, the team has become one of the most successful and profitable franchises in the league, winning the NBA championship in 2011.

Shark Tank: Cuban is also well-known for his role as one of the "sharks" on the popular TV show Shark Tank, where he invests in and mentors up-and-coming entrepreneurs.

Tech Investor: Cuban is a prolific tech investor, having

invested in numerous successful startups, including CyberDust (a messaging app), Xpire (a social media management tool), and Unikrn (an esports betting platform).

Political Views: Cuban has been outspoken on a range of political issues, including healthcare reform, tax policy, and immigration. He has also considered running for political office, including a potential presidential run in 2020.

Philanthropy: Cuban is a noted philanthropist and has donated millions of dollars to various causes and charities over the years, including the Center for Public Integrity and the Fallen Patriot Fund. He has also pledged to donate the majority of his wealth to charity after he passes away.

Overall, Mark Cuban is a fascinating and multifaceted figure, known for his success as a businessman, investor, and media personality, as well as his outspoken views on a range of political and social issues.

ADAM D'ANGELO

Is an American entrepreneur and businessman who has made a significant impact in the tech industry through his innovation, work, and tactics. He is widely considered one of the most influential business minds of our time and has been credited with creating some of the most important technological advancements of the 21st century.

Born in 1984, D'Angelo was raised in Palo Alto, California, in the heart of Silicon Valley. He attended the prestigious Phillips Exeter Academy before going on to study computer science at California Institute of Technology (Caltech). During his time at Caltech, D'Angelo became fascinated with artificial intelligence and machine learning, which would go on to shape his future career path.

D'Angelo's first job was at Facebook, where he joined as one of the early employees in 2004. As the company grew, D'Angelo quickly rose through the ranks and became the company's first chief technology officer (CTO) in 2008. During his time at Facebook, D'Angelo played a crucial role in developing many of the site's most important features, including the News Feed and the company's mobile platform.

However, D'Angelo is perhaps best known for his work on Facebook's question-and-answer platform, which would eventually become Quora. In 2009, D'Angelo left Facebook to start his own company, and he used his experience working on the Q&A platform at Facebook to launch Quora the following year.

Quora quickly became one of the most popular Q&A platforms on the internet, with millions of users asking and answering questions on a wide range of topics. D'Angelo's focus on creating a platform that allowed users to share their knowledge and expertise with others was a key factor in Quora's success, and the platform is still widely used today.

However, D'Angelo's contributions to the tech industry go beyond just Facebook and Quora. He is also a co-founder of OpenAI, a research company focused on developing advanced AI technology that is safe and beneficial for humanity. OpenAI is at the forefront of research into AI ethics, and D'Angelo's work there has been instrumental in helping to shape the future of AI.

D'Angelo is known for his innovative approach to business, and his focus on creating products and services that are user-friendly and accessible to everyone. He is a firm believer in the power of technology to improve people's lives, and he has consistently worked to make technology more accessible and user-friendly.

One of D'Angelo's key tactics as a businessman is to focus on creating products and services that solve real problems for people. He believes that by focusing on the needs of users, rather than simply trying to create the next big thing, businesses can create products that are truly valuable and have a lasting impact.

D'Angelo's influence on the tech industry is undeniable, and his innovative approach to business has helped to shape the way we use technology today. His work at Facebook, Quora, and OpenAI has had a profound impact on the development of the internet and artificial intelligence, and his contributions will continue to shape these fields for years to come.

In conclusion, Adam D'Angelo is an influential businessman who has made a significant impact on the tech industry through his innovative approach to business, focus on user needs, and contributions to the development of important technological advancements. His work at Facebook, Quora, and OpenAI has been instrumental in shaping the way we use technology today, and his legacy will continue to inspire and influence future generations of entrepreneurs and business leaders.

D'Angelo is known for his innovative approach to business, and one of his key tactics is to focus on creating products and services that are user-friendly and accessible to everyone. He believes that the best way to create a successful business is to solve real problems for people, and he has consistently worked to make technology more accessible and user-friendly.

One way that D'Angelo achieves this is by focusing on simplicity. He believes that the best products are those that are easy to use and understand, and he strives to create products and services that are intuitive and straightforward. For example, Quora's interface is designed to be simple and easy to navigate, with a focus on making it easy for users to ask and answer questions.

Another key tactic that D'Angelo employs is to listen to his users. He believes that by listening to feedback and suggestions from users, businesses can create products that are more valuable and effective. For example, D'Angelo has spoken about how Quora's features and functionality have been shaped by feedback from users, and how this has helped to make the platform more useful and engaging.

D'Angelo is also known for his focus on creating a positive and collaborative work environment. He believes that a supportive and inclusive workplace is essential for creating innovative and successful products, and he has worked to create a culture at his companies that values collaboration, creativity, and diversity.

In terms of business ethics, D'Angelo is committed to creating products and services that are ethical and beneficial for society. He has been a vocal advocate for the responsible development of artificial intelligence, and has spoken about the need for AI to be developed in a way that is safe, ethical, and beneficial for all people.

D'Angelo is also committed to transparency and accountability in his business practices. For example, Quora has a policy of transparency when it comes to moderation and content policies, and the company regularly communicates with users about changes to its policies and practices.

Overall, Adam D'Angelo's work tactics and business ethic are focused on creating products and services that are user-friendly, ethical, and beneficial for society. He employs a range of tactics, including simplicity, user feedback, and collaboration, to create products that solve real problems for people. And he is committed to creating a positive and inclusive work environment, as well as promoting transparency and accountability in his business practices.

The one thing that he did, that an entrepreneur should follow to be great today

One key thing that entrepreneurs can learn from Adam D'Angelo is the importance of focusing on solving real problems for users. D'Angelo's approach to business is centered around creating products and services that are accessible, user-friendly, and genuinely helpful for people.

To be a great entrepreneur today, it's essential to have a deep understanding of the needs and desires of your target audience. This requires listening to feedback and staying attuned to the latest trends and developments in your industry.

Additionally, entrepreneurs can learn from D'Angelo's commitment to simplicity and user-centered design. In a world where technology can sometimes feel overwhelming and complex, it's more important than ever to create products and services that are easy to use and understand.

By taking a user-focused approach to business, and working tirelessly to create innovative products and services that meet real needs, entrepreneurs can follow in the footsteps of Adam D'Angelo and become truly influential business leaders.

Some additional details about Adam D'Angelo:

D'Angelo co-founded Quora, a question-and-answer website, in 2009. Quora has since become one of the most popular Q&A websites on the internet, attracting millions of users from around the world.

Before co-founding Quora, D'Angelo was the Chief Technology Officer (CTO) at Facebook. He worked closely with Mark Zuckerberg to develop many of the site's key features, including the News Feed and the Like button.

D'Angelo is a self-taught programmer and has been interested in computers and technology since a young age. He began teaching himself to code when he was just 12 years old.

D'Angelo has been recognized for his contributions to the tech industry, receiving accolades such as Forbes' 30 Under 30 in Technology and the World Economic Forum's Young Global Leader award.

In addition to his work at Quora, D'Angelo is an investor and advisor to a number of tech startups, including Instacart and Asana.

D'Angelo is also known for his interest in artificial intelligence (AI). He has spoken extensively about the potential benefits and risks of AI, and is committed to promoting responsible AI development.

D'Angelo is originally from Palo Alto, California, and attended Phillips Exeter Academy before studying computer science at the California Institute of Technology (Caltech).

WALT DISNEY

I s widely recognized as one of the most innovative and influential businessmen of the 20th century. His visionary approach to storytelling and entertainment revolutionized the world of animation and filmmaking, and his legacy continues to shape the global media landscape today. In this essay, we will explore Walt Disney's life and business career, focusing on his innovation mindset, work ethic, and tactics, and examining why he is widely regarded as one of the most influential business minds of all time.

Walt Disney was born in Chicago, Illinois in 1901. From an early age, he showed a keen interest in drawing and storytelling, and he would often entertain his classmates with his drawings and imaginative stories. After high school, Disney briefly attended art school in Chicago, but he dropped out and moved to California to pursue his dream of becoming an animator.

In 1923, Disney founded the Disney Brothers Studio in Hollywood with his older brother Roy. The company started out producing short animated films, which were distributed through a network of theaters. Disney was a natural innovator, constantly pushing the boundaries of animation and experimenting with new techniques and technologies. One of his early breakthroughs was the creation of the first synchronized sound cartoon, Steamboat Willie, which premiered in 1928 and featured the now-iconic character of Mickey Mouse.

Disney's success with Steamboat Willie and other early films established him as a major player in the animation industry, and he continued to innovate and push the envelope with each new project. In 1937, he released Snow White and the Seven Dwarfs, the first full-length animated feature film. The film was a massive success, grossing over $8 million (equivalent to over $150 million today) and establishing Disney as a major force in the entertainment industry.

Throughout his career, Disney was known for his relentless work ethic and tireless pursuit of perfection. He was famously hands-on with all aspects of his business, from story development and character design to animation and sound design. He would often work 18-hour days, sleeping on a cot in his office to maximize his productivity.

In addition to his work ethic, Disney was also a master of marketing and branding. He was an early adopter of cross-promotion, using his characters and stories to sell merchandise, books, and other products. He also recognized the power of the Disney brand and worked tirelessly to protect and promote it. He famously said, "I only hope that we never lose sight of one thing – that it was all started by a mouse."

Disney's influence extended far beyond the entertainment industry. He was a pioneer of the theme park industry, opening Disneyland in Anaheim, California in 1955. The park was an immediate success, and it spawned a whole new industry of theme parks and amusement parks around the world. Disney's vision for Disneyland and his attention to detail and immersive storytelling have set the standard for theme parks to this day.

Perhaps the most enduring legacy of Walt Disney, however, is his commitment to innovation and his unwavering belief in the power of imagination. He was never content to rest on his laurels or repeat past successes. Instead, he was always looking for new ways to tell stories and create experiences that would captivate and delight audiences.

Disney once said, "We keep moving forward, opening new doors, and doing new things, because we're curious and curiosity keeps leading us down new paths." This spirit of curiosity and innovation is at the heart of Disney's legacy and has inspired countless business leaders and entrepreneurs around the world.

In conclusion, Walt Disney was a true visionary and a trailblazer in the entertainment industry. His commitment to innovation, his tireless work ethic, and his marketing and branding savvy helped him build a media empire that continues to shape the global media landscape today.

Walt Disney had a long and varied career as a businessman and entrepreneur, and there are many details and anecdotes that help to illustrate his innovation mindset, work ethic, and tactics.

One notable aspect of Disney's career was his ability to take risks and think outside the box. For example, when he first started working in the animation industry in the 1920s, he recognized that there was a gap in the market for animated shorts that could be shown before feature films in theaters. At the time, most animated shorts were made for children and shown in matinees. But Disney saw the potential for creating high-quality animated shorts that would appeal to all audiences and could be shown alongside live-action films. This led him to develop the now-famous "Silly Symphonies" series of animated shorts, which were hugely successful and helped to establish Disney as a major player in the animation industry.

Another example of Disney's innovative thinking was his approach to character development. Rather than simply creating one-dimensional cartoon characters, he saw the potential for creating complex, multi-dimensional characters with their own personalities and backstories. This led him to develop characters like Mickey Mouse, Donald Duck, and Goofy, who are still beloved by audiences today. Disney also recognized the power of characters in building a brand and creating merchandise, and he was an early adopter of cross-promotion and licensing deals.

Disney's commitment to quality and attention to detail were also key factors in his success. He was famously meticulous about every aspect of his films and theme parks, from the script and storyboards to the animation and sound design. He was known for his perfectionism and would often demand multiple re-takes of scenes until he was satisfied with the final product. This dedication to quality helped to set Disney apart from its competitors and established the company as a leader in the entertainment industry.

Another notable aspect of Disney's career was his ability to adapt and evolve with changing technologies and cultural trends. For example, in the 1950s and 1960s, as television became increasingly popular, Disney recognized the potential for creating TV shows that would appeal to the younger ages.

The one thing that Disney did, that an entrepreneur should follow to be great

Disney's success can be attributed to several factors, but one key thing that an entrepreneur should follow to be great today is Disney's commitment to storytelling.

Disney has always been a master at telling compelling stories that resonate with people of all ages and backgrounds. From their iconic animated movies like "Snow White" and "The

Lion King" to their theme parks and attractions like "Star Wars: Galaxy's Edge," Disney has always been able to create immersive experiences that transport people to another world.

As an entrepreneur, it's important to remember that customers don't just buy products or services - they buy experiences. By focusing on storytelling and creating immersive experiences that truly engage your audience, you can differentiate yourself from the competition and build a loyal following of customers who are passionate about your brand.

So, whether you're creating a new product, building a website, or launching a marketing campaign, think about how you can weave a compelling story into everything you do. By doing so, you'll be able to capture people's attention and create a lasting impression that sets you apart from the crowd.

Some anecdote stories about Disney's work and tactics:

Disneyland's Hidden Mickey: In the 1970s, Imagineer John Hench noticed that a lot of guests were looking for hidden images of Mickey Mouse throughout the park. He started hiding them intentionally in various locations, like the shape of a Mickey head formed by the arrangement of rocks or flowers. This became known as the "Hidden Mickey" and has since become a beloved tradition in all Disney parks worldwide.

Disneyland's "Plussing": Walt Disney was known for his commitment to excellence and always pushing for improvement. One of his techniques was called "plussing," which involved taking a ride or attraction and adding little details to make it even better. For example, when they were building the Pirates of the Caribbean ride, Walt suggested adding the sound of the pirate's parrot, which was initially left out of the design.

The Creation of Snow White: In 1934, Disney took a huge risk by creating the first-ever feature-length animated movie, Snow White and the Seven Dwarfs. Many people thought it was a bad idea and that nobody would want to watch a full-length cartoon. However, Walt was determined to make it a success and poured all his resources into the project. It ended up being a massive hit and paved the way for future animated movies.

The Importance of Attention to Detail: Disney is famous for its attention to detail, and it's not just in the big attractions or rides. Even the trash cans in the park are meticulously designed to fit with the theme of each land. Disney knows that every little detail matters in creating a truly immersive experience for its guests.

The Power of Storytelling: Finally, Disney's commitment to storytelling can be seen in all its creations. Whether it's a movie, ride, or attraction, everything is built around a compelling narrative that captures people's imagination and transports them to another world. This commitment to storytelling is a key reason why Disney has remained so popular and successful for so many years.

JACK DORSEY

is a renowned businessman and entrepreneur who co-founded two of the most popular tech companies in the world: Twitter and Square. His innovative ideas and contributions to the tech industry have earned him a place among the most influential business minds in history.

Early Life and Education:

Jack Dorsey was born on November 19, 1976, in St. Louis, Missouri. As a child, he was fascinated with computers and the internet and spent most of his time tinkering with electronic gadgets. He attended Bishop DuBourg High School, where he became interested in dispatch routing and created a simple program to track emergency vehicles.

After high school, Dorsey moved to New York City and attended New York University, but dropped out before completing his degree. During this time, he worked as a programmer and developed a messaging platform that allowed users to communicate with each other through the internet.

Career and Innovation:

In 2006, Dorsey co-founded Twitter, a social media platform that allows users to send short messages known as "tweets" to their followers. Twitter quickly gained popularity, and by 2012, it had over 500 million registered users. Dorsey was responsible for developing the platform's initial concept and was the first CEO of the company.

Dorsey's innovative ideas didn't stop with Twitter. In 2009, he founded Square, a mobile payment company that allows small businesses to accept credit card payments using a small device that attaches to a smartphone or tablet. Square revolutionized the way small businesses process payments and quickly became a major player in the payment processing industry.

Dorsey's work at both Twitter and Square has been characterized by his focus on simplicity and user experience. He has a talent for distilling complex ideas down to their essential components and creating products that are easy to use and understand. This approach has been instrumental in the success of both companies.

Tactics and Strategies:

Dorsey's success as a businessman is also due in part to his ability to identify and implement effective tactics and strategies. For example, at Twitter, he created a simple, user-friendly interface that allowed users to quickly and easily send and receive messages. This made Twitter accessible to a wider audience and helped to drive its rapid growth.

At Square, Dorsey focused on creating a product that would appeal to small businesses, a segment of the market that had traditionally been underserved by larger payment processing companies. He developed a pricing strategy that was transparent and easy to understand, which helped to build trust with small business owners.

Dorsey's emphasis on innovation, simplicity, and user experience has helped to set him apart from other business leaders. His ability to identify and implement effective tactics and strategies has been a key factor in the success of both Twitter and Square.

Conclusion:

Jack Dorsey's contributions to the tech industry have earned him a place among the most influential business minds of all time. His innovative ideas and focus on simplicity and user experience have helped to revolutionize the way we communicate and process payments. Dorsey's ability to identify and implement effective tactics and strategies has been a key factor in the success of both Twitter and Square. His legacy as a businessman and entrepreneur is sure to endure for generations to come.

Jack Dorsey's work tactics and business ethics have been instrumental in his success as an entrepreneur and businessman. Here are some key details about his approach:

Emphasis on Simplicity:

One of the most notable aspects of Dorsey's approach to business is his emphasis on simplicity. He believes that products should be easy to use and understand, and he has a talent for distilling complex ideas down to their essential components. This is evident in the user interfaces of both Twitter and Square, which are clean, intuitive, and easy to navigate.

Focus on User Experience:

Dorsey is also known for his focus on user experience. He understands that a product's success depends on its ability to meet the needs and expectations of its users. At Twitter, he created a platform that allowed users to send and receive messages quickly and easily. At Square, he developed a payment processing system that was transparent and easy to use, which helped to build trust with small business owners.

Transparency:

Another key aspect of Dorsey's business ethic is transparency. He believes that companies should be open and honest about their operations and pricing structures. At Square, he developed a pricing strategy that was transparent and easy to understand, which helped to build trust with small business owners. He has also been open about his own struggles with anxiety and stress, which has helped to break down the stigma around mental health issues in the tech industry.

Focus on Innovation:

Dorsey is always looking for new and innovative ways to solve problems and improve the user experience. He is not afraid to take risks and try new things, which has led to some of his most successful business ventures. For example, he was one of the first to recognize the potential of mobile payments, which led him to found Square.

Collaborative Approach:

Finally, Dorsey's approach to business is collaborative. He understands that success is not achieved alone and that a team effort is required. He has been known to work closely with his employees and encourages them to share their ideas and feedback. This collaborative approach has helped to create a culture of innovation and creativity at both Twitter and Square.

In summary, Jack Dorsey's work tactics and business ethics are characterized by his emphasis on simplicity, user experience, transparency, innovation, and collaboration. These principles have been instrumental in his success as an entrepreneur and businessman and have helped to shape the culture of both Twitter and Square.

The one thing that he did, that an entrepreneur should follow to be great today

One of the most important things that Jack Dorsey did as an

entrepreneur was to identify a problem and develop a simple and elegant solution for it. He recognized that there was a need for a platform that would allow people to send short messages quickly and easily, which led him to create Twitter. Similarly, he saw an opportunity to simplify the payment processing system for small businesses, which led to the creation of Square.

Therefore, one key thing that entrepreneurs can learn from Jack Dorsey is the importance of identifying a problem or a need in the market and developing a solution that is simple, intuitive, and easy to use. This involves conducting market research, understanding your target audience, and being willing to take risks and innovate to create a product or service that truly meets their needs. Additionally, it is important to have a strong vision and a clear understanding of your business goals, and to build a collaborative team that shares your vision and is committed to achieving those goals. By following these principles, entrepreneurs can increase their chances of success and create businesses that have a meaningful impact on the world.

Some additional details about Jack Dorsey:

Early Career:

Jack Dorsey was born on November 19, 1976, in St. Louis, Missouri. He attended the University of Missouri-Rolla (now the Missouri University of Science and Technology) for two years before transferring to New York University. While in college, he developed a fascination with dispatch routing, which would later inspire his work on Twitter.

Co-Founder of Twitter:

Dorsey co-founded Twitter in 2006 with Biz Stone and Evan Williams. Originally, the platform was designed as a way for individuals to send short, 140-character messages to a group of friends. However, it quickly grew in popularity and became a major social media platform, used by millions of people around the world.

Square:

In 2009, Dorsey co-founded Square, a payment processing company that makes it easy for small businesses to accept credit card payments. Square's innovative technology allows merchants to accept payments using their mobile devices, and it has become an essential tool for small business owners around the world.

Philanthropy:

Dorsey is a dedicated philanthropist and has donated millions of dollars to various causes over the years. In 2020, he announced that he was donating $1 billion to charity through his Start Small LLC fund, with a focus on COVID-19 relief efforts, girls' health and education, and universal basic income.

Other Ventures:

In addition to Twitter and Square, Dorsey has been involved in a number of other ventures over the years. He co-founded the podcast platform Odeo, which was later sold to Google, and he also launched a new cryptocurrency called Bitcoin. He has also been involved in various other technology and business ventures, and is known for his innovative and entrepreneurial spirit.

Overall, Jack Dorsey is a highly successful entrepreneur and businessman who has made a major impact on the tech industry. His work on Twitter and Square has revolutionized the way that people communicate and do business, and his dedication to philanthropy has made a difference in the lives of countless people around the world.

GEORGE EASTMAN

Was an American inventor, entrepreneur, and philanthropist who founded the Eastman Kodak Company and revolutionized the photography industry. He is widely regarded as one of the most influential business minds in history, and his innovations and tactics have had a lasting impact on the business world.

Eastman was born in 1854 in Waterville, New York, and grew up in Rochester, where he attended public schools. He started working at the age of 14 to support his family after his father's death, and worked various jobs before he landed a position as a bookkeeper at the Rochester Savings Bank. However, he soon became interested in photography and started experimenting with photographic chemicals and equipment in his spare time.

In 1880, Eastman founded the Eastman Dry Plate and Film Company, which produced photographic plates for professional photographers. He was not satisfied with the existing technology, which was bulky and difficult to use, so he began experimenting with a new type of film that would be more portable and easy to handle. In 1884, he introduced the first flexible roll film, which revolutionized the photography industry and made photography accessible to the masses.

Eastman's innovation didn't stop with the roll film. He also invented the first portable camera, the Kodak, in 1888. This camera was pre-loaded with enough film for 100 exposures and could be sent back to the company for processing and printing. The tagline for the Kodak was "You press the button, we do the rest," which appealed to amateur photographers who wanted to capture their own memories but didn't want to deal with the complicated processes of developing and printing their own photos.

Eastman's marketing tactics were also revolutionary. He believed in creating a brand that people could trust, and he invested heavily in advertising to promote the Kodak brand. He also introduced a loyalty program called the "Kodak Girl," which featured young women dressed in white promoting the Kodak camera at various events.

In addition to his innovations in the photography industry, Eastman was also a shrewd businessman. He believed in treating his employees well and paying them a fair wage, and he also believed in giving back to the community. He established the Eastman Savings and Loan Association to help his employees save money, and he also donated millions of dollars to various causes, including education and medical research.

Eastman's impact on the photography industry and on business in general cannot be overstated. His innovations in film and cameras paved the way for the development of the motion picture industry, and his marketing tactics and brand-building strategies have been studied and emulated by businesses around the world.

In conclusion, George Eastman was a true innovator and visionary who revolutionized the photography industry and set the standard for modern business practices. His roll film and portable camera inventions, as well as his marketing tactics and brand-building strategies, have had a lasting impact on the business world, and he is rightfully considered one of the most influential business minds of all time.

One of Eastman's key work tactics was his focus on research and development. He believed that innovation was crucial to the success of his business and dedicated significant resources to R&D. For example, in 1891, he established the Kodak Research Laboratories, which employed a team of scientists and engineers who worked on developing new photographic materials and processes. This commitment to innovation allowed Eastman to stay ahead of his competitors and maintain his dominance in the photography industry.

Another important aspect of Eastman's business ethic was his belief in treating his employees well. He recognized that his workers were the backbone of his business and made sure that they were paid a fair wage and had good working conditions. He also believed in providing opportunities for his employees to advance their careers and encouraged them to take on new challenges and responsibilities.

Eastman was also known for his philanthropy and believed in giving back to the community. He donated millions of dollars to various causes, including education, medical research, and the arts. He also established the Eastman School of Music at the University of Rochester and the Eastman Dental Dispensary, which provided free dental care to those in need.

In terms of his business tactics, Eastman was a master of marketing and brand-building. He recognized the importance of creating a strong brand identity and invested heavily in advertising to promote the Kodak brand. He also pioneered the use of testimonials and endorsements from satisfied customers, which helped to build trust and credibility for the brand.

Another key business tactic of Eastman's was his focus on customer service. He believed in providing a high level of service to his customers and went to great lengths to ensure their satisfaction. For example, when customers had problems with their cameras, Eastman would personally respond to their letters and often sent them a replacement camera free of charge.

Finally, Eastman was a strategic thinker and believed in taking a long-term view of his business. He was willing to invest in new technologies and infrastructure, even if it meant taking on debt in the short term. This allowed him to position his company for long-term success and maintain his dominance in the photography industry for decades.

Overall, George Eastman's work tactics and business ethic were characterized by a commitment to innovation, a focus on treating employees well, a dedication to philanthropy and community service, a mastery of marketing and brand-building, a focus on customer service, and a long-term strategic outlook. These traits helped him to build a successful and enduring business empire and establish himself as one of the most influential business minds in history.

The one thing that he did, that an entrepreneur should follow to be great today

There are several things that George Eastman did that modern entrepreneurs can learn from, but if I had to pick one, I would say that his commitment to innovation is the most important. Eastman was always looking for new and better ways to do things, and he recognized that innovation was key to staying ahead of the competition. He was not content to rest on his laurels, and instead continually invested in research and development to create new products and technologies.

In today's fast-paced and constantly changing business

environment, this commitment to innovation is more important than ever. Entrepreneurs who are able to think creatively and come up with new ideas and solutions will be better positioned to succeed.

To follow in Eastman's footsteps, entrepreneurs should make innovation a key priority in their business. This means dedicating resources to research and development, encouraging a culture of creativity and experimentation, and constantly looking for new ways to improve their products or services.

Entrepreneurs should also be willing to take risks and embrace failure as part of the innovation process. Eastman was not afraid to invest in new technologies or take on debt in order to pursue his vision, and modern entrepreneurs should be similarly bold and willing to take calculated risks.

Overall, George Eastman's commitment to innovation is a timeless lesson that can inspire and guide entrepreneurs today. By embracing innovation and staying true to their vision, entrepreneurs can build successful and enduring businesses that make a lasting impact on the world.

Some additional interesting facts and accomplishments about George Eastman:

Eastman was born in 1854 in Waterville, New York, and grew up in a family that struggled financially. As a teenager, he dropped out of school to work and support his family.

In the late 1800s, photography was a relatively new technology, and cameras were expensive and complicated to use. Eastman saw an opportunity to simplify the process and make photography more accessible to the masses.

In 1888, Eastman introduced the Kodak camera, which was a small, lightweight box camera that could take 100 photographs without the need for reloading. The camera was preloaded with a roll of film, and after taking the photos, customers could send the entire camera back to Kodak for processing and printing.

Eastman's Kodak camera was a huge success and revolutionized the photography industry. It made photography more affordable and accessible, and helped to popularize the concept of snapshot photography.

Eastman was also a pioneer in the field of motion picture film. In 1891, he introduced the first flexible, transparent film that could be used for motion pictures. This technology helped to create the film industry as we know it today. In addition to his business accomplishments, Eastman was a major philanthropist. He donated millions of dollars to various causes, including education, medical research, and the arts.

Eastman struggled with depression later in life and ultimately took his own life in 1932. However, his legacy lived on through his company, which continued to be a major player in the photography industry for many decades.

Today, Eastman is widely regarded as one of the most influential business minds in history. He helped to create an industry and change the way we think about photography and motion pictures, and his commitment to innovation and philanthropy continue to inspire entrepreneurs and philanthropists around the world.

THOMAS ALVA EDISON

is widely regarded as one of the most influential business minds in history. His remarkable innovation and creativity not only helped him build a vast and successful empire but also transformed the world in profound ways. Edison's legacy as an entrepreneur, inventor, and businessman is remarkable, and his impact on society is still being felt today.

Edison was born in Milan, Ohio in 1847. From an early age, he showed an interest in science and technology, and by the age of 14, he had already set up his own laboratory in his basement. However, it wasn't until he moved to Menlo Park, New Jersey, in 1876 that Edison began to achieve significant success in his entrepreneurial endeavors.

Edison was a prolific inventor, holding more than 1,000 patents in his lifetime. Among his most notable inventions were the phonograph, the motion picture camera, and the electric light bulb. However, Edison was not content to simply invent things; he also had a keen business sense and an unwavering commitment to bringing his inventions to market.

One of Edison's most notable business tactics was his focus on the importance of research and development. He believed that innovation was the key to success and spent a great deal of time and money developing new products and improving existing ones. Edison also recognized the importance of teamwork and collaboration in business, and he surrounded himself with talented individuals who shared his passion for innovation.

Another significant aspect of Edison's business approach was his willingness to take risks. Edison was not afraid to try new things, even if they were unproven or unpopular. For example, when he was developing the electric light bulb, many people doubted that it could ever be a viable alternative to gas lighting. However, Edison persevered, conducting countless experiments until he found a way to create a long-lasting, practical electric light bulb.

Edison also had a talent for marketing and promotion, and he knew how to create a buzz around his inventions. For example, when he was developing the phonograph, he made sure to demonstrate it to as many people as possible, including prominent politicians and celebrities. This helped to generate interest and excitement around the product, which helped to drive sales.

Edison's focus on research and development, willingness to take risks, and marketing savvy all contributed to his remarkable success as a businessman. However, perhaps his greatest strength was his ability to think outside the box and approach problems in unconventional ways. For example, when he was developing the electric light bulb, Edison tried countless different materials and filament shapes, constantly pushing the boundaries of what was possible. He was not afraid to challenge conventional wisdom or to take a different approach than other inventors.

Edison's innovation and creativity not only transformed the business world but also had a profound impact on society as a whole. His inventions and innovations helped to usher in the modern age of electricity and paved the way for countless other technological advancements. Edison's legacy as an entrepreneur and inventor continues to inspire people around the world to this day.

In conclusion, Thomas Alva Edison was one of the most influential business minds in history. His focus on innovation and research and development, willingness to take risks, marketing savvy, and unconventional approach to problem-solving all contributed to his remarkable success as an entrepreneur and inventor. Edison's impact on society cannot be overstated, and his legacy continues to inspire people around the world to push the boundaries of what is possible.

Thomas Edison had a number of work tactics and business ethics that contributed to his success as an entrepreneur and inventor. Here are some additional details:

The importance of iteration: Edison was a firm believer in the power of iteration, or the process of repeating a sequence of operations in order to improve a product or process. He famously said, "I have not failed. I've just found 10,000 ways that won't work." Edison recognized that the path to success was rarely straightforward, and that it often required a willingness to experiment and iterate until the right solution was found.

The value of hard work: Edison was known for his tireless work ethic, often working long hours and sacrificing his personal life in order to pursue his inventions. He believed that success was earned through hard work and dedication, and he expected the same level of commitment from his employees.

A focus on practicality: While Edison was a prolific inventor, he was also very practical in his approach. He believed that an invention was only truly valuable if it could be brought to market and have a tangible impact on people's lives. As a result, he was always looking for ways to make his inventions more practical and applicable to everyday use.

A commitment to collaboration: Edison recognized that innovation was rarely a solo endeavor, and he surrounded himself with talented individuals who could help him bring his inventions to life. He believed in the power of teamwork and collaboration, and he encouraged his employees to work together and share their ideas in order to achieve their goals.

A willingness to embrace failure: Edison was not afraid to fail, and he recognized that failure was often an essential part of the innovation process. He believed that every failure was an opportunity to learn and improve, and he encouraged his employees to view their failures in the same way.

A focus on customer needs: Despite his reputation as a brilliant inventor, Edison never lost sight of the fact that his inventions were ultimately intended to meet the needs of his customers. He was always thinking about how his inventions could make people's lives better and more convenient, and he was constantly looking for ways to improve his products based on customer feedback.

Overall, Edison's work tactics and business ethics were characterized by a willingness to experiment, iterate, and collaborate in pursuit of practical solutions that could make a real impact on people's lives. His commitment to hard work, customer needs, and a willingness to embrace failure made him one of the most influential business minds of all time, and his legacy continues to inspire entrepreneurs and inventors to this day.

The one thing that he did, that an entrepreneur should follow to be great

One thing that entrepreneurs can learn from Thomas Edison

is the value of persistence and the ability to overcome failure. Edison faced numerous setbacks and failures throughout his career, but he never gave up on his goals. Instead, he continued to experiment, iterate, and refine his inventions until he achieved success.

Entrepreneurs today can take inspiration from Edison's perseverance and apply it to their own endeavors. Starting a business is rarely easy, and setbacks and failures are almost inevitable. However, by adopting Edison's mindset of persistence, entrepreneurs can learn to view failure as a learning opportunity and to keep pushing forward even in the face of adversity.

Another lesson that entrepreneurs can learn from Edison is the importance of collaboration and teamwork. Edison recognized that he could not achieve his goals alone, and he surrounded himself with talented individuals who could help him bring his ideas to life. Today's entrepreneurs can similarly benefit from working with others and building a team that can help them achieve their goals.

Finally, Edison's focus on practicality and meeting customer needs is another lesson that entrepreneurs can learn from. In today's fast-paced business environment, it can be easy to get caught up in the latest trends and technologies without considering whether they truly meet the needs of customers. By taking a page from Edison's book and prioritizing practicality and customer needs, entrepreneurs can ensure that their innovations are truly impactful and valuable.

Here are a few more interesting facts about Thomas Edison:

Edison was a prolific inventor: Edison was known for his numerous inventions, which included the phonograph, the motion picture camera, and the incandescent light bulb, among others. He held over 1,000 patents during his lifetime and was constantly working on new ideas.

He was a self-taught inventor: Edison did not have a formal

education and was largely self-taught. He began working as a telegraph operator at a young age and used his spare time to experiment with new inventions.

Edison was a savvy businessman: In addition to his inventions, Edison was also a successful businessman. He founded the Edison Electric Light Company in 1878, which eventually became General Electric. He was also a shrewd marketer, using public demonstrations and exhibitions to generate interest in his inventions.

Edison was a mentor to other inventors: Edison recognized the value of collaboration and was a mentor to other inventors, including Nikola Tesla. Despite their differences, Edison encouraged Tesla's work and even offered to buy some of his patents.

Edison was a philanthropist: Later in life, Edison became involved in philanthropy and donated money to a variety of causes. He also founded the Edison Institute (now the Henry Ford Museum) to preserve and showcase technological innovations.

Edison was a prolific reader: Despite his lack of formal education, Edison was an avid reader and believed in the power of self-education. He reportedly read every book in the library of the Menlo Park laboratory where he conducted many of his experiments.

Overall, Thomas Edison was a remarkable individual who made significant contributions to the fields of science, technology, and business. His legacy as a prolific inventor, savvy businessman, and mentor to others continues to inspire entrepreneurs and innovators today.

DANIEL EK

is a Swedish entrepreneur and businessman who is best known as the co-founder and CEO of the popular music streaming service, Spotify. He was born on February 21, 1983, in Stockholm, Sweden. From a young age, Daniel was interested in technology and entrepreneurship. He began his career in the tech industry as a teenager, creating and selling websites.

In 2006, Daniel founded Advertigo, an online advertising company. Advertigo quickly became successful and was acquired by Tradedoubler, a digital marketing company, in 2007. After the acquisition, Daniel continued to work at Tradedoubler as the Chief Technology Officer.

However, Daniel's true passion was music. He had always been a fan of music and had even played in a band when he was younger. In 2006, he had the idea of creating a music streaming service that would allow users to listen to any song they wanted, without having to download it. He discussed the idea with his friend, Martin Lorentzon, and together they founded Spotify in 2008.

Spotify was initially launched in Sweden, but quickly expanded to other countries. The service was an instant hit and quickly became the most popular music streaming service in the world. Today, Spotify has over 365 million monthly active users in over 170 countries. The company has also become a major player in the music industry, working with record labels and artists to help them reach new audiences.

One of the key reasons for Daniel's success as a businessman is his innovative mindset. He is always looking for new and creative ways to solve problems and improve his products. For example, when Spotify was first launched, it was a desktop-only service. However, Daniel saw the potential for mobile devices and quickly developed a mobile app for the service. This helped Spotify reach a whole new audience and cement its position as the leading music streaming service.

Another reason for Daniel's success is his strong work ethic. He is known for working long hours and being very hands-on with the day-to-day operations of his company. He is also very focused on the user experience and is constantly looking for ways to improve it. This has helped Spotify maintain its position as the top music streaming service, despite competition from other companies like Apple Music and Amazon Music.

Daniel is also known for his tactical approach to business. He is very strategic in his decision-making and is always thinking about the long-term impact of his choices. For example, when Spotify was first launched, it faced a lot of resistance from the music industry. However, Daniel was able to negotiate deals with record labels that allowed Spotify to legally stream their music. This was a major coup for the company and helped it establish itself as a legitimate player in the music industry.

Finally, Daniel's success can also be attributed to his leadership skills. He is known for being a very hands-on CEO, and is heavily involved in the day-to-day operations of his company. He is also very supportive of his employees and is committed to creating a positive work culture. This has helped Spotify attract and retain top talent, which has been crucial to its success.

In conclusion, Daniel Ek is undoubtedly one of the most influential business minds of our time. His innovative mindset, strong work ethic, tactical approach, and leadership skills have all contributed to his success as the co-founder and CEO of Spotify. His vision for a music streaming service that could revolutionize the industry has been realized, and he has had a major impact on the way we listen to music today. Daniel Ek's story is a testament to the power of entrepreneurship and the potential for innovation to change the world.

One of Daniel's key work tactics is his focus on data-driven decision-making. He is known for analyzing data to inform his business decisions, including everything from product development to marketing strategies. This approach has allowed him to make informed decisions and avoid making decisions based solely on gut feelings or intuition. For example, when Spotify was first launched, Daniel relied heavily on data to understand how users were interacting with the service and what features they wanted. This helped him make improvements to the service that were well-received by users.

Another work tactic that Daniel employs is his ability to balance long-term goals with short-term objectives. He is known for being strategic in his decision-making and always thinking about the long-term impact of his choices. However, he also recognizes the importance of achieving short-term objectives and is able to balance these two goals effectively. For example, when negotiating deals with record labels, Daniel was able to strike a balance between getting the best possible deal for Spotify while also ensuring that the company had enough content to attract users in the short term.

Daniel's business ethics are also a key factor in his

success as a businessman. He is known for being honest and transparent in his dealings with others, including his employees, partners, and customers. He values integrity and believes in treating others with respect and fairness. For example, when negotiating deals with record labels, Daniel was committed to paying artists and songwriters fairly for their work. He also worked to establish partnerships with record labels that were mutually beneficial for both parties.

Another key aspect of Daniel's business ethics is his commitment to innovation and creativity. He is always looking for new and creative ways to solve problems and improve his products. He encourages his employees to think outside the box and take risks, even if it means failing occasionally. This approach has led to many of Spotify's key innovations, such as the Discover Weekly feature, which uses machine learning to create personalized playlists for users.

In terms of how he did things, Daniel is known for being a hands-on CEO who is heavily involved in the day-to-day operations of his company. He is known for being responsive to feedback from his employees and customers, and for being willing to make changes to the service based on that feedback. He also places a strong emphasis on user experience and is constantly looking for ways to improve the service for his users. For example, when the company first launched in the United States, Daniel spent several months living in New York City to better understand the market and the needs of American users.

Overall, Daniel Ek's work tactics and business ethics have played a major role in his success as a businessman. His focus on data-driven decision-making, ability to balance long-term goals with short-term objectives, commitment to honesty and transparency, and dedication to innovation and creativity have all contributed to his success as the co-founder and CEO of Spotify.

The one thing that he did, that an entrepreneur should follow to be great today

While there are many things that Daniel Ek has done that could be emulated by aspiring entrepreneurs, one of the most important things that sets him apart is his relentless focus on solving a specific problem and his commitment to delivering value to his customers.

When he started Spotify, Daniel recognized that the music industry was in a state of flux, with many consumers turning to illegal file-sharing services to access music. Rather than trying to fight against this trend, he saw an opportunity to create a legal, affordable, and convenient alternative that would meet the needs of music lovers.

This focus on solving a specific problem and delivering value to his customers has been a key driver of Spotify's success. By keeping the user experience at the forefront of everything he does, Daniel has been able to build a loyal customer base and attract new users through word-of-mouth recommendations.

For aspiring entrepreneurs, this is an important lesson to keep in mind. Rather than trying to build a business around a product or service that you are passionate about, it is important to start by identifying a real-world problem that needs to be solved. By focusing on delivering value to your customers and addressing their needs, you can build a successful and sustainable business that has a real impact on people's lives.

In short, if there is one thing that an entrepreneur should follow to be great today, it is to start by identifying a problem that needs to be solved, and then focus relentlessly on delivering value to your customers. This approach has been key to Daniel Ek's success, and it can be applied to any industry or market.

Some additional facts about Daniel Ek:

He co-founded Spotify in 2006 with Martin Lorentzon, a Swedish entrepreneur and investor.

Prior to founding Spotify, Daniel worked as a developer for companies such as Tradera, a Swedish online auction site, and Stardoll, a social gaming platform.

Daniel is known for being a voracious reader, and has cited books such as "The Lean Startup" by Eric Ries and "The Hard Thing About Hard Things" by Ben Horowitz as influential in his thinking about entrepreneurship and business.

In 2018, Daniel signed the Giving Pledge, committing to donate the majority of his wealth to philanthropic causes over the course of his lifetime.

Daniel is a proponent of the idea of a "mission-driven" company, which he defines as a business that is motivated by a desire to make a positive impact on the world, rather than simply maximizing profits.

In addition to his work with Spotify, Daniel has served on the boards of several other companies, including KRY, a Swedish digital healthcare startup, and the non-profit organization Stockholm Chamber Orchestra.

Daniel has been recognized with numerous awards and accolades for his work with Spotify, including being named one of Time magazine's 100 most influential people in the world in 2013.

Despite his success, Daniel is known for being down-to-earth and approachable. He has been described by colleagues and employees as a good listener and an effective communicator, and is known for valuing the input of others in his decision-making.

Overall, Daniel Ek is a fascinating figure in the world of business and entrepreneurship, with a unique approach to building companies and creating value for his customers. His focus on innovation, data-driven decision-making, and commitment to solving real-world problems has made him one of the most influential business leaders of his generation.

LARRY ELLISON

is a name synonymous with the world of business, and for good reason. Over the course of his career, Ellison has built one of the most successful software companies in history and has established himself as a true visionary in the tech industry. Let's dive deeper into his life as a businessman, focusing on his innovation mind, work, tactics, and why he is considered one of the most influential business minds of all time.

Early Life and Education

Lawrence Joseph Ellison was born on August 17, 1944, in New York City. He was raised in a single-parent household in the South Shore neighborhood of Chicago. Ellison's mother was an unwed 19-year-old woman who gave him up for adoption. He was adopted by his great aunt and uncle, who lived in Chicago. His adoptive father was an Italian-American who was a government employee and his adoptive mother was a Jewish-American.

Ellison showed an early interest in technology, building his first computer program at the age of 13. After high school, he attended the University of Illinois at Urbana-Champaign but dropped out after his second year. He then moved to California, where he held various odd jobs, including working for the aerospace company Ampex.

The Birth of Oracle

In 1977, Ellison co-founded Software Development Laboratories with two partners. The company's initial goal was to develop a relational database management system (RDBMS) based on a research paper Ellison had read. The product, which they called Oracle, quickly became the company's focus.

Ellison's vision was to create a system that could handle large amounts of data and be accessible to non-technical users. Oracle's success was due in part to the fact that it was the first RDBMS to run on multiple platforms, making it accessible to a wider audience.

Ellison's Tactics and Work Ethic

Ellison's success can be attributed to his innovative mind and his willingness to take risks. He has been known to say that "you have to act and you have to be willing to fail. If you're not failing, you're not trying hard enough."

Ellison is also known for his aggressive tactics in business. He once said that "I enjoy competition. I enjoy competing with Microsoft, I enjoy competing with IBM, I enjoy competing with SAP." This competitive spirit has led Oracle to acquire numerous companies over the years, including PeopleSoft, Siebel Systems, and Sun Microsystems.

In addition to his tactics, Ellison's work ethic is legendary. He is known for his long hours and dedication to his company. He has been known to work through the night and has even been spotted sleeping under his desk.

Ellison's Impact on the Tech Industry

Ellison's impact on the tech industry cannot be overstated. Oracle has become one of the largest software companies in the world, with revenue exceeding $40 billion in 2023. The company's products are used by businesses of all sizes and in a wide range of industries.

In addition to Oracle's success, Ellison has also been a

pioneer in cloud computing. He was one of the first to recognize the potential of cloud computing and invested heavily in the technology. Today, Oracle Cloud is one of the leading cloud platforms, providing businesses with a wide range of services, including infrastructure as a service (IaaS), platform as a service (PaaS), and software as a service (SaaS).

Ellison's philanthropy

Ellison is also known for his philanthropic efforts. He has donated billions of dollars to charity, including his own Ellison Medical Foundation, which focuses on research into age-related diseases. In addition, he has signed The Giving Pledge, committing to give away at least half of his wealth to charitable causes.

Larry Ellison is known for his aggressive tactics and his willingness to take risks. He has been known to go head-to-head with competitors like Microsoft and IBM, often making bold moves that have paid off in the long run.

One of Ellison's most famous tactics is his acquisition strategy. Oracle has acquired dozens of companies over the years, often at a premium price. These acquisitions have allowed Oracle to expand its product offerings and stay competitive in a rapidly changing tech landscape.

Ellison is also known for his work ethic. He has been known to work long hours and has been spotted sleeping under his desk on occasion. He expects the same level of dedication from his employees and has been known to push them to their limits.

Despite his aggressive tactics, Ellison is also known for his attention to detail. He is a hands-on CEO who is deeply involved in every aspect of his company's operations. He has been known to pore over every detail of a project, even going so far as to rewrite code himself.

Another notable aspect of Ellison's business ethic is his

willingness to take risks. He has been known to make bold moves that others might shy away from, such as investing heavily in cloud computing before it was a mainstream technology. This willingness to take risks has paid off for Ellison and for Oracle, allowing them to stay ahead of the curve in a fast-paced industry.

Finally, Ellison is known for his focus on results. He has a reputation for being direct and to-the-point, and he expects his employees to deliver results. He has been known to make tough decisions, such as laying off employees or divesting businesses, in order to ensure that Oracle stays on track.

In summary, Larry Ellison's work tactics and business ethic are characterized by aggressive tactics, attention to detail, a willingness to take risks, and a focus on results. These traits have helped him build one of the most successful software companies in history and have earned him a reputation as one of the most influential business minds of all time.

The one thing that he did, that an entrepreneur should follow to be great today

There are many things that Larry Ellison did throughout his career that contributed to his success, and it's difficult to pinpoint just one thing that entrepreneurs should follow to be great today. However, one aspect of Ellison's approach that could be particularly valuable to entrepreneurs is his willingness to embrace change and take risks.

Ellison was never content to rest on his laurels or maintain the status quo. Instead, he was always looking for ways to innovate and disrupt the industry. He was an early adopter of cloud computing, for example, even when many others were skeptical of its potential. This willingness to embrace change and take risks helped Ellison and Oracle stay ahead of the curve and maintain a competitive edge.

For entrepreneurs today, this same approach could be key to success. In a rapidly changing business landscape, it's important to be open to new ideas and technologies, and to be willing to take calculated risks in order to stay ahead of the competition. This could mean investing in new technologies, exploring new markets, or experimenting with new business models.

Of course, it's important to balance this willingness to take risks with careful planning and a solid understanding of the market and industry trends. But by following Ellison's lead and embracing change and innovation, entrepreneurs can increase their chances of success and build companies that truly disrupt the industry.

A few more interesting things about Larry Ellison:

Ellison was a college dropout: Ellison attended the University of Illinois at Urbana-Champaign for just one term before dropping out. He later attended the University of Chicago for a short time before dropping out again.

He was a pilot: Ellison has had a long-standing interest in aviation and has been a licensed pilot since the 1980s. He even founded his own aviation company, the now-defunct Airline Hawaii, in the 1990s.

Ellison is a philanthropist: In addition to his work at Oracle, Ellison is also known for his philanthropic efforts. He has donated millions of dollars to various causes, including medical research, education, and wildlife conservation. In 2010, he pledged to give away 95% of his fortune to charity.

He's a sports enthusiast: Ellison is a passionate sports fan and has been involved in various sports-related ventures over the years. He sponsored a sailing team that won the America's Cup in 2010 and was also rumored to be interested in buying an NBA team at one point.

Ellison has a reputation for being a bit of a maverick: Ellison's approach to business and life in general has often been characterized as unconventional and even maverick-like. He's known for his aggressive tactics, willingness to take risks, and tendency to go against the grain. For example, he famously dropped out of college twice, and he's been known to challenge established business practices and industry norms.

HENRY FORD

Was an American industrialist and entrepreneur who founded the Ford Motor Company. He is widely considered to be one of the most influential business minds in history, as his innovative methods and entrepreneurial tactics revolutionized the automotive industry and transformed the way people work and live.

Early Life and Career:

Henry Ford was born in 1863 in a farming community near Detroit, Michigan. He grew up on a farm and had a strong interest in mechanics and engineering from an early age. In 1891, he became an engineer for the Edison Illuminating Company, where he developed his interest in electricity and machinery. During his time at the company, Ford began to experiment with his own designs for internal combustion engines.

Ford's Innovation Mind:

Ford's innovation mind is one of the key reasons for his success. He was constantly looking for new and better ways to do things, and he was not afraid to take risks. Ford was an expert in mass production, and he is often credited with creating the modern assembly line. This innovation allowed Ford to produce automobiles on a large scale and at a low cost. It also allowed him to pay his workers a higher wage, which helped to boost productivity and reduce turnover.

Work and Tactics:

Ford's work and tactics were based on his belief in the importance of efficiency and productivity. He was known for his focus on detail and his ability to streamline operations to reduce waste and increase output. Ford was also a strong believer in the power of automation, and he used machines and technology to speed up production and reduce costs.

One of the most famous examples of Ford's tactics is the Model T. This car was designed to be affordable and easy to maintain, which made it a popular choice for consumers. Ford was able to produce the Model T on a massive scale, which helped to drive down the price and make it accessible to a wider audience.

Why he would be considered amongst the most influential business minds:

Henry Ford's impact on the automotive industry cannot be overstated. His innovative methods and entrepreneurial tactics transformed the way cars were produced and sold, and his legacy lives on today. Ford's work helped to create a middle class in America, as the affordability of the Model T allowed more people to own cars and travel further distances.

Ford's influence also extended beyond the automotive industry. His focus on efficiency and productivity inspired other business leaders to adopt similar methods, and his ideas helped to shape the modern business landscape.

In conclusion, Henry Ford was one of the most influential business minds in history. His innovation mind, work, and tactics revolutionized the automotive industry and transformed the way people work and live. His impact on the world is still felt today, and his legacy serves as an inspiration to entrepreneurs and business leaders everywhere.

Henry Ford was known for his unique work tactics and

business ethics, which played a significant role in his success as an entrepreneur. Here are some key examples:

The Assembly Line: Ford's introduction of the assembly line was a game-changer in the manufacturing industry. By breaking down the production process into small, repetitive tasks, Ford was able to speed up the production process and reduce costs. This allowed him to produce cars faster and more efficiently, making them more affordable for the average person.

Standardization: Ford believed in standardization and simplification. He applied this principle to all aspects of his business, from the production process to the design of his cars. By standardizing parts and processes, Ford was able to reduce costs and improve efficiency. He famously declared that customers could have any color Model T they wanted, as long as it was black.

Continuous Improvement: Ford was constantly looking for ways to improve his business. He would regularly review his production processes and make changes to improve efficiency. This philosophy of continuous improvement became a hallmark of the Ford Motor Company, and it helped to keep the company at the forefront of the industry.

Employee Welfare: Ford believed that happy employees were productive employees. He introduced a $5-a-day wage for his workers, which was double the industry standard at the time. He also implemented a profit-sharing plan, which gave workers a share of the company's profits. This helped to reduce turnover and increase productivity, as workers felt valued and invested in the success of the company.

Business Ethics: Ford believed in conducting business with honesty and integrity. He was known for his straightforward approach to business, and he expected the same from his suppliers and partners. Ford also believed in paying his suppliers on time and treating them fairly, which helped to build long-term relationships based on trust and mutual respect.

Overall, Henry Ford's work tactics and business ethics were based on simplicity, efficiency, and a strong focus on the customer. His innovative ideas revolutionized the manufacturing industry, and his commitment to employee welfare and business ethics set a high standard for future generations of business leaders.

The one thing that he did, that an entrepreneur should follow to be great

One key thing that entrepreneurs can learn from Henry Ford's success is the importance of innovation and continuous improvement. Ford was constantly looking for new and better ways to do things, and he was not afraid to take risks or challenge the status quo. This mindset allowed him to create groundbreaking innovations like the assembly line, which revolutionized the manufacturing industry and changed the way cars were produced and sold.

Today, entrepreneurs can follow in Ford's footsteps by embracing innovation and seeking out new opportunities for growth and improvement. This might involve investing in new technologies or exploring new business models, or simply challenging conventional wisdom and finding ways to do things differently.

In addition to innovation, entrepreneurs can also learn from Ford's commitment to employee welfare and business ethics. By treating their employees fairly, paying suppliers on time, and conducting business with honesty and integrity, entrepreneurs can build a strong reputation and establish long-term relationships based on trust and mutual respect.

Ultimately, the key to following in Henry Ford's footsteps

as an entrepreneur is to maintain a focus on innovation, efficiency, and customer satisfaction, while also upholding strong ethical values and a commitment to employee welfare. By doing so, entrepreneurs can build successful businesses that leave a lasting impact on their industry and the world.

Some additional facts about Henry Ford and his legacy as a businessman:

Ford was a pioneer of mass production techniques: As mentioned earlier, Ford is widely credited with revolutionizing the manufacturing industry by introducing mass production techniques such as the assembly line. His innovations allowed for the efficient and affordable production of goods, and helped to establish the United States as a manufacturing powerhouse.

He was a self-made man: Ford came from humble beginnings and worked his way up to become one of the most successful entrepreneurs of his time. He had a strong work ethic and was always looking for ways to improve himself and his business.

He had a strong interest in technology: Ford was fascinated by machinery and technology from a young age, and spent much of his career experimenting with new technologies and innovations. This passion for technology helped him to stay ahead of his competitors and create groundbreaking products that changed the world.

He was a philanthropist: In addition to his success as a businessman, Ford was also known for his philanthropic work. He founded the Ford Foundation, which has donated millions of dollars to various causes over the years. He also established the Ford Motor Company Fund, which supports education, community development, and other charitable causes.

He had a complicated legacy: While Ford is widely recognized as one of the most influential businessmen of all time, his legacy is also somewhat complicated. He was known for his anti-Semitic views and his support of eugenics, which have drawn criticism in recent years. However, it is important to acknowledge both the positive and negative aspects of his legacy in order to fully understand his impact on the business world and beyond.

SIMON FULLER

is a name that is well-known in the entertainment industry, particularly in the music industry. As a businessman, he has made a name for himself by creating and executing innovative ideas that have transformed the way people consume entertainment. He has been the driving force behind some of the most successful music acts of the past few decades, including the Spice Girls and American Idol.

Fuller's career began in the music industry in the 1980s. He started off working as a talent manager and quickly became known for his ability to spot new talent and turn them into stars. In the early 1990s, he founded his own management company, 19 Entertainment, which would go on to become one of the most successful talent management companies in the world.

One of Fuller's earliest successes was with the Spice Girls. He put together the group in 1994 and helped them become one of the biggest music acts of the 1990s. Their success was due in part to Fuller's innovative marketing tactics. He created an image for the group that was fun, colorful, and empowering, and he marketed them to a young female demographic. He also recognized the power of merchandise and helped the Spice Girls launch a range of products, from dolls to clothing to books.

Fuller's success with the Spice Girls led to other opportunities in the music industry. He worked with a number of other successful acts, including Annie Lennox and Kelly Clarkson. But his biggest success came with American Idol, which he created in 2002. The show quickly became a cultural phenomenon and helped to launch the careers of countless music stars.

One of the keys to Fuller's success has been his ability to innovate. He has always been willing to take risks and try new things, even when they seem unconventional. For example, when he launched American Idol, many people in the music industry were skeptical. They didn't think that a reality TV show could produce real music stars. But Fuller believed in the concept and was willing to invest time and money to make it work.

Another key to Fuller's success has been his ability to think outside the box. He has always been willing to challenge conventional wisdom and come up with new and creative ways to market his talent. For example, when he was working with the Spice Girls, he realized that their fans wanted more than just music. They wanted a lifestyle. So he helped the group launch a range of products that allowed fans to buy into the Spice Girls brand.

Finally, Fuller's success can be attributed to his tireless work ethic. He is known for being a hard worker who is always willing to go the extra mile to make things happen. He is also known for his attention to detail and his ability to stay focused on the big picture while also keeping an eye on the details.

In conclusion, Simon Fuller is one of the most influential business minds of our time. His ability to spot new talent, innovate, and think outside the box has transformed the music industry and made him one of the most successful businessmen in the world. His work with the Spice Girls and American Idol have made him a household name, and his legacy will continue to inspire future generations of entrepreneurs and businessmen.

Simon Fuller is known for his innovative approach to business, which is characterized by a number of key tactics and strategies.

One of the most important tactics that Fuller employs is his focus on building strong relationships with his clients. He is known for taking a personal interest in the careers of the people he works with, and he is always looking for ways to help them succeed. He understands that success in the entertainment industry is often dependent on personal relationships, and he has built a reputation for being a loyal and supportive mentor to his clients.

Another key aspect of Fuller's approach to business is his ability to identify emerging trends and capitalize on them. He has a keen eye for talent and is always on the lookout for the next big thing. He is not afraid to take risks and invest in projects that others might see as unconventional or risky. This willingness to take chances has helped him stay ahead of the curve and make a name for himself as a visionary leader in the entertainment industry.

Fuller is also known for his attention to detail and his focus on creating a cohesive brand image for his clients. He understands that success in the entertainment industry is not just about talent, but also about marketing and branding. He is a master at creating a clear and consistent brand message that resonates with audiences and helps to build a loyal fan base.

One of the key ways that Fuller has been able to achieve success is through his use of technology. He has always been an early adopter of new technologies, and he has been quick to embrace social media and other digital platforms as a way to reach new audiences and connect with fans. He has also been a pioneer in the use of data analytics and other tools to help him make informed business decisions and identify new opportunities.

Finally, Fuller is known for his strong work ethic and his relentless pursuit of excellence. He is a hands-on leader who is deeply involved in all aspects of his business, and he is always pushing himself and his team to do better. He is not content to rest on his laurels, and he is always looking for ways to improve and innovate.

Overall, Simon Fuller's success as a businessman can be attributed to his focus on building strong relationships, his ability to identify emerging trends, his attention to detail, his use of technology, and his strong work ethic. These tactics and strategies have helped him achieve unparalleled success in the entertainment industry and have cemented his place as one of the most influential business minds of our time.

The one thing that he did, that an entrepreneur should follow to be great today

There are many things that entrepreneurs can learn from Simon Fuller's approach to business. However, if I had to highlight one key thing that sets Fuller apart and that entrepreneurs should follow to be great today, it would be his willingness to take risks and pursue unconventional ideas.

Throughout his career, Fuller has been willing to take chances on projects and ideas that others might have dismissed as too risky or unorthodox. For example, he was one of the first people to recognize the potential of reality television and was instrumental in creating the hugely successful show "Pop Idol" (which was later adapted for American audiences as "American Idol").

Fuller's willingness to take risks and pursue unconventional ideas has helped him stay ahead of the curve and make a name for himself as a visionary leader in the entertainment industry. He has never been afraid to challenge the status quo and try new things, even when others were skeptical.

In today's fast-paced and rapidly changing business landscape, taking calculated risks and embracing innovation is more important than ever. Entrepreneurs who are willing to think outside the box and pursue unconventional ideas are more likely to succeed in today's competitive marketplace.

Of course, it's important to note that taking risks should always be done in a calculated and strategic way. Entrepreneurs should carefully evaluate the potential risks and rewards of any new idea or project before committing resources to it. But, ultimately, it is often those who are willing to take risks and pursue unconventional ideas that achieve the greatest success in business.

A few more things to know about Simon Fuller:

He started his career as a talent manager: Fuller began his career in the music industry in the early 1980s as a talent manager, working with acts such as The Spice Girls, S Club 7, and Annie Lennox.

He is the creator of the "Idol" franchise: Fuller is perhaps best known for creating the "Idol" franchise, which includes shows such as "Pop Idol," "American Idol," and "Idol Gives Back." These shows have been hugely successful around the world and have helped launch the careers of many music stars.

He has also been involved in the fashion industry: In addition to his work in the music and entertainment industries, Fuller has also been involved in the fashion industry. He founded the clothing line 19RM and has worked with designers such as Roland Mouret.

He is a philanthropist: Fuller is known for his philanthropic efforts, particularly through his involvement with the "Idol Gives Back" charity campaign. He has also been involved in efforts to fight malaria and other diseases in Africa.

He is a serial entrepreneur: Over the course of his career, Fuller has launched a number of successful businesses, including XIX Entertainment, which is a management and production company that represents a wide range of talent in the entertainment industry.

He has won numerous awards: Fuller has been recognized for his contributions to the entertainment industry with numerous awards, including an Emmy Award and a star on the Hollywood Walk of Fame.

Overall, Simon Fuller's career has been characterized by innovation, risk-taking, and a relentless pursuit of excellence. His contributions to the music and entertainment industries have been significant, and he has helped shape the careers of many of the biggest stars in the world. His success as a businessman and entrepreneur serves as an inspiration to aspiring entrepreneurs everywhere.

BILL GATES

is undoubtedly one of the most influential business minds of all time. As the co-founder of Microsoft, he revolutionized the personal computer industry and changed the way we work and communicate.

Early Life and Career:

Bill Gates was born in Seattle, Washington in 1955. He showed an early aptitude for technology, programming his first computer game at the age of 13. After attending Harvard University for two years, he dropped out to start Microsoft with his childhood friend Paul Allen in 1975.

Innovation and Tactics:

Gates' innovation and tactics in the early days of Microsoft were instrumental in the company's success. One of his key innovations was the development of the operating system MS-DOS, which became the standard operating system for IBM-compatible personal computers. This made Microsoft a dominant player in the computer software industry and established Gates as a visionary entrepreneur.

Gates was also known for his aggressive business tactics, which sometimes led to legal challenges. One notable example was the antitrust lawsuit brought against Microsoft by the U.S. Department of Justice in 1998. The lawsuit accused Microsoft of monopolistic practices and bundling its

Internet Explorer web browser with its Windows operating system to stifle competition. Despite the legal challenges, Gates' tenacity and vision allowed Microsoft to continue to innovate and dominate the industry.

Work Ethic:

Gates' work ethic is also legendary. In the early days of Microsoft, he was known for pulling all-nighters and working tirelessly to develop new products and expand the company's reach. Even after he stepped down as CEO of Microsoft in 2000, he continued to be involved in the company's strategic direction and product development.

Philanthropy:

In addition to his contributions to the tech industry, Gates is also known for his philanthropy. The Bill and Melinda Gates Foundation, which he established with his wife in 2000, is one of the world's largest charitable organizations, focused on global health and education initiatives. In recent years, Gates has also been a vocal advocate for issues such as climate change and vaccine development.

Legacy:

Gates' impact on the tech industry and the world at large is difficult to overstate. Microsoft's dominance in the computer software industry paved the way for the personal computer revolution and the explosion of the internet. His philanthropic work has also had a significant impact on global health and education, helping to improve the lives of millions of people around the world.

One of Gates' key work tactics was his focus on results. He believed that success was achieved through hard work and the ability to deliver tangible results. Gates was known for his intense focus on meeting deadlines and delivering high-quality products. He set ambitious goals for himself and his team, and was not afraid to take risks in pursuit of those goals.

Another important tactic that Gates employed was his ability to pivot when necessary. He recognized early on that the tech industry was rapidly evolving and that Microsoft needed to adapt to stay ahead of the curve. He was not afraid to abandon projects that were not working or to change the direction of the company in order to stay competitive.

Gates also had a reputation for being a tough negotiator. He was known for his ability to drive a hard bargain and to get what he wanted out of business deals. He was not afraid to walk away from negotiations if he felt that the terms were not in Microsoft's best interests.

Despite his tough negotiating tactics, Gates also had a strong sense of ethics and integrity. He believed that honesty and transparency were essential in business dealings, and he was committed to building long-term relationships based on mutual trust and respect. He was also a strong advocate for corporate social responsibility, and he believed that businesses had a responsibility to give back to the community and to address social and environmental issues.

Another key aspect of Gates' business ethic was his commitment to innovation. He recognized early on that innovation was the key to success in the tech industry, and he encouraged his team to push the boundaries and to constantly explore new ideas and technologies. He also believed in investing heavily in research and development, even if it meant taking short-term financial risks.

Finally, Gates was a strong believer in the power of collaboration. He recognized that no one person could achieve success alone, and he fostered a culture of teamwork and collaboration at Microsoft. He encouraged his team members to share ideas and to work together to achieve common goals.

In summary, Gates' work tactics and business ethic were

characterized by his focus on results, his ability to pivot when necessary, his tough negotiating tactics, his commitment to ethics and integrity, his belief in innovation, and his emphasis on collaboration. These qualities helped to make him one of the most influential business minds of all time.

In conclusion, Bill Gates is undoubtedly one of the most influential business minds of all time. His innovation, tactics, work ethic, and philanthropy have made a lasting impact on the tech industry and the world at large. His legacy as a visionary entrepreneur and philanthropist will continue to inspire future generations of business leaders.

The one thing that he did, that an entrepreneur should follow to be great

There are several things that entrepreneurs can learn from Bill Gates' success. However, if I had to choose just one thing that entrepreneurs should follow to be great today, it would be Gates' relentless focus on innovation.

Throughout his career, Gates was always pushing the boundaries and exploring new ideas and technologies. He recognized that innovation was the key to success in the tech industry, and he was not afraid to take risks in pursuit of that innovation.

For entrepreneurs today, the ability to innovate is more important than ever. In a rapidly changing business landscape, those who are able to identify and capitalize on emerging trends and technologies are the ones who will succeed. Entrepreneurs who are willing to take risks, to experiment with new ideas, and to adapt to changing market conditions are

will thrive in today's competitive environment.

Gates' approach to innovation was not just about developing new products or technologies, but also about constantly refining and improving existing ones. He recognized that there was always room for improvement, and he was committed to delivering products that were both innovative and user-friendly.

Entrepreneurs who want to follow in Gates' footsteps should focus on fostering a culture of innovation within their organizations. This means creating an environment where employees feel empowered to share ideas, take risks, and experiment with new technologies and business models. It also means staying up-to-date with the latest trends and developments in the industry and being willing to adapt quickly to changing market conditions.

In addition to innovation, Gates' success as an entrepreneur was also due in part to his ability to build strong relationships and to communicate his vision effectively. Entrepreneurs who are able to build a strong network of partners, investors, and customers, and who are able to communicate their vision and goals clearly and effectively, are more likely to succeed in the long run.

In summary, the one thing that entrepreneurs can learn from Bill Gates' success is the importance of innovation. By focusing on innovation and constantly pushing the boundaries of what is possible, entrepreneurs can stay ahead of the competition and build successful businesses that have a lasting impact on the world.

Some additional details about Bill Gates and his life as a businessman:

Early Life: Bill Gates was born in Seattle, Washington in 1955. His father was a lawyer and his mother was a teacher. Gates showed an early interest in technology, and was first introduced to computers at the age of 13.

Founding of Microsoft: In 1975, Gates co-founded Microsoft

with his childhood friend Paul Allen. They began by developing software for the Altair 8800, an early personal computer. Microsoft quickly became one of the most successful software companies in the world.

Development of MS-DOS and Windows: Microsoft's first major success was the development of MS-DOS, the operating system that was used by IBM's first personal computer. Later, Microsoft developed the Windows operating system, which became the dominant operating system for personal computers around the world.

Business Strategy: Gates was known for his aggressive business tactics, including his focus on controlling the platform that software ran on. This strategy helped to make Microsoft one of the most successful companies in the world, but also drew criticism and antitrust lawsuits.

Philanthropy: After stepping down as CEO of Microsoft in 2000, Gates focused on philanthropy through the Bill and Melinda Gates Foundation. The foundation works to improve global health, reduce poverty, and increase access to education and technology.

Personal Life: Gates is married to Melinda Gates, with whom he has three children. He is known for his love of reading, and is an avid collector of art and rare books.

Net Worth: As of 2023, Gates has a net worth of over $100 billion, making him one of the richest people in the world.

In summary, Bill Gates is a complex figure who has had a significant impact on the technology industry and on the world as a whole. He is known for his aggressive business tactics, his focus on innovation, and his philanthropic work through the Bill and Melinda Gates Foundation.

DAVID GEFFEN

is a prominent American businessman and entertainment industry executive, known for his exceptional business acumen, innovative thinking, and successful ventures. His career spans several decades, during which he has demonstrated his entrepreneurial spirit and an unwavering commitment to excellence. His achievements have earned him a place among the most influential business minds of all time. In this article, we will explore the life and accomplishments of David Geffen, highlighting his innovation mindset, work, tactics, and why he is considered one of the most influential businessmen of all time.

Early Life and Career:

David Geffen was born on February 21, 1943, in Brooklyn, New York. He grew up in a Jewish family and attended the University of Texas at Austin but dropped out after his freshman year. He moved to Los Angeles in the mid-1960s and began working in the entertainment industry. His first job was at the William Morris Agency, where he worked as a mailroom clerk. Later, he went on to work as a talent agent and music manager.

Innovation Mindset:

David Geffen is known for his innovative thinking and risk-taking. One of his most significant innovations was the creation of Asylum Records, a label that he founded in 1971.

Asylum Records was the first label that focused on the singer-songwriter genre, which had previously been ignored by other record labels. This innovation turned out to be a massive success, as the label signed several big-name artists, including Joni Mitchell, Jackson Browne, and the Eagles.

Geffen also founded Geffen Records in 1980, which went on to sign artists like Guns N' Roses, Nirvana, and Aerosmith, among others. His keen sense of the market and ability to identify trends and opportunities have made him a legendary figure in the music industry.

Work and Tactics:

David Geffen's work ethic and business tactics have played a significant role in his success. He is known for his unwavering commitment to excellence and his willingness to work hard to achieve his goals. Geffen is also known for his ability to build and maintain relationships, which has been critical to his success in the entertainment industry.

One of his most notable tactics is his negotiating skills. Geffen is a tough negotiator who is not afraid to walk away from a deal if it does not meet his expectations. His ability to get the best possible deal for himself and his clients has made him one of the most respected businessmen in the industry.

Another one of his tactics is his ability to adapt to changing circumstances. Geffen has never been afraid to try something new or take a risk. He has always been willing to pivot when necessary, which has allowed him to stay ahead of the curve and remain successful.

David Geffen's work tactics and business ethics were key factors in his success as a businessman. Here are some additional details about his approach:

Attention to detail: Geffen was known for his hands-on approach to his business ventures. He paid close attention to all aspects of his artists' careers, from the recording of their albums to the marketing and promotion of their music. He was involved in all aspects of the creative process, ensuring that the final product was of the highest quality.

Focus on innovation: Geffen was always looking for new and innovative ways to approach the entertainment industry. He recognized the importance of marketing and promotion and invested heavily in these areas, using music videos as a tool to promote his artists. He also negotiated deals with his artists that were more favorable to them than the standard deals offered by other record labels.

Risk-taking: Geffen was not afraid to take risks in his business ventures. When he started Asylum Records, he focused on singer-songwriters, a genre that was not widely popular at the time. He also invested heavily in music videos, a medium that was relatively new in the industry.

Integrity: Geffen was known for his honesty and integrity in his business dealings. He was committed to treating his artists fairly and ensuring that they received the compensation they deserved. He also had a reputation for being straightforward and direct in his communication.

Strategic partnerships: Geffen understood the importance of strategic partnerships in building his business. He formed partnerships with other industry leaders, such as Warner Communications, which he sold Asylum Records to. He also formed partnerships with other businesses outside of the music industry, such as when he co-produced the hit Broadway musical "Dreamgirls."

Philanthropy: Geffen's philanthropic efforts were a reflection of his business ethics. He was committed to giving back to the community and supporting causes he believed in, such as AIDS research and education, cancer research, and the arts.

In summary, David Geffen's work tactics and business ethics were characterized by attention to detail, a focus on innovation, risk-taking, integrity, strategic partnerships, and philanthropy. These qualities helped him become one of the most successful and influential business minds of all time.

The one thing that he did, that an entrepreneur should follow to be great today

It is difficult to pinpoint just one thing that David Geffen did that an entrepreneur should follow to be great today, as his success was the result of a combination of factors. However, if there is one thing that stands out, it would be his ability to recognize the potential of new and innovative ideas and to act on them.

Geffen was not afraid to take risks and was always looking for new and innovative ways to approach the entertainment industry. He recognized the importance of marketing and promotion and invested heavily in these areas, using music videos as a tool to promote his artists. He also negotiated deals with his artists that were more favorable to them than the standard deals offered by other record labels.

In today's rapidly changing business landscape, it is more important than ever to be able to recognize the potential of new and innovative ideas and to act on them. The ability to adapt to change and to stay ahead of the curve can make all the difference in the success of a business.

Therefore, if there is one thing that an entrepreneur can learn from David Geffen, it would be to embrace innovation and to be open to taking risks. By doing so, they can increase their chances of success and stay ahead of the competition in an ever-changing business landscape.

Some additional details about David Geffen:

Early life: David Geffen was born in Brooklyn, New York, in 1943. His father was a garment industry salesman, and his mother worked in a Brooklyn public school. Geffen grew up in a Jewish family and was the youngest of three siblings.

Career beginnings: Geffen got his start in the entertainment industry as a talent agent, representing clients such as Laura Nyro and Crosby, Stills & Nash. He later went on to co-found Asylum Records in 1971, which became known for its roster of singer-songwriters. In 1975, Geffen founded Geffen Records, which went on to become one of the most successful record labels of the 1980s and 1990s. The label's roster included acts such as Guns N' Roses, Aerosmith, and Nirvana.

Business ventures: In addition to Asylum Records, Geffen went on to co-found Geffen Records in 1980, which became one of the most successful record labels of the 1980s and 1990s. Geffen was involved in the production of several hit Broadway shows, including "Dreamgirls," "Cats," and "M. Butterfly." He also produced several successful films, including "Risky Business," "Little Shop of Horrors," and "Beetlejuice." He also co-founded DreamWorks SKG in 1994, a film studio that produced such hits as "American Beauty" and "Saving Private Ryan."

Personal life: Geffen is known for his philanthropy, particularly his support of AIDS research and education. In 2018, he donated $150 million to the David Geffen School of Medicine at UCLA, which was renamed in his honor. He is also known for his lavish lifestyle, owning multiple homes and yachts.

Honors and awards: Geffen has received numerous honors and awards throughout his career, including induction into the Rock and Roll Hall of Fame in 2010 and the American Academy of Arts and Sciences in 2014.

Geffen has a reputation for being media-shy and rarely gives interviews. In fact, he once famously said, "I'm not a public person. I'm really shy. I'm not interested in being a personality."

Overall, David Geffen is an icon in the entertainment industry and a testament to what can be achieved through hard work, innovation, and a dedication to one's craft. His impact on the industry is still felt today, and he continues to inspire entrepreneurs and business leaders to strive for greatness.

KATHARINE GRAHAM

Was an American businesswoman who is widely regarded as one of the most influential media moguls of the 20th century. She served as the publisher of The Washington Post for more than two decades, during which time she transformed the newspaper from a struggling local publication into one of the most respected and powerful media outlets in the world. Graham's innovative approach to journalism, her shrewd business tactics, and her unwavering commitment to freedom of the press have earned her a place among the most influential business minds of all time.

Born in New York City in 1917, Katharine Graham grew up in a privileged and well-connected family. Her father, Eugene Meyer, was a successful financier and served as the chairman of the Federal Reserve during the Great Depression. After graduating from the University of Chicago, Graham worked briefly as a journalist for the San Francisco News before marrying Philip Graham, a young lawyer who would later become the owner of The Washington Post.

In 1948, Philip Graham purchased The Washington Post, which at the time was a struggling local newspaper with a small circulation. Katharine Graham initially had little involvement in the newspaper's operations, but after her husband's sudden death in 1963, she took over as publisher and began to transform the paper into a major force in American journalism.

One of Graham's most significant innovations was her decision to publish the Pentagon Papers, a top-secret government report on the Vietnam War that had been leaked to The New York Times. Despite intense pressure from the Nixon administration to suppress the documents, Graham decided to publish them in The Washington Post, risking legal action and even imprisonment. The decision was a bold and risky move, but it helped to establish The Washington Post as a fearless and independent voice in American journalism.

Graham also played a key role in uncovering the Watergate scandal, which eventually led to the resignation of President Richard Nixon. In 1972, a group of men broke into the Democratic National Committee headquarters at the Watergate complex in Washington, D.C. The Washington Post, under Graham's leadership, aggressively pursued the story and eventually uncovered a web of corruption and cover-up that reached the highest levels of the Nixon administration. The reporting helped to expose the truth about Watergate and to restore faith in the power of the press to hold government officials accountable.

Throughout her tenure as publisher of The Washington Post, Graham was known for her shrewd business tactics and her ability to navigate complex political and social issues. She was a master negotiator, often brokering deals with powerful figures in politics and business, and she was never afraid to take risks in pursuit of the truth. She was also a trailblazer for women in business, breaking down barriers and paving the way for future generations of female leaders.

In recognition of her achievements, Graham was awarded numerous honors, including the Presidential Medal of Freedom and the Pulitzer Prize for her memoir, "Personal

History." She was also the first woman to serve as the president of the American Newspaper Publishers Association and the first female member of the Pulitzer Prize Board.

In conclusion, Katharine Graham was a true visionary and a trailblazer in the world of business and journalism. Her innovative approach to journalism, her shrewd business tactics, and her unwavering commitment to freedom of the press have earned her a place among the most influential business minds of all time. Graham's legacy continues to inspire journalists and business leaders around the world, and her contributions to the field of media and communications will be felt for generations to come.

Katharine Graham was known for her strategic business tactics and her unwavering commitment to journalistic integrity. She was a trailblazer for women in business, breaking down barriers and paving the way for future generations of female leaders. Here are some additional details about her work tactics and business ethics:

Empowering her staff: One of Graham's key strategies was to empower her staff to take risks and pursue stories that other newspapers might shy away from. She believed that the best way to build a successful media organization was to cultivate a team of talented journalists and editors who were passionate about their work and committed to the ideals of journalistic integrity.

Fostering an environment of innovation: Graham was always looking for ways to innovate and stay ahead of the competition. She was quick to embrace new technologies and platforms, and she encouraged her staff to experiment with new forms of storytelling and multimedia content. Under her leadership, The Washington Post became one of the first newspapers to embrace digital publishing, and the paper's website became one of the most popular news sites on the internet.

Putting journalistic integrity first: Graham was deeply committed to the principles of journalistic integrity and was willing to take risks to protect the freedom of the press. She famously refused to back down in the face of government pressure to suppress the Pentagon Papers and other stories that were critical of the Nixon administration. She believed that the role of the media was to hold those in power accountable and to provide the public with accurate and unbiased information.

Cultivating relationships with powerful figures: Graham was known for her ability to cultivate relationships with powerful figures in politics, business, and the media. She used these relationships to build alliances, broker deals, and advance her own agenda. However, she also knew when to take a stand and was not afraid to challenge those in power when she believed it was necessary.

Leading by example: Perhaps the most important aspect of Graham's business ethics was her leadership style. She led by example, setting a high standard for journalistic integrity and ethical behavior. She was deeply respected by her staff and was known for her unwavering commitment to the principles of honesty, transparency, and accountability.

In summary, Katharine Graham was a visionary leader who was committed to journalistic integrity, innovation, and ethical business practices. She empowered her staff, fostered an environment of innovation, put journalistic integrity first, cultivated relationships with powerful figures, and led by example. Her legacy continues to inspire journalists and business leaders around the world, and her contributions to the field of media and communications will be felt for generations to come.

The one thing that she did,

*that an entrepreneur should
follow to be great today*

There are many valuable lessons that entrepreneurs can learn from Katharine Graham's life and work, but one of the most important is her commitment to empowering her staff and fostering an environment of innovation.

In today's fast-paced business world, it can be easy to get caught up in the day-to-day tasks of running a company and lose sight of the big picture. But successful entrepreneurs understand that the key to long-term success is to build a strong team of talented and passionate employees who are committed to achieving a common goal.

Like Katharine Graham, entrepreneurs should focus on empowering their employees to take risks and pursue their ideas. This can mean creating a culture of innovation and experimentation, where employees feel encouraged to try new things and explore new opportunities.

Additionally, entrepreneurs should be committed to fostering an environment of open communication and collaboration. By actively soliciting feedback from their employees and creating opportunities for cross-functional collaboration, entrepreneurs can tap into the collective creativity and intelligence of their team.

In short, the most important thing that entrepreneurs can learn from Katharine Graham is the importance of building a strong team and creating a culture of innovation and empowerment. By doing so, they can not only achieve greater success in the short term but also build a company that will thrive for years to come.

Some additional details about Katharine Graham's life and legacy:

Early life and education: Katharine Meyer was born in 1917 in New York City to Eugene Meyer, a prominent financier, and

Agnes Meyer, a civic leader and philanthropist. She attended private schools in New York City and went on to study at the University of Chicago, where she earned a bachelor's degree in 1938.

Career at The Washington Post: After college, Graham worked briefly as a reporter for the San Francisco News before returning to New York to work for the Herald Tribune. In 1948, she married Philip Graham, who would later become the publisher of The Washington Post. After her husband's sudden death in 1963, Katharine took over as publisher and transformed the struggling newspaper into a leading national publication.

Role in the Watergate scandal: One of the most defining moments of Graham's career came during the Watergate scandal, which began in 1972. The Washington Post's coverage of the scandal played a key role in exposing the corrupt practices of the Nixon administration and ultimately led to the resignation of President Nixon in 1974.

Philanthropy and civic engagement: Throughout her life, Graham was deeply committed to philanthropy and civic engagement. She served on the boards of numerous nonprofit organizations, including the Metropolitan Museum of Art, the Kennedy Center, and the American Red Cross. In 1998, she established the Katharine Graham Fellowship at Harvard University to support aspiring journalists.

Honors and recognition: Graham's contributions to journalism and civic life were widely recognized during her lifetime. She received numerous awards, including the Presidential Medal of Freedom and the Pulitzer Prize for biography. In 1997, she was inducted into the National Women's Hall of Fame.

In summary, Katharine Graham was a pioneering journalist and publisher who transformed The Washington Post into one of the most respected newspapers in the world. She played a key role in exposing the Watergate scandal and was a passionate advocate for philanthropy and civic engagement. Her legacy continues to inspire journalists and business leaders around the world, and her contributions to the field of media and communications will be felt for generations to come.

EDWARD H. HARRIMAN

Was a prominent American businessman and railroad executive who lived from 1848 to 1909. He is widely regarded as one of the most influential business minds of his time, and his impact on the railroad industry has had a lasting effect on American business and transportation.

Harriman's career in the railroad industry began in the late 1800s, when he took over the Union Pacific Railroad. Under his leadership, the company underwent a dramatic transformation, with Harriman implementing a series of innovative strategies to improve its operations and profitability.

One of Harriman's most significant innovations was his development of the concept of the "system railroad." This involved consolidating several smaller railroads into a single, unified system, which allowed for greater efficiency and reduced costs. This concept was a major departure from the prevailing business model of the time, which relied on independent, smaller railroads that competed with each other for business.

Harriman's system railroad model proved to be highly successful, and he soon expanded his holdings to include other major railroads, including the Southern Pacific and the Illinois Central. He also invested heavily in new technology and infrastructure, such as modernized locomotives and upgraded track systems.

In addition to his business innovations, Harriman was also known for his aggressive and sometimes controversial tactics. He was not afraid to take on competitors or challenge regulators, and he was known for his willingness to engage in tough negotiations and aggressive price-cutting.

Despite his sometimes controversial reputation, Harriman's impact on the railroad industry was undeniable. He helped to transform the industry from a fragmented and inefficient system to a streamlined, efficient network that connected the country and helped to drive economic growth.

Harriman's legacy as a businessman and innovator continues to be felt today. His concept of the system railroad remains a fundamental part of the modern transportation system, and his emphasis on efficiency and technology has become a guiding principle for businesses across a range of industries.

In recognition of his achievements, Harriman has been posthumously inducted into the Railway Hall of Fame and is widely regarded as one of the most influential business leaders in American history. His innovations and leadership have inspired generations of entrepreneurs and business leaders to think boldly and embrace new ideas in their pursuit of success.

Edward H. Harriman was born in 1848 in New York City, the son of a prominent railroad executive. He grew up around railroads and developed a fascination with them at a young age.

Harriman's career in the railroad industry began in the late 1800s, when he acquired a major stake in the Union Pacific Railroad. At the time, the company was in serious financial trouble, but Harriman saw an opportunity to turn it around.

One of Harriman's first moves was to install a new management team and implement a series of cost-cutting measures. He also invested heavily in new technology, such as modernized locomotives and more efficient track systems.

Under Harriman's leadership, the Union Pacific quickly became one of the most efficient and profitable railroads in the country. He continued to expand his holdings, acquiring other major railroads and consolidating them into a single, unified system.

Harriman's business acumen was not limited to the railroad industry, however. He was also an avid investor, and he made successful investments in a range of industries, including banking, mining, and steel.

Despite his successes, Harriman was not without controversy. He was known for his aggressive tactics and willingness to take on competitors and regulators alike. He also had a reputation for being ruthless with his employees, and he was not afraid to lay off workers or cut wages in order to improve the bottom line.

Despite these controversies, Harriman's impact on the railroad industry and American business more broadly cannot be overstated. He was a true innovator who transformed the way that railroads were operated and managed, and his legacy continues to be felt today.

The one thing that Harriman did, that an entrepreneur should follow to be great

One thing that entrepreneurs can learn from Edward H. Harriman's success is his willingness to take risks and think big. Harriman was not afraid to make bold moves, such as consolidating multiple railroads into a single system or investing in new technologies that could potentially revolutionize the industry.

Harriman also understood the importance of having a strong and capable team to execute his vision. He carefully selected top talent and gave them the resources and support they needed to succeed.

Another key lesson from Harriman is his focus on efficiency and cost-cutting. He recognized that in order to succeed in a competitive market, it was essential to continually find ways to do things better and more efficiently.

Finally, Harriman's relentless drive and determination are also traits that entrepreneurs can emulate. He was a tireless worker who never gave up in the face of challenges or setbacks, and he was always looking for ways to improve and grow his business. By adopting this same level of dedication and persistence, entrepreneurs can overcome obstacles and achieve their own goals and ambitions.

Here are some additional details about Edward H. Harriman's life and career:

Harriman was a self-made man who began his career as a stockbroker, eventually becoming one of the wealthiest and most powerful men in America. He was known for his shrewd business sense, as well as his ability to cultivate strong relationships with influential politicians and financiers.

In addition to his work in the railroad industry, Harriman was also involved in other businesses, including banking and real estate. He was a savvy investor who was always looking for new opportunities to grow his wealth and influence.

Harriman was a firm believer in the power of technology to transform industries and improve efficiency. He was an early adopter of new technologies in the railroad industry, such as the use of automatic signals and air brakes, and he also invested in other cutting-edge technologies of the day, such as electric power and telegraphy.

Harriman was a tough negotiator who was not afraid to use his considerable wealth and influence to get what he wanted. He was known for his aggressive business tactics, and he often clashed with competitors and regulators who stood in his way.

Despite his reputation as a hard-nosed businessman, Harriman was also known for his philanthropic endeavors. He donated large sums of money to charity, and he also supported a number of cultural and educational institutions.

Harriman was known for his ability to turn around struggling businesses. In the late 1800s, he took over the Union Pacific Railroad, which was then in serious financial trouble, and within a few years, he had transformed it into a profitable enterprise.

Harriman was also an early adopter of new technologies. He recognized the potential of the telegraph to improve communication and efficiency in the railroad industry, and he invested heavily in laying new telegraph lines along his railroads.

Harriman was not only a successful businessman, but also a noted philanthropist. He donated generously to causes such as education, healthcare, and the arts, and he helped fund the construction of several important public buildings, including the New York Public Library and the American Museum of Natural History.

In addition to his business interests, Harriman was an avid outdoorsman and conservationist. He helped create several national parks, including Yellowstone and Mount Rainier, and he was a strong advocate for preserving America's natural resources.

Harriman's legacy continued long after his death. His son, W.

Averell Harriman, became a prominent diplomat and served as the U.S. Ambassador to the Soviet Union during World War II, and his granddaughter, Pamela Harriman, was a noted political figure and ambassador in her own right.

Overall, Edward H. Harriman was a complex and influential figure in American business history. By studying his life and career, entrepreneurs can learn valuable lessons about the importance of technology, negotiation, philanthropy, and more.

REED HASTINGS

is a visionary entrepreneur and businessman who has been instrumental in shaping the future of the entertainment industry. He is the co-founder and CEO of Netflix, a company that has revolutionized the way we consume and enjoy movies and television shows.

Early Life and Education

Reed Hastings was born on October 8, 1960, in Boston, Massachusetts. He grew up in a military family and spent most of his childhood moving around the world. He attended high school in Brussels, Belgium, and graduated from Bowdoin College in 1983 with a degree in mathematics.

After graduation, Hastings joined the Peace Corps and spent two years teaching high school math in Swaziland, a small country in southern Africa. This experience gave him a unique perspective on education and the challenges faced by developing countries.

Early Career

After returning to the United States, Hastings worked briefly as a software engineer before starting his first company, Pure Software, in 1991. Pure Software provided debugging tools for software developers and quickly became a leader in its field. In 1997, Pure Software merged with another company to form Rational Software, which was later acquired by IBM.

Netflix

In 1997, Hastings founded Netflix along with Marc Randolph, a former colleague from Pure Software. At the time, Netflix was a DVD-by-mail rental service that allowed customers to rent movies and TV shows without ever leaving their homes. The company was an instant success, and by 2002, it had grown to over 600,000 subscribers.

In 2007, Netflix introduced a new service that would change the entertainment industry forever: streaming video. With the advent of high-speed internet and advances in video compression technology, Netflix was able to offer its subscribers access to thousands of movies and TV shows instantly, without the need for physical media.

This innovation was a game-changer, and it wasn't long before other companies, such as Amazon and Hulu, followed suit. Today, Netflix is the world's leading streaming video service, with over 200 million subscribers in more than 190 countries.

Innovation Mindset

One of the reasons why Reed Hastings is considered one of the most influential business minds of all time is his innovation mindset. Hastings is a true believer in the power of technology to disrupt traditional industries and create new opportunities.

At Netflix, Hastings has always been focused on innovation, pushing his team to think outside the box and come up with new ways to delight customers. He famously once said, "Our job is to entertain and delight the world. If we don't do that, we'll be out of business."

Work and Tactics

Hastings is known for his unconventional management style, which emphasizes transparency and autonomy. He believes in giving his employees the freedom to make decisions and take risks, even if it means making mistakes along the way.

Hastings also believes in the power of data-driven decision-making. At Netflix, he has built a culture of experimentation, where every decision is based on data and analysis. This approach has allowed Netflix to stay ahead of the competition and continuously improve its service.

Another tactic that Hastings has used to great effect is the "freemium" model, which offers a basic service for free and charges for additional features. This model has been a key factor in Netflix's success, as it allows the company to attract new customers while generating revenue from its most loyal fans.

Conclusion

Reed Hastings is a true innovator and one of the most influential business minds of all time. His vision and leadership have transformed the entertainment industry and paved the way for new opportunities in the digital age.

Through his work at Netflix, Hastings has shown the power of technology to disrupt traditional industries and create new business models. His unconventional management style and focus on data-driven decision-making have helped Netflix stay ahead of the competition.

Reed Hastings is known for his unconventional management style, which emphasizes transparency, autonomy, and a focus on results. Here are some of the key work tactics and business ethics that Hastings has used to build a successful company:

Radical Candor

Hastings is a proponent of "radical candor," which is the practice of giving direct, honest feedback to employees. He believes that this approach helps to build trust and encourages employees to take ownership of their work.

Data-Driven Decision Making

Hastings is a big believer in data-driven decision making. At Netflix, he has built a culture of experimentation and A/B testing, where every decision is based on data and analysis. This approach has allowed Netflix to stay ahead of the competition and continuously improve its service.

Autonomy and Responsibility

Hastings believes in giving his employees autonomy and responsibility. He has famously said, "We're a team, not a family." This means that he expects his employees to take ownership of their work and make decisions that are in the best interest of the company.

Embracing Failure

Hastings believes that failure is an important part of the innovation process. He encourages his employees to take risks and try new things, even if it means making mistakes along the way. This approach has allowed Netflix to innovate and stay ahead of the competition.

Focus on the Customer

Hastings believes that the customer should be at the center of everything a company does. He has built a culture at Netflix that is focused on delighting customers and delivering value. This focus on the customer has been a key factor in Netflix's success.

Frequent Communication

Hastings believes in frequent communication and transparency. He sends regular company-wide emails that provide updates on the state of the business and encourage feedback from employees. This approach helps to build trust and keeps everyone aligned around the company's goals.

Long-Term Thinking

Hastings takes a long-term view of business strategy. He is

willing to invest in new initiatives and take risks that may not pay off in the short term, but have the potential to create significant value in the future. This approach has allowed Netflix to stay ahead of the curve and maintain its position as a leader in the entertainment industry.

Overall, Reed Hastings has built a company that is focused on innovation, experimentation, and customer delight. His unconventional management style and focus on data-driven decision making have helped to create a culture that is agile, adaptable, and forward-thinking. These tactics and business ethics have helped to make Reed Hastings one of the most influential business minds of all time.

The one thing that he did, that an entrepreneur should follow to be great today

One thing that entrepreneurs can learn from Reed Hastings is the importance of having a strong customer focus. Hastings has built Netflix with the goal of providing a better experience for customers, and this has been a key factor in the company's success.

Entrepreneurs today can learn from Hastings' focus on customer delight by making sure that their businesses are built with the needs and wants of customers in mind. This involves understanding the target audience and creating products or services that solve a real problem or fulfill a genuine need.

Entrepreneurs can also adopt Hastings' emphasis on data-driven decision making. By using data to inform business decisions, entrepreneurs can make more informed choices that are more likely to lead to success. This means investing in data analytics tools and platforms, and making sure that all decisions are backed up by data and analysis.

Finally, entrepreneurs can learn from Hastings' embrace of failure as a necessary part of the innovation process. This means being willing to take risks and try new things, even if there is a chance of failure. By embracing failure, entrepreneurs can learn from their mistakes and improve their products or services over time.

In summary, entrepreneurs can learn from Hastings by focusing on the customer, using data-driven decision making, and embracing failure as a part of the innovation process. By adopting these principles, entrepreneurs can build businesses that are more likely to succeed in today's competitive marketplace.

Some additional details about Reed Hastings and his career as a businessman:

Early Career

Before founding Netflix, Hastings worked as a software engineer at companies like Adaptive Technology and Pure Software. In 1991, he founded his first company, Pure Atria, which specialized in software development tools. Pure Atria was eventually acquired by Rational Software in 1997 for $700 million.

The Birth of Netflix

Hastings founded Netflix in 1997 as a DVD-by-mail rental service. The idea for the company came to him after he was charged a $40 late fee for returning a movie rental to Blockbuster. He saw an opportunity to create a better customer experience by allowing customers to rent DVDs online without late fees.

Innovations at Netflix

Under Hastings' leadership, Netflix has introduced a number of innovative ideas that have disrupted the entertainment industry. These include the creation of original content, the use of algorithms to suggest personalized recommendations, and the development of a streaming service that has largely replaced DVD rentals.

Netflix's Growth

Netflix has grown rapidly under Hastings' leadership, with the company now boasting over 200 million subscribers in more than 190 countries. The company's market capitalization has also skyrocketed, making it one of the most valuable media companies in the world.

Philanthropy

Hastings is also known for his philanthropic work. In 2016, he launched a $100 million education fund to support education reform efforts. He has also made significant donations to organizations focused on social justice, including the Black Lives Matter movement.

Board Memberships

Hastings serves on the board of a number of companies and organizations, including Facebook, the KIPP Foundation, and the California State Board of Education. He is known for his outspoken views on education reform and has advocated for changes to the public education system in the United States.

Overall, Reed Hastings is a successful entrepreneur and business leader who has made a significant impact on the entertainment industry. His focus on customer delight, data-driven decision making, and innovation have helped to make Netflix one of the most successful companies of all time.

WILLIAM RANDOLPH HEARST

Was a businessman and media mogul who revolutionized the newspaper industry in the late 19th and early 20th centuries. His innovative tactics and business acumen made him one of the most influential entrepreneurs of all time.

Hearst was born in San Francisco in 1863, the only child of wealthy mining magnate George Hearst. After attending Harvard University for two years, he dropped out and began working as a journalist for the San Francisco Examiner, which his father had recently acquired. Hearst quickly rose through the ranks at the newspaper, eventually becoming its owner and publisher in 1887.

Under Hearst's leadership, the Examiner became known for its sensationalist reporting and eye-catching headlines. Hearst realized that the public was hungry for scandal and sensational stories, and he gave it to them in spades. He pioneered the use of "yellow journalism," a term coined to describe the practice of using exaggerated headlines and lurid illustrations to attract readers.

Hearst's sensationalism paid off in a big way. The Examiner's circulation skyrocketed, and Hearst soon acquired other newspapers, including the New York Journal and the

Chicago American. He also purchased magazines such as Cosmopolitan and Good Housekeeping.

Hearst's empire continued to grow throughout the early 20th century, and he became one of the wealthiest men in America. He used his wealth and influence to pursue a variety of causes, including politics. Hearst ran unsuccessfully for mayor of New York City in 1905 and for governor of New York in 1906.

Despite his political ambitions, Hearst's true passion was always journalism. He used his newspapers to champion causes he believed in, including the fight against the Spanish-American War and the campaign for women's suffrage. He also used his newspapers to attack his enemies, both real and perceived, and to push his own political agenda.

Hearst was a master of innovation, both in terms of content and technology. He was one of the first newspaper publishers to use photographs to illustrate his stories, and he was also an early adopter of color printing. He introduced the comic strip to American newspapers, and he was a pioneer in the use of radio and newsreels as sources of news.

Hearst's influence on the media landscape of the 20th century cannot be overstated. His use of sensationalism and his willingness to blur the line between news and entertainment helped to shape the modern media landscape. He also helped to create a new model for the newspaper industry, one that relied on advertising revenue rather than subscriptions to pay the bills.

Despite his many accomplishments, Hearst's legacy is not without controversy. He was often accused of using his newspapers to further his own interests and to manipulate public opinion. His role in the Spanish-American War, in particular, has been the subject of much debate. Some historians argue that his newspapers played a significant role in drumming up public support for the war, while others maintain that he was simply responding to public sentiment.

Despite these controversies, there is no denying that Hearst was one of the most influential businessmen and entrepreneurs of all time. His innovative tactics and his willingness to take risks helped to shape the modern media landscape, and his impact is still felt today.

William Randolph Hearst was known for his ruthless business tactics, but he was also a shrewd businessman who understood the importance of innovation and risk-taking in the media industry.

One of Hearst's key tactics was to use his newspapers to promote his own interests and agenda. He was not afraid to use his newspapers to attack his enemies or to push his own political views. He also used his newspapers to promote his own business interests, such as his real estate holdings.

Hearst was also a master of sensationalism. He understood that the public was hungry for scandal and sensational stories, and he was not afraid to give it to them. His newspapers often featured lurid headlines and exaggerated stories designed to shock and grab the reader's attention. This approach was not without controversy, and Hearst was often accused of prioritizing entertainment over journalism.

Despite his sensationalism, Hearst was also committed to journalism and the pursuit of truth. He was a strong advocate for the First Amendment and believed that the press had a responsibility to keep the public informed about the issues of the day. He also used his newspapers to champion causes he believed in, such as the fight for women's suffrage and workers' rights.

In terms of business ethic, Hearst was not above using questionable tactics to get what he wanted. He was known for his cutthroat business practices, and he was not afraid to use his wealth and influence to get what he wanted. However, he was also willing to take risks and innovate in order to stay ahead of his competitors. He was an early adopter of new technologies, such as radio and newsreels, and he was always looking for new ways to attract readers and advertisers.

Hearst also had a strong sense of civic duty. He believed that it was the responsibility of the wealthy to give back to society, and he used his wealth and influence to support a variety of charitable causes. He was a strong supporter of education and the arts, and he donated generously to universities and cultural institutions.

In summary, Hearst was a businessman who was not afraid to take risks and innovate in order to stay ahead of his competitors. He used his newspapers to promote his own interests and agenda, and he was known for his sensationalism and cutthroat business practices. However, he was also committed to journalism and the pursuit of truth, and he believed in using his wealth and influence to support charitable causes and give back to society.

The one thing that he did, that an entrepreneur should follow to be great today

One thing that entrepreneurs can learn from William Randolph Hearst is the importance of innovation and taking calculated risks. Hearst was always looking for new ways to attract readers and advertisers, and he was an early adopter of new technologies such as radio and newsreels. He was not afraid to try new things and take risks, even if it meant deviating from the traditional ways of doing things.

In today's rapidly changing business environment, innovation and risk-taking are essential for entrepreneurs who want to stay ahead of the competition. This means being open to new ideas, experimenting with new technologies and business models, and being willing to pivot if something is not working. It also means being comfortable with uncertainty and ambiguity, and not being afraid to fail.

Another lesson that entrepreneurs can learn from Hearst is the importance of persistence and perseverance. Hearst faced many setbacks and obstacles in his career, but he never gave up. He was tenacious and determined, and he never let failure deter him from pursuing his goals. This kind of resilience and perseverance is essential for entrepreneurs who want to overcome the inevitable challenges and obstacles that come with building a successful business.

In summary, entrepreneurs can learn from William Randolph Hearst's innovative and risk-taking mindset, as well as his persistence and perseverance in the face of obstacles. By being open to new ideas, taking calculated risks, and staying focused on their goals, entrepreneurs can build successful businesses that stand the test of time.

Some more interesting facts about William Randolph Hearst:

Hearst was born into a wealthy family and inherited a newspaper from his father. However, he did not rest on his family's wealth and instead worked tirelessly to expand the Hearst Corporation into a media empire.

Hearst was known for his lavish lifestyle and his extravagant spending. He owned multiple mansions, including Hearst Castle in California, and he was a collector of art and antiques.

Hearst was a major political player in his time and was known for using his newspapers to promote his own political agenda. He was a staunch Democrat and ran for office several times, including a failed bid for President in 1904.

Hearst was an early advocate for environmental conservation and played a major role in the creation of the Save the Redwoods League, a nonprofit organization dedicated to protecting California's redwood forests. Hearst was a patron of the arts and supported many artists and writers during his lifetime. He also founded the Hearst National Writing Contest, which provided opportunities for aspiring writers to gain recognition and launch their careers.

Hearst was involved in a bitter feud with fellow media mogul Joseph Pulitzer, with the two engaging in a fierce rivalry for control of the newspaper industry. This rivalry was the inspiration for the musical "Newsies" and the film "Citizen Kane." Despite his reputation for sensationalism and yellow journalism, Hearst was also committed to investigative journalism and was responsible for breaking several major news stories during his career.

Overall, William Randolph Hearst was a complex and multifaceted individual who left a lasting impact on the worlds of media, politics, and philanthropy. While his methods and tactics may have been controversial, there is no denying his place as one of the most influential and innovative businessmen of his time.

HUGH HEFNER

born in 1926, was an American entrepreneur, publisher, and founder of Playboy Enterprises, Inc. He was known for his innovative ideas and bold marketing tactics, which helped him build a multi-million-dollar empire and establish himself as one of the most influential businessmen of all time.

Hefner's entrepreneurial journey began in the early 1950s when he worked as a copywriter for Esquire magazine. However, he soon realized that the magazine was not catering to the needs of young men like himself. He saw an opportunity to create a new type of publication that combined sex, humor, and quality journalism, and thus Playboy magazine was born.

Hefner's innovative mind was apparent from the very beginning. He not only created a magazine that was different from anything else on the market but also came up with unique marketing tactics to promote it. For instance, the first issue of Playboy featured a nude photo of Marilyn Monroe, which helped to generate buzz and sales. Hefner also created the Playboy Bunny, an iconic symbol of the brand, which became a cultural phenomenon in the 1960s and 70s.

Hefner was also a pioneer in the use of technology in the publishing industry. He was one of the first publishers to embrace the potential of digital media, and Playboy was one of the first magazines to have its own website. He also launched the Playboy Channel, a cable television network that featured adult-oriented programming, which was a revolutionary concept at the time.

However, Hefner's success was not just the result of his innovative ideas and marketing tactics. He was also a shrewd businessman who knew how to leverage his brand to generate revenue. Playboy Enterprises, Inc. expanded beyond the magazine and television channels and became a lifestyle brand, with products ranging from clothing to home entertainment systems. Hefner also invested in real estate, including the famous Playboy Mansion in Los Angeles, which he used to entertain celebrities and business associates.

Despite criticism and controversy surrounding his work, Hefner remained committed to his vision of a more open and liberated society. He used his magazine to promote civil rights, freedom of speech, and other progressive causes. He was also a philanthropist, supporting organizations that focused on education, health, and social justice.

Hugh Hefner's impact on the business world cannot be overstated. He revolutionized the publishing industry, pioneered the use of digital media, and created a brand that became a cultural icon. He was not afraid to take risks, challenge the status quo, and push boundaries, which helped him to stay ahead of the curve and remain relevant for decades. His legacy as a businessman and entrepreneur will continue to inspire future generations.

In conclusion, Hugh Hefner was an influential businessman and entrepreneur who made a significant impact on the publishing and media industries. His innovative ideas, marketing tactics, and shrewd business sense helped him to create a multi-million-dollar empire that became a cultural icon. He was also committed to promoting progressive causes and philanthropy, making him a complex and multifaceted figure. Hefner's legacy is one of creativity, risk-taking, and boldness, and his contributions to the business world will be remembered for generations to come.

Hugh Hefner was known for his unconventional and bold work tactics, which played a key role in his success as a businessman. Here are some of the ways in which he approached his work and business:

Embracing Risks: Hefner was not afraid to take risks and pursue new ideas, even if they were considered controversial or risky. For instance, he launched Playboy magazine in the conservative 1950s, when the idea of a publication that featured nude photos and sexual content was considered scandalous. He also invested in new technology and media formats, such as digital media and cable television, which were unproven at the time.

Innovative Marketing: Hefner was a master of marketing, and he used creative and bold tactics to promote his brand. For instance, he used provocative imagery and the concept of the Playboy Bunny to create an iconic brand identity. He also created themed parties and events at the Playboy Mansion, which helped to build buzz and generate media attention.

Strong Brand Identity: Hefner understood the power of a strong brand identity, and he worked hard to build and maintain the Playboy brand. He was known for his attention to detail and his insistence on quality, which helped to establish the Playboy logo and brand as a symbol of sophistication and luxury.

Diversification: Hefner was not content with just publishing a magazine, and he sought to diversify his business interests. He expanded into other media formats, such as television and home entertainment systems, and he also invested in real estate and other ventures. This diversification helped to reduce his business risk and ensure the longevity of his brand.

Commitment to Values: Despite the controversial nature of his work, Hefner was committed to promoting certain values and causes through his business. For instance, he used his magazine to promote civil rights and free speech, and he supported organizations that focused on education and social justice. He also advocated for sexual liberation and challenged traditional gender roles, which was groundbreaking at the time.

In terms of his business ethics, Hefner was known for his personal integrity and honesty. He was a hands-on CEO who was involved in every aspect of his business, and he was respected by his employees for his leadership style. He was also committed to treating his employees fairly and providing them with a positive work environment.

However, it is important to note that Hefner's work was not without controversy, and he faced criticism for his portrayal of women and his promotion of a hedonistic lifestyle. Some critics argued that his work was exploitative and objectifying, and that it perpetuated harmful stereotypes and attitudes. Despite this criticism, Hefner remained committed to his vision of a more liberated and open society, and he continued to innovate and push boundaries throughout his career.

*The one thing that he did,
that an entrepreneur should
follow to be great today*

One of the key things that entrepreneurs can learn from Hugh Hefner is his willingness to take risks and pursue new ideas, even if they are controversial or unproven. Hefner was not afraid to challenge conventional wisdom and push the boundaries of what was acceptable in his industry. He was a visionary who saw opportunities where others did not, and he was willing to invest his time, money, and reputation to pursue those opportunities.

Today, in a rapidly changing business environment where disruption and innovation are essential for success, entrepreneurs need to be willing to take risks and pursue new ideas in order to stay ahead of the competition. This means being open to new technologies, new business models, and new ways of thinking about problems.

Another important lesson from Hefner's life is the importance of building a strong brand identity. Hefner understood the power of branding and used creative marketing tactics to build a strong and iconic brand that stood the test of time. Entrepreneurs today can learn from Hefner's commitment to quality and attention to detail, and strive to create a brand that is instantly recognizable and highly valued by customers.

Finally, Hefner's commitment to social causes and his advocacy for free speech and civil rights serves as a reminder that entrepreneurs have a responsibility to use their influence and resources to promote positive change in society. In today's business environment, consumers are increasingly looking for companies that share their values and are committed to making a positive impact on the world. Entrepreneurs who are able to align their business goals with social causes and create a sense of purpose beyond profit will be better positioned to succeed in the long term.

Some additional things about Hugh Hefner:

Entrepreneurial Spirit: Hefner had an entrepreneurial spirit from a young age. While working as a copywriter for Esquire magazine, he recognized an opportunity to create a new men's magazine that focused on the urban lifestyle. He raised funds from family and friends and used his own furniture as collateral to start Playboy magazine.

Philanthropy: Hefner was known for his philanthropic activities and donated millions of dollars to various causes throughout his life. He supported organizations focused on civil rights, free speech, and social justice, as well as organizations focused on education and the arts.

Personal Life: Hefner was married three times and had numerous romantic relationships throughout his life. He lived in the Playboy Mansion with multiple girlfriends, which was the subject of much media attention. Hefner also had a passion for collecting and was an avid collector of artwork, antiques, and memorabilia.

Business Challenges: Despite his success, Hefner faced numerous challenges throughout his career. He battled censorship laws and was arrested multiple times on obscenity charges. He also faced financial challenges in the 1970s when the magazine industry experienced a downturn. However, Hefner was able to navigate these challenges and adapt his business to changing circumstances.

Legacy: Hefner's impact on popular culture and the media industry is undeniable. He created a brand that has become an iconic symbol of the 20th century and his influence can still be seen in today's media landscape. Hefner's vision of a more liberated and open society, while controversial at times, was groundbreaking and paved the way for future generations.

CONRAD HILTON

Was an American hotelier and businessman, born in 1887 in San Antonio, New Mexico. He was the founder of the Hilton Hotels chain and is widely regarded as one of the most influential entrepreneurs and businessmen of the 20th century. He was born on December 25, 1887, in San Antonio, New Mexico, and grew up in a devout Catholic family. He was the second of eight children and had four sisters and three brothers.

Hilton's business career began in the early 1900s when he opened a small hotel in Cisco, Texas. Over the years, he gradually built up his hotel business, acquiring more properties and expanding his operations. However, it was not until the 1940s that Hilton achieved real success, with the opening of his first luxury hotel, the Roosevelt Hotel in New York City.

Hilton's success as a businessman was due to his innovative thinking and tireless work ethic. He was constantly looking for new ways to improve his hotels, and he was always willing to take risks in order to achieve his goals. For example, he was one of the first hoteliers to install televisions in guest rooms, recognizing the potential for this technology to enhance the guest experience.

Another innovation that Hilton introduced was the concept of the "airport hotel." He recognized the need for convenient, high-quality accommodation for travelers, and in the 1950s he began building hotels near major airports. This was a radical idea at the time, but it proved to be a huge success, and Hilton's airport hotels quickly became some of the most popular and profitable in the world.

Hilton was also a master of marketing and publicity. He understood the importance of branding and was one of the first hoteliers to use television advertising to promote his hotels. He also made sure that his hotels were always in the news, hosting high-profile events and attracting famous guests.

However, Hilton's success was not just down to his innovation and marketing skills. He was also a shrewd businessman who understood the importance of financial management. He was always looking for ways to reduce costs and increase efficiency, and he was not afraid to make tough decisions, such as selling off underperforming hotels or cutting staff when necessary.

Hilton's legacy as a businessman and entrepreneur is undeniable. He built a hotel empire that has continued to thrive long after his death, with more than 6,000 properties in 119 countries around the world. He was also a pioneer in the hospitality industry, introducing many of the concepts and innovations that are now taken for granted.

Furthermore, Hilton's impact on the business world extends beyond the hotel industry. He was a role model for many entrepreneurs and businessmen, demonstrating that with hard work, innovation, and a willingness to take risks, it is possible to achieve great success. His influence can be seen in the many businesses that have followed in his footsteps, from other hotel chains to tech startups and beyond.

Hilton was known for his work tactics and business ethics, which played a significant role in his success as a businessman. One of his key business tactics was his ability to identify opportunities and capitalize on them. He was always on the lookout for new opportunities to expand his business, whether it was by acquiring existing hotels or by building new ones. He was also known for his ability to negotiate deals and to find creative solutions to problems.

Hilton's business ethic was centered on hard work, honesty, and integrity. He believed in leading by example and was not afraid to roll up his sleeves and work alongside his employees. He was a hands-on leader who was involved in every aspect of his business, from the design of the hotels to the training of the staff. He believed that the success of his business was a team effort and that everyone had a role to play.

Hilton was also committed to providing the best possible service to his customers. He believed that the customer was king and that his hotels should provide the highest level of comfort and convenience. He was constantly looking for ways to improve his hotels and to enhance the guest experience. He was also known for his attention to detail, which was reflected in everything from the design of the hotels to the quality of the food and the cleanliness of the rooms.

Another key aspect of Hilton's business ethic was his willingness to take risks. He was not afraid to invest in new hotels or to enter new markets, even if it meant taking on significant financial risk. He believed that taking calculated risks was essential for business growth and success.

Hilton's work tactics and business ethics were also reflected in his management style. He believed in empowering his employees and giving them the freedom to make decisions. He also believed in treating his employees with respect and in providing them with opportunities for professional development.

In summary, Hilton's work tactics and business ethics

were centered on identifying opportunities, hard work, honesty, integrity, customer service, attention to detail, willingness to take risks, and empowering employees. These tactics and ethics played a significant role in his success as a businessman and continue to inspire and influence entrepreneurs and business leaders today.

The one thing that he did, that an entrepreneur should follow to be great today

There are several things that Conrad Hilton did that entrepreneurs today can follow to be great, but if I had to choose one, I would say that it is his unwavering commitment to customer service.

Hilton believed that the customer was king, and he made it his top priority to provide the highest level of comfort and convenience to his guests. He was constantly looking for ways to improve his hotels and to enhance the guest experience. He believed that satisfied customers were the key to his success and that word-of-mouth advertising was the most effective way to attract new customers.

Today, in the age of social media and online reviews, customer service is more important than ever. Entrepreneurs who prioritize customer service and make it their top priority are more likely to attract and retain customers, build a loyal customer base, and ultimately achieve long-term success.

So, if there is one thing that entrepreneurs should follow to be great today, it is to prioritize customer service above all else. By focusing on providing exceptional customer service and constantly looking for ways to improve the customer experience, entrepreneurs can build a strong brand, increase customer loyalty, and ultimately achieve their business goals.

Some more interesting facts and accomplishments about Conrad Hilton:

Conrad Hilton was born on December 25, 1887, in San Antonio, New Mexico, and was one of seven children. His father was a Norwegian immigrant who ran a general store.

Hilton started his career as a banker but soon realized that his true passion was in the hotel business. In 1919, he purchased his first hotel, the Mobley Hotel in Cisco, Texas, and soon after, he began acquiring more hotels.

Hilton is credited with revolutionizing the hotel industry by introducing several innovations, including the first hotel to offer room service, the first hotel to use air conditioning in the public areas, and the first hotel to install televisions in guest rooms.

In 1943, Hilton founded the Hilton Hotels Corporation, which would eventually become one of the largest hotel chains in the world. He was the CEO of the company until 1966, and during his tenure, he oversaw the construction of many iconic hotels, including the Hilton Hawaiian Village and the Beverly Hilton.

Hilton was a philanthropist who believed in giving back to the community. In 1944, he established the Conrad N. Hilton Foundation, which has since donated over $2 billion to various charitable causes around the world.

Hilton was also a devout Catholic and a member of the Knights of Malta, a Catholic organization that provides humanitarian aid to people in need. He was known for his generosity and his commitment to helping others.

Hilton was married twice and had eight children. His son, Barron Hilton, succeeded him as the CEO of the Hilton Hotels Corporation and continued to grow the business after his father's death.

Overall, Conrad Hilton was a visionary businessman and philanthropist who revolutionized the hotel industry and left a lasting legacy.

RYAN HOOVER

is a successful entrepreneur and businessman who has had a significant impact on the tech industry. He is best known as the founder of Product Hunt, a website and community that showcases new products and startups. Hoover's innovative approach to building and scaling companies has earned him a reputation as one of the most influential business minds of our time.

Hoover's career in tech began in his early twenties when he co-founded an email marketing tool called Playhaven. The startup quickly gained traction, and within a few years, it was acquired by a larger company. This early success set the stage for Hoover's future endeavors.

In 2013, Hoover launched Product Hunt, which quickly became one of the most popular websites for discovering new startups and products. The platform has since been acquired by AngelList, but it continues to thrive under Hoover's leadership.

One of the things that sets Hoover apart as a businessman is his ability to spot trends and build products that tap into them. He has a keen eye for emerging technologies and consumer behavior, which has allowed him to build successful businesses in some of the most exciting areas of tech.

For example, in 2016, Hoover launched Ship, a platform

that helps businesses create and launch their own chatbots. This was at a time when chatbots were just starting to gain traction, and Ship quickly became one of the most popular tools for building them.

Hoover's success as an entrepreneur is also due to his focus on community-building. He understands the importance of creating a loyal and engaged user base, and he has used this approach to build successful businesses time and time again.

Product Hunt is a great example of this. The platform is not just a directory of new startups and products; it's also a vibrant community of entrepreneurs, investors, and early adopters. Hoover has fostered this community by creating a culture of collaboration and openness, which has helped to attract some of the most innovative minds in tech.

Another area where Hoover excels is in his marketing tactics. He understands the power of storytelling and has used this to great effect in his businesses. For example, when launching Product Hunt, Hoover used his personal blog to share his vision for the platform and build anticipation. This helped to generate buzz and attract early adopters.

Hoover has also been successful in using social media to build his personal brand and promote his businesses. He has a large following on Twitter and is known for his engaging and insightful posts on entrepreneurship and tech.

In conclusion, Ryan Hoover is a highly influential business mind who has made significant contributions to the tech industry. His ability to spot trends, build communities, and use marketing tactics to build successful businesses has earned him a reputation as one of the most innovative and forward-thinking entrepreneurs of our time. Whether launching new startups or advising others on their own businesses, Hoover's impact will continue to be felt for years to come.

Ryan Hoover's work tactics and business ethics are an

important part of what makes him such a successful and influential entrepreneur.

One of the key tactics that Hoover employs is his focus on experimentation and iteration. He is a big believer in the "fail fast, learn fast" approach to building businesses. This means that he encourages his teams to try out new ideas quickly, and if they don't work, to move on to the next idea just as quickly.

Hoover also emphasizes the importance of staying nimble and adaptable in the face of changing circumstances. He understands that the tech industry moves quickly and that startups need to be able to pivot and change direction when necessary. This is a mindset that he has instilled in his teams and that has contributed to the success of his businesses.

Another important aspect of Hoover's work tactics is his emphasis on data-driven decision making. He believes that businesses should rely on data and metrics to guide their decision making, rather than relying on intuition or gut feelings. This approach has helped him to make informed decisions about where to invest resources and which products or features to prioritize.

In terms of his business ethics, Hoover is known for his transparency and openness. He believes in being honest with his team members, investors, and customers, even when the news is not good. This has helped to build trust and loyalty among those who work with him.

Hoover is also committed to building diverse and inclusive teams. He understands the value of having a range of perspectives and experiences on his team and has made a concerted effort to hire people from a variety of backgrounds. This is reflected in the culture of his companies, which are known for being welcoming and supportive of all team members.

Finally, Hoover is committed to giving back to the

community. He has mentored countless entrepreneurs and has been an advocate for improving access to education and resources for underrepresented groups in tech. He understands that he has been fortunate to achieve success in the industry, and he is committed to using his platform to help others achieve their goals as well.

Overall, Ryan Hoover's work tactics and business ethics reflect a commitment to innovation, transparency, and inclusivity. His approach has helped him to build successful businesses and to earn the respect and admiration of his peers in the tech industry.

The one thing that he did, that an entrepreneur should follow to be great

It's difficult to point to just one thing that Ryan Hoover did as an entrepreneur that all aspiring business leaders should follow to be great today. However, if I had to choose one key takeaway from Hoover's success, it would be his emphasis on building strong communities around his businesses.

Hoover's approach to community building has been a major factor in the success of his ventures, from Playhaven to Product Hunt. He understands that in order to build a successful business, it's not enough to simply create a great product or service. You also need to build a community of users and supporters who are passionate about what you're doing.

By building a strong community around your business, you can create a network of loyal customers and advocates who will help you spread the word about your product or service. This can be especially powerful in the tech industry, where word-of-mouth recommendations can be incredibly influential.

To build a strong community, you need to focus on creating a culture of collaboration and openness. This means engaging with your users and customers, listening to their feedback, and responding to their needs. You also need to be transparent and honest about your goals and your progress, which can help to build trust and loyalty.

In addition, you need to create opportunities for your community to engage with each other, whether that's through online forums, in-person meetups, or other channels. By fostering a sense of connection and belonging among your users, you can create a powerful network that will help to support your business over the long term.

So, if there's one thing that entrepreneurs can learn from Ryan Hoover's success, it's the importance of building strong communities around your business. By doing so, you can create a powerful network of supporters and advocates who will help you achieve your goals and drive your business forward.

Some additional things about Ryan Hoover:

Early career: Before becoming a successful entrepreneur, Ryan Hoover began his career as a software developer. He worked for various tech companies, including Microsoft, and eventually co-founded his first startup, Playhaven, in 2009.

Product Hunt: Hoover's most well-known venture is Product Hunt, which he co-founded in 2013. Product Hunt is a community-driven platform for discovering and sharing new products, and it quickly gained a loyal following among tech enthusiasts and early adopters. The platform was eventually acquired by AngelList in 2016.

Founder Collective: In addition to his work as an entrepreneur, Hoover is also a venture partner at Founder Collective, a seed-stage venture capital firm. In this role, he helps to identify and invest in promising startups.

Writing: Hoover is also an avid writer and has written extensively about entrepreneurship and startup culture. He has a popular blog where he shares his thoughts on a range of topics, from product development to community building.

Mentoring: Hoover is known for his willingness to mentor other entrepreneurs and to share his knowledge and experience with others. He has mentored countless startup founders and has been a vocal advocate for improving access to resources and education in the tech industry.

Awards and recognition: Hoover's contributions to the tech industry have not gone unnoticed. He has been recognized as one of the top young entrepreneurs by publications like Forbes and Business Insider, and he has been named to the Forbes 30 Under 30 list in both the technology and media categories.

Overall, Ryan Hoover is a highly respected figure in the tech industry, known for his innovation, community building, and commitment to mentoring and education.

TONY HSIEH

is certainly an interesting figure to include in your list of the most influential entrepreneurs and businessmen of all time. He was a pioneer in the tech industry, and his innovative thinking and approach to business made him stand out in the crowded world of startups. Let's take a closer look at his life and work.

Tony Hsieh was born on December 12, 1973, in Illinois. He grew up in the Bay Area, and attended Harvard University, where he graduated with a degree in Computer Science. After college, Hsieh worked for Oracle, but soon realized that he wanted to start his own company. In 1996, he co-founded LinkExchange, an online advertising network that was sold to Microsoft for $265 million just three years later.

With the proceeds from the sale of LinkExchange, Hsieh became an angel investor and started investing in various startups, including Zappos, an online shoe retailer. In 2004, Hsieh joined Zappos as CEO, and under his leadership, the company grew rapidly. He transformed Zappos from a small startup into a billion-dollar enterprise, with a reputation for excellent customer service and a unique company culture.

One of the key factors that set Zappos apart was Hsieh's focus on delivering happiness. He believed that if his employees were happy, they would provide better service to customers, which would lead to greater success for the company. To this end, Hsieh invested heavily in employee training, and even created a "culture book" that outlined the company's values and mission. He also encouraged his employees to have fun and be creative, and he was known for throwing wild parties at the company's Las Vegas headquarters.

But Hsieh's commitment to customer service was perhaps his greatest innovation. He believed that the key to success in e-commerce was to provide an exceptional customer experience, and he was willing to do whatever it took to achieve that goal. For example, Zappos offered free shipping and free returns, and even allowed customers to return shoes up to a year after purchase. Hsieh believed that these policies would build customer loyalty, and he was right. Zappos became known for its exceptional customer service, and the company's sales soared.

In 2009, Hsieh sold Zappos to Amazon for $1.2 billion. But rather than retire, he remained at the company and continued to innovate. He launched the "Holacracy" management system, which eliminated traditional hierarchy in favor of a more fluid, self-organizing structure. He also invested in a variety of startups and launched the Downtown Project, an initiative aimed at revitalizing downtown Las Vegas.

Tragically, Hsieh passed away in November 2020, at the age of 46. But his legacy lives on. He is remembered as a visionary entrepreneur who was ahead of his time. He was a pioneer in e-commerce and customer service, and his innovative approach to business inspired countless others. His commitment to happiness and his belief in the power of culture and community continue to be an inspiration to entrepreneurs and business leaders around the world.

In conclusion, Tony Hsieh was a true innovator and a force to be reckoned with in the world of business. His commitment to customer service, employee happiness, and community building set him apart from his peers, and his influence can still be felt in the tech industry and beyond. His legacy serves as a reminder that innovation, creativity, and a willingness to take risks are the keys to success in business.

Tony Hsieh was known for his unique approach to business and his strong work ethic. Here are some additional details about his tactics and business ethics:

Focus on customer service: As I mentioned earlier, Hsieh believed that exceptional customer service was the key to success in e-commerce. He implemented policies such as free shipping and free returns, and he encouraged his employees to go above and beyond to make customers happy. This approach paid off, as Zappos became known for its outstanding customer service.

Employee happiness: Hsieh believed that happy employees were essential to the success of any business. He invested heavily in employee training and created a culture that valued creativity, fun, and community. He even developed a "culture book" that outlined the company's values and mission. This focus on employee happiness helped to create a loyal and motivated workforce.

Strong work ethic: Hsieh was known for his tireless work ethic. He was often the first person to arrive at the office in the morning and the last person to leave at night. He was also willing to take risks and make bold decisions in order to grow the company.

Innovation: Hsieh was constantly looking for new and innovative ways to do things. He was an early adopter of online advertising and e-commerce, and he was always looking for ways to improve the customer experience. He also launched the "Holacracy" management system, which was a radical departure from traditional management.

Community building: Hsieh was passionate about building community, both within his company and in the wider world. He launched the Downtown Project in Las Vegas, which aimed to revitalize the city's downtown area through investments in technology, education, and small businesses. He also encouraged his employees to get involved in charitable activities and community service.

Authenticity: Hsieh was known for being authentic and transparent in his business dealings. He believed in being honest and open with customers and employees, and he was not afraid to admit when things went wrong. This approach helped to build trust and loyalty with his stakeholders.

Overall, Tony Hsieh's business tactics and ethics were centered around delivering happiness to customers, employees, and the wider community. He believed in taking risks, being innovative, and creating a positive and authentic company culture. His approach to business continues to inspire entrepreneurs and business leaders around the world.

The one thing that he did, that an entrepreneur should follow to be great today

While there are many things that Tony Hsieh did that entrepreneurs could learn from, perhaps the most important lesson he taught is the value of creating a strong company culture. Hsieh recognized early on that a company's culture could be a powerful tool for attracting and retaining talented employees, as well as for building a loyal customer base.

To create a strong company culture, Hsieh focused on several key areas, including employee happiness, community building, and innovation. He invested heavily in employee training and development, and he encouraged his employees to be creative and take risks. He also built a sense of community within the company, which helped to foster a strong sense of teamwork and collaboration.

At the same time, Hsieh was willing to take bold risks and make unconventional decisions in order to grow the company. He was not afraid to try new things or to pivot the business when necessary. By creating a strong company culture that emphasized creativity, community, and innovation, Tony Hsieh was able to build one of the most successful e-commerce businesses in the world. Today, entrepreneurs can learn from his example by focusing on creating a culture that fosters employee happiness, community building, and innovation, and by being willing to take bold risks to achieve success.

A few more things about Tony Hsieh:

Early career: Before he founded Zappos, Hsieh had a successful career as a tech entrepreneur. He co-founded LinkExchange, an online advertising network, which he sold to Microsoft for $265 million in 1998. He then became an angel investor and invested in several startups, including Ask Jeeves (now known as Ask.com).

Downtown Project: In addition to his work at Zappos, Hsieh was also involved in a project to revitalize downtown Las Vegas. The Downtown Project aimed to create a vibrant and connected community in the city's historic downtown area, with a focus on technology, education, and small business development. Hsieh invested $350 million of his money in the project, which included investments in businesses, real estate, and community spaces.

Holacracy: Hsieh was a proponent of the "Holacracy" management system, which he implemented at Zappos in 2013. Holacracy is a decentralized management structure that distributes decision-making power throughout the organization. It is designed to be more flexible and adaptable than traditional hierarchies, and it places a strong emphasis on individual autonomy and accountability.

Philanthropy: Hsieh was a generous philanthropist, and he donated millions of dollars to charitable causes throughout his career. He was particularly passionate about education, and he established the Downtown Project's "100% of Kids" initiative, which aimed to ensure that all children in the downtown Las Vegas area had access to high-quality education.

Overall, Tony Hsieh was a visionary entrepreneur who made a significant impact in the tech and e-commerce industries. He was known for his innovative ideas, his strong work ethic, and his commitment to building community and fostering employee happiness. His legacy continues to inspire entrepreneurs around the world.

MA HUATENG

also known as Pony Ma, is a Chinese entrepreneur who is best known as the co-founder and CEO of Tencent, one of the world's largest internet companies. Born in 1971 in Guangdong, China, Ma started his career as a software developer before co-founding Tencent in 1998 with four other co-founders. Tencent's flagship product is the social media platform WeChat, which has over a billion users worldwide.

Ma's innovation mind can be seen in his early recognition of the potential of the internet as a tool for communication and commerce. He and his co-founders started Tencent with the goal of creating an online platform that would allow people to communicate with each other in real-time. Their first product was an instant messaging service called OICQ (later renamed QQ), which quickly became popular in China. However, they didn't stop there and continued to innovate with new products and services that expanded Tencent's reach and influence.

One of Ma's most notable innovations was the development of WeChat. Launched in 2011, WeChat is now much more than just an instant messaging app. It has become an all-in-one platform that allows users to chat, make payments, book appointments, play games, and much more. WeChat has become an essential part of daily life for millions of people in

China and has even started to gain popularity in other parts of the world.

Ma's work ethic and tactics have also contributed to his success as a businessman. He is known for being a hard worker and for setting ambitious goals for Tencent. He has a hands-on approach to management and is involved in many aspects of the company's operations. He also values teamwork and collaboration, which has helped to foster a culture of innovation and creativity at Tencent.

Another key tactic that Ma has employed is strategic investment. Tencent has invested in a wide range of companies and startups over the years, including Tesla, Snap, and Epic Games. By investing in these companies, Tencent has been able to diversify its business and expand into new markets.

Ma's impact on the business world is undeniable. Tencent is now one of the largest and most successful internet companies in the world, with a market capitalization of over $1 trillion. Ma's innovations and leadership have helped to shape the way people communicate and do business online, not just in China but around the world. He has been recognized for his achievements with numerous awards and honors, including being named one of Time magazine's 100 most influential people in the world.

In conclusion, Ma Huateng is an influential businessman who has had a significant impact on the business world through his innovation mind, work, and tactics. His early recognition of the potential of the internet, his hands-on approach to management, and his strategic investments have all contributed to the success of Tencent and his status as one of the most influential business minds of our time.

Ma Huateng is known for his strong work ethic and commitment to excellence. He is known to work long hours and is deeply involved in the day-to-day operations of

Tencent. He has also set ambitious goals for the company, which has helped to drive its success.

One of Ma's key tactics is a focus on innovation and creativity. He encourages his employees to think outside the box and to come up with new and innovative ideas. Tencent has a dedicated research and development team that is focused on developing new technologies and products. Ma himself is known for his passion for technology and is always looking for new ways to improve Tencent's products and services.

Another important aspect of Ma's business ethic is his emphasis on teamwork and collaboration. He believes that the key to success is working together and building strong relationships with colleagues and partners. Tencent has a collaborative culture that encourages employees to work together and share ideas.

In addition to innovation and teamwork, Ma is also known for his strategic investments. Tencent has invested in a wide range of companies and startups, both in China and abroad. This has helped to diversify Tencent's business and expand its reach into new markets. Ma is known for his ability to identify promising companies and to make strategic investments that will benefit Tencent in the long term.

Ma is also known for his philanthropic work. In 2016, he established the Ma Huateng Global Foundation, which is focused on supporting education, healthcare, and environmental initiatives. He has also made significant donations to various causes in China, including disaster relief efforts.

Overall, Ma Huateng's work tactics and business ethic are characterized by a focus on innovation, teamwork, and strategic investments. His commitment to excellence and his passion for technology have helped to drive the success of Tencent and his status as one of the most influential business minds of our time.

The one thing that he did, that an entrepreneur should follow to be great today

It's difficult to pinpoint just one thing that Ma Huateng did that an entrepreneur should follow to be great today, as his success is the result of a combination of factors. However, one key aspect of Ma's approach that entrepreneurs could learn from is his emphasis on innovation and creativity.

Ma's focus on innovation has been a driving force behind Tencent's success. He has always been willing to take risks and to try new things, and this has helped to keep Tencent at the forefront of the rapidly evolving technology landscape. He has also fostered a culture of innovation within the company, encouraging his employees to think creatively and to come up with new and innovative ideas.

Entrepreneurs can learn from Ma's approach by prioritizing innovation and creativity in their own businesses. By staying open to new ideas and technologies, entrepreneurs can stay ahead of the competition and continue to grow and evolve over time. This might involve investing in research and development, encouraging employees to experiment and take risks, and staying up-to-date with the latest trends and developments in their industry.

In addition to innovation, Ma's emphasis on teamwork and collaboration is another key aspect of his approach that entrepreneurs could learn from. By building strong relationships with colleagues and partners, entrepreneurs can leverage the skills and expertise of others to achieve their goals. This might involve networking, building partnerships, or collaborating with other businesses in their industry.

Overall, entrepreneurs looking to emulate Ma's success

should focus on innovation, creativity, and collaboration. By staying open to new ideas and working closely with others, they can build successful businesses that are capable of adapting and evolving over time.

A few more interesting facts about Ma Huateng:

Ma is also known by his nickname "Pony Ma". This nickname was given to him by a friend and is a reference to his love of horse riding.

Ma was born in 1971 in Chaoyang, Guangdong Province, China. He grew up in a small village and later moved to Shenzhen to attend college.

Ma co-founded Tencent in 1998 with several classmates from college. The company started as an instant messaging service and has since grown to become one of the largest and most influential technology companies in the world.

Ma is one of the wealthiest people in China, with a net worth of over $60 billion as of 2023. He has been named one of Time magazine's 100 most influential people and was also ranked among Forbes' list of the world's most powerful people.

Ma is a strong advocate for internet freedom and has spoken out against censorship and government control of the internet. He has also been involved in several philanthropic efforts, including the establishment of the Ma Huateng Global Foundation.

Ma is a member of the Chinese People's Political Consultative Conference, a political advisory body in China. He has also been recognized for his contributions to science and technology, receiving the prestigious China Reform Friendship Medal in 2018.

Ma is a self-described introvert and has spoken openly about his struggles with public speaking. Despite this, he is known for his leadership and vision, and has been credited with driving Tencent's growth and success over the years.

Overall, Ma Huateng is a fascinating and influential figure in the world of business and technology, known for his innovation, leadership, and commitment to excellence.

ARIANA HUFFINGTON

is a prominent Greek-American businesswoman, author, and media mogul who has made a significant impact on the world of business and entrepreneurship. She is the co-founder of The Huffington Post, a popular online news and opinion website, and the founder and CEO of Thrive Global, a company focused on promoting well-being and reducing stress and burnout in the workplace.

Born in Athens, Greece in 1950, Ariana Stassinopoulos (as she was then known) moved to England at the age of 16 to attend Cambridge University. After graduating, she began a career as a journalist, working for publications such as The Sunday Times and The Economist. In the 1980s, she moved to the United States and became a political commentator and television personality.

In the early 2000s, Ariana Huffington saw an opportunity to create a new kind of media company that would combine the speed and reach of the internet with the journalistic standards and quality of traditional media. In 2005, she co-founded The Huffington Post with Kenneth Lerer and Jonah Peretti. The website quickly became a huge success, attracting millions of readers with its mix of news, opinion, and entertainment content. It was acquired by AOL in 2011 for $315 million.

Ariana Huffington's success with The Huffington Post demonstrated her innovative thinking and her ability to identify new trends and opportunities in the world of business. She also showed a talent for building and leading teams of talented individuals, as the website's success was due in large part to the many writers and editors who contributed to it.

After leaving The Huffington Post in 2016, Ariana Huffington founded Thrive Global, a company focused on promoting health and well-being in the workplace. The company provides a range of tools and resources for individuals and organizations looking to reduce stress and burnout and improve their overall well-being. Thrive Global has been successful in part because of the growing awareness of the importance of mental health and well-being in the workplace, and Ariana Huffington's innovative approach to addressing this issue.

In addition to her work as a businesswoman and entrepreneur, Ariana Huffington is also a successful author and public speaker. She has written numerous books on topics such as personal growth, politics, and business, and is a sought-after speaker on topics related to leadership, entrepreneurship, and well-being.

Overall, Ariana Huffington's innovative thinking, entrepreneurial spirit, and ability to identify and capitalize on new trends and opportunities in the world of business make her one of the most influential business minds of our time. Her success with The Huffington Post and Thrive Global demonstrate her ability to create and lead successful companies, while her advocacy for well-being and mental health in the workplace has helped to shape the conversation around these important issues.

Ariana Huffington is known for her strong work ethic

and her focus on promoting well-being and balance in the workplace. Here are some additional details about her work tactics and business ethics:

Prioritizing Sleep and Well-being: Ariana Huffington has been a vocal advocate for the importance of getting enough sleep and taking care of one's physical and mental health. She has written books and given speeches on the topic, and her company Thrive Global provides resources and tools to help individuals and organizations improve their well-being.

Embracing Failure: Ariana Huffington has talked openly about the failures and setbacks she has experienced throughout her career. She sees failure as an opportunity for growth and learning, and encourages others to embrace it as well.

Collaboration and Teamwork: Ariana Huffington understands the value of collaboration and teamwork, and has built successful companies by bringing together talented individuals from a variety of backgrounds. She has also emphasized the importance of creating a positive and supportive work culture.

Innovation and Disruption: Ariana Huffington has demonstrated a willingness to embrace new ideas and technologies, and to disrupt traditional industries. The Huffington Post was a groundbreaking example of how the internet could change the media landscape, and Thrive Global has challenged the traditional approach to workplace well-being.

Social Responsibility: Ariana Huffington has emphasized the importance of using business as a force for good, and has spoken out on a range of social and political issues. She has used her platform to advocate for causes such as gender equality and climate change.

Overall, Ariana Huffington's work tactics and business ethics are centered around the idea of promoting well-being and balance, while also being innovative and disruptive. She values collaboration and teamwork, and sees failure as an opportunity for growth. She also prioritizes social responsibility, and uses her platform to advocate for important causes. These values have been integral to her success as an entrepreneur and business leader.

The one thing that she did, that an entrepreneur should follow to be great

It's difficult to point to just one thing that Ariana Huffington did that an entrepreneur should follow to be great today, as her success is the result of a combination of factors such as her innovative thinking, work ethic, and focus on well-being and balance. However, if I had to identify one key takeaway from Ariana Huffington's career that entrepreneurs can learn from, it would be the importance of embracing new technologies and disrupting traditional industries.

Ariana Huffington recognized early on the potential of the internet to transform the media industry, and she created The Huffington Post to take advantage of this trend. By combining traditional journalistic standards with the speed and reach of the internet, she created a new kind of media company that disrupted the traditional newspaper and magazine model.

Similarly, with Thrive Global, Ariana Huffington is disrupting the traditional approach to workplace well-being by using technology to provide resources and tools to individuals and organizations. She recognized the growing importance of mental health and well-being in the workplace, and she created a company that leverages technology to address this issue.

Today, with the rapid pace of technological change,

entrepreneurs need to be able to recognize and adapt to new trends and technologies in order to stay ahead of the curve. By embracing new technologies and disrupting traditional industries, entrepreneurs can create innovative solutions that meet the needs of today's consumers and businesses. This is a key lesson that can be learned from Ariana Huffington's career.

Some additional facts and accomplishments about Ariana Huffington:

She is a prolific author: Ariana Huffington has written over 15 books, covering a range of topics including politics, women's issues, and well-being. Some of her most well-known books include "The Sleep Revolution," "Thrive," and "On Becoming Fearless."

She has been recognized for her achievements: Ariana Huffington has been named to numerous lists of the world's most influential people, including Time magazine's list of the 100 Most Influential People in the World, Forbes' list of the Most Powerful Women, and the Financial Times' list of the Top 50 Women in World Business.

She is a strong advocate for gender equality: Ariana Huffington has been a vocal advocate for women's rights and gender equality throughout her career. She has spoken out on issues such as the gender pay gap, women's representation in politics and business, and sexual harassment in the workplace.

She is a political commentator: Prior to launching The Huffington Post, Ariana Huffington was a political commentator and commentator for various news outlets, including CNN and MSNBC. She has also run for political office, making an unsuccessful bid for Governor of California in 2003.

She is a philanthropist: Ariana Huffington is involved in a number of charitable organizations and causes. She serves on the board of directors for a number of non-profit organizations, including the Center for Public Integrity and the Committee to Protect Journalists. She has also launched several initiatives aimed at supporting underserved communities and improving well-being.

Overall, Ariana Huffington is a highly accomplished entrepreneur, author, and advocate. Her work has had a significant impact on a variety of fields, from media and technology to well-being and gender equality. Her dedication to innovation, collaboration, and social responsibility are qualities that have helped her to achieve success and make a positive impact on the world.

HOWARD HUGHES

Was one of the most iconic and influential businessmen of the 20th century, known for his innovative ideas, strategic tactics, and unparalleled vision. Born on December 24, 1905, in Houston, Texas, Hughes was a true pioneer who revolutionized several industries during his lifetime.

Hughes' early years were marked by privilege, as his father was a successful businessman who made a fortune in the oil industry. This allowed Hughes to receive an excellent education, and he was sent to private schools where he excelled in mathematics and science. However, it wasn't until he inherited his father's company, Hughes Tool Company, at the age of 19, that he truly began to make his mark on the business world.

From the very beginning, Hughes was a visionary entrepreneur who was never satisfied with the status quo. He quickly realized that the aviation industry was ripe for disruption, and he set his sights on developing faster, more efficient airplanes. Hughes' innovations in aviation were unparalleled, and he went on to create some of the most advanced and groundbreaking aircraft of his time.

One of his most famous aircraft was the H-1 Racer, which set the world speed record in 1935 at a staggering 352 miles per hour. Hughes continued to push the boundaries of aviation, and in 1947, he piloted the Hughes H-4 Hercules, also known as the "Spruce Goose," on its first and only flight. The Spruce Goose was the largest aircraft ever built at the time, with a wingspan of 320 feet, and it was a testament to Hughes' boundless creativity and innovative spirit.

But Hughes was not content with just dominating the aviation industry. He also made significant contributions to the entertainment industry, producing and directing several successful films, including the classic "Hell's Angels." His work in film led him to create a new sound system that revolutionized the movie industry, and his innovations in this area earned him several Oscars.

Hughes' success was not just due to his innovative mind, but also his shrewd business tactics. He was a master at identifying profitable opportunities and seizing them quickly. For example, he acquired the controlling interest in TWA airlines in 1939 and turned the struggling airline into a profitable venture within a few short years. Hughes' ability to see the potential in a business and take decisive action to make it successful was one of his greatest strengths.

Hughes was also a perfectionist who demanded excellence from himself and his employees. He was notorious for his attention to detail and his insistence on quality, which helped to set his businesses apart from his competitors. He was constantly testing new ideas and methods, and he was not afraid to take risks to achieve his goals.

Despite his many accomplishments, Hughes' later years were marked by personal struggles and controversy. He became increasingly reclusive and battled with mental health issues, which led to his eventual withdrawal from public life. However, his impact on the business world and his contributions to aviation, film, and entertainment cannot be overstated.

In conclusion, Howard Hughes was a true innovator and

a visionary entrepreneur who left an indelible mark on the business world. His contributions to aviation, film, and entertainment were groundbreaking, and his strategic business tactics and attention to detail set him apart from his competitors. His legacy continues to inspire entrepreneurs and businessmen to this day, and his influence on the business world will undoubtedly be felt for generations to come.

Howard Hughes' work tactics and business ethics were as unique as his personality. He was known for being a hands-on leader who was involved in every aspect of his businesses. He demanded excellence from himself and his employees and was relentless in his pursuit of perfection. Here are some specific examples of his work tactics and business ethics:

Attention to Detail: Hughes was famous for his attention to detail, which extended to every aspect of his businesses. He was known for spending countless hours poring over blueprints, scrutinizing every detail to ensure that everything was perfect. He would even conduct his own crash tests to determine the strength and durability of his aircraft. This attention to detail helped to set his businesses apart from his competitors and contributed to his success.

Innovation: Hughes was an innovator who was constantly pushing the boundaries of what was possible. He was not content to simply follow in the footsteps of others, but was always looking for ways to improve and innovate. For example, he developed new materials and technologies to make his aircraft faster and more efficient, and he created a new sound system that revolutionized the movie industry.

Risk-Taking: Hughes was not afraid to take risks to achieve his goals. He was willing to invest his own money and take on significant debt to fund his businesses and projects. For example, he spent millions of dollars of his own money to develop the H-1 Racer, a risky move that paid off when the aircraft set a world speed record.

Long-Term Thinking: Hughes was a strategic thinker who always had an eye on the long-term. He was not interested in short-term gains but was focused on building sustainable businesses that would last for generations. For example, when he acquired TWA airlines, he made significant investments in modernizing the fleet and improving customer service, even though it took several years for the investments to pay off.

Personal Involvement: Hughes was a hands-on leader who was involved in every aspect of his businesses. He would personally test his aircraft and would visit his factories to ensure that everything was running smoothly. He was also known for hiring the best and brightest minds in the industry and giving them the resources and support they needed to succeed.

Ethical Conduct: Despite his reputation for being a maverick, Hughes was a principled businessman who conducted himself with integrity. He was known for being fair and honest in his dealings with employees, suppliers, and partners. He was also committed to safety, both for his employees and his customers, and he invested heavily in safety technology and training.

In conclusion, Howard Hughes was a driven, innovative, and ethical businessman who left an indelible mark on the business world. His attention to detail, innovation, risk-taking, long-term thinking, personal involvement, and ethical conduct helped to set him apart from his competitors and contributed to his success. His legacy continues to inspire entrepreneurs and businessmen to this day, and his influence on the business world will undoubtedly be felt for generations to come.

The one thing that he did,

*that an entrepreneur should
follow to be great today*

It's difficult to point to just one thing that Howard Hughes did as an entrepreneur that others should follow to be great today, as his success was the result of a combination of many factors. However, if there is one key lesson that can be learned from Hughes' approach to business, it is his relentless pursuit of innovation.

Hughes was a visionary who was constantly pushing the boundaries of what was possible, and he was not content to simply follow in the footsteps of others. He was always looking for ways to improve and innovate, whether it was developing new technologies, creating new materials, or finding new ways to do things. He had a passion for his work that drove him to continually strive for excellence, and he was never satisfied with the status quo.

In today's fast-paced and rapidly evolving business landscape, innovation is more important than ever. Entrepreneurs who want to be successful need to be able to adapt quickly to changing circumstances and find new and better ways to meet the needs of their customers. They need to be willing to take risks and think outside the box, and they need to have a relentless drive to improve and innovate.

Innovation can take many forms, from developing new products and services to improving existing ones, to finding more efficient ways of doing things. It requires a willingness to experiment and take risks, and it requires a deep understanding of the needs and desires of your customers.

So, if there is one thing that entrepreneurs should follow from Howard Hughes' example, it is his relentless pursuit of innovation. By constantly pushing the boundaries of what is possible, entrepreneurs can create new opportunities for themselves and their businesses, and stay ahead of the competition in an ever-changing business landscape.

Some more interesting facts about Howard Hughes:

Hughes was a self-made billionaire. He inherited a fortune from his father, but he built his own businesses from scratch and became one of the wealthiest men in the world. At the peak of his career, he had a net worth of more than $1 billion, which would be the equivalent of several billion dollars today.

Hughes was a prolific inventor. He held more than 300 patents in his lifetime, including patents for aircraft designs, electronic devices, and medical equipment. He was constantly tinkering and experimenting, and his inventions helped to revolutionize several industries.

Hughes was a movie producer and director. He founded Hughes Productions in the 1940s and produced several successful films, including "The Outlaw" and "The Conqueror". He also directed several films himself, including "Hell's Angels" and "The Front Page".

Hughes was a record-breaking aviator. He set several speed and distance records in the 1930s and 1940s, including a record-breaking flight around the world in 1938. He was also a skilled pilot and often flew his own aircraft.

Hughes was a reclusive figure in later life. In the 1950s and 1960s, he became increasingly reclusive and withdrew from public life. He suffered from several health problems, including obsessive-compulsive disorder, and became dependent on prescription drugs. He spent much of his later life in seclusion, living in hotel suites and communicating with the outside world through intermediaries.

Hughes was the subject of several high-profile legal battles. In the 1970s, several people claimed to be heirs to his fortune, and there were several lawsuits over his estate. His estate was eventually divided among his surviving relatives, but the legal battles continued for many years after his death.

In conclusion, Howard Hughes was a fascinating figure who achieved great success in multiple industries. He was a self-made billionaire, a prolific inventor, a movie producer and director, a record-breaking aviator, and a reclusive figure in later life. His life and career were marked by both triumphs and tragedies, and his legacy continues to inspire entrepreneurs and innovators to this day.

LEE IACOCCA

Was a prominent businessman and automobile industry executive who had a significant impact on the industry through his innovative approach, management style, and business strategies. Iacocca was born on October 15, 1924, in Allentown, Pennsylvania, and died on July 2, 2019, in Bel Air, California. Throughout his career, he demonstrated a remarkable talent for leadership, innovation, and a strong work ethic that set him apart from his peers.

Early Life and Education:

Lee Iacocca was born to Italian immigrant parents and grew up in a blue-collar family in Allentown, Pennsylvania. From an early age, he showed an interest in mechanics and engineering, which led him to pursue a degree in industrial engineering at Lehigh University. After graduation, Iacocca went on to attend Princeton University, where he earned a master's degree in mechanical engineering.

Career at Ford:

After completing his education, Iacocca began his career at Ford Motor Company in 1946. He quickly rose through the ranks at the company, and by the early 1960s, he had become one of the top executives at Ford. During his time at Ford, Iacocca was responsible for several major initiatives that helped the company become one of the most successful automobile manufacturers in the world.

One of Iacocca's most significant contributions to the automobile industry was the development of the Ford Mustang. In the early 1960s, Iacocca recognized that there was a market for a small, sporty car that was both affordable and stylish. He convinced Ford to develop the Mustang, and the car was an immediate success when it was introduced in 1964. The Mustang went on to become one of the most iconic cars of the 1960s and is still popular today.

In addition to the Mustang, Iacocca also played a key role in the development of other successful Ford models, such as the Pinto and the Escort. He was known for his innovative approach to automobile design and his ability to identify and capitalize on emerging trends in the market.

Career at Chrysler:

In 1978, Iacocca was hired as the CEO of Chrysler Corporation, which was on the brink of bankruptcy at the time. Under his leadership, the company underwent a massive restructuring that included layoffs, plant closures, and the sale of non-core assets. Iacocca also introduced several new models, such as the minivan, which helped the company turn a profit and become one of the most successful automobile manufacturers in the world.

One of Iacocca's most notable achievements at Chrysler was the development of the K-car platform. The K-car was a compact, front-wheel-drive platform that was used as the basis for several Chrysler models, including the Dodge Aries, Plymouth Reliant, and Chrysler LeBaron. The K-car was a huge success and helped Chrysler become profitable again after years of losses.

In addition to his innovative approach to automobile design, Iacocca was also known for his management style and business strategies. He was a charismatic leader who was able to motivate his employees and build strong relationships with suppliers and customers. He also believed in the importance of advertising and marketing, and he was responsible for several memorable ad campaigns during his time at Chrysler.

Conclusion:

Lee Iacocca was a true innovator and one of the most influential businessmen of all time. His contributions to the automobile industry, particularly his work at Ford and Chrysler, had a lasting impact on the industry and helped shape the modern automobile as we know it today. Iacocca was a visionary leader who was able to identify emerging trends in the market and capitalize on them, and his innovative approach to automobile design set him apart from his colleagues.

Lee Iacocca was known for his strong work ethic, innovative approach, and effective management style, which set him apart from his peers in the automobile industry. Here are some more details about his work tactics and business ethics:

Strong Leadership: Iacocca was a charismatic leader who had a clear vision for his companies and was able to communicate that vision to his employees. He was known for his ability to motivate his team and build strong relationships with suppliers and customers.

Innovative Approach: Iacocca was a true innovator who was always looking for ways to improve his companies and their products. He was responsible for several groundbreaking designs, such as the Ford Mustang and the K-car platform, which helped his companies stay ahead of the competition.

Effective Management: Iacocca was a hands-on manager who was involved in every aspect of his companies' operations. He was known for his attention to detail and his ability to make quick, informed decisions. He also believed in the importance of teamwork and collaboration, and he worked closely with his employees to achieve their goals.

Marketing and Advertising: Iacocca understood the importance of marketing and advertising in the automobile industry. He was responsible for several memorable ad campaigns, such as the "Imported from Detroit" campaign for Chrysler, which helped his companies build brand awareness and loyalty.

Business Ethics: Iacocca was a firm believer in the importance of honesty and integrity in business. He was known for his ethical approach to business and for treating his employees, customers, and suppliers with respect and fairness.

Focus on Profitability: Iacocca was always focused on the bottom line and on making his companies profitable. He was willing to take risks and make tough decisions, such as the layoffs and plant closures he implemented at Chrysler, in order to achieve that goal.

In summary, Lee Iacocca was a talented businessman who was known for his strong work ethic, innovative approach, and effective management style. He believed in the importance of leadership, teamwork, marketing, and ethical business practices, and he was always focused on profitability and improving his companies. These tactics and business ethics made him one of the most influential business minds of all time.

The one thing that he did, that an entrepreneur should follow to be great today

There are many things that Lee Iacocca did that entrepreneurs could learn from, but one thing that stands out is his ability to take calculated risks and innovate in the face of adversity.

Iacocca was faced with several challenges throughout his career, such as the declining sales at Ford and the near-bankruptcy of Chrysler. However, he was able to overcome these challenges by taking bold, calculated risks and introducing innovative products and strategies.

For example, at Ford, he championed the development of the Mustang, which became a huge success and helped turn the company's fortunes around. At Chrysler, he introduced the K-car platform and the minivan, which helped the company regain its footing and become profitable again.

Entrepreneurs can learn from Iacocca's example by being willing to take calculated risks and innovate in the face of adversity. This may involve developing new products or services, exploring new markets or distribution channels, or finding ways to differentiate themselves from their competitors. It may also involve being willing to make tough decisions, such as cutting costs or laying off employees, in order to stay profitable and competitive.

Ultimately, the key to success as an entrepreneur is being able to adapt to changing circumstances and take bold, calculated risks when necessary. By following Iacocca's example, entrepreneurs can increase their chances of success and achieve their goals.

Some more interesting facts about Lee Iacocca:

He was born in Allentown, Pennsylvania in 1924, to Italian immigrant parents.

He attended Lehigh University, where he earned a degree in industrial engineering.

He began his career at Ford Motor Company in 1946, where he rose through the ranks to become the company's president in 1970.

He is credited with leading the development of several iconic Ford models, including the Mustang and the Pinto.

In 1978, he was fired from Ford after a power struggle with Henry Ford II.

He was hired as CEO of Chrysler Corporation in 1978, at a time when the company was facing bankruptcy.

He introduced several successful models at Chrysler, including the K-car platform and the minivan.

He is credited with turning Chrysler around and making it profitable again.

He became a well-known public figure during his time at Chrysler, appearing in several television commercials for the company.

He was also known for his philanthropy, supporting causes such as diabetes research and the restoration of the Statue of Liberty.

He wrote several books, including his autobiography, "Iacocca: An Autobiography," which became a bestseller.

He passed away in 2019 at the age of 94, leaving behind a legacy as one of the most influential businessmen of the 20th century.

STEVE JOBS

Was indeed one of the most influential businessmen and entrepreneurs of all time. He co-founded Apple Inc. and was instrumental in transforming it into one of the world's most successful companies.

Steve Jobs was born in San Francisco in 1955, and was adopted by Paul and Clara Jobs. He grew up in Mountain View, California, which was then known as the heart of Silicon Valley. Jobs showed an early interest in electronics and computing and, after dropping out of college, he and Steve Wozniak founded Apple in 1976 in Jobs' parents' garage.

The first product that Apple launched was the Apple I, which was essentially a kit computer that customers had to assemble themselves. However, it was the launch of the Apple II in 1977 that really put Apple on the map. The Apple II was the first personal computer with color graphics and a built-in keyboard, and it became a huge success.

Jobs was known for his innovative mind and his ability to anticipate what consumers would want before they even knew it themselves. One of his most famous quotes was "You can't just ask customers what they want and then try to give that to them. By the time you get it built, they'll want something new."

Jobs was also known for his perfectionism and his obsession

with design. He believed that every detail of a product, from the hardware to the software to the packaging, should be perfect. This attention to detail was evident in the design of the Apple II and all subsequent Apple products.

In 1985, Jobs left Apple after a power struggle with the board of directors. He went on to found NeXT Computer, a company that focused on developing high-end workstations for the education and business markets. However, NeXT never achieved the same level of success as Apple, and in 1996, Apple bought NeXT, bringing Jobs back into the fold.

Jobs returned to Apple as CEO and immediately set about transforming the company. He streamlined the product line, focusing on a few core products rather than a confusing array of options. He also introduced new products, such as the iMac, which was a huge success due to its colorful design and easy-to-use interface.

However, it was the launch of the iPod in 2001 that really put Apple back on top. The iPod was a revolutionary product that allowed users to carry their entire music library with them wherever they went. It was also the beginning of Apple's foray into digital media, which would eventually lead to the launch of the iPhone and the iPad.

Jobs' tactics were often controversial, and he was known for being a difficult person to work with. However, there is no denying that his innovation and vision transformed Apple into one of the world's most valuable companies. He was a master of branding and marketing, and his presentations, such as the famous iPhone launch in 2007, were legendary.

Sadly, Jobs was diagnosed with pancreatic cancer in 2003 and passed away in 2011 at the age of 56. However, his legacy lives on, not only at Apple but in the wider world of business and technology.

In conclusion, Steve Jobs was a truly innovative and influential businessman. His attention to detail, obsession with design, and ability to anticipate what consumers would want made him a true visionary. While his tactics were often controversial, there is no denying that his contributions to the world of business and technology have been immense. Steve Jobs will always be remembered as one of the most important figures in the history of entrepreneurship and business.

Steve Jobs was known for being a very demanding boss, with a reputation for being difficult to work with. However, his work tactics and business ethic were a key part of his success.

One of the key tactics that Jobs employed was to focus on a small number of products and make them the best they could possibly be. Rather than trying to offer a wide range of products with varying degrees of quality, Jobs believed in honing in on a few key products and ensuring that they were perfect. This allowed Apple to create products that were not only of exceptional quality but also easy to use, as the company had put a lot of effort into making them as user-friendly as possible.

Jobs also believed in creating products that people didn't even know they wanted yet. Rather than asking customers what they wanted and then trying to deliver that, Jobs believed in developing products that would create a need that didn't previously exist. This was evident in products like the iPod, which allowed people to carry their entire music library with them, and the iPhone, which transformed the mobile phone industry by making smartphones accessible to the masses.

Another key aspect of Jobs' work tactics was his attention to design. Jobs believed that not only did products need to be functional, but they also needed to look good. This focus on design was evident in all of Apple's products, from the iMac to the iPhone, and it was a key part of the company's success. Jobs believed that good design was not only aesthetically pleasing but also functional, and that every detail of a product needed to be perfect.

In terms of his business ethic, Jobs was known for being a tough negotiator and a demanding boss. He expected a lot from his employees and was known for pushing them to their limits. However, he was also known for being fiercely loyal to his team and for putting the needs of the company ahead of his own personal interests. He was also very focused on creating a brand that people could identify with, and he was instrumental in creating the cult-like following that Apple has today.

Another important aspect of Jobs' business ethic was his focus on innovation. Jobs believed that Apple needed to constantly innovate in order to stay ahead of the competition, and he was not afraid to take risks in order to do so. This focus on innovation was evident in products like the iPod, the iPhone, and the iPad, which all represented major advances in their respective fields.

In conclusion, Steve Jobs' work tactics and business ethic were a key part of his success as a businessman and entrepreneur. He focused on creating exceptional products that were not only functional but also looked great and were easy to use. He was also very focused on creating a strong brand identity and fostering a culture of innovation within the company. While he was known for being a tough boss, his loyalty to his team and his dedication to the success of the company were unwavering. Steve Jobs will always be remembered as one of the most innovative and influential business minds of all time.

The one thing that he did, that an entrepreneur should follow to be great

One thing that entrepreneurs can learn from Steve Jobs is his focus on creating products that people didn't even know they wanted yet. This approach to innovation involved anticipating the needs of customers and developing products that would create a demand for something that didn't previously exist. Jobs believed that this approach was key to creating products that would change the world, and his success with products like the iPod, iPhone, and iPad proves that he was right.

To follow in Jobs' footsteps, entrepreneurs should focus on understanding their customers' needs and anticipating what they will want in the future. This involves doing extensive market research, observing trends, and being willing to take risks in order to create something truly innovative. Entrepreneurs should be willing to think outside the box and challenge conventional wisdom in order to create products that will truly change the game.

In addition to this focus on innovation, entrepreneurs can also learn from Jobs' attention to design and his dedication to creating a strong brand identity. By focusing on creating products that not only function well but also look great and are easy to use, entrepreneurs can create products that stand out in a crowded market. And by building a strong brand identity and fostering a culture of innovation within their companies, entrepreneurs can create the kind of lasting impact that Jobs was able to achieve with Apple.

Here are some lesser-known anecdotes about his approach to work:

Attention to detail: Steve Jobs was known for his obsessive attention to detail. He was known to scrutinize even the smallest details of a product, such as the curvature of a button or the color of a font.

Simplicity: Jobs had a passion for simplicity. He believed that simplicity was the key to creating products that were both elegant and easy to use. He famously said, "Simple can be harder than complex: You have to work hard to get your thinking clean to make it simple."

Failure is not an option: Steve Jobs was not afraid to take risks and was determined to succeed at any cost. He once said, "I'm convinced that about half of what separates the successful entrepreneurs from the non-successful ones is pure perseverance."

Empathy: Although he was known for his demanding work style, Jobs also had a strong sense of empathy for his customers. He believed that understanding their needs and desires was crucial to creating successful products.

Personal style: Jobs was known for his personal style, which included a black turtleneck, blue jeans, and New Balance sneakers. He wore this outfit almost every day, which helped him save time and focus on more important tasks.

Work-life balance: Jobs was known to be a workaholic, often working long hours and weekends. However, he also believed in taking time off to recharge and pursue other interests, such as traveling or practicing yoga.

Leadership: Jobs was a charismatic leader who inspired his team to achieve their best work. He believed in surrounding himself with talented individuals who shared his vision and passion for innovation.

Overall, Steve Jobs' work ways and ethics were driven by his passion for innovation, attention to detail, and relentless pursuit of excellence.

PETER JONES

is a British entrepreneur, businessman, and television personality known for his innovation, business tactics, and keen eye for investment opportunities. Born on March 18, 1966, in Maidenhead, Berkshire, England, he began his career in business at the young age of 16 when he started a computer business from his bedroom.

Jones' early foray into the world of business was a sign of things to come. Over the years, he has built an impressive business empire and has become one of the most successful and influential entrepreneurs in the United Kingdom. His unique approach to business, coupled with his innovative ideas, has earned him a reputation as a savvy businessman with a keen eye for investment opportunities.

One of the keys to Jones' success has been his willingness to take risks. He has never been afraid to take on new challenges and is always looking for ways to push the boundaries of what is possible. This has led him to invest in a wide range of businesses, from technology startups to real estate ventures. He has also launched his own companies, including Phones International Group, Wines4Business.com, and the Peter Jones Foundation.

Another important factor in Jones' success has been his ability to think outside the box. He has always been a creative thinker and has come up with some truly innovative ideas over the years. For example, he was one of the first entrepreneurs to recognize the potential of the internet and started selling computer equipment online back in the early 1990s, long before the e-commerce boom.

Jones' success as a businessman has not gone unnoticed. In 2008, he was awarded a CBE (Commander of the Order of the British Empire) for his services to business. He has also been honored with numerous other awards, including the Ernst & Young Entrepreneur of the Year Award in 2006 and the BT Enterprise Award in 2009.

One of the reasons why Jones is considered one of the most influential business minds of all time is his work as a mentor and investor. In 2005, he became a dragon on the popular television show, "Dragons' Den," where he invested in a range of startups and helped to mentor young entrepreneurs. He also launched his own show, "Peter Jones Meets...," where he interviewed some of the most successful business people in the world and offered insights into their success.

Jones' investment philosophy is based on finding the right people and backing them with the resources they need to succeed. He looks for entrepreneurs who have a clear vision, a solid business plan, and the passion and drive to make it happen. He is not afraid to offer tough love and will push his investments to their limits to help them reach their full potential.

Overall, Peter Jones is a true innovator and one of the most influential business minds of all time. His willingness to take risks, think outside the box, and invest in the right people has helped him build a business empire and become a leader in the business world. His work as a mentor and investor has also helped to inspire a new generation of entrepreneurs and business people.

Peter Jones has built his success on a strong set of work tactics and business ethics that have helped him to stay focused, motivated, and driven. Here are some of the key strategies he has employed:

Focus on the long-term: Jones is a firm believer in the power of long-term planning. He has always looked beyond short-term gains and focused on building sustainable businesses that can weather any storm. This means he is willing to make sacrifices in the short-term in order to secure long-term success.

Take calculated risks: Jones is not afraid to take risks, but he always approaches them with a calculated mindset. He conducts thorough research and analysis before making any investment, and he is always looking for ways to minimize his risk exposure.

Embrace innovation: Innovation has been a hallmark of Jones' career. He is always on the lookout for new ideas and technologies that can disrupt established industries and create new opportunities. He is willing to experiment with new business models and approaches, even if they are untested or unconventional.

Build a strong team: Jones understands that he cannot build a successful business alone. He has always surrounded himself with talented and motivated people who share his vision and work ethic. He is a firm believer in the power of collaboration and teamwork.

Have a clear vision: Jones has a clear and compelling vision for his businesses. He knows what he wants to achieve and has a plan in place to get there. He communicates his vision clearly and passionately, inspiring his team to work towards a common goal.

Stay grounded: Despite his success, Jones remains grounded and humble. He understands the importance of hard work and persistence, and he is always willing to roll up his sleeves and get involved in the day-to-day operations of his businesses.

Give back: Jones is a strong believer in the importance of giving back. He has launched the Peter Jones Foundation, which supports young people from disadvantaged backgrounds to start their own businesses. He is also involved in a range of other charitable initiatives, including supporting cancer research and animal welfare causes.

These work tactics and business ethics have helped Peter Jones to build an impressive business empire and become one of the most influential business minds of all time. His dedication, passion, and willingness to take risks have set him apart from other entrepreneurs, and his commitment to innovation and long-term planning has helped him to stay ahead of the curve.

The one thing that he did, that an entrepreneur should follow to be great today

One of the most important things that Peter Jones has done throughout his career is to constantly seek out and embrace innovation. He has always been on the lookout for new technologies, business models, and opportunities to disrupt established industries and create new value. This focus on innovation has allowed him to stay ahead of the curve and build successful businesses that are able to adapt and thrive in rapidly changing markets.

For entrepreneurs today, this same focus on innovation is crucial. In today's fast-paced business world, innovation is not just a competitive advantage, it is a necessity. Entrepreneurs who are able to stay ahead of the curve and identify new opportunities for growth and innovation are the ones who will be most successful.

To follow in Peter Jones' footsteps, entrepreneurs should focus on three key areas:

Be curious: Always be on the lookout for new ideas and technologies that can help you to innovate and grow your business.

Be open-minded: Don't be afraid to experiment with new business models and approaches, even if they are untested or unconventional.

Be willing to take risks: Innovation often involves taking risks, but calculated risks can lead to great rewards. Always approach new opportunities with a calculated mindset, but be willing to take the leap when the potential payoff is high.

By focusing on innovation and taking these three steps, entrepreneurs can follow in the footsteps of Peter Jones and build successful businesses that are able to adapt and thrive in today's rapidly changing business landscape.

Some more interesting facts about Peter Jones:

He started his first business at the age of 16: Jones began his entrepreneurial journey early, launching his first business selling tennis equipment at the age of 16.

He has a background in computer science: Before becoming an entrepreneur, Jones studied computer science at the University of Northumbria in Newcastle.

He made his first million at the age of 28: Jones made his first million by the age of 28, through a series of successful business ventures in the technology sector.

He is a successful television personality: In addition to his business ventures, Jones is also a well-known television personality in the UK. He has appeared on a number of shows, including the BBC's "Dragon's Den" and "American Inventor."

He has invested in a wide range of businesses: Jones has invested in a diverse range of businesses throughout his career, including technology startups, fashion brands, and food and beverage companies.

He is passionate about entrepreneurship education: Jones is a strong advocate for entrepreneurship education, and he has launched several initiatives to support young people in starting their own businesses.

He has faced some setbacks: Despite his success, Jones has faced some setbacks in his career, including the failure of a technology company he founded in the 1990s. However, he has always bounced back and continued to pursue new opportunities for growth and innovation.

Overall, Peter Jones is an inspiring figure in the world of entrepreneurship, known for his passion, innovation, and dedication to building successful businesses. His story serves as an inspiration to aspiring entrepreneurs around the world.

LYN JURICH

Was born in Palo Alto, California, in 1979. She graduated from the University of California, Berkeley with a degree in political economy. After college, she worked in finance for several years before co-founding Sunrun in 2007 with her business partner, Ed Fenster.

Sunrun was created with the goal of making solar power more accessible and affordable for homeowners. Jurich and Fenster recognized the potential for residential solar power to become a major source of energy, but they also understood that the upfront costs of installing solar panels were prohibitively expensive for many people. To solve this problem, they came up with a business model that allowed homeowners to lease solar panels from Sunrun rather than purchasing them outright.

This innovative business model was a game-changer for the residential solar industry. Sunrun's leasing program made it possible for more people to switch to solar power, which helped to reduce carbon emissions and promote sustainability. In addition to the leasing program, Sunrun also offers installation and maintenance services for solar panels.

Under Jurich's leadership, Sunrun has become one of the largest residential solar companies in the United States, with operations in 22 states. The company has installed over 4.5 gigawatts of solar power capacity and has saved its customers over $300 million on their energy bills.

Jurich's success as an entrepreneur and businesswoman is due in large part to her innovative thinking and willingness to take risks. She saw an opportunity to disrupt the traditional energy industry and create a more sustainable future, and she took bold steps to make that vision a reality. Her business model has been replicated by other companies in the industry, and it has helped to make solar power more accessible and affordable for millions of people.

In addition to her work at Sunrun, Jurich is also a vocal advocate for clean energy and sustainable living. She has spoken at numerous conferences and events about the importance of renewable energy and the need to reduce carbon emissions. She has also served on the board of directors for the Solar Energy Industries Association, a trade association for the solar industry.

Jurich's accomplishments as a businesswoman and entrepreneur have earned her numerous awards and accolades. She has been named one of Fortune's Most Powerful Women Entrepreneurs and was included on Forbes' list of America's Richest Self-Made Women. She has also been recognized for her philanthropic work, including her support of organizations that promote clean energy and environmental sustainability.

In conclusion, Lyn Jurich is an influential businesswoman and entrepreneur who has had a major impact on the residential solar industry. Her innovative thinking and willingness to take risks have helped to make solar power more accessible and affordable for millions of people, while also promoting sustainability and reducing carbon emissions. She is a true visionary and an inspiration to others in the business world.

Lyn Jurich is known for her innovative thinking and her commitment to sustainability and clean energy. Her business tactics and ethics have been shaped by these core values, and they have played a major role in the success of Sunrun and her other ventures.

One of Jurich's key business tactics is a focus on customer satisfaction. She understands that in order to build a successful business, it is essential to prioritize the needs and desires of the customer. Sunrun's leasing program, for example, was designed with the goal of making solar power more accessible and affordable for homeowners, which has been a major factor in the company's growth and success.

Jurich is also a strong believer in the power of collaboration and teamwork. She recognizes that no one person can accomplish great things alone, and she works hard to foster a culture of collaboration and mutual support within her company. Sunrun has a highly engaged and motivated workforce, and Jurich has been instrumental in creating an environment where employees feel valued and supported.

Another key business tactic that Jurich employs is a willingness to take risks and try new things. She understands that innovation requires a willingness to experiment and try new approaches, even if they don't always work out. This willingness to take risks has been a major factor in Sunrun's success, as well as in Jurich's own personal career.

In addition to her business tactics, Jurich is known for her strong business ethics. She is committed to sustainability and clean energy, and she has worked hard to ensure that Sunrun operates in an ethical and responsible manner. The company has a strong track record of environmental stewardship, and it is committed to reducing carbon emissions and promoting sustainability.

Jurich is also committed to creating a diverse and inclusive workplace. She recognizes the importance of building a team that reflects a wide range of perspectives and experiences, and she has taken steps to ensure that Sunrun is a welcoming and inclusive environment for all employees.

Overall, Lyn Jurich's work tactics and business ethics are rooted in a commitment to innovation, sustainability, collaboration, and ethical responsibility. These core values have been instrumental in her success as a businesswoman and entrepreneur, and they continue to drive her work today.

The one thing that she did, that an entrepreneur should follow to be great today

thing that Lyn Jurich did as an entrepreneur that others could follow to be great today is to identify and pursue an opportunity that aligns with their core values and passions. Jurich recognized the potential for residential solar power to become a major source of energy, but more importantly, she was driven by a deep-seated commitment to sustainability and a desire to make a positive impact on the environment.

By focusing on a goal that aligned with her values and passions, Jurich was able to build a successful business that has had a major impact on the residential solar industry. Her passion and commitment have also helped to inspire others and create a sense of purpose and meaning for her employees and customers.

Entrepreneurs who want to be great today should take a similar approach by identifying an opportunity that aligns with their core values and passions. This could involve pursuing a business idea that solves a social or environmental problem, or it could simply involve pursuing a passion or interest that they feel strongly about.

By pursuing a goal that aligns with their values and

passions, entrepreneurs can tap into a sense of purpose and meaning that can help to sustain them through the ups and downs of building a business. They can also create a stronger connection with their customers and employees by demonstrating a genuine commitment to a cause or purpose that resonates with them.

Ultimately, Lyn Jurich's example shows that entrepreneurs who are driven by a sense of purpose and passion can achieve great things and create a positive impact on the world around them.

A few more things about Lyn Jurich:

Jurich co-founded Sunrun, a residential solar company, in 2007 along with her business partner Edward Fenster. The company provides homeowners with solar panels that are leased through a power purchase agreement, which allows customers to pay for the energy they use rather than the cost of the panels themselves.

Prior to founding Sunrun, Jurich worked as an investment banker at Goldman Sachs and as a venture capitalist at Foundation Capital. Her experience in finance and investing helped to shape her understanding of the solar industry and the potential for growth in the residential solar market.

Jurich has been recognized as a leader in the clean energy industry, and she has received numerous awards and honors for her work. In 2019, she was named one of Fortune's "Most Powerful Women" in business, and in 2020, she was listed as one of Time's "100 Most Influential People in the World."

In addition to her work at Sunrun, Jurich is also involved in a number of other ventures and organizations. She serves on the board of directors for the California Clean Energy Fund and is a member of the National Renewable Energy Laboratory's Energy Systems Integration Advisory Council.

Jurich is committed to promoting sustainability and clean

energy, both through her work at Sunrun and through her personal life. She is an advocate for electric vehicles and has installed solar panels on her own home, which is powered entirely by renewable energy.

Jurich is a graduate of Stanford University, where she earned a Bachelor of Arts degree in International Relations and an MBA from the Stanford Graduate School of Business.

HENRY J. KAISER

Was a prolific American industrialist, shipbuilder, and businessman who was instrumental in the development of various industries in the early 20th century. He was born on May 9, 1882, in Sprout Brook, New York, and was the son of German immigrant parents. Kaiser had a passion for entrepreneurship and a vision to revolutionize industries through innovation, which set him apart from his contemporaries.

Kaiser's first foray into the business world was in 1914 when he founded his first construction company, Henry J. Kaiser Co., in partnership with his friend, J.A. Harvey. The company was successful, but it was in the shipbuilding industry that Kaiser made his mark. During World War II, the US government commissioned him to build a fleet of ships for the war effort. This was no easy feat, as the US had not built a new ship in over 20 years. Kaiser stepped up to the challenge, and his company produced over 1,500 ships in just four years.

Kaiser's success in shipbuilding was largely due to his innovative ideas and tactics. He was a forward-thinking businessman who was always looking for ways to improve his products and processes. He recognized the potential of mass production and introduced assembly-line techniques to shipbuilding, which significantly increased efficiency and reduced costs. Kaiser also pioneered the use of prefabrication techniques, which allowed his company to build ships faster and with greater precision.

Another of Kaiser's innovations was the development of the "Liberty Ship," a standardized cargo ship that was designed to be produced quickly and efficiently. These ships were crucial to the Allied war effort, as they could carry essential supplies across the Atlantic without the risk of being sunk by enemy submarines. The success of the Liberty Ships was a testament to Kaiser's vision and ingenuity, and they played a significant role in the outcome of the war.

Kaiser's influence extended beyond shipbuilding, and he was involved in various industries, including construction, steel, aluminum, and health care. He was a pioneer in the development of the modern American health care system and established the Kaiser Permanente Health Care Program in 1945. This program was designed to provide affordable health care to workers and their families and was a model for other health care providers.

One of the reasons why Kaiser is considered one of the most influential businessmen of all time is his ability to adapt and innovate in response to changing circumstances. During World War II, he recognized the need for a new approach to shipbuilding, and he was able to develop new techniques and processes that revolutionized the industry. He was also a visionary who saw the potential for new industries and was willing to take risks to make them a reality.

Kaiser was also a master of public relations and understood the importance of promoting his brand and image. He was a charismatic and energetic leader who was able to inspire and motivate his employees to achieve their best work. He was also a philanthropist who believed in giving back to his community and supported various charitable organizations throughout his life.

After the success of his shipbuilding ventures during World War II, Kaiser turned his attention to other industries, including aluminum production, construction, and automobile manufacturing. He founded the Kaiser-Frazer Corporation, which produced cars under the Kaiser and Frazer brand names. However, the venture was not as successful as his shipbuilding business, and he eventually sold the company in the 1950s.

Kaiser's success in shipbuilding was not just due to his innovative ideas and tactics, but also his ability to manage large-scale projects efficiently. He was a master of logistics and had a keen eye for detail. He understood the importance of maintaining a steady supply of materials and labor and was able to keep his production lines running smoothly, even under the most challenging conditions.

Kaiser was also a shrewd businessman who understood the importance of building strong relationships with his suppliers and customers. He was known for his fair and honest dealings, and his word was his bond. He believed in treating his employees well and providing them with good working conditions, which helped to foster a sense of loyalty and commitment to his company.

In addition to his business ventures, Kaiser was also a philanthropist who believed in giving back to his community. He established the Kaiser Family Foundation in 1948, which supports various charitable causes, including health care, education, and the arts. He also donated millions of dollars to universities and other institutions, including the University of California, Berkeley, and the Kaiser Foundation Hospitals.

Kaiser's legacy as a businessman and entrepreneur continues to inspire others to this day. His innovative ideas and tactics, his ability to adapt to changing circumstances, and his commitment to his employees and community are all qualities that have made him one of the most influential business minds of all time.

In conclusion, Henry J. Kaiser was a true innovator and visionary who revolutionized the shipbuilding industry and made significant contributions to various other industries. His innovative ideas and tactics, his ability to adapt to changing circumstances, and his charismatic leadership style set him apart from his contemporaries and made him one of the most influential businessmen of all time. His legacy continues to inspire entrepreneurs and business leaders to this day.

The one thing that Kaiser did, that an entrepreneur should follow to be great

If there was one thing that entrepreneurs could learn from Henry J. Kaiser to be great today, it would be his willingness to innovate and take risks.

Throughout his career, Kaiser was constantly looking for new ways to improve his products and processes. He was not content to simply follow the status quo, but instead sought to challenge conventional thinking and push the boundaries of what was possible. This spirit of innovation and experimentation allowed him to stay ahead of his competitors and revolutionize industries.

Kaiser was also willing to take risks and pursue opportunities that others might have deemed too risky or uncertain. For example, he was one of the few shipbuilders who were willing to take on the challenge of building a fleet of ships for the US government during World War II. Many others thought it was an impossible task, but Kaiser saw it as an opportunity to innovate and make a difference.

In today's fast-paced and rapidly changing business

environment, entrepreneurs need to be willing to take risks and embrace new ideas and technologies. The ability to adapt and innovate is essential for staying competitive and thriving in today's economy. By following in Kaiser's footsteps and taking a proactive approach to innovation and risk-taking, entrepreneurs can position themselves for success and achieve their goals.

Some more details about Henry J. Kaiser and his life as a businessman:

Kaiser was born in 1882 in Sprout Brook, New York. His father was a manufacturer of construction equipment, and Kaiser developed an early interest in engineering and construction.

In the early 1900s, Kaiser moved to the western United States and became involved in the construction industry. He started his own construction company in 1914 and quickly established a reputation for innovation and efficiency.

During World War II, Kaiser was one of the leading shipbuilders in the United States. He built a fleet of Liberty ships, which were used to transport troops and supplies to Europe and the Pacific. His company was able to build these ships at a faster rate and lower cost than any other shipbuilder at the time.

After the war, Kaiser turned his attention to other industries, including aluminum production, construction, and automobile manufacturing. He founded the Kaiser-Frazer Corporation, which produced cars under the Kaiser and Frazer brand names. Although the venture was not as successful as his shipbuilding business, it demonstrated Kaiser's willingness to take risks and explore new industries.

In addition to his business ventures, Kaiser was also a philanthropist and supporter of various charitable causes. He established the Kaiser Family Foundation in 1948, which supports health care, education, and the arts. He also donated millions of dollars to universities and other institutions.

Kaiser's success in shipbuilding during World War II was largely due to his innovative approach to production. He introduced a number of new techniques and technologies, such as prefabrication and welding, which allowed his shipyards to produce ships at a much faster rate than his competitors. He also pioneered the use of mass production techniques in shipbuilding, which helped to reduce costs and increase efficiency.

Kaiser was also a pioneer in the field of healthcare. In 1938, he founded the Kaiser Permanente health plan, which was one of the first integrated health care systems in the United States. The plan provided comprehensive medical care to workers in his shipyards and other industries, and later expanded to serve the general public. Today, Kaiser Permanente is one of the largest healthcare providers in the country, with more than 12 million members.

In addition to his work in shipbuilding and healthcare, Kaiser was also involved in a number of other industries. He was a major producer of aluminum during World War II and later founded the Kaiser Aluminum and Chemical Corporation. He also built several large-scale construction projects, including the Hoover Dam and the Grand Coulee Dam.

Throughout his career, Kaiser was known for his commitment to his employees and his community. He believed in providing his workers with good wages and benefits, and he established a number of programs to promote worker health and safety. He also donated millions of dollars to charitable causes and established several foundations to support education, healthcare, and the arts.

Kaiser died in 1967 at the age of 85. He is remembered as one of the most innovative and influential business minds of the

20th century. His legacy continues to inspire entrepreneurs and business leaders today.

TRAVIS KALANICK

Is widely recognized as one of the most influential entrepreneurs of the modern era. He is best known for co-founding Uber, the ride-hailing company that has revolutionized the transportation industry. However, Kalanick's path to success was not an easy one, and his career has been marked by both triumphs and controversies.

Kalanick was born on August 6, 1976, in Los Angeles, California. He grew up in a family of entrepreneurs and was exposed to the world of business from a young age. His mother worked as a retail advertising executive, while his father was a civil engineer who started his own construction company.

As a teenager, Kalanick showed an early interest in technology and computers. He taught himself how to code and built his first computer game when he was just 14 years old. He attended the University of California, Los Angeles, but dropped out after just one year to pursue his entrepreneurial ambitions.

Kalanick's first major venture was Scour, a file-sharing service he co-founded in 1998. The platform allowed users to share music, videos, and other files online, but it was quickly shut down due to copyright infringement issues. Despite this setback, Kalanick continued to pursue his passion for technology and entrepreneurship.

In 2007, Kalanick co-founded Uber, along with Garrett Camp. The idea for the company came about when Kalanick and Camp were attending a technology conference in Paris and couldn't find a taxi. They realized that there was a need for a more efficient and convenient way to get around cities, and the idea for Uber was born.

Under Kalanick's leadership, Uber grew at an unprecedented rate. The company expanded to more than 600 cities around the world and was valued at over $60 billion at its peak. Kalanick was known for his aggressive tactics and willingness to take risks in order to grow the company. He was also a strong advocate for innovation, constantly pushing his team to develop new products and services that would set Uber apart from its competitors.

However, Kalanick's tenure at Uber was not without controversy. The company faced numerous legal and regulatory challenges, as well as accusations of sexual harassment and discrimination within the workplace. Kalanick was forced to step down as CEO in 2017, amid mounting pressure from investors and the public.

Despite the challenges he faced at Uber, there is no denying the impact that Kalanick has had on the business world. His innovative thinking and willingness to take risks have inspired countless entrepreneurs to pursue their own ventures. He has also challenged traditional business models and disrupted entire industries, paving the way for a new era of innovation and entrepreneurship.

In conclusion, Travis Kalanick's life as a businessman is a testament to the power of innovation and determination. From his early days as a teenage coder to his groundbreaking work at Uber, Kalanick has consistently pushed the boundaries of what is possible in the world of business. While his tenure at Uber may have been marked by controversy, there is no denying the impact he has had on the way we think about entrepreneurship and innovation. For these reasons, he deserves a place among the most influential business minds of all time.

Travis Kalanick is known for his aggressive work tactics and innovative approach to business. Here are some key details about his work tactics and business ethics:

Relentless Pursuit of Growth: Kalanick has always been focused on growth and expansion. He was willing to take bold risks and make big bets in order to grow Uber at an unprecedented rate. His aggressive tactics included engaging in price wars with competitors, expanding into new markets quickly, and taking on regulatory authorities to gain a foothold in the transportation industry.

Innovative Thinking: Kalanick is a true innovator, always looking for new ways to improve and expand his business. He was constantly challenging his team to come up with new products and services that would set Uber apart from its competitors. His innovative thinking led to the development of new features such as UberPOOL, UberEATS, and self-driving cars.

Disruption of Traditional Business Models: Kalanick disrupted the traditional business models of the taxi and transportation industry by introducing a new way of getting around cities. His idea of using technology to connect riders with drivers and make the process more convenient and efficient was a game-changer.

Data-Driven Decision Making: Kalanick is known for his data-driven decision making. He relied heavily on data analytics to make informed decisions about how to grow and scale his business. He used data to identify areas of opportunity, target new markets, and optimize pricing and supply.

Work Ethic: Kalanick is known for his intense work ethic and dedication to his business. He was often described as a workaholic, putting in long hours and pushing his team to work just as hard. He was driven by a passion for innovation and a desire to create something truly revolutionary.

Risk-Taking: Kalanick was not afraid to take risks in order to achieve his goals. He was willing to put everything on the line to grow Uber and was known for his willingness to fight back against competitors and regulators.

Controversies: While Kalanick's aggressive tactics and innovative thinking have earned him praise from many, they have also led to controversies. He has been accused of engaging in unethical practices such as tracking journalists and lying to regulators. His tenure at Uber was also marked by accusations of sexual harassment and discrimination within the workplace.

In summary, Travis Kalanick's work tactics and business ethics were characterized by a relentless pursuit of growth, innovative thinking, disruption of traditional business models, data-driven decision making, an intense work ethic, risk-taking, and controversies. These qualities have made him one of the most influential business minds of our time, inspiring countless entrepreneurs to push the boundaries of what is possible in the world of business.

The one thing that he did, that an entrepreneur should follow to be great today

One thing that entrepreneurs can learn from Travis Kalanick's approach to business is his relentless pursuit of growth and innovation. He was not content with simply creating a successful company, but instead was always looking for new ways to expand and improve his business.

Entrepreneurs today can follow this example by never settling for the status quo and always looking for ways to innovate and improve their products or services. This requires a willingness to take risks and to think outside the box.

Another key lesson that can be learned from Kalanick's approach to business is the importance of data-driven decision making. By relying on data to inform his business decisions, he was able to identify opportunities, target new markets, and optimize pricing and supply.

Entrepreneurs today can follow this example by leveraging data analytics to make informed decisions about their business. This means collecting and analyzing data on customer behavior, market trends, and other key metrics in order to make strategic decisions that will help drive growth and success.

Overall, the key takeaway from Travis Kalanick's approach to business is the importance of innovation, growth, and data-driven decision making. By following these principles, entrepreneurs can build successful businesses that are truly transformative in their industries.

Some more interesting facts about Travis Kalanick:

Early Entrepreneurial Spirit: Kalanick showed an entrepreneurial spirit from a young age, starting his first business at the age of 18. The company, called Scour, was a file-sharing service that was eventually sued for copyright infringement.

Experience at Red Swoosh: Before founding Uber, Kalanick was the CEO of another startup called Red Swoosh. The company was a peer-to-peer content delivery network that was eventually acquired by Akamai Technologies in 2007.

Passion for Politics: Kalanick has a passion for politics and has been involved in political campaigns and causes. He worked as a strategist for the 2004 re-election campaign of President George W. Bush and was involved in efforts to legalize marijuana in California.

Philanthropic Efforts: Kalanick has been involved in philanthropic efforts throughout his career. He launched the UberMILITARY initiative, which helps veterans and their families find work in the tech industry. He has also donated to various causes, including cancer research and education initiatives.

Self-Driving Car Technology: Kalanick has been a vocal proponent of self-driving car technology and has invested heavily in the development of autonomous vehicles. He believes that self-driving cars will eventually replace human drivers and transform the transportation industry.

Personal Controversies: Kalanick's personal life has been marked by controversies, including accusations of misogyny and sexist behavior. He has also been criticized for his aggressive business tactics and for fostering a toxic workplace culture at Uber.

Investment Ventures: After leaving Uber, Kalanick founded a venture capital firm called 10100, which focuses on investing in companies in the areas of real estate, e-commerce, and innovations in China and India.

These are just a few of the many interesting facts and facets of Travis Kalanick's life and career. Despite the controversies surrounding his tenure at Uber, his impact on the transportation industry and his entrepreneurial spirit make him an influential figure in the world of business.

INGVAR KAMPRAD

is widely regarded as one of the most influential business minds of all time. He was the founder of IKEA, one of the largest furniture retailers in the world. Kamprad's life and work provide a fascinating case study on entrepreneurship, innovation, and business success.

Kamprad was born in 1926 in Sweden. He showed an entrepreneurial spirit from an early age, selling matches to his neighbors when he was just five years old. As a teenager, Kamprad started selling other household items such as pens, wallets, and picture frames. In 1943, at the age of 17, Kamprad founded IKEA with a small loan from his father.

From the beginning, Kamprad's approach to business was unique. He was obsessed with efficiency and cost-cutting, and he applied these principles to every aspect of the IKEA business. For example, he noticed that the traditional furniture retailing model involved a lot of expensive overhead costs, such as large showrooms and salespeople. Kamprad's solution was to create self-serve showrooms where customers could browse the furniture without assistance. This not only saved money but also allowed customers to take their time and make their own decisions.

Another example of Kamprad's innovative thinking was his use of flat-pack furniture. Instead of selling fully assembled furniture, IKEA began selling furniture in pieces that customers could assemble themselves. This approach not only saved money on shipping costs but also allowed customers to take pride in their own ability to build something.

Kamprad was also a master of marketing. He knew that IKEA's success depended on its ability to connect with customers and create a strong brand. He developed a unique advertising style that emphasized IKEA's Swedish heritage and its commitment to affordable, functional furniture. He also created a sense of community among IKEA customers, encouraging them to share their decorating tips and ideas.

One of Kamprad's most enduring legacies is his commitment to sustainability. Long before it became fashionable, Kamprad recognized the importance of using environmentally friendly materials and reducing waste. He also believed in making quality furniture that would last for generations, rather than disposable products that would need to be replaced every few years.

Kamprad's business tactics were not without controversy, however. In the 1990s, IKEA was accused of using child labor to produce its products in developing countries. Kamprad took responsibility for the issue and vowed to make changes to ensure that all IKEA products were ethically produced.

Despite this setback, Kamprad's impact on the world of business is undeniable. He transformed the furniture industry, creating a new model of efficient, affordable, and stylish furniture retailing. He also demonstrated the power of branding and marketing in creating a successful business. And he showed that sustainability and social responsibility can be profitable and practical business practices.

In conclusion, Ingvar Kamprad's life and work are a testament to the power of innovation, hard work, and creative thinking in the world of business. He revolutionized the furniture industry and created a lasting legacy of affordable, functional, and sustainable products. His commitment to efficiency, cost-cutting, and marketing helped him build one of the largest and most successful companies in the world. And his influence continues to be felt today, inspiring new generations of entrepreneurs to follow in his footsteps.

One of Ingvar Kamprad's most notable work tactics was his focus on efficiency and cost-cutting. He was a firm believer in the idea that every penny saved was a penny earned, and he applied this principle to every aspect of the IKEA business. For example, he would reuse shipping containers to transport furniture and encouraged his employees to save paper by using both sides of the sheet.

Kamprad also had a unique approach to product development. Instead of relying on a small group of designers to create new products, he would encourage his employees to come up with ideas. He believed that anyone could have a good idea and that the best way to innovate was to have a diverse group of people contributing to the process.

In terms of business ethics, Kamprad was known for his strong commitment to sustainability and social responsibility. He recognized that businesses had a responsibility to minimize their impact on the environment and to treat their employees fairly. He was an early adopter of renewable energy sources and was committed to using environmentally friendly materials in the production of IKEA products.

Kamprad was also deeply committed to providing affordable products to his customers. He believed that everyone should be able to afford stylish and functional furniture, regardless of their income. To achieve this goal, he implemented a number of cost-cutting measures, such as using self-service showrooms and selling flat-pack furniture.

Another key aspect of Kamprad's business ethic was his

commitment to quality. He believed that IKEA products should be durable and long-lasting, rather than disposable. This was reflected in the company's policies on product development and manufacturing, which emphasized the use of high-quality materials and production processes.

Overall, Kamprad's work tactics and business ethic were characterized by a focus on efficiency, innovation, sustainability, affordability, and quality. His commitment to these principles helped him build one of the largest and most successful companies in the world, and his influence continues to be felt today in the business world and beyond.

The one thing that he did, that an entrepreneur should follow to be great today

There are many things that Ingvar Kamprad did that entrepreneurs can learn from, but if I had to choose one, it would be his commitment to innovation.

Kamprad was always looking for ways to improve his products, processes, and business model. He was not afraid to challenge the status quo and was always willing to experiment with new ideas. This commitment to innovation allowed him to create a truly unique and successful business that disrupted the furniture industry.

Today, entrepreneurs face a rapidly changing business landscape, with new technologies and business models emerging all the time. To succeed in this environment, it's essential to be innovative and willing to take risks. Entrepreneurs who are willing to challenge the status quo and experiment with new ideas are more likely to succeed than those who stick to the same old formula.

So, the one thing that entrepreneurs can learn from Ingvar Kamprad is to embrace innovation and make it a central part of their business strategy. By doing so, they can create truly innovative products, services, and business models that set them apart from the competition and drive success.

HERB KELLEHER

Was a true legend in the world of business and entrepreneurship. He is best known for co-founding Southwest Airlines in 1971, a low-cost airline that has grown to become one of the most successful airlines in the world. Kelleher's impact on the airline industry and business in general is undeniable, and he is widely considered to be one of the most innovative and influential business minds of all time.

Born in 1931 in Camden, New Jersey, Kelleher grew up in a family of lawyers. After attending law school at New York University, he moved to Texas in the early 1960s to practice law. It was in Texas that he first became involved in the airline industry, when he represented a client who was being sued by another airline. Kelleher was fascinated by the airline industry, and he soon began to see the potential for a low-cost airline that could serve the underserved markets in Texas.

Kelleher co-founded Southwest Airlines with his business partner, Rollin King, in 1971. The airline was an instant success, offering low fares, frequent flights, and a fun, customer-focused experience. Kelleher was instrumental in developing Southwest's unique business model, which focused on keeping costs low while providing excellent service to customers. He believed that happy employees would lead to happy customers, and he worked tirelessly to create a culture at Southwest that was both fun and productive.

One of Kelleher's most innovative and influential tactics was the use of a single type of airplane, the Boeing 737. By standardizing its fleet, Southwest was able to save money on maintenance and training, and it was also able to negotiate better deals with Boeing. This allowed the airline to offer lower fares than its competitors, while still maintaining a high level of safety and reliability.

Kelleher was also a master of marketing and public relations. He understood the power of word-of-mouth advertising, and he encouraged his employees to have fun and be themselves while interacting with customers. This led to a highly positive reputation for Southwest, and the airline became known for its friendly, down-to-earth service. Kelleher himself was also a highly visible and charismatic spokesperson for the airline, appearing in numerous commercials and publicity events.

Throughout his career, Kelleher remained focused on his core values of putting employees and customers first. He believed that a happy workforce was key to a successful business, and he went to great lengths to create a culture at Southwest that was both fun and productive. He also believed in the importance of innovation and continuous improvement, and he was constantly looking for ways to make Southwest more efficient and customer-friendly.

Kelleher's legacy as an influential business mind is evident in the success of Southwest Airlines, which has grown to become one of the largest and most profitable airlines in the world. His focus on customer service, employee satisfaction, and innovation has inspired countless other businesses, both within and outside of the airline industry. Kelleher's leadership and vision continue to be celebrated and studied by business leaders and entrepreneurs around the world.

In conclusion, Herb Kelleher was a true visionary and innovator in the world of business. His focus on customer service, employee satisfaction, and innovation helped to revolutionize the airline industry and inspire countless other businesses. Kelleher's legacy as an influential business mind is evident in the success of Southwest Airlines and the countless entrepreneurs and business leaders who have been inspired by his example. He will always be remembered as a true pioneer and legend in the world of business.

Kelleher was known for his strong work ethic, and he believed in leading by example. He was often seen working long hours and was known to be very hands-on in the day-to-day operations of Southwest Airlines. Kelleher was a firm believer in the importance of teamwork, and he worked hard to foster a culture of collaboration and communication within the company.

One of Kelleher's key business tactics was to keep costs low. He believed that offering low fares was the key to success in the airline industry, and he worked hard to find ways to reduce costs while maintaining a high level of service. In addition to standardizing the airline's fleet, Kelleher also implemented a number of other cost-saving measures, such as using secondary airports, negotiating favorable fuel contracts, and keeping advertising costs low by relying on word-of-mouth marketing.

Another important aspect of Kelleher's business strategy was his focus on customer service. He believed that happy customers were the key to success in any business, and he worked hard to create a culture at Southwest Airlines that was focused on meeting the needs of customers. Kelleher was known for his "fun-loving" personality, and he encouraged his employees to have fun and be themselves while interacting with customers. He also believed in giving employees the autonomy to make decisions and solve problems on their own, which helped to create a more responsive and customer-friendly culture at the airline.

Kelleher was also known for his commitment to employee satisfaction. He believed that happy employees were the key to a successful business, and he went to great lengths to create a work environment that was both fun and productive. Kelleher believed in treating employees like family, and he was known for his hands-on approach to management. He was often seen walking around the office, talking to employees, and listening to their concerns. Kelleher also believed in the importance of recognition and rewards, and he implemented a number of employee incentive programs to encourage high performance and reward exceptional work.

Finally, Kelleher was known for his strong business ethics. He believed in honesty, integrity, and transparency, and he worked hard to create a culture at Southwest Airlines that was grounded in these values. Kelleher was also a firm believer in corporate responsibility, and he implemented a number of initiatives to reduce the airline's impact on the environment and give back to the communities it served.

Overall, Herb Kelleher's work tactics and business ethics were characterized by a strong focus on teamwork, cost control, customer service, employee satisfaction, and corporate responsibility. He was a visionary leader who was known for his hands-on approach to management and his commitment to creating a culture of innovation, continuous improvement, and fun. Kelleher's legacy as an influential business mind will continue to be felt for generations to come.

*The one thing that he did,
that an entrepreneur should*

follow to be great today

Herb Kelleher's success as an entrepreneur was built on a number of key factors, including his focus on low costs, customer service, employee satisfaction, and strong business ethics. However, if there was one thing that entrepreneurs could learn from Kelleher, it would be his emphasis on company culture.

Kelleher believed that a strong company culture was essential for success in business, and he worked hard to create a culture at Southwest Airlines that was fun, collaborative, and customer-focused. He believed that happy employees were the key to a successful business, and he went to great lengths to create a work environment that was both productive and enjoyable.

To follow Kelleher's example, entrepreneurs today should focus on building a strong company culture that values teamwork, innovation, and customer service. This means hiring employees who share your values and vision for the company, and creating an environment that fosters collaboration, communication, and creativity.

Entrepreneurs should also prioritize employee satisfaction, recognizing that happy employees are more productive, engaged, and committed to the company's success. This means investing in employee training and development, recognizing and rewarding outstanding performance, and creating a work-life balance that allows employees to thrive both professionally and personally.

In addition, entrepreneurs should prioritize their customers, working hard to create products and services that meet their needs and exceed their expectations. This means listening to customer feedback, engaging with them on social media and other platforms, and constantly striving to improve the customer experience.

Finally, entrepreneurs should prioritize strong business

ethics, recognizing that honesty, integrity, and transparency are essential for building trust with employees, customers, and other stakeholders. This means being transparent about the company's finances and operations, treating employees and customers with respect, and giving back to the community in meaningful ways.

By following Kelleher's example and focusing on these key principles, entrepreneurs can build strong, successful companies that make a positive impact in the world.

A few more things about Herb Kelleher that might be of interest:

Herb Kelleher co-founded Southwest Airlines in 1967 with Rollin King. Kelleher served as the CEO of Southwest from 1982 to 2001 and remained active in the company until his death in 2019.

Kelleher was a lawyer by trade and initially became involved with Southwest Airlines when he helped the company fight a lawsuit that was trying to prevent them from operating in Texas.

Kelleher was known for his unconventional leadership style, which included wearing Hawaiian shirts, engaging in public stunts and pranks, and appearing in humorous ads for the airline.

Kelleher was a strong advocate for deregulation in the airline industry, arguing that it would lead to increased competition and lower fares for consumers.

Under Kelleher's leadership, Southwest Airlines grew from a small regional carrier to one of the largest and most successful airlines in the world. The company was known for its low fares, high customer satisfaction, and strong company culture.

Kelleher received numerous awards and accolades throughout his career, including being named one of the

"100 Most Influential People in the World" by Time Magazine in 1999.

Kelleher was also known for his philanthropic work, including his support of various charitable organizations and his advocacy for issues such as education, health care, and poverty alleviation.

Overall, Herb Kelleher was a charismatic and innovative leader who made a significant impact on the airline industry and on business more broadly. His legacy continues to inspire entrepreneurs and business leaders around the world to this day.

ADNAN KHASHOGGI

Was a Saudi Arabian businessman who rose to prominence in the 1970s and 1980s as one of the world's richest men. He is best known for his work as an international arms dealer, but he was also involved in a wide range of other industries, including real estate, aviation, and media.

Khashoggi was born in Mecca, Saudi Arabia in 1935. His father, Mohammed Khashoggi, was a doctor and advisor to King Abdul Aziz Al Saud, the founder of modern Saudi Arabia. Khashoggi studied in the United States, earning a degree in business administration from Chico State College in California.

Khashoggi began his business career in the 1960s, when he established a small company that imported American-made cars into Saudi Arabia. However, it was his work as an international arms dealer that brought him the most success and notoriety. Khashoggi was known for his ability to negotiate large-scale arms deals between various countries, often acting as a middleman between governments and defense contractors.

Khashoggi's innovation mind was evident in his business tactics. He was known for his ability to think outside the box and find creative solutions to complex problems. For example, in the 1970s, he arranged for the sale of American-made fighter planes to Iran, which was under an arms embargo at the time. Khashoggi was able to use a loophole in the law to make the deal happen, by arranging for the planes to be delivered to Israel first, and then transferred to Iran.

In addition to his work in the arms industry, Khashoggi was involved in a wide range of other businesses. He invested heavily in real estate, purchasing properties around the world, including the famous New York Plaza Hotel. He also owned a private jet charter company, and was a major shareholder in a number of media companies, including the Spanish-language television network, Univision.

Khashoggi's tactics were not without controversy, and he was often criticized for his involvement in arms deals that fueled conflicts around the world. He was also accused of illegal activities, including bribery and money laundering, and was the subject of several high-profile scandals.

Despite these controversies, Khashoggi is still considered to be one of the most influential business minds of all time. His ability to navigate complex international deals and his innovative business tactics have inspired generations of entrepreneurs and businessmen. Khashoggi's legacy is a reminder that success in business often requires a willingness to take risks and think outside the box.

In conclusion, Adnan Khashoggi was a Saudi Arabian businessman who achieved great success as an international arms dealer, real estate investor, and media mogul. His innovative business tactics and ability to think outside the box have inspired generations of entrepreneurs and businessmen. While his tactics were not without controversy, his legacy as a trailblazer in the world of business is undeniable.

One of Khashoggi's most notable business tactics was his ability to negotiate complex international deals. He was known for his exceptional networking skills and his ability to build relationships with people in positions of power around the world. This allowed him to facilitate deals between governments and defense contractors, often acting as a middleman and taking a cut of the profits.

Khashoggi was also a master of creative problem-solving, and was always on the lookout for innovative ways to get around obstacles. For example, when he arranged for the sale of American-made fighter planes to Iran, he found a loophole in the law that allowed him to make the deal happen. By arranging for the planes to be delivered to Israel first, and then transferred to Iran, he was able to get around the arms embargo that was in place at the time.

Khashoggi was also known for his shrewd negotiating tactics. He was a tough negotiator who was not afraid to walk away from a deal if he didn't feel like he was getting what he wanted. He was also a skilled strategist who was always thinking several steps ahead, anticipating the moves of his opponents and coming up with counter-strategies to gain the upper hand.

However, Khashoggi's business tactics were not without controversy. He was accused of engaging in illegal activities, including bribery and money laundering, and was the subject of several high-profile scandals. Some critics accused him of exploiting his connections to people in positions of power to secure business deals that were not in the best interests of the countries involved.

Despite these controversies, Khashoggi was generally regarded as a shrewd and successful businessman. He was known for his hard work and determination, and his willingness to take risks in pursuit of his goals. He was also a philanthropist who donated generously to a wide range of charitable causes, including hospitals, universities, and cultural organizations.

In terms of his business ethics, Khashoggi was known for his insistence on honesty and integrity. He believed in building relationships based on trust and mutual respect, and he expected the people he worked with to uphold the same high standards. He was also committed to giving back to society and using his wealth and influence to make a positive impact on the world.

In conclusion, Adnan Khashoggi was a shrewd and successful businessman who was known for his innovative business tactics, his tough negotiating skills, and his commitment to honesty and integrity. While his tactics were not without controversy, his legacy as a trailblazer in the world of business is undeniable. His ability to navigate complex international deals and his willingness to take risks in pursuit of his goals continue to inspire entrepreneurs and businessmen around the world.

The one thing that he did, that an entrepreneur should follow to be great today

Adnan Khashoggi had many qualities and tactics that made him a successful entrepreneur, but if I had to pick one thing that stands out, it would be his ability to build and leverage a powerful network of contacts.

Khashoggi was known for his exceptional networking skills, which allowed him to build relationships with people in positions of power around the world. He used these connections to facilitate deals between governments and defense contractors, often acting as a middleman and taking a cut of the profits.

In today's business world, networking is just as important as it was in Khashoggi's time. Building a strong network of contacts can provide entrepreneurs with access to valuable resources and opportunities, as well as help them to gain insight into the latest trends and innovations in their industry.

To follow in Khashoggi's footsteps, entrepreneurs should focus on building and maintaining strong relationships with people in their industry, as well as with potential customers, investors, and mentors. This can be done through attending industry events and conferences, joining professional organizations, and using social media to connect with others in their field.

However, it's important to note that networking is not just about making connections for personal gain. Like Khashoggi, entrepreneurs should focus on building relationships based on trust and mutual respect. They should be willing to offer their help and support to others in their network, and be generous with their time and resources.

In short, if there's one thing that entrepreneurs can learn from Adnan Khashoggi, it's the importance of building and leveraging a powerful network of contacts. By focusing on building relationships based on trust and mutual respect, entrepreneurs can gain access to valuable resources and opportunities that can help them to achieve their goals and make a positive impact on the world.

A few more interesting facts about Adnan Khashoggi:

He was born in Mecca, Saudi Arabia in 1935, into a wealthy family with Turkish and Saudi ancestry. His father was a doctor and his mother was a member of the influential Saudi Arabian family that would later become the Khashoggi family.

Khashoggi was educated in Egypt and later attended Stanford University in California, where he studied political science and business.

After completing his education, Khashoggi began working

for his family's business, which was involved in construction, real estate, and other industries. He eventually branched out on his own and founded his own company, Triad Holding Company, which became one of the largest privately-held companies in the world.

In the 1970s and 1980s, Khashoggi was one of the world's richest men, with a personal fortune estimated at over $4 billion.

Khashoggi was a flamboyant figure who loved luxury and was known for his extravagant lifestyle. He owned several yachts, including the 282-foot Nabila, which was featured in the James Bond film "Never Say Never Again," and he had a personal collection of exotic animals that included tigers, elephants, and gazelles.

In addition to his business activities, Khashoggi was also a philanthropist who donated generously to a wide range of charitable causes, including hospitals, universities, and cultural organizations.

Khashoggi's business empire suffered a significant blow in the 1990s, as a result of the Gulf War and the collapse of the Soviet Union, which had been a major customer for his arms deals. He was also implicated in a number of scandals, including allegations of bribery and money laundering.

Khashoggi passed away in 2017 at the age of 81, leaving behind a legacy as one of the most influential and controversial businessmen of the 20th century.

DARA KHOSROWSHAHI

is an Iranian-American businessman who has made a name for himself as a leading innovator in the tech industry. As the CEO of Uber, he has transformed the ride-hailing company into a global behemoth that has revolutionized the way people get around.

Born in Tehran, Iran in 1969, Khosrowshahi immigrated to the United States with his family during the Iranian Revolution in 1978. Growing up in a new country, he learned to adapt quickly and developed an entrepreneurial spirit from a young age. He graduated from Brown University with a degree in electrical engineering in 1991 and began his career in finance, working for investment bank Allen & Company.

Khosrowshahi's first foray into the tech industry was in 1998 when he joined online travel company Expedia as Vice President of Strategic Planning. He quickly rose through the ranks, becoming CEO in 2005. Under his leadership, Expedia expanded globally and diversified its business, acquiring several other travel companies and launching a successful advertising platform. Khosrowshahi's innovation and strategic thinking helped to position Expedia as a leader in the online travel industry.

In 2017, Khosrowshahi was appointed CEO of Uber, taking over from controversial founder Travis Kalanick. The ride-hailing company was facing a slew of controversies and legal challenges, including accusations of sexual harassment, discrimination, and regulatory violations. Khosrowshahi was tasked with cleaning up Uber's image and turning the company around.

One of Khosrowshahi's first moves as CEO was to launch an "180 Days of Change" initiative, which aimed to improve Uber's relationship with drivers and address some of their biggest concerns, such as pay and working conditions. He also oversaw a major restructuring of the company's executive team, bringing in a number of new hires and promoting existing employees.

Under Khosrowshahi's leadership, Uber has continued to innovate and expand its business. The company has launched new products, such as Uber Eats and Uber Freight, and expanded into new markets, such as electric scooters and bike sharing. Khosrowshahi has also made a concerted effort to improve Uber's relationship with regulators and local governments, working to address concerns about safety, privacy, and labor rights.

Khosrowshahi's innovative approach to business and his ability to adapt quickly to changing circumstances have made him one of the most influential business minds of our time. He has demonstrated an unwavering commitment to customer satisfaction, employee well-being, and social responsibility, all while maintaining a focus on growth and profitability. His leadership at Uber has transformed the company into a global powerhouse and set a new standard for innovation and excellence in the tech industry.

Overall, Dara Khosrowshahi's contributions to the tech industry and his leadership at Uber make him a strong candidate for inclusion on any list of the most influential entrepreneurs and businessmen of all time. His innovative mindset, strategic thinking, and commitment to social responsibility have set him apart from his peers and established him as a true leader in his field. Dara Khosrowshahi is known for his innovative work tactics and strong business ethics. Here are a few key aspects of his approach:

Customer-centric focus: One of Khosrowshahi's top priorities is delivering a positive customer experience. He has emphasized the importance of listening to customer feedback and addressing their concerns, as well as creating new products and services that meet their needs. This focus on customer satisfaction has been a driving force behind Uber's success.

Collaborative leadership: Khosrowshahi is known for his collaborative leadership style. He has encouraged open communication and teamwork among employees, and has emphasized the importance of diversity and inclusion in the workplace. He has also worked closely with regulators and local governments to address concerns and build positive relationships.

Innovation: Khosrowshahi is a strong believer in innovation and has worked to position Uber as a leader in the tech industry. He has overseen the launch of new products and services, such as Uber Eats and Uber Freight, and has expanded the company's offerings to include electric scooters and bike sharing. He has also made investments in emerging technologies, such as self-driving cars and flying taxis.

Strong business ethics: Khosrowshahi has been vocal about his commitment to ethical business practices. He has emphasized the importance of transparency and accountability, and has taken steps to address concerns about data privacy and security. He has also been a vocal supporter of social responsibility and has taken steps to address issues such as climate change and income inequality.

Adaptability: Finally, Khosrowshahi is known for his ability to adapt quickly to changing circumstances. He has faced a number of challenges during his time at Uber, including regulatory scrutiny and legal challenges, but has remained focused on finding solutions and moving the company forward. He has shown a willingness to make tough decisions and pivot the company's strategy when necessary.

Overall, Dara Khosrowshahi's work tactics and business ethic are focused on delivering a positive customer experience, fostering a collaborative and inclusive workplace culture, driving innovation, maintaining strong ethical standards, and adapting to changing circumstances. These approaches have helped him to succeed in the competitive tech industry and establish himself as one of the most influential business minds of our time.

The one thing that he did, that an entrepreneur should follow to be great today

There are many things that Dara Khosrowshahi has done throughout his career that could serve as inspiration for entrepreneurs looking to make their mark. However, one key aspect of his approach that stands out is his willingness to embrace change and take bold risks.

Throughout his tenure at Uber, Khosrowshahi has faced numerous challenges and obstacles, from regulatory hurdles to fierce competition from rival companies. In response, he has consistently demonstrated a willingness to take bold risks and make significant changes to the company's strategy. For example, he oversaw the acquisition of Jump, a bike-share startup, and has invested heavily in developing new technologies such as self-driving cars.

Khosrowshahi's approach is a reminder that successful entrepreneurs must be willing to take risks and embrace change in order to achieve their goals. They must be willing to pivot their strategies quickly, experiment with new ideas, and make tough decisions in the face of uncertainty. This ability to adapt and evolve is essential in today's fast-paced business world, where competition is fierce and disruption is constant.

So, if there's one thing that entrepreneurs can learn from Dara Khosrowshahi, it's that they must be willing to take risks and embrace change in order to succeed in today's business landscape. By doing so, they can stay ahead of the curve and position themselves for long-term success.

Some additional details about Dara Khosrowshahi's career and accomplishments:

Prior to his role at Uber, Khosrowshahi served as CEO of Expedia Group, a travel technology company. During his tenure, he oversaw the acquisition of several major travel brands, including Orbitz, Travelocity, and HomeAway.

Khosrowshahi was born in Iran and immigrated to the United States with his family as a child. He attended Brown University, where he studied engineering.

Khosrowshahi has been recognized for his leadership and business accomplishments, receiving accolades such as the EY Entrepreneur of the Year award and inclusion on Forbes' list of the World's 100 Most Powerful People. In addition to his role at Uber, Khosrowshahi serves on the boards of several other companies, including The New York Times Company and Convoy, a digital freight network.

Khosrowshahi has been vocal about his commitment to social responsibility and has taken steps to address issues such as climate change and income inequality. Under his leadership, Uber has made commitments to reduce its carbon footprint and support driver earnings.

Khosrowshahi is known for his down-to-earth personality and approachable leadership style. He has been described as approachable and personable, and has prioritized building positive relationships with his employees and stakeholders.

Overall, Dara Khosrowshahi's career has been marked by his innovative approach, willingness to take risks, and commitment to social responsibility. His success at Uber and Expedia Group has established him as one of the most influential business leaders of our time.

PHIL KNIGHT

born in 1938, is an American entrepreneur, businessman, and the co-founder of Nike, Inc. His contribution to the world of business and entrepreneurship is immense and he is regarded as one of the most influential business minds of all time.

Knight was born in Portland, Oregon, and after completing his education at the University of Oregon, he went on to complete his MBA from Stanford University in 1962. After completing his studies, Knight went on a trip to Japan where he discovered a new type of athletic shoe called the Tiger Shoe, which was made by the Japanese company, Onitsuka Co.

Recognizing the potential of the shoe, Knight approached the company with a proposition to sell the shoes in the United States. Onitsuka agreed and Knight started selling the shoes from the back of his car, under the name Blue Ribbon Sports. The business quickly took off and Knight soon found himself running a successful company.

In 1971, Knight decided to rebrand the company as Nike, Inc. The new name was inspired by the Greek goddess of victory, Nike. The company started manufacturing its own line of shoes and soon became a household name in the world of sports.

One of Knight's most significant contributions to the world

of business and entrepreneurship is his innovation mindset. He was never afraid to take risks and try new things, which is evident in the way he took Blue Ribbon Sports and turned it into Nike, Inc. He was always looking for new ways to improve his business, which is why Nike became one of the most innovative companies in the world.

Another key factor that contributed to Knight's success was his work ethic. He was incredibly driven and passionate about his business and was willing to put in the long hours and hard work necessary to make it a success. He also surrounded himself with a team of talented and dedicated individuals who shared his vision and helped him achieve his goals.

Knight was also known for his tactical approach to business. He was a master strategist who always had a plan and was able to execute it flawlessly. He was able to anticipate trends in the market and respond to them quickly, which is why Nike has remained at the forefront of the athletic shoe industry for decades.

One of the reasons why Knight is considered one of the most influential business minds of all time is because of the impact he has had on the world of sports. Nike has revolutionized the way athletes train and compete, and has become an integral part of the athletic culture. The company's innovative products and marketing campaigns have inspired athletes around the world to push themselves to new heights and achieve their goals.

Knight's contribution to philanthropy is also worth mentioning. He and his wife have donated millions of dollars to various charitable causes, including education and healthcare. Knight has also been a vocal advocate for social justice and has used his platform to bring attention to important issues affecting society.

In conclusion, Phil Knight is an exceptional businessman

who has made an indelible mark on the world of sports and entrepreneurship. His innovative mindset, work ethic, and tactical approach to business have been instrumental in the success of Nike, Inc. His philanthropy and advocacy for social justice further demonstrate his commitment to making the world a better place. It is no surprise that Knight is considered one of the most influential business minds of all time, and his legacy will continue to inspire future generations of entrepreneurs and businessmen.

Phil Knight's work tactics and business ethic played a significant role in his success as an entrepreneur and businessman. Here are some additional details about these aspects of his approach to business:

Innovative mindset: As mentioned earlier, Knight was always looking for new ways to improve his business. He was willing to take risks and try new things, even if they seemed unconventional at the time. For example, one of his early marketing tactics was to give free shoes to Olympic athletes, which helped to promote the brand and generate buzz. He also invested heavily in research and development, which allowed Nike to develop cutting-edge products that set them apart from their competitors.

Focus on quality: Knight was known for his commitment to quality, and this was reflected in everything that Nike produced. He was determined to create the best products possible, and he was willing to invest time and money to ensure that every product met his high standards. This focus on quality helped to build trust with customers, which was essential for the long-term success of the brand.

Tactical approach: Knight was a master strategist who always had a plan. He was able to anticipate trends in the market and respond to them quickly, which helped Nike to stay ahead of the competition. For example, when Nike started to face competition from Reebok in the 1980s, Knight responded by launching a new line of products called Air Jordans. This move not only helped to boost sales, but it also helped to cement Nike's status as the leader in the athletic shoe industry.

Attention to detail: Knight was known for his meticulous attention to detail. He understood that even small details could have a big impact on the success of a product or marketing campaign. For example, he was involved in every aspect of the design process for Nike shoes, from the materials used to the way they were stitched together. He also paid close attention to the branding and marketing of the products, ensuring that everything was consistent with the Nike brand.

Hard work and dedication: Knight was incredibly driven and passionate about his business. He was willing to put in the long hours and hard work necessary to make Nike a success. He also surrounded himself with a team of talented and dedicated individuals who shared his vision and helped him achieve his goals.

Overall, Phil Knight's work tactics and business ethic were characterized by a commitment to innovation, quality, strategic thinking, attention to detail, and hard work. These qualities helped to establish Nike as one of the most successful and influential companies in the world, and they continue to inspire entrepreneurs and businessmen today.

The one thing that he did, that an entrepreneur should follow to be great today

It's difficult to point to just one thing that Phil Knight did that all entrepreneurs should follow, as there were many aspects of his approach to business that contributed to his success. However, if I had to pick one thing, it would be his willingness to take risks and pursue his vision, even in the face of adversity.

Throughout his career, Knight encountered numerous obstacles and setbacks. He faced intense competition from established brands, struggled with cash flow issues in the early days of Nike, and had to deal with legal disputes and public relations challenges. However, despite these challenges, Knight remained committed to his vision of building a world-class athletic shoe company. He was willing to take risks, try new things, and pursue unconventional ideas, even if they seemed risky or untested.

This willingness to take risks and pursue his vision was essential for Knight's success as an entrepreneur. It allowed him to stay ahead of the competition, create new markets, and build a brand that was recognized around the world. Today, as entrepreneurs face an increasingly competitive and fast-paced business environment, this same willingness to take risks and pursue a bold vision is more important than ever. Whether it's developing new products, entering new markets, or pursuing innovative business models, entrepreneurs who are willing to take risks and pursue their vision are most likely to achieve great success, like Phil Knight did with Nike.

A few more interesting facts and details about Phil Knight:

Early Life and Education: Phil Knight was born on February 24, 1938, in Portland, Oregon. He grew up in a middle-class family and attended Cleveland High School. He went on to study accounting at the University of Oregon, where he was a member of the track and field team.

Founding of Nike: Phil Knight co-founded Nike, originally known as Blue Ribbon Sports, in 1964 with his former track coach, Bill Bowerman. The company started out as a distributor of Japanese athletic shoes in the United States. Knight's early sales strategy involved selling shoes out of the trunk of his car at track meets and calling on high school coaches in the Pacific Northwest.

Marketing Innovations: Phil Knight was instrumental in developing many of the marketing strategies that helped to make Nike one of the most recognized brands in the world. For example, Nike was one of the first companies to use celebrity endorsements in their marketing campaigns, starting with the signing of basketball player Michael Jordan in 1984. Nike also developed the "Just Do It" advertising campaign, which has become one of the most iconic slogans in advertising history.

Philanthropy: In addition to his work with Nike, Phil Knight has also been involved in numerous philanthropic endeavors. He has donated millions of dollars to his alma mater, the University of Oregon, and he has also supported medical research and environmental causes through the Knight Foundation.

Leadership Style: Phil Knight was known for his hands-on leadership style and his willingness to take risks. He was deeply involved in every aspect of Nike's operations, from product design to marketing strategy. He was also known for his ability to inspire and motivate his employees, many of whom remained loyal to the company for years.

Legacy: Phil Knight's legacy as an entrepreneur and businessman is hard to overstate. Under his leadership, Nike grew from a small distributor of athletic shoes into a global brand with revenues of over $30 billion. Knight's innovative approach to business, his focus on quality and attention to detail, and his willingness to take risks and pursue his vision have inspired countless entrepreneurs and business leaders around the world.

RAY KROC

is one of the most influential businessmen of all time, and is widely credited with revolutionizing the fast food industry. Kroc was born in 1902 in Oak Park, Illinois, and grew up in a middle-class family. After graduating from high school, he worked a variety of odd jobs before landing a job as a traveling salesman for the Lily-Tulip Cup Company in the 1920s.

It was during his time as a traveling salesman that Kroc first came into contact with the fast food industry. He would often stop at roadside diners and hamburger stands while on the road, and was struck by the efficiency and profitability of these businesses. He saw an opportunity to bring this same efficiency to the wider world, and in 1954 he began working with the McDonald brothers to franchise their fast food concept.

Kroc's innovation mind was key to the success of the McDonald's franchise. He recognized that the key to profitability in the fast food industry was to streamline the production process, and he spent years refining the McDonald's system to make it faster, more efficient, and more profitable. He introduced a range of new innovations to the McDonald's model, including the use of standardized equipment and ingredients, a focus on cleanliness and hygiene, and the implementation of a rigorous training program for franchisees.

One of Kroc's most important innovations was the creation of the Franchise Realty Corporation (later renamed the McDonald's Corporation) in 1959. This allowed Kroc to buy out the McDonald brothers and take full control of the franchise system, giving him the power to make sweeping changes and expand the brand around the world. Kroc was a master of branding and marketing, and he used his skills to build McDonald's into one of the most recognizable and successful brands in the world.

Kroc's work and tactics were also instrumental in the success of McDonald's. He was a tireless worker, often putting in 18-hour days to build the business. He was also a shrewd negotiator, and was able to secure favorable deals with suppliers and franchisees alike. Kroc's ability to balance his entrepreneurial vision with his attention to detail and hard work was key to his success as a businessman.

There are many reasons why Ray Kroc is considered one of the most influential business minds of all time. Perhaps the most important is his ability to identify and capitalize on opportunities. Kroc saw the potential of the fast food industry long before most other people, and he was able to turn this vision into a hugely successful business. He also had the foresight to recognize the value of the McDonald's brand, and worked tirelessly to build it into the global behemoth it is today.

Kroc's willingness to take risks was also a key factor in his success. He was not afraid to make bold moves, such as buying out the McDonald brothers and taking control of the franchise system. He also invested heavily in marketing and advertising, which helped to build the brand and drive sales. Kroc understood that in business, as in life, sometimes you need to take risks in order to succeed.

Finally, Kroc's commitment to innovation and continuous

improvement was critical to the success of McDonald's. He was always looking for ways to make the business more efficient and profitable, and was not afraid to experiment with new ideas. This willingness to innovate and adapt helped McDonald's stay ahead of the competition and remain a leader in the fast food industry for decades.

In conclusion, Ray Kroc is one of the most influential business minds of all time. His innovation mind, work and tactics, and commitment to continuous improvement were instrumental in the success of McDonald's and the fast food industry as a whole.

Kroc started out as a struggling milkshake machine salesman: After serving in World War I, Kroc tried his hand at a variety of jobs, including paper cup salesman, pianist, and radio DJ. In the 1950s, he began selling milkshake machines for the Multimixer Corporation. It was during this time that he met the McDonald brothers and became interested in their fast food concept.

Kroc was in his 50s when he first got involved with McDonald's: Kroc was 52 years old when he met the McDonald brothers and began working with them to franchise their concept. This is a testament to the fact that it's never too late to start a successful business.

Kroc initially struggled to get McDonald's off the ground: Despite his enthusiasm for the McDonald's concept, Kroc faced numerous obstacles in his efforts to franchise the business. He was turned down by countless investors and lenders, and had to mortgage his own home to raise funds for the first franchise location.

Kroc was a hands-on leader who focused on the details: Kroc was known for his attention to detail and his hands-on approach to leadership. He visited franchise locations regularly and was always looking for ways to improve the McDonald's system. He also had a reputation for being a demanding boss who expected a lot from his employees.

Kroc was a philanthropist who gave generously to charity: In addition to his business pursuits, Kroc was also a generous philanthropist. He donated millions of dollars to various causes over the course of his life, including the construction of a hospital and a performing arts center in his hometown of Oak Park, Illinois.

Kroc was a controversial figure who drew criticism for his business practices: While Kroc is widely recognized as a successful businessman and innovator, he also drew criticism for his aggressive business tactics. Some accused him of exploiting franchisees and putting profits ahead of people. However, others argue that his success was simply a result of his relentless drive and his commitment to innovation.

Kroc's legacy continues to shape the fast food industry: Even decades after his death in 1984, Kroc's legacy continues to shape the fast food industry. McDonald's remains one of the most successful and recognizable brands in the world, and its business model has been emulated by countless other chains. While Kroc's methods may not be universally admired, there's no denying that his impact on the world of business has been enormous.

The one thing that Kroc did, that an entrepreneur should follow to be great

One thing that entrepreneurs could learn from Ray Kroc is the importance of persistence and determination in the face of adversity. Kroc faced numerous obstacles and setbacks in his efforts to franchise McDonald's, but he never gave up. He was willing to mortgage his home and put everything on the line to make his vision a reality.

This kind of persistence is essential for entrepreneurs who want to achieve great things. Starting a business is never easy, and there will always be challenges and setbacks along the way. But by staying focused on your goals and refusing to give up, you can overcome those challenges and achieve success.

Another thing that entrepreneurs could learn from Kroc is the importance of innovation. Kroc saw the potential in the McDonald's concept and worked tirelessly to improve and expand it. He was always looking for ways to innovate and stay ahead of the competition.

Innovation is essential for any business that wants to succeed in today's fast-paced and constantly changing business environment. By constantly pushing the boundaries and coming up with new and better ways of doing things, entrepreneurs can stay ahead of the curve and build successful businesses that stand the test of time.

Here are a few more interesting facts about Ray Kroc:

Kroc was a self-made millionaire: Kroc's success with McDonald's made him a very wealthy man. At the time of his death in 1984, his net worth was estimated to be around $600 million.

Kroc was a marketing genius: Kroc was a master of marketing and advertising. He was responsible for many of the iconic McDonald's slogans and jingles, such as "You deserve a break today" and "Two all-beef patties, special sauce, lettuce, cheese, pickles, onions, on a sesame seed bun."

Kroc was a risk-taker: Kroc was not afraid to take risks and try new things. For example, he was one of the first fast food entrepreneurs to embrace automation and introduce things like milkshake machines and french fry cookers to his restaurants.

Kroc was a big believer in the power of teamwork: Kroc

recognized that the success of McDonald's was due in large part to the teamwork and collaboration of his employees. He was known for his motto, "None of us is as good as all of us."

Kroc was a voracious reader: Kroc was a lifelong learner and was known to be an avid reader. He often read business and self-help books to stay up-to-date on the latest trends and ideas.

PIERS M. WOLF

ESTÉE LAUDER

Was a trailblazing entrepreneur and one of the most influential business minds of the 20th century. Born Josephine Esther Mentzer in Queens, New York in 1908, she was the daughter of Hungarian immigrants. From an early age, she was fascinated with beauty and cosmetics, and she would go on to build one of the world's most successful beauty brands.

Lauder's innovative mind was evident from the beginning of her career. In the 1930s, she began mixing her own creams and lotions in her kitchen, using natural ingredients like lanolin and honey. She would test her products on her friends and family, and soon her homemade creams were in high demand. In 1946, Lauder and her husband Joseph launched Estée Lauder Companies, with just four products - Super-Rich All-Purpose Cream, Creme Pack, Cleansing Oil, and Skin Lotion.

From the outset, Lauder was a master of marketing and promotion. She recognized the power of word-of-mouth advertising and would give her products away to her friends and acquaintances, encouraging them to share their experiences with others. She also cultivated relationships with prominent women in society, offering them her products and asking them to spread the word to their friends and colleagues.

Lauder was always focused on innovation, and she was constantly looking for new products and new markets to conquer. In the 1950s, she launched Youth-Dew, a bath oil that could also be used as a perfume, and it became a sensation. She also developed a line of men's grooming products, Aramis, which proved to be highly successful.

One of Lauder's most significant contributions to the beauty industry was her emphasis on skincare. She recognized that skincare was an essential part of any beauty regimen, and she developed a range of skincare products that became bestsellers. She also pioneered the use of gift-with-purchase promotions, which are now a standard marketing tactic in the beauty industry.

Lauder's business tactics were also groundbreaking. She was a firm believer in the power of the department store, and she forged strong partnerships with stores like Saks Fifth Avenue and Neiman Marcus. She would spend hours in these stores, training the sales staff and educating them about her products. She also developed a loyal following among her own employees, who were known as "Estée's girls," and who were trained to provide exceptional customer service.

Lauder's legacy is undeniable. Today, Estée Lauder Companies is a multibillion-dollar enterprise, with brands like MAC, Clinique, and Bobbi Brown under its umbrella. Lauder's impact on the beauty industry is immeasurable, and her marketing and promotional tactics have become standard practice in the industry. She was a true visionary and an inspiration to generations of entrepreneurs and businesspeople.

In conclusion, Estée Lauder was a true pioneer in the beauty industry and one of the most influential business minds of all time. She was an innovator, a marketing genius, and a trailblazer for women in business. Her dedication to quality products, customer service, and innovation has made her an enduring icon of the beauty industry and a role model for entrepreneurs everywhere. She will always be remembered as one of the most significant and influential businesspeople of the 20th century.

Estée Lauder's work tactics and business ethics were integral to her success and have become part of her enduring legacy. Here are some more details about how she approached her work and the principles that guided her business practices:

Quality products: Lauder was passionate about creating high-quality products that delivered on their promises. She believed that if a product didn't work, customers would not come back for more. This commitment to quality helped establish her brand's reputation for excellence.

Word-of-mouth marketing: Lauder recognized the power of word-of-mouth advertising and understood that happy customers were her best advocates. She would often give her products away to friends and acquaintances, asking them to share their experiences with others. This strategy helped to build a loyal customer base and helped her brand grow through positive recommendations.

Department store partnerships: Lauder was a firm believer in the power of department stores and forged strong partnerships with them. She would spend hours in stores training the sales staff and educating them about her products. This personal touch helped to create a strong relationship between her brand and the department stores that carried her products.

Gift-with-purchase promotions: Lauder pioneered the use of gift-with-purchase promotions, where customers would receive a free gift with the purchase of a certain product or dollar amount. This tactic was highly effective in driving sales and has since become a standard marketing practice in the beauty industry.

Focus on skincare: Lauder recognized early on that skincare

was an essential part of any beauty regimen and developed a range of skincare products that became bestsellers. She also educated her customers on the importance of taking care of their skin, which helped to establish her brand as a leader in the skincare category.

Exceptional customer service: Lauder believed in the importance of providing exceptional customer service and trained her employees to deliver it. Her sales staff, known as "Estée's girls," were trained to provide personalized service and make customers feel valued.

Innovation: Lauder was always looking for new products and markets to conquer. She was a pioneer in developing products like Youth-Dew and Aramis and was constantly experimenting with new ingredients and formulations.

Strong work ethic: Lauder was known for her tireless work ethic and dedication to her brand. She was often the first one in the office and the last one to leave, and she would spend hours testing and developing new products.Overall, Estée Lauder's work tactics and business ethics were grounded in a commitment to quality, innovation, and exceptional customer service. She believed in the power of personal relationships and partnerships and was constantly looking for ways to improve her brand and expand her reach. These principles helped her to build a global beauty empire and establish herself as one of the most influential business minds of all time.

The one thing that she did, that an entrepreneur should follow to be great

There are many things that Estée Lauder did that entrepreneurs can learn from, but if I had to pick just one thing, it would be her relentless pursuit of quality. Lauder was deeply committed to creating products that delivered on their promises and would go to great lengths to ensure that every product was of the highest quality. She believed that if a product didn't work, customers would not come back for more, and that the key to success was creating products that customers loved and trusted.

This focus on quality is just as important today as it was during Lauder's time. In today's crowded marketplace, customers have more choices than ever before, and they expect products that are not only effective but also safe, sustainable, and ethical. By making quality a top priority, entrepreneurs can differentiate themselves from their competitors and build a loyal customer base that will help drive their success.

To follow in Lauder's footsteps, entrepreneurs should focus on creating products that meet a real need, that are innovative, and that are designed with the customer in mind. They should be willing to invest time and resources into testing and refining their products, and they should be open to feedback from their customers and willing to make changes as needed. By doing so, they can build a brand that stands for quality, excellence, and trust, just as Estée Lauder did.

Here are a few more things about Estée Lauder that may be of interest:

Early beginnings: Estée Lauder, whose real name was Josephine Esther Mentzer, was born in Queens, New York in 1906. She grew up in a family of entrepreneurs and was exposed to the world of business from an early age.

Love of beauty: Lauder had a lifelong love of beauty and was fascinated by the ways in which makeup and skincare products could enhance a person's appearance. As a teenager, she experimented with creating her own creams and lotions, using ingredients from her father's hardware store.

Early sales tactics: Lauder's first foray into business came when she was still a teenager. She would sell her homemade products to her friends and family, and she would also go door-to-door in her neighborhood, offering free makeovers to anyone who would let her.

Marriage and partnership: In 1930, Lauder married Joseph Lauder, a businessman who would later become her business partner. Together, they launched the Estée Lauder company in 1946, with a focus on creating high-quality skincare and makeup products.

Persistence and determination: Lauder's road to success was not always easy, and she faced many obstacles along the way. However, she was persistent and determined, and she never gave up on her dream of building a successful beauty empire.

Philanthropy: Lauder was a generous philanthropist and was deeply committed to giving back to her community. She established the Breast Cancer Research Foundation in 1993, which has since become one of the largest private funders of breast cancer research in the world.

Legacy: Estée Lauder's legacy lives on today, not only in the products that bear her name but also in the values and principles that guided her business practices. She was a trailblazer in the beauty industry and a true pioneer in the world of entrepreneurship, and her contributions continue to inspire and motivate entrepreneurs around the world.

WILLIAM LEVER

1st Viscount Leverhulme, was a British businessman and entrepreneur who is best known for founding Lever Brothers, a company that would later become part of Unilever. He was a pioneer in the field of soap manufacturing and was widely recognized as one of the most innovative and influential business minds of his time.

Early Life and Career

William Lever was born in Bolton, England in 1851, the seventh child of a grocer. He left school at the age of 16 and began working in his father's grocery store, where he gained an appreciation for the importance of quality and customer service. In 1885, he founded Lever Brothers with his brother James, with the goal of manufacturing high-quality soap at an affordable price.

Innovation and Expansion

Lever was a true innovator who was constantly experimenting with new techniques and technologies to improve his products and processes. He was one of the first soap manufacturers to use glycerin in his soap, which made it less harsh and more moisturizing. He also introduced the concept of branding, using the name "Sunlight" to market his soap and creating a distinctive yellow packaging that became instantly recognizable to consumers.

Lever was also a pioneer in the field of employee welfare, providing housing, healthcare, and education for his workers. He believed that happy and healthy employees would be more productive and loyal, and he was committed to creating a positive work environment that would benefit both his workers and his company.

Lever's innovative approach to business paid off, and Lever Brothers grew rapidly in the late 19th and early 20th centuries. The company expanded its product lines to include other household goods such as margarine, and it opened factories and offices around the world. Lever also became involved in politics and philanthropy, using his wealth and influence to support causes such as education, public health, and women's suffrage.

Legacy

William Lever is widely regarded as one of the most influential business leaders of his time, and his innovative ideas and approach to business continue to inspire entrepreneurs today. His focus on quality, branding, and employee welfare set a new standard for corporate responsibility and helped to establish the importance of these concepts in modern business.

Lever was also a pioneer in the field of marketing and advertising, recognizing the importance of building a strong brand and creating a loyal customer base. His use of the "Sunlight" brand and distinctive packaging helped to establish the importance of branding in modern marketing, and his innovative approach to advertising helped to create the modern advertising industry.

In addition to his business accomplishments, Lever was also a philanthropist and social reformer, using his wealth and influence to support a wide range of causes. He founded the Port Sunlight model village in England, which provided housing and amenities for his workers, and he was a vocal supporter of public health, education, and women's rights.

Conclusion

William Lever was a true visionary and innovator whose contributions to the field of business continue to be felt today. His focus on quality, branding, and employee welfare helped to set a new standard for corporate responsibility and established the importance of these concepts in modern business. His pioneering work in marketing and advertising helped to create the modern advertising industry, and his philanthropy and social reform efforts helped to improve the lives of countless people around the world. For these reasons and more, he is widely regarded as one of the most influential business minds of his time.

Lever was known for his interest in art and design, and he was a patron of the arts throughout his life. He was particularly interested in the Arts and Crafts movement, which emphasized traditional craftsmanship and design. He collected art and furniture, and he commissioned artists and designers to create pieces for his home and his businesses.

In addition to his work in soap manufacturing, Lever was also involved in politics and government. He was elected to the British Parliament in 1906 as a member of the Liberal Party, and he served as a member of Parliament for nearly 20 years. He was a vocal advocate for social reform, and he used his position in government to push for policies that would improve the lives of working-class people.

Lever was a supporter of women's rights and was a member of the Women's Social and Political Union, which was a leading organization in the women's suffrage movement in Britain. He believed that women should have the right to vote and to participate fully in public life, and he used his wealth and influence to support the cause.

Lever was also interested in public health and was a supporter of the public health movement in Britain. He believed that good hygiene and sanitation were essential for the health and well-being of people, and he used his businesses to promote these ideas. For example, he developed a system for providing clean water to his workers, and he provided health care and education to his employees to help prevent the spread of disease.

Lever was an avid traveler and explorer, and he was particularly interested in the natural world. He was a member of the Royal Geographical Society and supported scientific expeditions to remote parts of the world. He also established a research laboratory at his soap factory to study the properties of soap and other household products.

These are just a few examples of the many interests and activities of William Lever, which illustrate his diverse and multifaceted personality. He was a true Renaissance man who was passionate about many different things, and his life and work continue to inspire people around the world today.

The one thing that Lever did, that an entrepreneur should follow to be great

One thing that entrepreneurs can learn from William Lever is his focus on the needs and desires of his customers. Lever was known for his keen understanding of what consumers wanted, and he used this knowledge to create products and marketing campaigns that were tailored to their needs and desires.

To achieve this, Lever invested heavily in market research and customer feedback. He hired experts to study consumer trends and preferences, and he used this information to develop new products and improve existing ones. He also created innovative marketing campaigns that resonated with consumers, using techniques such as colorful packaging, catchy slogans, and celebrity endorsements.

Entrepreneurs today can follow Lever's example by taking a customer-centric approach to their business. This means focusing on understanding their customers' needs, preferences, and pain points, and using this information to create products and services that meet those needs. Entrepreneurs should invest in market research and customer feedback, and use these insights to continuously improve their products and marketing strategies.

By taking a customer-centric approach, entrepreneurs can build strong relationships with their customers, create products that people truly want and need, and ultimately, build a successful and sustainable business.

Here are some additional details about William Lever's life and work:

Lever was a pioneer in the field of marketing and advertising. He recognized the importance of creating a strong brand identity and using advertising to build brand awareness and loyalty. He was one of the first business leaders to use advertising on a large scale, and he created memorable marketing campaigns that helped establish his brand as a household name.

In addition to his work in soap manufacturing, Lever was also involved in other industries, including food and agriculture. He invested in farmland and dairy farms, and he developed innovative techniques for preserving and packaging food products. He also created a line of food products under the brand name "Lever Brothers", including margarine, cheese, and other dairy products.

Lever was a philanthropist who believed in giving back to society. He established a number of charitable foundations and organizations, including the Leverhulme Trust, which supports research and education in a variety of fields. He also created a number of initiatives to improve the lives of his employees, including providing housing, healthcare, and education to his workers and their families.

Lever was a proponent of environmental conservation and sustainability. He believed that businesses had a responsibility to protect the environment and use natural resources in a responsible and sustainable way. He invested in renewable energy sources, such as hydroelectric power, and he created initiatives to reduce waste and pollution in his factories.

Lever was also a supporter of international peace and cooperation. He believed that economic cooperation and cultural exchange could help promote understanding and peace between nations, and he supported initiatives to promote international trade and diplomacy.

These are just a few examples of the many interests and activities of William Lever, which illustrate his broad and far-reaching impact on business, society, and culture. His legacy continues to inspire entrepreneurs and business leaders around the world today.

HENRY LUCE

Was an American businessman and media magnate who co-founded Time magazine and revolutionized the publishing industry in the 20th century. Here is a closer look at his life, work, and why he is considered one of the most influential business minds of his time.

Early Life and Education

Henry Luce was born in Tengchow, China, in 1898. His parents were both missionaries, and he spent much of his childhood in China before returning to the United States to attend school. He went on to attend Yale University, where he became involved in journalism and wrote for the student newspaper.

Innovation in Publishing

After graduating from Yale in 1920, Luce and his friend Briton Hadden began work on a new type of magazine that would cover the news in a more comprehensive and engaging way. Their idea was to create a weekly magazine that would summarize the most important news stories of the week and present them in an accessible and entertaining format.

Their magazine, Time, was an immediate success, and it quickly became one of the most popular publications in the

United States. Luce and Hadden went on to launch several other successful magazines, including Fortune and Life, which helped to shape the way that Americans consumed news and information.

In addition to his innovative approach to publishing, Luce was also known for his keen business sense and his ability to spot new trends and opportunities. He was a master at marketing and advertising, and he understood the importance of building strong relationships with advertisers and readers alike.

Social and Political Activism

Despite his success in the business world, Luce was also deeply committed to social and political activism. He was a strong supporter of the civil rights movement and used his publications to advocate for social justice and equality.

Luce was also a strong advocate for American interventionism in world affairs, and he used his publications to promote American values and ideals around the world. He was a staunch anti-communist and believed that the United States had a responsibility to lead the world in the fight against communism and totalitarianism.

Legacy

Today, Henry Luce is remembered as one of the most influential business minds of the 20th century. His innovative approach to publishing, his keen business sense, and his commitment to social and political activism helped to shape the way that Americans consume news and information.

Luce's publications helped to define the American Century, and his ideas and ideals continue to shape American society and culture to this day. His legacy serves as an inspiration to entrepreneurs and business leaders around the world, and his commitment to social responsibility and political activism is a reminder of the power of business to effect positive change in the world.

Early Career: Before co-founding Time magazine, Luce worked as a reporter for the Chicago Daily News and later as a correspondent for the New York Times in China. It was during his time in China that he developed his interest in international affairs and began to see the potential for a new type of news magazine.

Cultural Impact: Luce's magazines had a significant impact on American culture, helping to define the American Century and shaping the way that Americans thought about their country and the world. His magazines were known for their high-quality journalism, stunning photography, and engaging storytelling, and they helped to create a sense of shared national identity among Americans.

Political Influence: Luce was a powerful political figure in his time, and he used his publications to advance his political views and promote American interests around the world. He was a close friend of several U.S. presidents, including Franklin Roosevelt and Dwight Eisenhower, and he played an influential role in shaping American foreign policy during the Cold War era.

Personal Life: Luce was married to Clare Boothe Luce, a prominent writer and politician, and the two were known for their high-profile social life and influential connections. Luce was also a devout Christian and was deeply committed to his faith, which he saw as a guiding force in his life and work.

Philanthropy: In addition to his work in publishing and politics, Luce was also a committed philanthropist and gave generously to a variety of causes throughout his life. He established the Henry Luce Foundation, which supports a range of educational, cultural, and religious organizations, and he was known for his generous support of the arts and humanities.

The one thing that Luce did, that an entrepreneur should follow to be great

One thing that entrepreneurs can learn from Henry Luce is the importance of innovation and staying ahead of the curve. Luce was a true visionary who saw the potential for a new type of news magazine and was willing to take risks to bring his vision to life. He was always looking for new ideas and opportunities, and he was not afraid to experiment and try new things.

For entrepreneurs today, this means staying on top of emerging trends and technologies, and being willing to take calculated risks to stay ahead of the competition. It also means being open to new ideas and perspectives, and being willing to adapt and evolve as the market and consumer preferences change.

Another key lesson from Luce's life and work is the importance of having a strong sense of purpose and vision. Luce was deeply committed to his mission of creating a new type of news magazine that would inform and engage readers in a fresh and exciting way. He believed in the power of media to shape public opinion and drive positive change, and he was driven by a sense of purpose and mission that went beyond mere profit.

For entrepreneurs today, this means having a clear sense of purpose and mission that goes beyond the bottom line. It means understanding the impact that your business can have on the world, and being committed to creating value for customers and society as a whole. By staying focused on your purpose and vision, and by being open to new ideas and opportunities, you can create a truly innovative and impactful business that can change the world for the better.

Some more interesting facts and details about Henry Luce:

Educational Background: Luce attended Yale University, where he was a member of the secret society Skull and Bones. He was an excellent student and won several awards for his writing and journalism skills.

Magazine Empire: Luce's publishing empire eventually grew to include not only Time magazine, but also Fortune, Life, and Sports Illustrated. These magazines became some of the most popular and influential publications of the 20th century, shaping American culture and public opinion.

Journalism Innovator: Luce was a true innovator in the field of journalism, introducing new techniques and technologies that would revolutionize the industry. For example, he was one of the first publishers to use color photography in magazines, and he was also an early adopter of electronic typesetting and computer technology.

Political Views: Luce was known for his conservative political views, and he used his magazines to promote a pro-American, anti-communist agenda. He was a vocal supporter of the Vietnam War and an opponent of the Civil Rights Movement, positions that would later be controversial and criticized.

Legacy: Henry Luce is widely regarded as one of the most influential business leaders and media moguls of the 20th century. His innovative ideas and entrepreneurial spirit transformed the publishing industry, and his magazines helped to shape American culture and public opinion in profound ways. His legacy continues to inspire entrepreneurs and innovators around the world today.

JACK MA

Is an iconic figure in the business world, renowned for his innovative approach and entrepreneurial success. Born in Hangzhou, China in 1964, Ma was raised in a modest family and had a humble beginning. Despite the initial setbacks in his career, he persevered and eventually founded one of the world's most successful e-commerce companies, Alibaba Group.

Ma's innovative mindset and work ethic have been the driving force behind his incredible success. From an early age, he had a passion for learning and exploring new ideas. This led him to pursue higher education in the United States, where he was exposed to the latest developments in the technology industry.

After returning to China, Ma worked as an English teacher for several years, during which he gained a deeper understanding of the Chinese market and its potential. He was quick to identify the potential of the internet as a tool for business, and in 1999, he founded Alibaba with a group of friends.

At the time, China had a small e-commerce market, and most businesses were conducted offline. However, Ma saw the potential for online sales and built Alibaba as a platform to connect Chinese manufacturers with global buyers. His vision was to create an open, accessible, and efficient online marketplace, and he pursued it relentlessly.

One of the keys to Ma's success was his ability to spot opportunities where others saw only challenges. For example, he recognized the potential of mobile technology to revolutionize e-commerce and invested heavily in mobile payments and logistics, which gave Alibaba a significant competitive advantage.

Ma also prioritized innovation and encouraged his team to think outside the box. He famously stated that "you should learn from your competitors, but never copy them." Instead, he urged his team to find new and innovative solutions to the challenges they faced.

Another important factor in Ma's success was his ability to build a strong team and cultivate a positive company culture. He believed that a successful business is built on trust, and he worked hard to establish a culture of transparency, integrity, and collaboration at Alibaba.

Ma's tactics were not without controversy, however. Critics have accused Alibaba of engaging in anti-competitive practices and of promoting counterfeit goods on its platform. Ma has also faced criticism for his close ties to the Chinese government and for his outspoken support of China's political leadership.

Despite these criticisms, it is hard to deny the incredible impact that Ma has had on the global business landscape. Under his leadership, Alibaba grew from a small startup to a multinational corporation with over 100,000 employees and a market value of over $500 billion.

Ma's influence extends far beyond Alibaba, however. He has been a vocal advocate for entrepreneurship and has inspired countless aspiring business leaders around the world. He has also been actively involved in philanthropy, supporting initiatives in education, the environment, and public health.

In conclusion, Jack Ma is undoubtedly one of the most influential business minds of our time. His innovative mindset, work ethic, and tactical approach have enabled him to build one of the world's most successful companies, and his impact on the global business landscape is undeniable. Despite the controversies that have surrounded him, his legacy as a visionary entrepreneur and a champion of innovation and entrepreneurship is assured.

Jack Ma's work tactics and business ethics played a crucial role in his success as an entrepreneur. Here are some more details on his approach:

Focus on the customer: Ma believed that the customer should always come first. He understood that building a successful business requires a deep understanding of the customer's needs and preferences. To achieve this, he encouraged his team to constantly listen to feedback and make improvements based on customer input.

Embrace failure: Ma was not afraid of failure and often spoke about the importance of learning from one's mistakes. He believed that setbacks were opportunities to learn and improve, and that entrepreneurs should be willing to take risks and experiment with new ideas.

Think big: Ma had a bold vision for Alibaba from the beginning. He recognized the potential of the internet to transform the way business was done, and he set out to create a platform that would connect businesses all over the world. He was not content with a small market share or limited growth, and he encouraged his team to think big and pursue ambitious goals.

Innovate constantly: Ma was a firm believer in the power of innovation. He understood that in order to stay ahead of the competition, businesses needed to constantly innovate and adapt to new technologies and market trends. He encouraged his team to be creative and to explore new ideas and approaches.

Foster a positive company culture: Ma recognized the importance of building a strong team and fostering a positive company culture. He believed that a successful business was built on trust, transparency, and collaboration, and he worked hard to create a culture that encouraged these values.

Build strong partnerships: Ma understood the value of building strong partnerships and relationships. He sought out strategic partnerships with other businesses and governments to expand Alibaba's reach and influence. He also worked closely with his team to build strong relationships with suppliers and customers, which helped to establish Alibaba as a trusted and reliable business partner.

Be adaptable: Ma recognized that the business landscape was constantly changing, and he emphasized the importance of being adaptable and flexible. He encouraged his team to be open to new ideas and to be willing to pivot when necessary.

Overall, Jack Ma's approach to business was characterized by a focus on the customer, a willingness to take risks and embrace failure, a commitment to innovation and continuous improvement, and a dedication to building strong partnerships and a positive company culture. These tactics and ethics were key factors in his success as an entrepreneur and have inspired countless others in the business world.

The one thing that he did, that an entrepreneur should follow to be great today

One of the most important things that Jack Ma did as an entrepreneur, which other entrepreneurs can learn from and follow, is his commitment to innovation.

Ma believed that in order to succeed in the highly competitive business landscape, one must constantly innovate and adapt to new technologies and market trends. He encouraged his team at Alibaba to be creative and to explore new ideas and approaches. This approach allowed Alibaba to stay ahead of the competition and to become a leader in the e-commerce industry.

In today's rapidly changing business world, innovation remains critical for entrepreneurs looking to build successful businesses. By continuously innovating, entrepreneurs can stay ahead of the competition, better serve their customers, and create new opportunities for growth.

Therefore, if an entrepreneur wants to be great today, they should prioritize innovation in their business strategy. They should constantly seek out new ideas, experiment with new technologies, and challenge themselves and their team to think outside the box. By doing so, they can stay relevant and competitive in the market, and build a successful and sustainable business over the long term.

A few more interesting things about Jack Ma and his entrepreneurial journey:

Humble beginnings: Ma came from humble beginnings and faced numerous obstacles early in his career. He failed his college entrance exam twice before finally being admitted to Hangzhou Teacher's Institute. After graduation, he applied for dozens of jobs and was rejected from all of them, including KFC. He eventually found work teaching English, which helped him develop his language skills and expand his horizons.

A chance encounter: Ma's journey into entrepreneurship began with a chance encounter with the internet. In 1995, he visited the United States as part of a government delegation and was introduced to the internet for the first time. He immediately recognized its potential to transform the way business was done and set out to create a platform that would connect Chinese businesses with the world.

Building Alibaba: Ma founded Alibaba in 1999 with a small group of friends in his apartment in Hangzhou, China. The company started as a business-to-business (B2B) marketplace, connecting Chinese manufacturers with overseas buyers. Over time, Alibaba expanded into other areas, including consumer-to-consumer (C2C) e-commerce with Taobao, and payment services with Alipay.

Overcoming challenges: Ma and Alibaba faced numerous challenges over the years, including fierce competition, regulatory hurdles, and an economic slowdown in China. However, Ma remained committed to his vision and his principles, and he worked tirelessly to overcome these challenges and build a successful and sustainable business.

Philanthropy: Ma is known for his philanthropic efforts, particularly through the Jack Ma Foundation. In 2014, he launched the Rural Teacher Initiative, which aims to improve education and training for teachers in rural areas of China. In 2019, he announced plans to donate $145 million to support research in the field of artificial intelligence.

Overall, Jack Ma's entrepreneurial journey is a testament to the power of persistence, vision, and innovation. Despite facing numerous obstacles and challenges, he remained committed to his principles and his vision, and he built one of the world's most successful and influential companies.

JOHN MACKEY

is an American entrepreneur, businessman, and co-founder of Whole Foods Market. He was born on August 15, 1953, in Houston, Texas. He is widely regarded as one of the most innovative and influential business leaders of his time. Mackey's entrepreneurial journey began when he was still in college, where he co-founded a vegetarian food store with his girlfriend.

Mackey's career as a businessman and entrepreneur took off when he co-founded Whole Foods Market in 1980 with his then-girlfriend, Renee Lawson Hardy, and two other partners. Whole Foods Market started as a small natural foods store in Austin, Texas, and has grown to become the world's leading retailer of natural and organic foods. The company operates more than 500 stores in North America, the UK, and Germany, and has a market capitalization of more than $20 billion.

One of Mackey's most significant contributions to the business world is his approach to conscious capitalism. Mackey believes that business should be a force for good and should prioritize the well-being of all stakeholders, including customers, employees, suppliers, and the community. He has written several books on the subject, including "Conscious Capitalism: Liberating the Heroic Spirit of Business," which he co-authored with Raj Sisodia.

Mackey's approach to conscious capitalism has influenced many other businesses and entrepreneurs, who have adopted his philosophy and principles. Mackey has also been a vocal critic of traditional capitalism, which he believes is focused solely on maximizing profits for shareholders at the expense of other stakeholders. Mackey's vision of conscious capitalism has inspired other businesses to prioritize sustainability, social responsibility, and ethical business practices.

In addition to his approach to conscious capitalism, Mackey is also known for his innovative management practices. Whole Foods Market has a unique decentralized management structure, where each store operates as an autonomous unit. This structure allows for more creativity and flexibility in each store, as managers can tailor their operations to the specific needs of their community.

Mackey is also an advocate of employee empowerment and has implemented several programs to promote employee well-being and engagement. For example, WFM offers its employees stock options and profit-sharing programs, which has helped to create a sense of ownership and loyalty among its workforce. Mackey also encourages his employees to be creative and innovative, which has led to many new offerings and initiatives.

Despite his success, Mackey has faced criticism and controversy throughout his career. In 2017, he faced backlash after comments he made about the Affordable Care Act, which he called "fascist." Mackey later apologized for his comments, saying that he regretted using the term and that he was passionate about improving healthcare in the United States.

In conclusion, John Mackey is a visionary businessman and entrepreneur who has had a significant impact on the business world. His approach to conscious capitalism has inspired many other businesses to prioritize social responsibility and sustainability. Mackey's innovative management practices and employee empowerment initiatives have helped to create a loyal and engaged workforce. Despite facing criticism and controversy, Mackey's legacy as one of the most influential business minds of his time is secure.

John Mackey's work tactics and business ethics are closely tied to his philosophy of conscious capitalism, which emphasizes the importance of ethical and sustainable business practices. Here are some specific examples of how Mackey has implemented these principles in his work:

Prioritizing Stakeholder Well-being: Mackey believes that businesses should prioritize the well-being of all stakeholders, including customers, employees, suppliers, and the community. WFM has implemented several programs to support this philosophy, such as offering high-quality products and services, providing fair wages and benefits to employees, and sourcing products from local suppliers to support the local economy.

Decentralized Management: WFM has a unique decentralized management structure, where each store operates as an autonomous unit. This structure allows for more creativity and flexibility in each store, as managers can tailor their operations to the specific needs of their community. This approach has been successful, as WFM has been able to adapt to local markets and expand rapidly while maintaining a strong corporate culture.

Innovation and Creativity: Mackey encourages his employees to be creative and innovative, which has led to many new product offerings and initiatives. For example, Whole Foods Market was one of the first retailers to introduce a large selection of organic and natural foods, which has become a major trend in the food industry. The company has also launched several new initiatives, such as the "Whole Planet Foundation," which provides microcredit loans to entrepreneurs in developing countries.

Employee Empowerment: Mackey has implemented several programs to promote employee well-being and engagement, including offering stock options and profit-sharing programs, which has helped to create a sense of ownership and loyalty among its workforce. Mackey also encourages his employees to take on leadership roles and make decisions at the store level, which has led to a more engaged and motivated workforce.

Sustainability: Whole Foods Market has been a leader in promoting sustainable business practices, such as reducing waste, conserving energy, and sourcing products from sustainable sources. Mackey has been a vocal advocate for environmental causes, such as promoting organic farming and reducing greenhouse gas emissions.

Overall, John Mackey's work tactics and business ethic are closely aligned with his philosophy of conscious capitalism, which prioritizes ethical and sustainable business practices. His emphasis on stakeholder well-being, innovation, employee empowerment, and sustainability has made him a highly influential business leader and a role model for many entrepreneurs and business owners.

The one thing that he did, that an entrepreneur should follow to be great today

One of the most important things that entrepreneurs can learn from John Mackey is the importance of prioritizing stakeholder well-being. Mackey has demonstrated that by focusing on the well-being of customers, employees, suppliers, and the community, businesses can create sustainable value and build long-term success.

One specific example of this principle in action is Whole Foods Market's emphasis on offering high-quality products and services. By providing customers with healthy, sustainable food options, the company has built a loyal customer base and become a leader in the organic and natural foods industry.

Entrepreneurs can also learn from Mackey's emphasis on employee empowerment and engagement. By offering employees stock options, profit-sharing programs, and opportunities for leadership and decision-making, businesses can create a more motivated and dedicated workforce.

Finally, entrepreneurs can learn from Mackey's emphasis on sustainability and social responsibility. By taking steps to reduce waste, conserve energy, and source products from sustainable sources, businesses can demonstrate their commitment to ethical and sustainable business practices, which can help to build a positive reputation and attract customers who share those values.

In summary, entrepreneurs can learn from John Mackey's focus on stakeholder well-being, employee empowerment, and sustainability in order to create successful and socially responsible businesses.

A few more things you might find interesting about John Mackey:

Mackey co-founded Whole Foods Market in 1980, along with his girlfriend at the time, Renee Lawson Hardy, and two other business partners. They opened their first store in Austin, Texas, with a focus on offering high-quality natural and organic foods.

Mackey has been a vocal advocate for conscious capitalism, which emphasizes the importance of creating value for all stakeholders, not just shareholders. He has written and spoken extensively about this philosophy, and has been a frequent guest on business and financial news programs.

In 2013, Mackey co-authored a book called "Conscious Capitalism: Liberating the Heroic Spirit of Business," which lays out the principles of conscious capitalism and provides examples of businesses that have successfully implemented these principles.

In 2017, Amazon acquired WFM for $13.7 billion, making it the company's largest acquisition to date. Mackey has continued to serve as CEO of WFM, and has emphasized the importance of maintaining the company's culture and values under Amazon's ownership.

In addition to his work with WFM, Mackey is involved in several philanthropic initiatives. He is a founding trustee of the Whole Planet Foundation, which provides microcredit loans to entrepreneurs in developing countries, and he has also donated to several other charitable organizations.

Mackey has been recognized with several awards and honors, including being named Ernst & Young's Entrepreneur of the Year in 2003 and the Natural Products Association's Lifetime Achievement Award in 2017.

Overall, John Mackey is a highly influential business leader who has made a significant impact on the food industry and the broader business community through his focus on conscious capitalism, stakeholder well-being, and sustainability.

ANDREW W. MELLON

Was an American financier, businessman, and philanthropist who is widely regarded as one of the most influential entrepreneurs and businessmen of all time. Mellon's innovative mind, work, and tactics enabled him to achieve remarkable success in both the business and political arenas, earning him a place in history as a titan of industry and a visionary leader.

Born in Pittsburgh, Pennsylvania, in 1855, Mellon was the son of Thomas Mellon, a successful lawyer and judge who would later found Mellon Bank. Andrew Mellon attended the Western University of Pennsylvania (now the University of Pittsburgh), where he earned a degree in economics before joining his father's law firm. However, it was in the financial sector where Mellon truly made his mark, eventually becoming one of the wealthiest men in the world.

Mellon's first major business venture was in the coal industry, where he and his brother Richard built a small coal mine into a major operation. Mellon's success in the coal industry led him to expand his business interests into other areas, including oil, steel, and finance. He also played a major role in the development of the aluminum industry, working closely with Charles Martin Hall to develop a more efficient process for producing aluminum.

Mellon's success as a businessman was due in large part to

his innovative mind and his willingness to take risks. He was one of the first entrepreneurs to use leverage as a means of expanding his business, borrowing large sums of money to fund his investments. He was also a strong believer in diversification, investing in a wide range of industries to spread his risk.

Another key element of Mellon's success was his ability to develop and implement effective business tactics. He was known for his meticulous attention to detail, carefully analyzing every aspect of his businesses to identify areas for improvement. He was also a master of financial management, using his knowledge of accounting and finance to make strategic investments and minimize risk.

Mellon's success as a businessman was not limited to his own ventures, however. He also played a major role in the development of the US economy as a whole. In the 1920s, Mellon served as Secretary of the Treasury under President Calvin Coolidge, where he implemented a series of policies designed to stimulate economic growth and promote investment. He was a strong advocate of tax cuts and deregulation, and his policies helped to fuel the economic boom of the 1920s.

Mellon's legacy as a businessman and innovator has endured long after his death in 1937. His work in the financial sector helped to shape the modern banking industry, while his contributions to the aluminum industry paved the way for the development of new technologies and materials. His leadership in government also had a lasting impact on the US economy, laying the groundwork for decades of growth and prosperity.

Andrew W. Mellon's work tactics and business ethic were driven by a combination of innovative thinking, strategic planning, and a relentless focus on efficiency and profitability. He was a meticulous planner and paid close attention to every aspect of his business operations. One of his core business principles was to minimize risk while maximizing return on investment, which he achieved by investing in a diverse range of industries and companies.

Mellon was a strong believer in the power of innovation to drive business growth and success. He recognized the potential of emerging technologies and industries, such as oil, steel, and railroads, and made strategic investments in these sectors to capitalize on their growth potential. He was also a pioneer in the use of financial leverage, using debt financing to expand his business operations and acquire new companies.

Another key aspect of Mellon's business philosophy was his commitment to ethical business practices. He believed that honesty, integrity, and transparency were essential for building strong and lasting relationships with customers, employees, and business partners. Mellon was known for his strict adherence to ethical standards, and he demanded the same from his employees and business associates.

In addition to his focus on innovation and ethics, Mellon was also known for his shrewd negotiating tactics. He was a master of deal-making and was renowned for his ability to strike profitable agreements with other business leaders. He was also skilled at identifying undervalued assets and businesses, and was not afraid to take calculated risks to acquire them.

Mellon's work tactics and business ethic were reflected in his impressive track record of success. He built a vast business empire that spanned multiple industries, including banking, oil, steel, and transportation. He was also a key player in the development of the modern American economy, and his contributions to the growth and expansion of the U.S. economy are still felt today.

The one thing that he did, that an entrepreneur should follow to be great today

One thing that entrepreneurs can learn from Andrew Mellon is the importance of investing for the long-term. Mellon was known for his patient and disciplined approach to investing, and he believed that the key to success in business was to identify companies with strong fundamentals and long-term growth potential.

Today, in the age of instant gratification and short-term thinking, it can be tempting for entrepreneurs to focus on quick wins and immediate returns. However, Mellon's example shows that taking a longer-term view can pay off in the end. By focusing on building sustainable businesses and investing for the long-term, entrepreneurs can create lasting value and have a greater impact on the world around them.

In addition to his focus on long-term investing, Mellon was also a strong advocate for innovation and entrepreneurship. He believed in taking risks and exploring new markets and opportunities. This spirit of entrepreneurship and willingness to take risks is also a valuable lesson for today's entrepreneurs, who must be willing to innovate and take calculated risks in order to succeed in an increasingly competitive business landscape.

A few more things about Andrew Mellon:

Mellon was a prominent banker and financier who played a key role in the development of the modern American financial system. He served as the Secretary of the Treasury under three different presidents: Warren G. Harding, Calvin Coolidge, and Herbert Hoover.

Mellon was a strong proponent of tax cuts as a means of spurring economic growth. He played a key role in the passage of the Revenue Act of 1921, which lowered the top marginal tax rate from 73% to 58%. He also supported the creation of the U.S. Bureau of the Budget, which was designed to improve the efficiency of government spending.

Mellon was a major art collector and philanthropist. He amassed one of the largest private art collections in the world, which included works by Rembrandt, Vermeer, and other Old Masters. He donated much of his collection to the National Gallery of Art in Washington, D.C., which was founded in large part thanks to his efforts.

Mellon was deeply committed to public service and civic engagement. He served as the president of the Carnegie Institute, which was dedicated to promoting education and the arts. He also founded the Mellon Institute of Industrial Research, which was focused on advancing scientific research and technological innovation.

Mellon was a devoted family man who had three children with his wife, Nora Mary McMullen. His daughter, Ailsa Mellon Bruce, carried on his legacy of philanthropy and became a major benefactor of the arts and education.

J.P. MORGAN

is widely regarded as one of the most influential businessmen of all time, having played a key role in the development of the modern financial system and the growth of American industry during the late 19th and early 20th centuries. Born in 1837 in Hartford, Connecticut, Morgan was the son of a successful banker and financier, and he quickly showed an aptitude for finance and business from a young age.

After attending private schools and receiving a degree from the University of Göttingen in Germany, Morgan joined his father's banking firm, J.S. Morgan & Co., in London. There, he quickly gained a reputation as a skilled financier and dealmaker, helping to arrange a number of high-profile mergers and acquisitions that helped to consolidate the banking industry in Europe.

In 1871, Morgan returned to the United States and established his own banking firm, J.P. Morgan & Co., which quickly became one of the most influential financial institutions in the country. Over the next few decades, Morgan would use his position as one of the most powerful bankers in America to shape the course of American industry and finance, playing a key role in the growth of the railroads, steel industry, and other key sectors of the economy.

One of Morgan's key innovations was his use of the

concept of "corporate finance" to fund large-scale projects and acquisitions. Rather than relying solely on the sale of stock or the issuance of bonds, Morgan developed a system of underwriting that allowed his firm to provide large sums of capital to corporations in exchange for a share of their profits. This allowed Morgan to play a key role in financing many of the largest and most successful companies of his time, including General Electric, U.S. Steel, and AT&T.

In addition to his role as a financier, Morgan was also a skilled negotiator and dealmaker, using his influence and connections to help broker many of the most important mergers and acquisitions of his time. Perhaps his most famous deal was the creation of U.S. Steel, which brought together several of the largest steel producers in the country into a single, vertically integrated company that was able to dominate the industry for decades.

Morgan was also a key figure in the development of the modern banking system, helping to establish the Federal Reserve System and serving as a key advisor to several presidents. He was known for his ability to bring together the most powerful figures in business and government to work towards common goals, and he used his influence to shape the course of American history in countless ways.

Despite his many achievements, Morgan was also a controversial figure, with some critics accusing him of using his immense power to manipulate markets and shape the course of American industry in ways that favored his own interests. Nevertheless, his legacy as a pioneer of modern corporate finance and a key figure in the development of the modern financial system is undeniable, and his influence continues to be felt in the world of business and finance to this day.

J.P. Morgan was known for his shrewd business tactics and his ability to make deals that benefited both himself and his clients. One of his key tactics was his use of leverage, both financial and political, to gain an advantage in negotiations. He was known for his ability to use his vast wealth and influence to persuade others to follow his lead, and he was often able to get his way through sheer force of will.

At the same time, Morgan was also a savvy risk manager, and he was not afraid to take calculated risks in pursuit of his goals. He was known for his ability to see the big picture and to identify opportunities that others might overlook, and he was often able to turn a potential crisis into a profitable opportunity through his skillful handling of financial markets and his vast network of contacts.

Despite his reputation as a ruthless businessman, Morgan was also known for his strict adherence to a code of business ethics that emphasized honesty, integrity, and fair dealing. He believed that a reputation for ethical behavior was essential to building long-term relationships with clients and business partners, and he was willing to walk away from deals that he believed were unethical or would damage his reputation.

One example of Morgan's ethical approach to business was his role in the Panic of 1907, a financial crisis that threatened to bring down the entire American financial system. Rather than simply looking out for his own interests, Morgan used his vast wealth and influence to stabilize the markets and prevent a complete collapse of the financial system. He worked closely with other bankers and government officials to provide emergency loans to struggling banks and businesses, and his efforts were credited with helping to prevent a catastrophic economic depression.

Morgan was also known for his philanthropic work, and he used his vast wealth to support a variety of charitable causes. He was a major supporter of the arts, education, and public health, and his donations helped to fund numerous cultural institutions and medical research centers.

In all of his dealings, Morgan emphasized the importance of building strong relationships with his clients and business partners, and he believed that long-term success in business depended on trust and mutual respect. He was known for his ability to listen carefully to the concerns and needs of others, and he was always willing to offer his advice and guidance to those who sought it.

Overall, J.P. Morgan's work tactics and business ethic were characterized by a combination of shrewdness, risk-taking, and ethical behavior. He was a master negotiator who was able to use his vast wealth and influence to get his way, but he also had a strict code of ethics that he believed was essential to building long-term relationships with clients and business partners. His legacy as one of the most influential business minds of all time is a testament to his skill, his vision, and his unwavering commitment to doing business the right way.

The one thing that he did, that an entrepreneur should follow to be great

There are many things that J.P. Morgan did that entrepreneurs can learn from, but if there is one thing that stands out, it is his ability to think long-term and to build strong relationships with his clients and business partners.

Morgan understood that in order to build a successful business, it was important to focus on long-term goals rather than short-term profits. He was willing to take risks and make investments that might not pay off immediately, but that he believed would benefit him and his clients in the long run. This approach allowed him to build a reputation as a trusted advisor who was always looking out for his clients' best interests.

In addition, Morgan was a master at building strong relationships with his clients and business partners. He was known for his ability to listen carefully to their concerns and needs, and to offer his advice and guidance based on his vast experience and knowledge. He believed that trust and mutual respect were essential to building long-term relationships, and he worked hard to earn the trust of everyone he dealt with.

Entrepreneurs today can learn a lot from Morgan's approach. By focusing on long-term goals and building strong relationships with clients and business partners, entrepreneurs can create a foundation for sustainable success that will last for years to come. They can also build a reputation as trusted advisors who are always looking out for their clients' best interests, which can help them attract and retain loyal customers and business partners.

Overall, the one thing that entrepreneurs can learn from J.P. Morgan is the importance of thinking long-term and building strong relationships with clients and business partners. By following these principles, entrepreneurs can create a solid foundation for success that will serve them well for years to come.

A few more things about J.P. Morgan:

Consolidation of the banking industry: One of Morgan's most significant contributions to the business world was his role in consolidating the banking industry. In the late 19th and early 20th centuries, the banking industry in the United States was highly fragmented, with thousands of small banks scattered across the country. Morgan recognized that this fragmentation was inefficient and made it difficult to provide large-scale financing for major projects. He set out to consolidate the industry through a series of mergers and acquisitions, and by the early 1900s, he had become one of the most powerful bankers in the world.

The creation of U.S. Steel: In 1901, Morgan played a key role in the creation of U.S. Steel, which was the first billion-dollar corporation in the world. The company was formed through a merger of several large steel companies, and Morgan helped to negotiate the deal and provide financing for the new company. U.S. Steel quickly became one of the most powerful and influential companies in the world, and it played a major role in the growth of the American economy.

The Panic of 1907: In 1907, the American financial system was on the brink of collapse due to a run on banks and a shortage of cash. Morgan played a key role in stabilizing the markets and preventing a complete economic collapse. He used his vast wealth and influence to provide emergency loans to struggling banks and businesses, and he worked closely with other bankers and government officials to restore confidence in the financial system.

Philanthropy: Throughout his life, Morgan was a generous philanthropist, and he donated large sums of money to support a variety of causes. He was a major supporter of the arts, education, and public health, and his donations helped to fund numerous cultural institutions and medical research centers. His philanthropic legacy lives on today through organizations such as the Morgan Library & Museum in New York City.

Overall, J.P. Morgan was one of the most influential and innovative business minds of his time. His contributions to the banking industry, his role in the creation of U.S. Steel, his efforts to stabilize the markets during the Panic of 1907, and his philanthropy all helped to shape the modern business world and have had a lasting impact on the global economy.

ELON MUSK

is an entrepreneur, inventor, and engineer whose work has transformed the fields of space exploration, electric cars, and renewable energy. He is widely recognized as one of the most innovative and influential business minds of our time, having co-founded and led several successful companies including PayPal, Tesla, SpaceX, and SolarCity.

Musk's innovation mindset can be traced back to his childhood, where he developed a keen interest in science and technology. He was born in South Africa in 1971 and grew up in Pretoria. Musk's father was an engineer, and his mother was a nutritionist and model. Musk showed a strong aptitude for science and technology from an early age and developed a fascination for computers and programming.

After completing his studies in South Africa, Musk moved to the United States to pursue his entrepreneurial ambitions. He enrolled at the University of Pennsylvania, where he earned degrees in physics and economics. While still a student, Musk co-founded his first company, Zip2, which provided online business directories and maps for newspapers.

After selling Zip2 for over $300 million, Musk went on to co-found PayPal, an online payment system that revolutionized the way people conduct financial transactions on the internet. PayPal's success led to its acquisition by eBay in

2002, for $1.5 billion.

Musk then turned his attention to the fields of electric cars, space exploration, and renewable energy. He co-founded Tesla Motors in 2003, which aimed to produce affordable, high-performance electric cars for the mass market. Tesla's electric cars have since become synonymous with sustainability and have helped to reduce the world's reliance on fossil fuels.

Musk also co-founded SpaceX in 2002, with the goal of reducing the cost of space exploration and making it more accessible to the public. SpaceX has since become one of the most successful private space exploration companies in history, having launched several spacecraft and satellites into orbit and successfully landed and reused its rockets.

In addition to his work at Tesla and SpaceX, Musk also co-founded SolarCity, which aimed to make solar energy more affordable and accessible to homeowners. SolarCity became one of the largest solar panel installation companies in the United States and was later acquired by Tesla.

One of the reasons why Elon Musk is considered one of the most influential business minds is his unique approach to business and his relentless pursuit of innovation. Musk has always been willing to take risks and pursue ambitious goals, even when they seem impossible. He has a long-term vision for the future and is willing to invest in and develop new technologies that will transform the way we live and work.

Musk's work at Tesla, SpaceX, and SolarCity has also helped to raise awareness about the urgent need to address climate change and reduce our dependence on fossil fuels. Musk has been a vocal advocate for renewable energy and has used his platform to encourage others to adopt sustainable practices and technologies.

In terms of tactics, Musk is known for his hands-on approach to leadership and his ability to inspire and motivate his employees. He has a reputation for being a demanding boss, but one who is deeply committed to the success of his companies and the vision he has for the future.

Musk's success as a businessman and innovator has not gone unnoticed, and he has received numerous awards and accolades throughout his career. In 2016, he was named one of Time Magazine's 100 Most Influential People, and in 2020, he became the world's richest person, with a net worth of over $200 billion.

In conclusion, Elon Musk is a true visionary whose innovation mindset, work ethic, and tactics have transformed multiple industries and inspired others to pursue ambitious goals. His focus on sustainability and renewable energy has helped to raise awareness about the urgent need to address climate change and reduce our dependence on fossil fuels.

Musk is known for his hands-on approach to leadership and his willingness to get involved in every aspect of his companies' operations. He has a reputation for being a demanding boss who expects nothing but the best from his employees. Musk is also known for his unconventional approach to problem-solving, which often involves challenging the status quo and coming up with creative solutions to complex problems.

One of Musk's most notable work tactics is his focus on vertical integration. Rather than relying on suppliers for key components, Musk has made a concerted effort to bring as much of the production process in-house as possible. This approach allows him to have greater control over the quality and cost of the final product. For example, at Tesla, Musk has invested heavily in the development of battery technology and has built his own battery factory to ensure a reliable supply of batteries for his electric cars.

Musk is also a firm believer in the power of iteration and

continuous improvement. He encourages his employees to take risks and experiment with new ideas, even if they fail. He has famously said, "If things are not failing, you are not innovating enough." Musk sees failure as an opportunity to learn and grow, and he encourages his employees to adopt the same mindset.

In terms of business ethics, Musk has a reputation for being transparent and honest with his customers and investors. He is known for his willingness to admit mistakes and take responsibility for his company's actions. For example, in 2018, Musk apologized to customers for production delays at Tesla and promised to make things right.

Musk is also committed to the idea of creating a better future for humanity. He sees his companies as a means to an end, rather than an end in themselves. He has stated that his goal is to "accelerate the advent of sustainable energy" and "make life multi-planetary." Musk's commitment to sustainability and space exploration has helped to inspire a new generation of entrepreneurs and innovators who share his vision for the future.

Overall, Elon Musk's work tactics and business ethic are characterized by a relentless focus on innovation, a willingness to take risks and experiment with new ideas, and a commitment to transparency and honesty. His unconventional approach to problem-solving and his hands-on approach to leadership have helped him to build some of the most successful companies of our time, and his focus on creating a better future for humanity has inspired millions around the world.

The one thing that he did, that an entrepreneur should follow to be great today

There are many things that Elon Musk has done throughout his career that entrepreneurs can learn from, but if there is one thing that stands out, it is his ability to think big and take bold risks.

Musk has a track record of pursuing audacious goals that others might view as impossible or impractical. For example, he founded SpaceX with the goal of reducing the cost of space travel and eventually making life multi-planetary. He also founded Tesla with the goal of accelerating the world's transition to sustainable energy. These are not small or easily achievable goals, but Musk has pursued them relentlessly, and his companies have achieved remarkable success.

One key lesson that entrepreneurs can learn from Musk is to be willing to take big risks in pursuit of a bold vision. This means having the courage to think beyond the conventional wisdom and pursue goals that others might view as unrealistic or unattainable. It also means being willing to invest significant resources and take calculated risks to make that vision a reality.

Of course, taking big risks also means that there is a higher chance of failure. But Musk has shown that even failures can be valuable learning experiences that can help entrepreneurs refine their vision and strategy. As he has famously said, "Failure is an option here. If things are not failing, you are not innovating enough."

In summary, if there is one thing that entrepreneurs can learn from Elon Musk, it is to be willing to think big and take bold risks in pursuit of a grand vision. This requires a combination of courage, perseverance, and a willingness to learn from both successes and failures.

A few more things you may find interesting about Elon Musk:

Musk was born and raised in South Africa before moving to the United States to attend college. He graduated from the University of Pennsylvania with degrees in physics and economics.

Before founding his own companies, Musk worked at a number of different tech startups, including Zip2 (which he co-founded) and PayPal (which he helped to create through his acquisition of X.com).

Musk is known for working incredibly long hours, often putting in 100-hour workweeks. He has said that he typically works from 8 am to 1 am every day.

In addition to his work with SpaceX and Tesla, Musk is also involved in several other companies and projects, including The Boring Company (which is developing underground tunnels for transportation) and Neuralink (which is working on developing brain-computer interfaces).

Musk has a reputation for being a bit of a maverick in the business world. He has clashed with investors, critics, and regulators at various points in his career, but he has always remained true to his vision and his principles.

Musk has been recognized for his many achievements with numerous awards and honors. He has been named to Time Magazine's list of the 100 most influential people in the world multiple times, and he has received numerous awards for his work in engineering, science, and innovation.

Despite his many successes, Musk has also faced significant challenges and setbacks throughout his career. He has dealt with production delays, technical failures, and other obstacles that would have deterred many other entrepreneurs. But he has always persevered, and he continues to push forward with his vision for a better future.

XAVIER NIEL

is a French entrepreneur and businessman who has made a name for himself in the tech industry. He is the founder of several successful startups, including Free, which revolutionized the French telecommunications industry. He is also an investor and has a significant stake in numerous companies, including French newspaper Le Monde.

Niel was born in Maisons-Alfort, France, in 1967. He grew up in a family of entrepreneurs and got his start in business at a young age. He dropped out of high school at age 18 to start his first company, a value-added service provider for Minitel, France's precursor to the internet. Niel's company quickly gained popularity and was eventually acquired by French telecom giant Matra.

After the sale of his first company, Niel went on to found Worldnet, a company that provided internet access to businesses in France. In 1999, he founded Free, a company that provided low-cost internet and phone services to consumers. Free's innovative business model, which relied on offering low-cost or even free services in exchange for other revenue streams such as advertising, disrupted the French telecommunications industry and made Niel a household name in France.

Niel's success with Free led to his involvement in other

companies, both as an investor and as a founder. He has invested in companies such as ride-sharing platform Uber and French music streaming service Deezer. He has also founded several other startups, including a coding school called 42 and a venture capital firm called Kima Ventures.

Niel's success as an entrepreneur and investor can be attributed to his innovative mindset and willingness to take risks. He has been known to invest in unconventional startups and has a keen eye for identifying disruptive technologies. He is also a vocal advocate for entrepreneurship and has worked to make it easier for startups to launch and succeed in France.

One of Niel's most significant contributions to the tech industry has been his role in making France a hub for tech startups. Through his involvement in 42, a coding school that offers free education to students, and Kima Ventures, which invests in startups, he has helped to cultivate a thriving startup ecosystem in France. This has led to the creation of numerous successful startups, including the French ride-sharing service BlaBlaCar.

Niel's tactics as a businessman have often been controversial, but they have also been effective. He has been known to take a hands-on approach to managing his companies and has been unafraid to make bold moves to achieve success. For example, when Free was struggling to gain a foothold in the French telecommunications market, Niel offered customers free internet access for a year. This move was risky, but it ultimately paid off and helped Free become a major player in the industry.

Overall, Xavier Niel's innovative mindset, willingness to take risks, and hands-on approach to business have made him one of the most influential entrepreneurs and businessmen of all time. His contributions to the tech industry, particularly in France, have been significant, and his tactics as a businessman have set him apart from his peers. Despite his controversial reputation, there is no denying that Niel has made a lasting impact on the business world and will continue to do so for years to come.

One of Niel's most notable work tactics is his willingness to take risks. He is not afraid to invest in unconventional startups or to take bold moves to achieve success. For example, when he founded Free, he decided to offer low-cost or even free services to consumers, which was a risky move given the traditional business models of the telecommunications industry. However, this move ultimately paid off and helped Free become a major player in the industry.

Another work tactic that sets Niel apart is his hands-on approach to managing his companies. He is known to be actively involved in the day-to-day operations of his startups, often working closely with his employees to ensure their success. This level of involvement has been key to the success of many of his companies, including Free and 42.

Niel is also known for his unconventional approach to business. He has a reputation for challenging established business models and disrupting traditional industries. For example, his investment in Uber, a ride-sharing platform that has disrupted the taxi industry, demonstrates his commitment to investing in disruptive technologies.

Niel's business ethics are also noteworthy. He has been known to speak out against unethical business practices and has advocated for greater transparency and accountability in the business world. He is committed to promoting entrepreneurship and making it easier for startups to succeed. This commitment is evident in his involvement with 42, a coding school that offers free education to students, and Kima Ventures, which invests in startups.

Despite his unconventional approach to business and

occasional controversial tactics, Niel is widely respected for his commitment to innovation and his contributions to the tech industry. He has demonstrated that it is possible to disrupt traditional industries and succeed in business without compromising one's ethical standards.

The one thing that he did, that an entrepreneur should follow to be great today

One thing that entrepreneurs today can learn from Xavier Niel is the importance of taking risks and being willing to disrupt traditional industries. Niel has never been afraid to challenge established business models or to invest in unconventional startups. He has demonstrated that by being bold and taking risks, it is possible to achieve significant success in business.

Another key lesson that entrepreneurs can learn from Niel is the value of being hands-on in the day-to-day operations of their companies. Niel is known for being actively involved in his startups, working closely with his employees to ensure their success. This level of involvement can help entrepreneurs to better understand their businesses and to identify areas for improvement.

Finally, entrepreneurs can learn from Niel's commitment to promoting entrepreneurship and making it easier for startups to succeed. His involvement with 42 and Kima Ventures demonstrates his commitment to supporting the next generation of entrepreneurs and to fostering a culture of innovation.

Overall, the key lesson that entrepreneurs can learn from Xavier Niel is the importance of being bold, hands-on, and committed to promoting innovation in the business world. By following his example, entrepreneurs can increase their chances of success and make a positive impact on the industries they operate in.

Some additional details about Xavier Niel:

Philanthropy: In addition to his business ventures, Xavier Niel is also known for his philanthropic work. He has donated millions of euros to charitable causes, including education and entrepreneurship initiatives. He is the founder of the NJJ Foundation, which supports education, cultural initiatives, and social innovation.

Business Ventures: Niel has been involved in several successful business ventures throughout his career. In addition to Free and 42, he is the co-founder of Kima Ventures, which has invested in over 400 startups around the world. He is also the founder of Station F, the world's largest startup campus, located in Paris.

Innovation: Niel is a firm believer in the power of innovation to drive progress and change. He has been involved in several projects that aim to promote innovation, including the creation of Ecole 42, a coding school that offers free education to students. Niel also established the Numa accelerator program, which helps startups to grow and develop.

Political Activism: Niel has been a vocal advocate for political reform in France. He has been critical of the country's traditional political parties and has called for greater transparency and accountability in government. In 2017, he launched a new political movement called "La French Tech" which aims to promote entrepreneurship and innovation in France.

Personal Life: Xavier Niel is a private individual and little is known about his personal life. He has been married twice and has two children. He is known for his love of motorcycles and has participated in several high-profile races, including the Bol d'Or.

Overall, Xavier Niel is a visionary entrepreneur who has made significant contributions to the tech industry and the business world as a whole. His commitment to innovation, hands-on approach to management, and philanthropic work make him a unique and inspiring figure in the world of business.

SIMON NIXON

Is a British entrepreneur who co-founded Moneysupermarket.com, a leading price comparison website that helps customers compare and switch between financial products such as insurance, credit cards, and mortgages. Born on February 18th, 1967 in Chester, Cheshire, Simon grew up in a family of entrepreneurs. His grandfather and father both ran successful businesses in the UK, and Simon followed in their footsteps to become one of the most influential business minds of his generation.

Nixon started his career as a trainee chartered accountant in London, but quickly realized that he was not suited for a career in the financial services industry. He left his job and began exploring various business ideas. In 1993, he co-founded a mail-order business called Nicholson Nixon, which sold compact discs and cassettes through mail-order catalogs. The business was profitable, but Nixon knew that he wanted to do something more innovative.

In 1999, Nixon founded Moneysupermarket.com with his business partner, Duncan Cameron. The idea behind the website was to make it easier for consumers to compare financial products and find the best deals. At the time, the financial services industry in the UK was fragmented and opaque, with customers struggling to compare different products and understand the fees and charges associated with them. Nixon saw an opportunity to disrupt the industry by creating a website that would bring transparency and simplicity to the market.

Moneysupermarket.com quickly became a huge success, with millions of visitors using the website to compare and switch between financial products. The company went public in 2007, and Nixon became a multimillionaire overnight. He remained involved in the business as a non-executive director until 2019, when he sold his remaining shares in the company.

One of the key reasons why Simon Nixon is considered one of the most influential business minds of his generation is his innovative approach to entrepreneurship. He saw a gap in the market and created a business that disrupted an industry that was ripe for change. His focus on simplicity, transparency, and customer empowerment was revolutionary at the time, and it paved the way for other entrepreneurs to create similar businesses in different markets.

Another reason why Nixon is influential is his work ethic and determination. He was not content with building a successful business and resting on his laurels. Instead, he continued to innovate and explore new business ideas, such as his investment in Startups.co.uk, a business support platform for entrepreneurs. He is also an active angel investor, supporting a number of startups in the UK and beyond.

Nixon's tactics as a businessman are also worth examining. He was not afraid to take risks and invest in new ideas, but he also knew when to cut his losses and move on. For example, he sold his stake in Nicholson Nixon when he realized that the business had reached its peak and was unlikely to grow further. He also recognized the potential of the internet early on, and invested heavily in Moneysupermarket.com at a time when many people were skeptical about the viability of online businesses.

In conclusion, Simon Nixon is one of the most influential business minds of his generation due to his innovative approach to entrepreneurship, his work ethic and continuous search for innovation.

One of the key tactics that Simon Nixon employed was his focus on building strong partnerships. He recognized that in order to create a successful price comparison website, he needed to have a wide range of financial products on offer. Therefore, he formed partnerships with various financial providers, such as banks, credit card companies, and insurance providers. These partnerships allowed Moneysupermarket.com to offer a comprehensive range of products to consumers, which in turn helped the company to become a leading player in the price comparison market.

Another tactic that Nixon employed was his focus on data-driven decision-making. He understood the importance of using data to make informed decisions about the direction of the company. Therefore, he invested heavily in data analysis and used this information to identify trends and opportunities in the market. This approach allowed Moneysupermarket.com to continually innovate and improve its services, ensuring that it remained a market leader.

In terms of business ethics, Simon Nixon was known for his transparency and honesty. He believed that trust was essential to building strong relationships with consumers and providers. Therefore, he made sure that all the information on the Moneysupermarket.com website was accurate and up-to-date, and that the company was transparent about its business practices.

Nixon also believed in treating his employees well. He understood that a happy and motivated workforce was essential to the success of the company. Therefore, he created a positive and supportive working environment, offering a range of benefits and opportunities for professional development. This approach helped to attract and retain top talent, which in turn helped to drive the company's success.

In terms of his personal work ethic, Nixon was known for his tenacity and determination. He was willing to take risks and put in long hours to ensure the success of his business ventures. He was also highly focused on his goals and was known for his ability to stay calm under pressure.

Overall, Simon Nixon's work tactics and business ethics were characterized by a focus on building strong partnerships, using data to inform decision-making, transparency and honesty, treating employees well, and a personal work ethic based on tenacity and determination. These factors, combined with his innovative mindset and willingness to take risks, helped to make him one of the most influential business minds of all time.

The one thing that he did, that an entrepreneur should follow to be great today

There are many things that an entrepreneur could learn from Simon Nixon's success, but if I had to pick one thing that he did exceptionally well, it would be his ability to focus on solving a specific problem in a unique and innovative way.

Nixon recognized that there was a problem with the way that financial products were being sold, and he saw an opportunity to create a price comparison website that would make it easier for consumers to compare and choose the best products for their needs. He then focused all his energy and resources on building the best possible solution to this problem, which led to the creation of

Moneysupermarket.com.

As an entrepreneur, it can be tempting to try and solve multiple problems at once or to pursue too many different ideas simultaneously. However, this approach can lead to a lack of focus and dilute your efforts. Instead, it's important to identify a specific problem that you are uniquely positioned to solve, and then focus all your resources and energy on developing the best possible solution to that problem.

So, if there's one thing that an entrepreneur should follow to be great today, it would be to focus on solving a specific problem in a unique and innovative way, just like Simon Nixon did with Moneysupermarket.com.

Some additional things about Simon Nixon that may be of interest:

Nixon co-founded Moneysupermarket.com in 1999 with Duncan Cameron. They started the company in Nixon's bedroom in Chester, UK, with just £100,000 in funding.

Nixon's initial idea for Moneysupermarket.com came after he had trouble finding the best deal for his car insurance. He realized that there was a need for a website that would allow consumers to compare financial products easily and quickly.

Nixon is known for his passion for sports cars and has owned several high-performance vehicles over the years. In fact, he once drove a Lamborghini across Europe to promote Moneysupermarket.com.

In 2017, Nixon sold a 6.5% stake in Moneysupermarket.com for £160 million, but he still retains a significant stake in the company.

Nixon has been recognized for his contributions to the business world with numerous awards, including Entrepreneur of the Year at the 2009 National Business Awards and the Outstanding Contribution to the Industry Award at the 2011 Moneyfacts Awards.

In addition to his work with Moneysupermarket.com, Nixon has also invested in several other businesses, including the property website OnTheMarket.com and the energy comparison website Love Energy Savings.

Nixon is a philanthropist and has donated millions of pounds to charitable causes. He established the Simon Nixon Foundation in 2010 to support education, health, and social welfare projects in the UK and around the world.

These are just a few additional facts about Simon Nixon. Despite his success, he remains relatively private and is known for shying away from the media spotlight.

ALFRED NOBEL

Is an influential figure in the world of business and entrepreneurship due to his innovative and revolutionary work in the fields of science and engineering, which led to the invention of dynamite and other powerful explosives. However, Nobel's contribution to the world was not limited to just the field of science; he was also an astute businessman who understood the importance of innovation, hard work, and strategy.

Nobel was born in Stockholm, Sweden, in 1833, and grew up in a family of engineers and inventors. His father, Immanuel Nobel, was a successful inventor and engineer who had invented several groundbreaking technologies, including the rotary lathe, which made it possible to mass-produce wooden pulleys and gears.

As a young man, Nobel showed an early interest in science and engineering, and he began experimenting with explosives at a young age. In 1867, he invented dynamite, which was a significant breakthrough in the field of explosives. Dynamite was a safer and more reliable explosive than the gunpowder that was commonly used at the time, and it quickly became popular with construction companies, miners, and military organizations around the world.

Nobel's success with dynamite made him a wealthy man, and he used his wealth to fund other innovative projects and ventures. He was a strong believer in research and development, and he invested heavily in scientific research and innovation.

Nobel's business tactics were also innovative and groundbreaking. He was a strong believer in free trade and competition, and he worked hard to make his products affordable and accessible to people around the world. He established manufacturing plants in several countries, including the United States, Germany, and Russia, which helped him to expand his business and reach a global audience.

Nobel was also an early proponent of corporate social responsibility. He believed that businesses had a responsibility to give back to the communities in which they operated, and he established several philanthropic organizations and foundations to support scientific research, education, and social welfare programs.

Despite his many contributions to the world of business and science, Nobel is perhaps best known for his creation of the Nobel Prizes, which he established in his will in 1895. The Nobel Prizes are awarded annually to individuals who have made significant contributions to the fields of physics, chemistry, medicine, literature, and peace.

Nobel's legacy as a businessman and entrepreneur is marked by his innovative spirit, his commitment to research and development, and his strong sense of social responsibility. His work with explosives revolutionized the construction, mining, and military industries, and his business tactics helped to establish the foundations of modern corporate strategy. His philanthropic efforts also helped to promote scientific research, education, and social welfare programs, and his creation of the Nobel Prizes has had a lasting impact on the world of science and academia.

In conclusion, Alfred Nobel was an influential businessman

and entrepreneur whose innovative work in the fields of science and engineering revolutionized the world of explosives and helped to establish the foundations of modern corporate strategy. His commitment to research and development, his business tactics, and his sense of social responsibility have had a lasting impact on the world of business and philanthropy, and his creation of the Nobel Prizes continues to inspire and recognize the achievements of individuals around the world.

n addition to his work in the field of explosives, Alfred Nobel was also involved in several other innovative projects and ventures throughout his life. Here are a few more details about his life and work:

Nobel was a polyglot who spoke several languages fluently, including Swedish, Russian, French, English, and German. This made it easier for him to conduct business in different parts of the world.

In addition to his work with explosives, Nobel also held over 350 patents for other inventions, including synthetic rubber, leather, and artificial silk.

Nobel was deeply interested in literature and the arts, and he wrote poetry and plays in his spare time. He also funded several literary prizes, including the Nobel Prize in Literature.

Nobel was an avid traveler, and he spent much of his life living and working in different parts of the world. He lived in Russia, France, Germany, and Italy, among other countries, and he established manufacturing plants and research facilities in many different locations.

Nobel was a lifelong pacifist who was deeply concerned about the destructive potential of his own inventions. He wrote several essays and articles about the need for disarmament and peace, and he established the Nobel Peace Prize in his will as a way to promote these ideals.

Nobel was known for his frugal lifestyle and his dedication to hard work. He often worked long hours in his laboratories and factories, and he was known to live modestly despite his immense wealth.

Nobel never married or had children, and he was known to be a solitary figure. However, he had many close friends and colleagues, and he was known for his generosity and kindness towards those who worked for him.

Overall, Alfred Nobel was a complex and multifaceted figure who made significant contributions to many different fields throughout his life. His legacy as an inventor, businessman, and philanthropist continues to inspire and influence people around the world today.

The one thing that Nobel did, that an entrepreneur should follow to be great

If there is one thing that entrepreneurs today can learn from Alfred Nobel's life and work, it is the importance of innovation and continuous learning.

Throughout his life, Nobel was constantly seeking out new ideas and pushing the boundaries of what was possible. He was never content to rest on his laurels or simply repeat what had been done before. Instead, he was always looking for ways to improve his products and processes, and he invested heavily in research and development as a way to stay ahead of the competition.

This commitment to innovation is a key trait that has been shared by many of the greatest entrepreneurs in history. From Thomas Edison to Steve Jobs, successful entrepreneurs have always been those who are willing to take risks, experiment with new ideas, and pursue innovation relentlessly.

In today's fast-paced and ever-changing business world, innovation is more important than ever. Entrepreneurs who are able to stay ahead of the curve and adapt to changing market conditions are the ones who are most likely to succeed. This requires a willingness to take risks, embrace failure, and constantly seek out new ideas and opportunities.

So if there is one thing that entrepreneurs today can learn from Alfred Nobel, it is to never stop innovating and learning. By staying curious, pushing boundaries, and seeking out new ideas, entrepreneurs can build the kind of businesses that truly change the world.

A few more interesting facts about Alfred Nobel and his life:

Nobel's father, Immanuel Nobel, was a successful inventor and engineer who played a major role in shaping his son's interest in science and technology.

Nobel's most famous invention, dynamite, was developed in the 1860s as a safer and more stable alternative to existing explosives. It revolutionized the mining and construction industries, and it played a major role in shaping the modern world.

Despite his success with dynamite, Nobel was deeply conflicted about the destructive potential of his invention. He was haunted by the fact that his creation was being used in war and violence, and he was determined to find ways to promote peace and disarmament.

Nobel's interest in promoting peace led him to establish the Nobel Peace Prize in his will. The prize is awarded annually to individuals or organizations who have made significant contributions to promoting peace and international understanding.

In addition to the Nobel Peace Prize, Nobel also established prizes in several other fields, including physics, chemistry, medicine, and literature. These prizes are now known collectively as the Nobel Prizes, and they are widely considered to be the most prestigious awards in their respective fields.

Nobel was a prolific writer and correspondent, and he left behind a large collection of letters, manuscripts, and other documents. These materials provide valuable insights into his life and work, and they continue to be studied by scholars and researchers today.

Nobel was a lifelong bachelor who had few close personal relationships. He was known to be somewhat reclusive and solitary, and he preferred to spend most of his time in his laboratories and factories.

Overall, Alfred Nobel was a complex and fascinating figure who made significant contributions to many different fields throughout his life. His legacy as an inventor, businessman, and philanthropist continues to inspire and influence people around the world today.

ARISTOTLE ONASSIS

1s one of the most prominent figures in the history of entrepreneurship and business. He was a Greek shipping magnate who rose to great heights in the 20th century through his innovative business tactics and a relentless work ethic.

Born in 1906 in Smyrna, Ottoman Empire (now known as Izmir, Turkey), Onassis grew up in a family of merchants and traders. His father, Socrates, was a successful tobacco merchant, and Onassis learned the basics of business from him at an early age. However, tragedy struck when Onassis was only 15 years old when his father died in a car accident. This forced him to leave school and take up his father's business, which he managed to grow significantly.

Onassis was a true innovator in the shipping industry. In the 1930s, he saw an opportunity to transport oil from the Middle East to Europe, which was a relatively new market at the time. He purchased his first oil tanker, the SS Sestos, and began transporting oil from Iran to Europe. He then expanded his fleet to include more tankers, which allowed him to become the largest independent oil tanker owner in the world.

Onassis was known for his relentless work ethic and his ability to take calculated risks. He once said, "The secret of business is to know something that nobody else knows."

He was always looking for ways to gain an edge over his competitors, whether it was by negotiating better deals, finding new markets, or developing new technologies.

Onassis also had a keen understanding of the importance of networking and building relationships. He was a charismatic and charming individual who was able to forge relationships with some of the most powerful people in the world. He became friends with many world leaders, including President John F. Kennedy and Winston Churchill, and he used these relationships to further his business interests.

Another aspect of Onassis's business strategy was his willingness to take on risk. He once said, "To succeed in business, you need a bit of luck and a lot of guts." He was not afraid to take on large-scale projects that others deemed too risky, such as building a pipeline from Saudi Arabia to the Mediterranean, or creating a luxury resort on a small Greek island.

Despite his many successes, Onassis was not without his share of controversies. He was known for his extravagant lifestyle, which included a private island, a luxurious yacht, and a string of high-profile romances. He also faced criticism for his business practices, including allegations of bribery and tax evasion.

Despite these controversies, Onassis is still widely regarded as one of the most influential business minds of all time. He revolutionized the shipping industry and paved the way for the modern oil tanker industry. He was a true innovator who was always looking for ways to gain an edge over his competitors. He was also a master networker and had an uncanny ability to forge relationships with some of the most powerful people in the world. His willingness to take risks and his relentless work ethic are traits that have inspired countless entrepreneurs and businesspeople over the years.

In conclusion, Aristotle Onassis was a true trailblazer in

the world of business. He was an innovator, a risk-taker, and a master networker. His contributions to the shipping industry and the modern oil tanker industry cannot be overstated. Despite his many controversies, he remains an icon in the world of business and an inspiration to entrepreneurs everywhere.

Some more details about his approach to business:

Negotiation Skills: Onassis was a skilled negotiator who could always get the best deal for himself. He was known for his ability to drive a hard bargain, and he would often spend hours negotiating a deal until he was satisfied with the terms. He also had a reputation for being tough but fair, and he was always willing to compromise when it was necessary.

Focus on Cost-Cutting: Onassis was always looking for ways to cut costs and increase profits. He believed that every penny saved was a penny earned, and he would often go to great lengths to reduce expenses. For example, he would buy older ships at a lower cost and then renovate them himself rather than buying new ones.

Risk-Taking: Onassis was never afraid to take risks, and he was always looking for the next big opportunity. He would often invest large sums of money in projects that others deemed too risky, such as building a pipeline from Saudi Arabia to the Mediterranean. He was also willing to take on debt if it meant expanding his business or gaining an advantage over his competitors.

Networking: Onassis was a master networker who understood the importance of building relationships. He was known for his charm and charisma, and he would often host lavish parties on his yacht to entertain his guests. He used these events as an opportunity to build relationships with some of the most powerful people in the world, including politicians, businessmen, and celebrities.

Innovation: Onassis was always looking for ways to innovate

and stay ahead of his competitors. He was one of the first businessmen to recognize the potential of the oil tanker industry, and he invested heavily in this area. He also developed new technologies and techniques to improve the efficiency of his ships and reduce costs.

Hard Work: Onassis was known for his incredible work ethic and his dedication to his business. He would often work 16-hour days, seven days a week, and he expected the same level of commitment from his employees. He once said, "If you want to succeed, you have to be willing to work harder than anyone else."

Attention to Detail: Onassis was a perfectionist who paid attention to even the smallest details. He believed that every aspect of his business was important, and he would often personally oversee every stage of a project to ensure that it was completed to his exacting standards.

Overall, Aristotle Onassis was a brilliant businessman who understood the importance of hard work, innovation, and networking. He was always looking for ways to gain an edge over his competitors, and he was never afraid to take risks if it meant expanding his business. His focus on cost-cutting, attention to detail, and negotiation skills also played a crucial role in his success.

The one thing that he did, that an entrepreneur should follow to be great today

One thing that entrepreneurs can learn from Aristotle Onassis is his willingness to take risks. Onassis was not afraid to take on projects that others deemed too risky, and he was always looking for the next big opportunity. This mindset allowed him to stay ahead of his competitors and to make significant gains in his industry.

In today's business landscape, taking risks can also be a key factor in achieving success. Many of the most successful entrepreneurs today have taken risks, whether it's launching a new product or service, entering a new market, or investing in a new technology. Of course, taking risks also involves careful planning and analysis to minimize the potential downsides.

Entrepreneurs can also learn from Onassis's focus on innovation. By continually looking for new ways to improve his business and stay ahead of the competition, Onassis was able to grow his empire and become one of the most successful businessmen of his time. Today's entrepreneurs should also prioritize innovation, whether it's through the development of new technologies or the creation of unique products or services.

Finally, Onassis's work ethic and attention to detail serve as an example for entrepreneurs today. To achieve success, it's important to work hard and pay attention to even the smallest details. This can mean putting in long hours, taking on challenging projects, and ensuring that every aspect of your business is operating at its best.

In summary, the willingness to take risks, a focus on innovation, and a strong work ethic are all key factors that entrepreneurs can learn from Aristotle Onassis. By following these principles, entrepreneurs can increase their chances of achieving success in their own businesses.

Some additional facts and insights about Aristotle Onassis:

Early Life: Onassis was born on January 15, 1906, in Smyrna, Turkey (now known as Izmir, Turkey). His family was wealthy and had business interests in the shipping industry.

Business Beginnings: Onassis began his career in the shipping industry at a young age, working for his family's business. In 1923, at the age of 17, he moved to Argentina to establish his own business, which included importing tobacco and exporting grain.

Oil Tankers: Onassis recognized the potential of the oil tanker industry early on, and he invested heavily in this area. He acquired his first oil tanker in 1948 and continued to expand his fleet over the next decade. By the 1960s, he was one of the largest oil tanker owners in the world.

Marriage to Jacqueline Kennedy: In 1968, Onassis married former First Lady Jacqueline Kennedy, who was still mourning the loss of her husband, President John F. Kennedy. The couple had a highly publicized relationship and were often photographed together.

Philanthropy: Onassis was known for his philanthropy and donated large sums of money to various causes throughout his life. He established the Alexander S. Onassis Public Benefit Foundation in memory of his son, who died in a plane crash in 1973.

Personal Life: Onassis was known for his extravagant lifestyle, which included owning several yachts, private islands, and homes around the world. He was also a notorious womanizer and had relationships with many famous women, including Maria Callas and Greta Garbo.

Legacy: Onassis is remembered as one of the most successful businessmen of the 20th century. He revolutionized the shipping industry and made significant contributions to the oil tanker industry. His legacy also includes his philanthropic work, which has continued through the Alexander S. Onassis Public Benefit Foundation.

LARRY PAGE

is one of the most influential businessmen and entrepreneurs of our time. He co-founded Google, which has become one of the largest and most powerful companies in the world, and has helped shape the internet as we know it today. In this essay, we will delve into his life and explore his innovation mind, work, and tactics, and why he is considered one of the most influential business minds of all time.

Early Life and Education

Larry Page was born on March 26, 1973, in East Lansing, Michigan, USA. His father, Carl Victor Page Sr., was a computer science professor at Michigan State University, and his mother, Gloria, was a computer programming instructor. From an early age, Page showed an interest in computers and technology, and he was always curious about how things worked. He attended the University of Michigan, where he earned a Bachelor of Science in computer engineering, and later went on to pursue a Ph.D. at Stanford University.

Innovation Mind

One of the key factors that set Page apart from other entrepreneurs is his innovative mindset. Page was always looking for new and better ways to do things, and he was never satisfied with the status quo. His passion for innovation led him to co-found Google with his friend Sergey

Brin in 1998. They wanted to create a search engine that was faster and more accurate than any other search engine on the market. They believed that the key to success was to deliver the best possible user experience, and they focused on developing an algorithm that could deliver the most relevant search results.

Work and Tactics

Page was known for his rigorous work ethic and attention to detail. He was deeply involved in the development of Google's search algorithm, and he was constantly looking for ways to improve it. He also played a key role in the development of Google's business model, which was based on advertising revenue. Page recognized that the more users Google had, the more valuable its advertising platform would be, and he worked tirelessly to expand the company's user base.

One of Page's most significant contributions to Google's success was his emphasis on data-driven decision-making. He believed that the key to making good decisions was to have access to accurate and timely data. He implemented a range of tools and techniques to collect and analyze data, which enabled Google to make more informed decisions about everything from product development to marketing.

Why He is Considered Amongst the Most Influential Business Minds

Page's impact on the business world has been enormous. He co-founded Google, which has become one of the most valuable companies in the world, with a market capitalization of over $1 trillion. He has been a driving force behind some of the most significant technological advancements of our time, including artificial intelligence and self-driving cars. His innovative mindset, rigorous work ethic, and emphasis on data-driven decision-making have set an example for entrepreneurs and business leaders around the world.

In addition to his contributions to the business world, Page has also been a philanthropist and a champion of social causes. He has donated billions of dollars to charity, and he has been a vocal advocate for issues such as climate change and renewable energy.

In conclusion, Larry Page is one of the most influential businessmen and entrepreneurs of our time. His innovative mindset, rigorous work ethic, and emphasis on data-driven decision-making have set an example for entrepreneurs and business leaders around the world. He co-founded Google, which has become one of the largest and most powerful companies in the world, and has helped shape the internet as we know it today. His contributions to the business world, as well as his philanthropy and advocacy for social causes, have made him a role model for future generations of business leaders.

One of Page's most significant contributions to Google's success was his emphasis on data-driven decision-making. He believed that the key to making good decisions was to have access to accurate and timely data. He implemented a range of tools and techniques to collect and analyze data, which enabled Google to make more informed decisions about everything from product development to marketing.

Page was also known for his rigorous work ethic and attention to detail. He was deeply involved in the development of Google's search algorithm, and he was constantly looking for ways to improve it. He would spend hours analyzing data, tweaking algorithms, and testing new approaches. He was not afraid to get his hands dirty and was known to dive into technical details to better understand the intricacies of Google's products and services.

Another tactic Page used to drive Google's success was his focus on user experience. He believed that the key to building a successful business was to provide users with the best possible experience. To achieve this, he pushed for a clean and simple user interface, fast and accurate search results, and an ad-free experience. This emphasis on user experience helped to differentiate Google from its competitors and contributed to the company's rapid growth.

Page was also known for his unconventional approach to business. He was not afraid to take risks and to think outside the box. For example, he introduced a "20% time" policy at Google, which allowed employees to spend 20% of their work time on projects of their choosing. This policy encouraged innovation and creativity and helped to drive many of Google's most successful products, such as Gmail and Google News.

Finally, Page was a firm believer in the power of collaboration. He worked closely with co-founder Sergey Brin to build Google, and he was known for his ability to build strong teams and foster a culture of innovation. He believed that the key to success was to surround oneself with the best people and to give them the freedom and resources to be creative and innovative.

In summary, Larry Page's work tactics and business ethic were characterized by his emphasis on data-driven decision-making, rigorous work ethic, focus on user experience, unconventional approach to business, and belief in the power of collaboration. These tactics and ethic helped him to co-found and lead one of the most successful and influential companies in the world and have made him a role model for future generations of business leaders.

The one thing that he did, that an entrepreneur should follow to be great

If we had to pick just one thing that an entrepreneur could

follow from Larry Page's example to be great today, it would be his focus on user experience.

Page was a strong believer in the idea that building a successful business requires providing users with the best possible experience. He understood that in the digital age, where competition is just a click away, user experience can be the key factor that separates successful companies from those that struggle to gain traction.

To follow Page's example, entrepreneurs should focus on understanding their users' needs and designing products and services that meet those needs in the most effective and efficient way possible. This means investing in user research, testing and refining products based on user feedback, and continually iterating to improve the user experience.

Entrepreneurs should also prioritize simplicity and ease of use. Page famously pushed for a clean and simple user interface at Google, and this approach has since become a hallmark of successful digital products and services. By making it easy for users to find what they need and accomplish their goals, entrepreneurs can build loyalty and create a positive reputation that will help them succeed over the long term.

Finally, entrepreneurs should be willing to take risks and think outside the box. Page was known for his unconventional approach to business, and this willingness to take risks and try new things was a key factor in Google's success. By being open to new ideas and willing to experiment, entrepreneurs can discover new opportunities and create innovative products and services that set them apart from the competition.

Some additional details about Larry Page that you may find interesting:

Larry Page was born on March 26, 1973, in East Lansing, Michigan. His parents were both computer science professors at Michigan State University, which helped to foster his early interest in technology.

Page attended Stanford University, where he earned a bachelor's degree in computer engineering and a master's degree in computer science. While at Stanford, he met Sergey Brin, with whom he would later co-found Google.

In 1998, Page and Brin launched Google from a garage in Menlo Park, California. Initially, Google was just a search engine, but it quickly grew into a company that offered a range of products and services, including email, online advertising, and mobile operating systems.

In addition to his work at Google, Page has been involved in a number of other ventures. He co-founded the X Prize Foundation, which awards cash prizes for breakthroughs in science and technology, and he is an investor in a number of startups, including Tesla and SpaceX.

Page is known for his interest in sustainability and environmental issues. He has invested in a number of renewable energy projects and has advocated for the use of clean energy to reduce carbon emissions and combat climate change.

In 2011, Page became the CEO of Google, taking over from Eric Schmidt. During his tenure as CEO, he oversaw the company's transition to Alphabet, a holding company that oversees Google and a number of other subsidiaries.

In 2019, Page stepped down as CEO of Alphabet, but he remains a member of the company's board of directors. He continues to be involved in a range of philanthropic and entrepreneurial activities, and his influence on the technology industry is widely recognized.

PIERS M. WOLF

SEAN PARKER

is a well-known entrepreneur and businessman who has been involved in numerous innovative companies that have disrupted various industries. He is best known for his involvement in Napster, Facebook, and Spotify, and his innovative mind, work, and tactics have made him one of the most influential business minds of all time.

Sean Parker was born in Virginia in 1979, and he grew up with a passion for computers and technology. He began programming at a young age, and he eventually dropped out of high school to pursue his entrepreneurial ambitions. His first major venture was Napster, a file-sharing service that he co-founded in 1999.

Napster was a revolutionary service that allowed users to share music files online. This was a game-changing innovation in the music industry, as it allowed people to access and share music more easily than ever before. However, Napster was also controversial, as it was accused of facilitating copyright infringement. The company faced legal challenges and was eventually shut down, but it paved the way for other innovative companies in the music industry.

After Napster, Parker became involved with Facebook, a social networking site that was founded in 2004. Parker became the first president of Facebook, and he was instrumental in the company's early growth and success. He helped to build the company's user base and develop its advertising strategy, and he played a key role in the company's eventual IPO in 2012.

Parker's work at Facebook was characterized by his innovative mind and his willingness to take risks. He was not afraid to challenge conventional wisdom and push the boundaries of what was possible. He was also known for his strategic thinking and his ability to see the big picture. He understood the power of social networking and how it could be used to connect people and build communities.

In addition to his work at Facebook, Parker was also involved with other innovative companies, such as Spotify. He became an early investor in Spotify and played a key role in the company's growth and success. Parker saw the potential for streaming music and believed that it could disrupt the traditional music industry. His vision and innovation helped to make Spotify one of the most successful music streaming services in the world.

Parker's success as a businessman and entrepreneur can be attributed to his innovative mind, his strategic thinking, and his willingness to take risks. He was not afraid to challenge conventional wisdom and push the boundaries of what was possible. He also had a deep understanding of technology and how it could be used to disrupt industries and create new opportunities.

Another key factor in Parker's success was his ability to build and maintain relationships. He was known for his charisma and his ability to connect with people, and he used this skill to build strong partnerships and collaborations. He was also a mentor to many young entrepreneurs and was always willing to share his knowledge and experience.

In conclusion, Sean Parker is one of the most influential business minds of all time. His innovative mind, strategic thinking, and willingness to take risks have made him a key player in the tech industry. His work with Napster, Facebook, and Spotify has disrupted multiple industries and paved the way for new opportunities. His ability to build relationships and mentor young entrepreneurs has also had a significant impact on the business world. Parker's legacy as a businessman and entrepreneur will continue to inspire future generations of innovators and disruptors.

Sean Parker's work tactics and business ethics are as important as his innovative mind in understanding why he is considered one of the most influential business minds of all time.

One of Parker's most distinctive work tactics was his ability to identify and capitalize on emerging trends. He has been involved in a number of businesses that have disrupted industries, such as Napster, Facebook, and Spotify. In each case, Parker recognized the potential of a new technology or trend, and he was able to turn it into a successful business. This ability to spot trends early and capitalize on them has been a key factor in Parker's success.

Another key tactic that Parker employed was his willingness to take risks. He was not afraid to challenge conventional wisdom and push the boundaries of what was possible. For example, Napster was a controversial service that was accused of facilitating copyright infringement, but Parker was willing to take the risk and launch the service anyway. Similarly, Parker was one of the early investors in Facebook, and he played a key role in the company's early growth and success. His willingness to take risks and challenge the status quo has been a hallmark of his career.

In addition to his work tactics, Parker is known for his business ethics. He has always been committed to transparency and honesty in his dealings with others. He has been open about his mistakes and shortcomings, and he has used these experiences to learn and grow as a businessperson. He has also been committed to creating businesses that have a positive impact on society. For example, he has been involved in efforts to combat climate change and promote renewable energy.

Parker's business ethic is also reflected in his leadership style. He has been described as a "servant leader" who puts the needs of his team first. He has been known to take a hands-on approach to management, working closely with his teams to understand their needs and help them achieve their goals. He has also been committed to fostering a culture of innovation and collaboration within his companies.

Finally, Parker is known for his ability to build and maintain relationships. He has been able to forge strong partnerships and collaborations throughout his career, and he has been a mentor to many young entrepreneurs. He has also been committed to giving back to the community, and he has been involved in a number of philanthropic efforts.

In summary, Sean Parker's work tactics and business ethic are characterized by his ability to spot trends early, take risks, and lead with transparency and integrity. He has always been committed to creating businesses that have a positive impact on society, and he has been a mentor and collaborator to many young entrepreneurs. These qualities have made him one of the most influential business minds of all time, and his legacy will continue to inspire future generations of innovators and disruptors.

The one thing that he did, that an entrepreneur should follow to be great today

It is difficult to point to just one thing that an entrepreneur should follow to be great today, as success in entrepreneurship often involves a combination of factors. However, one key takeaway from Sean Parker's success as an entrepreneur is his ability to identify and capitalize on emerging trends.

To be great as an entrepreneur today, it is important to be able to stay ahead of the curve and identify new opportunities before they become mainstream. This requires a deep understanding of your industry and a willingness to take calculated risks. By studying trends and being open to new ideas, you can position yourself to be at the forefront of innovation and disruption.

Another important lesson from Parker's success is his ability to build strong relationships and collaborations. In today's highly interconnected and fast-moving business world, it is essential to be able to forge partnerships and work collaboratively with others. By building a strong network of colleagues, partners, and mentors, you can tap into a wealth of knowledge and expertise that can help you navigate the challenges of entrepreneurship.

Finally, it is important to have a strong sense of purpose and commitment to making a positive impact on society. As Parker has demonstrated throughout his career, a focus on social responsibility can help to attract customers, partners, and employees who share your values and vision for the future.

In summary, to be a great entrepreneur today, it is important to stay ahead of the curve, build strong relationships and collaborations, and have a strong sense of purpose and commitment to social responsibility. By following these principles and taking inspiration from the success of entrepreneurs like Sean Parker, you can position yourself for success in today's ever-changing business landscape.

Some additional details about Sean Parker:

Sean Parker was born on December 3, 1979, in Virginia, USA.

He grew up in a middle-class family and showed an early interest in computers and programming.

Parker dropped out of high school and moved to California at the age of 16 to pursue his interests in technology. He eventually landed a job at a startup called Plaxo, where he worked as a software engineer.

Parker is best known for his role in co-founding Napster, a peer-to-peer file sharing service that revolutionized the music industry. Napster was launched in 1999 and quickly gained popularity, but it was also the subject of a high-profile lawsuit by the music industry that ultimately led to its demise.

After Napster, Parker went on to become an early investor in Facebook, where he played a key role in the company's early growth and success. He served as the company's first president and helped to shape its strategy and vision.

Parker has also been involved in a number of other successful startups, including Plaxo, Causes, and Airtime. He has been known for his ability to identify and capitalize on emerging trends, as well as his willingness to take risks and challenge conventional wisdom.

In addition to his work in technology, Parker is also known for his philanthropic efforts. He has been involved in a number of initiatives to promote environmental conservation and combat climate change, including the Parker Foundation, which he founded in 2015.

Parker has been married twice and has two children. He is known for his flamboyant style and has been described as a "party boy" by the media. However, he has also been praised for his creativity and vision as an entrepreneur, as well as his commitment to social responsibility.

KEVIN PLANK

is a prominent figure in the business world, known for founding Under Armour, a popular sportswear brand. His innovative mindset, tireless work ethic, and strategic tactics have helped him become one of the most influential business minds of our time.

Kevin Plank was born on August 13, 1972, in Kensington, Maryland. He attended the University of Maryland, where he played football and became frustrated with the way cotton T-shirts would become soaked with sweat during games. This sparked his idea for a moisture-wicking athletic shirt that would keep athletes dry and comfortable. In 1996, Plank founded Under Armour, with this concept at the forefront of his vision.

Plank's innovative mind was evident in the development of Under Armour. He took a material typically used for women's lingerie and adapted it for his moisture-wicking shirt. He also spent countless hours experimenting with different fabrics and designs until he found the perfect combination for his product. Plank's ability to take a simple idea and turn it into a successful business is a testament to his creativity and innovation.

However, it wasn't just Plank's innovative mind that led to the success of Under Armour. He also had a tireless work ethic that allowed him to put his ideas into action. He spent countless hours researching and developing his product, often sleeping in his car and using credit cards to finance his business. His determination and perseverance paid off when his product gained popularity among athletes and sports enthusiasts.

Plank also employed strategic tactics to grow his business. He focused on building relationships with athletes and coaches to gain endorsements and generate buzz about his product. He also targeted specific sports, such as football and lacrosse, where his product could make a significant impact. Plank's ability to identify his target market and develop a strategic marketing plan helped him establish Under Armour as a leading sportswear brand.

Under Plank's leadership, Under Armour went public in 2005, and the company has since expanded its product line to include footwear, accessories, and women's apparel. Today, Under Armour is a global brand with a market value of over $10 billion.

So why would Kevin Plank be considered amongst the most influential business minds? Firstly, his innovation mindset allowed him to develop a unique and game-changing product that revolutionized the sportswear industry. Secondly, his tireless work ethic and determination to succeed enabled him to turn his idea into a successful business. And finally, his strategic tactics in marketing and product development helped him grow his business into a global brand.

Plank's impact on the business world extends beyond Under Armour. He has also been an advocate for entrepreneurship and small businesses, serving as a member of the President's Advisory Council on Doing Business in Africa and as a member of the Board of Trustees of the University of Maryland College Park Foundation. He has also invested in and supported numerous startups and entrepreneurs, providing guidance and resources to help them succeed.

In conclusion, Kevin Plank is a prime example of a successful entrepreneur and businessman. His innovation mindset, tireless work ethic, and strategic tactics have allowed him to build a global brand that revolutionized the sportswear industry. His impact extends beyond his own business and has inspired countless entrepreneurs and startups. For these reasons, he is rightfully considered amongst the most influential business minds of all time.

Kevin Plank's work tactics and business ethics were instrumental in his success as an entrepreneur and businessman. Here are some additional details about how he approached his work and built his business:

Focus on Product Development: Plank's focus on product development was a key factor in Under Armour's success. He spent years researching and developing his moisture-wicking shirt, experimenting with different fabrics and designs until he found the perfect combination. Plank's attention to detail and commitment to creating a high-quality product helped him establish Under Armour as a leading sportswear brand.

Marketing Strategy: Plank's marketing strategy was also critical in building Under Armour's brand. He targeted specific sports where his product could make a significant impact, such as football and lacrosse. Plank also focused on building relationships with athletes and coaches to gain endorsements and generate buzz about his product. His targeted approach to marketing helped him establish Under Armour as a brand for serious athletes and sports enthusiasts.

Customer-centric approach: Plank also had a customer-centric approach to his business. He understood that athletes needed high-performance clothing that would allow them to perform at their best, and he focused on meeting those needs. Plank was always listening to feedback from his customers and making improvements to his products based on their suggestions. This approach helped him build a loyal customer base that trusted and relied on Under Armour's products.

Team building: Plank also understood the importance of building a strong team to support his business. He surrounded himself with talented individuals who shared his vision and values. He hired experts in product development, marketing, and finance, and empowered them to take ownership of their areas of expertise. Plank also fostered a culture of collaboration and creativity, encouraging his team to share ideas and work together to achieve the company's goals.

Strategic Partnerships: Plank's strategic partnerships were also instrumental in building Under Armour's brand. He partnered with high-profile sports teams, such as Notre Dame and Auburn, to gain exposure for his brand. He also partnered with retailers, such as Dick's Sporting Goods and Foot Locker, to expand Under Armour's reach and distribution channels. Plank's ability to identify and cultivate strategic partnerships helped him build a strong and recognizable brand.

Ethical Business Practices: Finally, Plank's ethical business practices were a key factor in his success. He always put his customers first, prioritizing their needs and satisfaction over profits. He also prioritized the well-being of his employees, offering competitive salaries and benefits and fostering a positive and inclusive workplace culture. Plank's commitment to ethical business practices helped him build a reputation as a responsible and trustworthy business leader.

Overall, Kevin Plank's work tactics and business ethics were characterized by a focus on product development, targeted marketing, customer-centric approach, team building, strategic partnerships, and ethical business practices. These strategies helped him build Under Armour into a global brand and establish himself as one of the most influential business minds of our time.

The one thing that he did, that an entrepreneur should follow to be great today

If I had to choose one thing that Kevin Plank did exceptionally well and that entrepreneurs today could follow to be great, it would be his relentless focus on innovation and product development.

Plank's success with Under Armour was largely due to his ability to identify a gap in the market and create a product that addressed a specific need. He recognized that athletes needed high-performance clothing that would keep them dry and comfortable during intense physical activity, and he spent years developing a product that would meet those needs.

To be great as an entrepreneur today, it's essential to have a similar focus on innovation and product development. Identify a problem that needs to be solved or a need that's not being met, and then work tirelessly to create a product or service that addresses that need in a unique and valuable way.

This approach requires a combination of creativity, perseverance, and a willingness to take risks. It also requires a deep understanding of your target market and their needs and preferences. By focusing on innovation and product development, entrepreneurs can create products and services that stand out in a crowded marketplace, build a loyal customer base, and establish themselves as leaders in their field.

Some additional details about Kevin Plank that you may find interesting:

Early Life: Kevin Plank was born in Maryland in 1972. He grew up playing football and wrestling and went on to play football at the University of Maryland.

Under Armour: Plank founded Under Armour in 1996, while he was still a student at the University of Maryland. The company started with a single moisture-wicking shirt, which Plank developed after noticing that his cotton shirts became heavy and uncomfortable when he sweated during football practice. Under Armour has since grown into a global brand that offers a wide range of sportswear and accessories.

Philanthropy: Plank is also known for his philanthropic work. He has donated millions of dollars to various causes, including cancer research and education. He also founded the Cupid Foundation, which supports programs and organizations that promote health and wellness.

Business Ventures: In addition to Under Armour, Plank has also been involved in other business ventures. He founded Sagamore Ventures, a venture capital firm that invests in early-stage companies. He also owns Sagamore Farm, a thoroughbred horse racing and breeding operation.

Leadership Style: Plank's leadership style is characterized by his vision, determination, and commitment to excellence. He is known for his focus on innovation and product development, as well as his ability to build strong teams and foster a culture of collaboration and creativity. Plank is also a strong believer in the importance of hard work, discipline, and perseverance.

Controversies: Plank has faced some controversies during his career, including allegations of sexual harassment and a lawsuit over trademark infringement. However, he has also been praised for his handling of these situations, including his public apologies and efforts to improve company culture.

Overall, Kevin Plank is a complex figure who has made a significant impact on the business world through his innovative approach to sportswear and his commitment to philanthropy and community building.

FRANCOIS HENRI PINAULT

is one of the most influential business minds of our time. He is the CEO and Chairman of Kering, a global luxury group that includes several well-known luxury brands such as Gucci, Yves Saint Laurent, and Bottega Veneta. He is also the founder of Artemis, a holding company that owns several major companies including Christie's auction house, and is involved in various other ventures. Pinault's innovative mind, strategic work, and tactical approach have made him one of the most successful businessmen of all time.

Pinault's business career began at the age of 23 when he joined his father's company, Pinault-Printemps-Redoute (PPR), a retail conglomerate that specialized in department stores, home furnishings, and catalog sales. Under his leadership, PPR underwent a transformation from a traditional retail company to a global luxury group, with a focus on high-end brands. Pinault's vision and innovative ideas were the driving force behind this transformation.

One of Pinault's most significant contributions to the business world is his ability to identify and acquire innovative brands. He has a reputation for recognizing the potential of new and emerging brands, and investing in them early on. For example, in 1999, Pinault acquired a majority stake in Gucci, a struggling Italian luxury brand. Pinault recognized the potential of Gucci's then-unknown designer Tom Ford, and under Pinault's leadership, the brand was transformed into a global luxury powerhouse. This acquisition and Pinault's strategic guidance of the brand paved the way for Kering's future success.

Pinault's innovative mind is also evident in his approach to sustainability. He recognized early on that sustainability was becoming a crucial issue in the fashion industry and took action to address it. Kering was the first luxury group to publish an environmental profit and loss account, which measures the environmental impact of the company's operations. Pinault has also championed sustainable practices within the company's brands and has encouraged them to adopt more sustainable methods of production.

Pinault's tactical approach to business is also noteworthy. He is known for his meticulous attention to detail and his ability to make difficult decisions. He is not afraid to make bold moves, such as divesting non-core businesses and focusing on luxury brands, even when it may not be the popular choice. His strategic vision and tactical approach have resulted in Kering's success as a global luxury powerhouse.

Pinault's work and tactics have not only been successful but have also set a precedent for other business leaders. His approach to sustainability has inspired other luxury brands to follow suit and adopt sustainable practices. His focus on acquiring innovative brands early on has become a model for other companies looking to expand their portfolio. His strategic and tactical approach to business has also been studied by business students and scholars, who look to him as an example of successful leadership.

In conclusion, Francois Henri Pinault's innovative mind, strategic work, and tactical approach have made him one of the most influential business minds of all time. His ability to identify and acquire innovative brands, his focus on sustainability, and his meticulous attention to detail have set a precedent for other business leaders. His contributions to the luxury industry have transformed it and made Kering a global powerhouse. It is without a doubt that Francois Henri Pinault deserves a place amongst the 100 most influential entrepreneurs and businessmen of all time.

Francois Henri Pinault's work tactics and business ethic are characterized by his attention to detail, strategic vision, and ethical leadership.

Attention to Detail:

Pinault is known for his meticulous attention to detail in all aspects of his business operations. He is known to thoroughly research and analyze each investment opportunity, and he pays close attention to the smallest details in every decision. His attention to detail has allowed him to make informed and strategic decisions that have resulted in the success of his business ventures.

Strategic Vision:

Pinault's strategic vision has been a key factor in his success. He is known for his ability to identify emerging trends in the luxury market and to position his businesses accordingly. He has a keen eye for talent and has been instrumental in the success of many designers and creative directors who have worked under his leadership. Pinault has also been able to leverage his company's success to acquire other innovative brands, further expanding his business empire.

Ethical Leadership:

Pinault is a strong proponent of ethical leadership and has incorporated this into his business operations. He is committed to sustainability and has championed sustainable practices within his company. He has also been a vocal advocate for corporate social responsibility, emphasizing the importance of giving back to communities and promoting diversity and inclusion within his company.

Pinault's business ethic is guided by his belief that business success should not come at the expense of social and environmental responsibility. He has demonstrated a commitment to sustainability and ethical practices, leading by example and inspiring others in the industry to follow suit.

One example of Pinault's ethical leadership is Kering's Environmental Profit and Loss (EP&L) report. Kering was the first luxury group to publish an EP&L report, which measures the environmental impact of the company's operations. This report is an important step in the fashion industry's efforts to address sustainability issues and has become a model for other companies to follow.

In addition to his commitment to sustainability, Pinault has also emphasized the importance of corporate social responsibility. He has made significant contributions to various philanthropic causes, including environmental conservation and disaster relief efforts. He has also championed diversity and inclusion within his company, promoting a culture of acceptance and equality.

Overall, Francois Henri Pinault's work tactics and business ethic are characterized by his attention to detail, strategic vision, and ethical leadership. His commitment to sustainability, corporate social responsibility, and ethical practices has set a precedent for other business leaders to follow, making him an influential figure in the business world.

The one thing that he did, that an entrepreneur should

follow to be great today

One thing that entrepreneurs can learn from Francois Henri Pinault is the importance of having a clear and long-term strategic vision. Pinault's success as a businessman can be attributed to his ability to identify emerging trends in the luxury market and to position his businesses accordingly. He has been able to make bold and strategic investments, such as the acquisition of Gucci in 1999, which has helped his company to become one of the world's leading luxury goods conglomerates.

Entrepreneurs today should focus on developing a clear and long-term strategic vision for their business. This involves staying informed about industry trends, identifying emerging opportunities, and taking calculated risks to position their business for long-term success. By having a clear vision, entrepreneurs can make informed and strategic decisions that align with their overall goals and objectives.

Another important aspect of Pinault's success is his commitment to ethical leadership and sustainability. In today's business climate, consumers are increasingly interested in supporting companies that prioritize ethical and sustainable practices. Entrepreneurs should take note of this and make sure that their business practices align with these values. By prioritizing ethical leadership and sustainability, entrepreneurs can build a loyal customer base and distinguish themselves from competitors.

Overall, the lesson that entrepreneurs can learn from Francois Henri Pinault is the importance of having a clear and long-term strategic vision and a commitment to ethical leadership and sustainability. By focusing on these principles, entrepreneurs can position their businesses for long-term success while also making a positive impact on society and the environment.

Some additional facts about Francois Henri Pinault:

Early Life and Education:

Francois Henri Pinault was born on May 28, 1962, in Rennes, France. He is the son of Francois Pinault, who founded Pinault SA, the holding company that eventually became Kering. Pinault attended the HEC Paris business school, where he studied economics and management.

Career: After completing his education, Pinault joined his father's company and worked his way up the ranks. In 1987, he became the CEO of Pinault SA, and in 1990, he took over as Chairman of the Board. Under his leadership, the company grew rapidly and expanded into new markets.

In 1999, Pinault orchestrated the acquisition of Gucci, which was struggling at the time. This move helped Pinault SA to become one of the world's leading luxury goods conglomerates, and the company eventually changed its name to Kering in 2013.

Today, Kering owns several luxury brands, including Gucci, Saint Laurent, Bottega Veneta, Balenciaga, and Alexander McQueen.

Personal Life:

Pinault is married to actress Salma Hayek, and the couple has a daughter together. Pinault also has two children from a previous marriage. In addition to his business and personal pursuits, Pinault is an avid art collector and is known for his support of contemporary artists.

Philanthropy:

Pinault is committed to philanthropy and has made significant contributions to various causes. He established the Kering Foundation in 2009, which is dedicated to combating violence against women. He has also been a supporter of environmental conservation efforts and disaster relief efforts, donating millions of dollars to various organizations over the years.

In 2019, Pinault pledged 100 million euros to help rebuild the Notre-Dame Cathedral in Paris after it was damaged in a fire. The donation was the largest individual contribution to the restoration effort.

Overall, Francois Henri Pinault is a prominent businessman and philanthropist who has made significant contributions to the luxury goods industry and beyond. His leadership and commitment to ethical practices have set a standard for other business leaders to follow, and his philanthropic efforts have had a positive impact on society and the environment.

MARJORIE MERRIWEATHER POST

Was a pioneering businesswoman who built a vast fortune in the food industry and was also known for her philanthropic activities. Born on March 15, 1887, in Springfield, Illinois, Post was the only child of Ella Letitia Merriweather and C. W. Post, the founder of Post Cereals.

After her father's death in 1914, Post inherited a significant portion of his estate, including his company, Postum Cereal Company. Post was only 27 years old when she inherited the company, and she quickly began to reshape it. One of the first things she did was to rename it to General Foods Corporation. This move allowed her to expand the company's product lines and eventually become one of the largest food companies in the world.

Post was not afraid to take risks in her business ventures. She invested in new technologies, such as the electric toaster, and introduced products that had not been seen before, such as Minute Tapioca and Jell-O. She also understood the importance of marketing and advertising, and she was one of the first to use radio commercials to promote her products.

Post's business acumen was not limited to the food industry. She also invested in other industries, such as real estate and aviation. In 1935, she became the first woman in the United States to own a private jet, a Lockheed Vega. She used this plane to travel to her various properties and business ventures.

Post was a shrewd negotiator and was known for her ability to strike deals. She acquired several prestigious properties, such as the Mar-a-Lago estate in Palm Beach, Florida, which she purchased for $100,000 in 1933. She also bought the Hutton House in Washington D.C., which she later donated to the government to be used as the official residence of the Vice President.

Post was not only focused on building her business empire; she was also a philanthropist who gave generously to charity. She donated millions of dollars to various causes, including medical research and education. In 1955, she established the Marjorie Merriweather Post Foundation, which continues to support charitable causes to this day.

Post's legacy as a businesswoman and innovator is significant. She was a trailblazer for women in business, and her success in a male-dominated industry paved the way for future generations of female entrepreneurs. Her risk-taking, innovation, and negotiation tactics were ahead of her time, and her philanthropic efforts have had a lasting impact on society.

In conclusion, Marjorie Merriweather Post was a woman ahead of her time. Her innovative mind, risk-taking tactics, and philanthropic efforts have made her one of the most influential business minds of all time. She was a trailblazer for women in business, and her legacy continues to inspire future generations of entrepreneurs.

Marjorie Merriweather Post was known for her strong work

ethic and business tactics that set her apart from other entrepreneurs of her time.

First and foremost, Post was a savvy negotiator. She had a keen eye for identifying undervalued assets and was not afraid to negotiate aggressively to secure them. For example, she purchased the Mar-a-Lago estate in Palm Beach, Florida, for a fraction of its original asking price, thanks to her shrewd negotiation skills.

Post was also an innovator who was always looking for new and better ways to do things. She invested in new technologies and was quick to adopt new marketing and advertising techniques. For example, she was one of the first to use radio commercials to promote her products, recognizing the potential of this emerging medium.

One of Post's most significant strengths was her ability to spot opportunities and take calculated risks. She was not afraid to invest in new ventures, such as aviation and real estate, and was always looking for ways to expand her business empire. This willingness to take risks helped her stay ahead of the competition and maintain her position as one of the most influential business minds of her time.

Post was also known for her attention to detail and her strong work ethic. She was involved in all aspects of her business, from product development to marketing and sales. She was a hands-on leader who believed in leading by example and was never afraid to get her hands dirty.

Finally, Post was a philanthropist who believed in giving back to society. She donated millions of dollars to various charitable causes throughout her life, including medical research, education, and the arts. She established the Marjorie Merriweather Post Foundation in 1955, which continues to support charitable causes to this day.

In summary, Marjorie Merriweather Post's work tactics and business ethics were characterized by her strong negotiation skills, innovative mindset, willingness to take risks, attention to detail, and dedication to philanthropy. These qualities set her apart from other entrepreneurs of her time and have helped cement her legacy as one of the most influential business minds in history.

The one thing that she did, that an entrepreneur should follow to be great today

Marjorie Merriweather Post's success as an entrepreneur was the result of many factors, but if there is one thing that entrepreneurs today can learn from her, it is her willingness to take calculated risks.

Post was not afraid to invest in new ventures and try out new ideas. She recognized that innovation was key to staying ahead of the competition and that taking calculated risks was necessary to achieve success. For example, she invested in new technologies like the electric toaster and introduced new products like Minute Tapioca and Jell-O.

Today's entrepreneurs can learn from Post's example by being willing to take calculated risks in their own businesses. This means doing thorough research and analysis before making a decision, but also being willing to take action and try out new ideas. Taking calculated risks can help entrepreneurs discover new opportunities and stay ahead of the competition in an ever-changing business landscape.

Another important lesson that entrepreneurs can learn from Post is the importance of hard work and attention to detail. Post was involved in all aspects of her business, from product development to marketing and sales. She believed in leading by example and was never afraid to get her hands dirty. Entrepreneurs who are willing to put in the hard work and attention to detail necessary to achieve success are more likely to achieve their goals.

In summary, the one thing that entrepreneurs can learn from Marjorie Merriweather Post is to be willing to take calculated risks. By doing so, they can discover new opportunities and stay ahead of the competition. Additionally, they can follow her example of hard work and attention to detail to ensure that they are putting in the effort necessary to achieve success.

Some additional interesting facts about Marjorie Merriweather Post:

Post was the daughter of C.W. Post, the founder of Post Cereals. When her father died in 1914, she inherited the company and became one of the wealthiest women in the world at the time.

Despite her wealth, Post was known for her humility and down-to-earth demeanor. She was often described as warm, approachable, and gracious.

Post was an avid art collector and amassed an impressive collection of paintings, sculptures, and other artworks over her lifetime. She donated her collection to the Smithsonian Institution, and it now forms the core of the museum's American Art collection.

Post was a trailblazer in the aviation industry and helped establish the first transcontinental air mail service in the United States. She was a pilot herself and used her personal plane to transport mail and other goods.

Post was also a pioneer in the field of frozen foods. She recognized the potential of frozen foods early on and helped popularize them by introducing products like Minute Tapioca and frozen dinners.

In addition to her business ventures, Post was deeply committed to philanthropy. She donated millions of dollars to various charitable causes throughout her life and established the Marjorie Merriweather Post Foundation to continue her philanthropic work after her death.

Overall, Marjorie Merriweather Post was a fascinating and accomplished individual who made significant contributions to the worlds of business, aviation, and the arts. Her legacy continues to inspire entrepreneurs and philanthropists today.

SUMNER REDSTONE

born Sumner Murray Rothstein, was a businessman and media magnate who was widely considered one of the most influential figures in the entertainment industry. He was born on May 27, 1923, in Boston, Massachusetts, to a Jewish family of Ukrainian and Russian descent. He began his business career as a lawyer before transitioning to the media industry, where he would make his mark as an innovator and leader.

Redstone's innovative mindset was evident from a young age. He graduated from Harvard University in 1944 and went on to earn a law degree from Harvard Law School in 1947. He initially worked as a law clerk and later as an attorney in Washington, D.C. before joining his father's theater chain, National Amusements, in 1954. Redstone quickly rose through the ranks at National Amusements, eventually becoming CEO in 1967.

Under Redstone's leadership, National Amusements expanded its reach and began acquiring a number of media companies, including Viacom, CBS, and Paramount Pictures. He was known for his shrewd negotiating tactics and his ability to identify undervalued assets. For example, in 1993, Redstone purchased a controlling stake in Viacom for $3.4 billion. At the time, Viacom was seen as a struggling company, but Redstone saw its potential and was able to turn it into a major media conglomerate.

Redstone was also an early proponent of the digital revolution and recognized the potential of the internet to transform the media industry. In 1995, he launched the first online movie rental service, MovieLink, which allowed users to download movies and watch them on their computers. While the service was ahead of its time and ultimately unsuccessful, it demonstrated Redstone's willingness to take risks and his foresight in identifying emerging trends.

One of Redstone's most notable achievements was his role in the creation of the modern movie theater experience. In the 1960s, he recognized that the traditional theater model, which relied on showing a single movie for an extended period, was becoming outdated. He began experimenting with the concept of "multiplex" theaters, which showed multiple movies simultaneously, and introduced stadium-style seating, which provided better views for moviegoers. These innovations helped to modernize the movie industry and are still in use today.

Redstone was also known for his tenacity and his unwillingness to back down from a fight. In 1987, he engaged in a bitter legal battle with his own family over control of National Amusements, which resulted in him being ousted from the company. However, he ultimately prevailed and regained control of the company in 1999. This episode demonstrated Redstone's determination and his willingness to fight for what he believed was right.

Overall, Sumner Redstone's life as a businessman was marked by his innovative mindset, his willingness to take risks, and his tenacity. He was able to identify undervalued assets and turn struggling companies into major players in the media industry. He was also a pioneer in the digital revolution and played a key role in modernizing the movie theater experience. While he was not without his controversies, his impact on the entertainment industry cannot be denied. He was truly one of the most influential business minds of his time.

Redstone was known for being a tough negotiator and a shrewd businessman. He had a reputation for being aggressive in his business dealings and was not afraid to take risks. He believed in the power of hard work and was known for putting in long hours and dedicating himself fully to his business pursuits.

One of Redstone's key business tactics was his ability to identify undervalued assets and turn them into profitable businesses. For example, when he acquired Viacom in 1993, the company was struggling and was undervalued by many investors. However, Redstone recognized its potential and was able to turn it into a major media conglomerate through a series of strategic acquisitions and investments.

Redstone was also known for his focus on innovation and his willingness to embrace new technologies and business models. He recognized the potential of the internet early on and was an early proponent of online movie rentals, launching the service MovieLink in 1995. He was also a pioneer in the development of multiplex theaters and introduced stadium-style seating to improve the movie-going experience.

In terms of business ethics, Redstone was known for his strong sense of loyalty and his commitment to his employees. He believed in treating people fairly and with respect, and he was known for being generous with his employees. For example, he would often give bonuses and stock options to employees who had been with his company for many years.

However, Redstone was also known for being a demanding boss and could be difficult to work for at times. He had high expectations for his employees and was not afraid to let them know when he was unhappy with their work. He also had a reputation for being quick to anger and could be ruthless in his pursuit of business success.

Overall, Sumner Redstone was a complex figure who combined a focus on innovation and risk-taking with a strong work ethic and a commitment to treating people fairly. While he could be difficult to work for at times, his impact on the media industry was significant, and he will be remembered as one of the most influential business minds of his time.

The one thing that he did, that an entrepreneur should follow to be great today

There are several things that Sumner Redstone did that entrepreneurs today could learn from. However, if I had to choose one thing that entrepreneurs should follow to be great today, it would be his ability to think outside the box and identify undervalued assets.

Redstone was known for his ability to see the potential in companies and assets that others had overlooked. He was not afraid to take risks and was willing to invest in companies that others considered to be too risky or undervalued. For example, when he acquired MTV in the 1980s, many people thought that the idea of a 24-hour music channel was crazy. However, Redstone recognized the potential of the channel and was able to turn it into a major success.

Today, there are many opportunities for entrepreneurs to identify undervalued assets and turn them into successful businesses. This could involve anything from developing a new technology to identifying an untapped market niche. By thinking outside the box and being willing to take calculated risks, entrepreneurs can follow in Redstone's footsteps and build successful businesses that have a significant impact on their industries.

A few more interesting facts about Sumner Redstone:

Redstone was born on May 27, 1923, in Boston, Massachusetts, and grew up in a Jewish family. His real name was Sumner Murray Rothstein, but he changed it to Redstone in 1940.

Redstone was a highly educated individual, earning a Bachelor of Arts degree from Harvard University in 1944 and a Bachelor of Laws degree from Harvard Law School in 1947.

Redstone's career in the media industry began in 1954 when he took over his father's drive-in movie theater business. He later expanded the business by building new theaters and acquiring other theater chains.

In 1987, Redstone acquired a controlling stake in Viacom, a media company that owned MTV, Nickelodeon, and Paramount Pictures. He later acquired CBS in 1999, creating a media conglomerate with a combined market value of over $80 billion.

Redstone was known for his love of fitness and exercise. He was an avid tennis player and practiced yoga daily.

Redstone was also known for his philanthropic activities, donating millions of dollars to various charities and organizations throughout his life. In 2003, he donated $18 million to the Boston University School of Law, which was later renamed in his honor as the Sumner M. Redstone Law School.In the 1950s, Redstone started a chain of drive-in movie theaters with his father-in-law, which eventually grew into National Amusements, a major cinema and media company.

In addition to Viacom, which he acquired in 1993, Redstone also owned CBS, Paramount Pictures, and a number of other media companies.

Redstone was involved in several high-profile legal battles over the years, including a dispute with his daughter Shari Redstone over control of his media empire.

In his later years, Redstone became increasingly reclusive and rarely made public appearances. He passed away in 2020 at the age of 97.

Despite his wealth and success, Redstone was known for his frugal lifestyle and was often seen driving himself to work in an old car.

Redstone was a major philanthropist and donated millions of dollars to various causes over the course of his life. He was particularly interested in supporting education and medical research.

JOHN D. ROCKEFELLER

Was born in 1839 in New York, and he was the second of six children. His father, William Rockefeller, was a businessman who owned a wholesale food business. Rockefeller grew up in a modest household and his family struggled financially. However, he displayed a strong work ethic from a young age and was determined to improve his circumstances.

Rockefeller's entrepreneurial spirit was evident from an early age. When he was just 16 years old, he began working as an assistant bookkeeper for a local produce commission merchant. He quickly demonstrated an aptitude for business and was promoted to bookkeeper after just six months. Within a year, he had saved up $50 (which was a considerable amount of money at the time) and decided to start his own business.

In 1859, Rockefeller went into partnership with a local businessman named Maurice Clark to create a wholesale produce firm called Clark & Rockefeller. The partnership was successful, and the two men soon expanded their business to include the shipping of grain and other commodities. In 1862, Rockefeller bought out his partner and became the sole owner of the firm, which he renamed Rockefeller & Andrews.

Rockefeller's real breakthrough came in the 1870s, when he began to focus on the oil industry. At the time, the oil industry was highly fragmented, with many small-scale producers and refiners operating independently. Rockefeller recognized that there was an opportunity to consolidate the industry and create a more efficient, profitable business model.

To achieve this goal, Rockefeller employed a number of innovative business tactics. Firstly, he built an extensive network of pipelines and railroads that allowed him to transport oil from the fields to his refineries and then to market. This gave him a significant cost advantage over his competitors, who had to rely on expensive transportation methods such as horse-drawn wagons.

Secondly, Rockefeller invested heavily in research and development, working to improve the efficiency of his refineries and develop new products such as gasoline. He also implemented strict cost controls throughout his business, focusing on maximizing efficiency and minimizing waste.

Perhaps most controversially, Rockefeller also engaged in a strategy known as "vertical integration". This involved buying up other companies at every stage of the oil production process, from the oil fields to the refineries to the marketing and distribution channels. By controlling every aspect of the industry, Rockefeller was able to exert significant control over the market and eliminate competition.

Rockefeller's tactics were highly successful, and he quickly became one of the wealthiest men in America. However, his business practices were also highly controversial, and he faced significant criticism for his ruthless tactics and alleged monopolistic behavior.

Despite this, Rockefeller's legacy as an innovator and business leader is undeniable. His focus on efficiency, cost control, and vertical integration helped to transform the oil industry and lay the foundations for the modern business landscape. His impact on the American economy and global business community has been profound, and he remains a significant figure in business history to this day.

In conclusion, John D. Rockefeller's life as a businessman was defined by his innovative mind, hard work, and tactics. He recognized the opportunity to consolidate the fragmented oil industry and create a more efficient, profitable business model. Through the use of pipelines and railroads, vertical integration, and strict cost controls, he transformed the oil industry and became one of the wealthiest men in America. Despite the controversies surrounding his business practices, Rockefeller's legacy as an influential business mind and innovator is undeniable, and his impact on the global business community continues to be felt today.

One of the key tactics that Rockefeller employed throughout his business career was a focus on efficiency and cost control. He was known for his attention to detail and his willingness to scrutinize every aspect of his business in order to identify areas where costs could be reduced. For example, he implemented strict accounting practices and closely monitored the performance of every department in his company.

Rockefeller was also a strong believer in the importance of research and development. He invested heavily in developing new products and improving the efficiency of his refineries. He also hired top scientists and engineers to work on projects aimed at increasing productivity and reducing waste.

Another key aspect of Rockefeller's business approach was his commitment to vertical integration. This involved acquiring companies at every stage of the oil production process, from exploration and drilling to refining and marketing. By controlling every aspect of the industry,

Rockefeller was able to eliminate competition and maximize his profits.

However, Rockefeller's business practices were not without controversy. Many critics accused him of engaging in monopolistic behavior and using his wealth and power to crush smaller competitors. His business practices were eventually investigated by the government, and in 1911, the U.S. Supreme Court ruled that his company, Standard Oil, was in violation of antitrust laws and ordered it to be broken up into smaller companies.

Despite these controversies, Rockefeller was known for his strong sense of business ethics. He believed in the importance of hard work, honesty, and fair dealing. He was a staunch advocate of philanthropy and donated vast sums of money to charitable causes throughout his life.

Rockefeller was also a strong believer in the importance of education. He founded the University of Chicago in 1890, which quickly became one of the leading research institutions in the United States. He also established the Rockefeller Institute for Medical Research (now known as Rockefeller University), which was dedicated to advancing medical knowledge and developing new treatments for diseases.

In summary, John D. Rockefeller's work tactics and business ethics were defined by his focus on efficiency, research and development, vertical integration, and a commitment to hard work, honesty, and fair dealing. Although his business practices were controversial, his impact on the global business community and his contributions to philanthropy and education have earned him a place among the most influential business minds of all time.

The one thing that he did,

that an entrepreneur should follow to be great

One thing that modern-day entrepreneurs could learn from John D. Rockefeller is the importance of strategic thinking and a long-term vision. Rockefeller was able to build his oil empire by thinking strategically and focusing on the big picture.

For example, he recognized early on that the oil industry was going to be a major player in the global economy, and he worked tirelessly to build his business around that vision. He also saw the value in controlling every aspect of the oil production process, from exploration and drilling to refining and marketing, and he pursued a strategy of vertical integration to achieve this goal.

Rockefeller's success was not just due to hard work and persistence, but also to his ability to think strategically and plan for the future. Today's entrepreneurs can learn from his example by developing a long-term vision for their businesses and thinking strategically about how to achieve their goals. This may involve investing in research and development, focusing on efficiency and cost control, and pursuing a strategy of vertical integration or other forms of business consolidation.

Ultimately, the key lesson that modern-day entrepreneurs can take from Rockefeller's success is the importance of strategic thinking and a long-term vision. By focusing on these principles, entrepreneurs can build successful businesses that stand the test of time and have a lasting impact on the world.

Some additional facts about John D. Rockefeller that may be of interest:

He was born into a modest family in upstate New York in 1839. His father was a traveling salesman and was frequently away from home, leaving Rockefeller and his siblings to be raised by their mother.

Rockefeller's first job was as an assistant bookkeeper in a Cleveland firm. He worked his way up to become a partner in the company, and then left to start his own business.

Rockefeller's first venture was in the produce industry, but he soon shifted his focus to the emerging oil industry. He formed the Standard Oil Company of Ohio in 1870 and quickly began acquiring other oil companies.

By the 1880s, Rockefeller had become the richest man in America and one of the wealthiest people in the world. His personal fortune was estimated to be worth more than $1 billion at the time of his death in 1937.

In addition to his business ventures, Rockefeller was also a philanthropist. He donated millions of dollars to various causes, including education, medical research, and the arts. He also established the Rockefeller Foundation, which continues to fund research and social programs around the world.

Despite his immense wealth, Rockefeller was known for his frugal lifestyle. He was often seen wearing simple, modest clothing and preferred to live in modest homes rather than extravagant mansions.

Rockefeller was a devout Baptist and believed strongly in the importance of giving back to the community. He once said, "I believe that every right implies a responsibility; every opportunity, an obligation; every possession, a duty."

Overall, John D. Rockefeller was a complex figure who made a significant impact on the worlds of business and philanthropy. Despite his controversial business practices, his contributions to the oil industry and his philanthropic work continue to be felt to this day.

ANITA RODDICK

Was a British businesswoman who founded The Body Shop, a cosmetics and personal care company that revolutionized the industry with its ethical and environmentally friendly approach. Roddick was born in 1942 in Littlehampton, England, and grew up in a family that valued social activism and entrepreneurship.

In the early 1970s, Roddick and her husband Gordon opened a small shop in Brighton, England, selling natural skincare products and cosmetics that they sourced from around the world. The shop was an instant success, and soon the couple had opened additional locations in London and other parts of the UK.

What set The Body Shop apart from other cosmetics companies of the time was its commitment to ethical and sustainable business practices. Roddick was passionate about environmentalism, animal rights, and fair trade, and she integrated these values into every aspect of her company. For example, The Body Shop was one of the first cosmetics companies to prohibit animal testing, and it sourced ingredients from sustainable and fair trade suppliers.

Roddick's innovative approach to business was not limited to her company's ethical practices, however. She was also a marketing genius, and she understood the importance of branding and storytelling in building a successful business.

The Body Shop's products were packaged in distinctive, eco-friendly containers, and they were marketed with clever and memorable slogans, such as "There are three billion women in the world who don't look like supermodels and only eight who do."

Roddick's entrepreneurial spirit and innovative tactics helped to make The Body Shop a global success. By the 1990s, the company had hundreds of stores in dozens of countries, and it was valued at billions of dollars. Roddick was widely recognized as one of the most influential businesspeople of her time, and she was awarded numerous honors for her achievements, including an OBE (Order of the British Empire) and a Damehood.

So why would Anita Roddick be considered amongst the most influential business minds of all time? Firstly, her commitment to ethical and sustainable business practices set a precedent for future generations of entrepreneurs. She demonstrated that it was possible to build a successful business while also making a positive impact on the world.

Secondly, Roddick's innovative marketing and branding tactics showed that a company's success is not just about the quality of its products, but also about the stories it tells and the values it embodies. She understood that consumers are increasingly drawn to companies that share their values and beliefs, and she was able to build a loyal following by appealing to this desire.

Finally, Roddick's success as a woman in a male-dominated industry was groundbreaking. She showed that women could be just as successful and innovative as men, and she inspired countless women around the world to pursue their entrepreneurial dreams.

In conclusion, Anita Roddick was an innovative and influential businesswoman whose commitment to ethical and sustainable business practices, innovative marketing tactics, and trailblazing leadership have earned her a place among the most influential business minds of all time. Her legacy continues to inspire and influence entrepreneurs around the world, and she will always be remembered as a visionary leader who changed the cosmetics industry and set an example for others to follow.

One of the key tactics that Roddick used in building The Body Shop was her focus on creating a distinctive brand identity. She believed that branding was critical to the success of any business, and she worked tirelessly to create a brand that was instantly recognizable and memorable. To do this, she drew on her passion for environmentalism, animal rights, and fair trade, and made these values the core of The Body Shop's brand identity. She also used striking and eco-friendly packaging and clever slogans to differentiate her products from those of other cosmetics companies.

Another important tactic that Roddick used was her emphasis on customer engagement. She believed that the best way to build a loyal customer base was to create a personal connection with each customer, and she encouraged her employees to engage with customers on a personal level. For example, she insisted that all of The Body Shop's products be displayed in open containers, so that customers could smell and sample them, and she encouraged her employees to share their personal experiences with the products and the company's values.

Roddick was also known for her commitment to ethical and sustainable business practices. She believed that a company's success should not come at the expense of the environment or of the people who produce its products. To this end, she made sure that The Body Shop's products were sourced from sustainable and fair trade suppliers, and she was one of the first cosmetics companies to prohibit animal testing. She also established The Body Shop Foundation, which supports charitable causes around the world.

In addition to her commitment to ethical and sustainable business practices, Roddick was also known for her leadership style. She was a hands-on leader who was deeply involved in every aspect of her company's operations, from product development to marketing to store design. She was also a strong advocate for her employees, and she believed that empowering her employees was critical to the success of her company. She encouraged her employees to share their ideas and opinions, and she created a culture of openness and transparency.

Overall, Anita Roddick's work tactics and business ethics were characterized by her commitment to creating a distinctive brand identity, engaging with her customers on a personal level, and prioritizing ethical and sustainable business practices. Her leadership style was hands-on, and she believed in empowering her employees and creating a culture of openness and transparency. These tactics and ethics were key to the success of The Body Shop and have had a lasting impact on the cosmetics industry and on the business world as a whole.

The one thing that she did, that an entrepreneur should follow to be great today

There are many things that Anita Roddick did as an entrepreneur that are worth emulating, but if I had to highlight just one thing that entrepreneurs today could learn from her, it would be her commitment to creating a brand with a strong purpose.

Anita Roddick recognized early on that consumers were looking for more than just a product when they shopped. They wanted to support companies that shared their values and that had a positive impact on the world. This led her to build The Body Shop around a clear purpose: to create high-quality, ethically-sourced beauty products that did not harm the environment or animals.

Roddick's commitment to purpose-driven branding was ahead of its time. Today, many successful companies are built around a strong sense of purpose, and studies have shown that purpose-driven brands tend to outperform their competitors. Customers are more likely to be loyal to brands that stand for something and that are working to make the world a better place.

Entrepreneurs today can learn from Roddick's example by focusing on building a brand with a strong purpose that resonates with customers. This means identifying a clear mission or set of values that your company stands for and making sure that everything you do is aligned with that mission. It also means being transparent and authentic about your purpose, and using it as a guiding principle for all of your business decisions.

In summary, Anita Roddick's commitment to purpose-driven branding is a lesson that entrepreneurs today can learn from. By building a brand with a strong sense of purpose, entrepreneurs can create a loyal customer base, differentiate themselves from their competitors, and make a positive impact on the world.

Some additional things about Anita Roddick that may be of interest:

Roddick was a pioneer in using her business as a platform for social activism. She believed that businesses had a responsibility to use their resources and influence to advocate for social and environmental causes. This led her to take public stances on issues such as animal testing, human rights, and environmental protection.

Roddick was a prolific writer and public speaker. She wrote several books, including "Business As Unusual" and "Take It Personally," which shared her experiences as an entrepreneur and her views on business and social activism. She also gave numerous speeches and interviews throughout her career, and was known for her frank and opinionated style.

Roddick's business success allowed her to pursue her philanthropic interests. She was a passionate advocate for human rights, environmental protection, and social justice, and used her resources to support numerous causes and organizations. In addition to founding The Body Shop Foundation, she was involved with organizations such as Amnesty International and Friends of the Earth.

Roddick was a lifelong learner who was always curious and eager to explore new ideas. She traveled extensively, and was known for her interest in different cultures and traditions. She also had a keen interest in science, and was an early supporter of alternative medicine and natural health remedies.

Roddick's impact on the cosmetics industry was significant. She helped to popularize the use of natural and ethically-sourced ingredients in cosmetics, and raised awareness about the environmental and social impacts of the cosmetics industry. Her legacy can be seen in the growing popularity of natural and organic beauty products, as well as in the increasing focus on sustainability and ethical sourcing in the cosmetics industry.

MEYER AMSCHEL ROTHSCHILD

born on February 23, 1744, was a German Jewish banker who is widely regarded as one of the most influential businessmen of all time. He was the founder of the Rothschild banking dynasty, which became one of the wealthiest and most powerful families in Europe during the 19th century.

Meyer Amschel Rothschild was born in the Jewish ghetto of Frankfurt, Germany. His father was a moneychanger, and Meyer Amschel learned the trade from him at a young age. He was a talented businessman, and by the time he was 19, he had already established a successful business in the textile trade.

Rothschild was not content with merely running a successful business, however. He had a vision of creating a powerful banking dynasty that would span across Europe. To achieve this goal, he began to develop innovative business strategies and tactics that would allow him to expand his business rapidly.

One of Rothschild's most significant innovations was his use of courier networks. He recognized that information was key to successful banking, and he set up a network of couriers who could carry messages and information quickly and securely across Europe. This allowed Rothschild to be one step ahead of his competitors, as he was able to gather information about market conditions and political events before anyone else.

Another key innovation that Rothschild introduced was the use of bonds. At the time, government bonds were not widely used as an investment vehicle. Rothschild recognized the potential of these bonds, however, and began to invest heavily in them. This allowed him to build up a vast fortune, as governments across Europe began to borrow money from him.

Rothschild also recognized the importance of strategic partnerships and alliances. He formed close relationships with other wealthy families and banking dynasties across Europe, which allowed him to access new markets and expand his business quickly. This network of alliances would become a critical factor in the success of the Rothschild banking dynasty.

Perhaps Rothschild's greatest strength as a businessman was his ability to adapt to changing circumstances. He recognized that the world was constantly changing, and he was always looking for new opportunities to grow his business. When the Napoleonic Wars broke out in Europe, for example, Rothschild quickly recognized the potential of funding both sides of the conflict. He was able to use his courier network to gain information about the war's progress and make strategic investments that would maximize his profits.

Rothschild's business tactics and strategies were not without controversy, however. Some accused him of being overly secretive and manipulative. There were also rumors that he had exploited his insider knowledge of the Battle of Waterloo to make a fortune. Despite these criticisms, however, there is no doubt that Rothschild was a highly innovative and influential businessman.

In conclusion, Meyer Amschel Rothschild was one of the most influential businessmen of all time. He was a highly innovative thinker who introduced many new strategies and tactics to the world of banking. His use of courier networks, investment in bonds, and strategic partnerships helped him to build a vast fortune and establish one of the most powerful banking dynasties in history. While his tactics were not without controversy, there is no doubt that his legacy as a business innovator will endure for generations to come.

Rothschild was born into a large family, and he was the fourth of eight children. His parents were both from prominent Jewish families in the Frankfurt ghetto, and they were involved in the money-changing business.

At the age of 13, Rothschild was sent to Hanover to train with a bank. He spent five years there, learning the ins and outs of banking and finance. After his training, he returned to Frankfurt to work with his father in the family business.

Rothschild was a savvy businessman from a young age. In addition to his work in the family business, he also began to trade in rare coins and antiques. He quickly established himself as a successful dealer, and his reputation as a shrewd businessman began to spread.

One of Rothschild's most significant early successes came during the French Revolutionary Wars. He was able to use his courier network to transport gold from England to Austria, where it was desperately needed to fund the war effort. This successful transaction helped to establish Rothschild's reputation as a reliable and trustworthy banker.

As Rothschild's wealth and influence grew, he began to invest heavily in real estate. He purchased several properties in Frankfurt and began to accumulate large tracts of land in other parts of Europe. His real estate holdings would eventually become one of the largest and most valuable parts of the Rothschild family's portfolio.

Despite his great wealth, Rothschild was known for his frugal habits. He was said to be incredibly careful with his money, and he was always looking for ways to save and invest. This frugality helped him to weather the many financial crises that occurred during his lifetime.

Rothschild was also known for his philanthropic work. He donated large sums of money to Jewish charities and helped to establish a number of Jewish institutions in Frankfurt. He was a strong advocate for Jewish rights and worked tirelessly to promote the interests of his community.

In addition to his success in business, Rothschild was also a devoted family man. He married his wife, Gutle Schnapper, in 1770, and they had 10 children together. Rothschild was known for his close relationships with his children, and he took great pride in their accomplishments.

Overall, Meyer Amschel Rothschild was a complex and fascinating figure. He was a highly successful businessman, a shrewd investor, and a philanthropist who was deeply committed to his community. His innovations in banking and finance helped to shape the modern world, and his legacy continues to inspire generations of entrepreneurs and investors.

The one thing that Rothschild did, that an entrepreneur should follow to be great

There are many things that an entrepreneur could learn from Meyer Amschel Rothschild's life and work. However, one of the most important lessons that could be taken from his experience is the importance of building a strong network.

Throughout his life, Rothschild was known for his extensive

network of contacts and his ability to cultivate relationships with people from all walks of life. He recognized that building a strong network was key to his success as a businessman, and he worked tirelessly to establish connections with influential people in the financial world.

Rothschild's network was built on trust, reputation, and a commitment to mutual benefit. He understood that by building relationships with other successful individuals, he could create opportunities for himself and his family.

For entrepreneurs today, the importance of building a strong network cannot be overstated. In today's hyper-connected world, networking is essential for anyone looking to succeed in business. By cultivating relationships with other entrepreneurs, investors, and industry leaders, an entrepreneur can gain access to new opportunities, ideas, and resources.

However, building a strong network is not just about making connections for the sake of it. Like Rothschild, successful entrepreneurs today need to focus on building relationships based on trust, mutual respect, and a commitment to creating value for all parties involved. By doing so, they can build a network that will help them achieve their goals and overcome the many challenges that come with starting and running a successful business.

Some more things about Rothschild

One of the key innovations that Rothschild introduced to the world of finance was the use of courier networks. In the early 19th century, communication between different parts of Europe was slow and unreliable. Rothschild recognized that by establishing a network of trusted couriers, he could get information and make transactions faster and more securely than his competitors.

Rothschild was also known for his ability to manage risk. He was always looking for ways to minimize his exposure to potential losses, and he was never afraid to take bold steps to protect his investments. For example, during the Napoleonic Wars, Rothschild was able to protect his wealth by spreading his investments across different countries and assets.

In addition to his success in finance, Rothschild was also known for his cultural interests. He was a patron of the arts, and he collected rare books, manuscripts, and other treasures. He was also a great lover of music, and he often hosted concerts and other cultural events in his home.

Despite his great wealth and success, Rothschild remained committed to his Jewish faith and his community. He was a major supporter of Jewish charities and institutions, and he was a strong advocate for Jewish rights. He used his wealth and influence to help promote the welfare of his fellow Jews, and he remained committed to this cause throughout his life.

Finally, it's worth noting that Rothschild's legacy extends far beyond his own lifetime. His five sons, who all went on to become successful bankers in their own right, helped to establish the Rothschild family as one of the most powerful and influential banking dynasties in Europe. Today, the Rothschild family continues to be one of the wealthiest and most influential families in the world, with interests in finance, industry, and philanthropy.

CHARLES SAATCHI

is a British businessman and art collector, born on June 9, 1943, in Baghdad, Iraq. He is known for co-founding Saatchi & Saatchi, one of the world's largest advertising agencies. He is also recognized as one of the most influential art collectors of contemporary art in the world. Saatchi has an exceptional ability to identify and nurture artistic talent, which has made him a prominent figure in the art world.

Saatchi began his career in advertising in the 1960s, working for different agencies before teaming up with his younger brother, Maurice Saatchi, to establish Saatchi & Saatchi in 1970. The company rapidly grew, and by the 1980s, it was one of the most successful advertising agencies in the world, with clients such as British Airways, Procter & Gamble, and Mars Inc. The Saatchi brothers revolutionized the advertising industry by creating advertisements that were not only memorable but also entertaining and thought-provoking. Their approach was to make people think and engage with their ads, rather than just trying to sell a product.

However, in 1995, Charles Saatchi was ousted from Saatchi & Saatchi, following disagreements with the company's board of directors. But, instead of dwelling on the setback, Saatchi turned his focus to the art world. In the late 1980s, he began collecting contemporary art, and by the 1990s, he had established himself as a prominent art collector, with a particular interest in British art. His collection included works by Damien Hirst, Tracey Emin, and Marc Quinn, among others.

Saatchi's approach to collecting art was as innovative as his advertising strategies. He was known for discovering unknown artists and promoting them, providing them with a platform to showcase their work. For instance, in 1997, he launched the Sensation exhibition at the Royal Academy of Arts in London, which featured the works of the Young British Artists, a group of emerging artists he had discovered. The exhibition was highly controversial, with some works being criticized for their provocative and explicit nature. However, it was also highly successful, attracting over 300,000 visitors.

Saatchi's influence in the art world extends beyond his personal collection and exhibitions. In 2010, he launched the Saatchi Gallery, a contemporary art museum in London that showcases emerging artists from around the world. The museum is known for its innovative approach to exhibiting art, with exhibitions being curated around themes rather than by artist or style. The Saatchi Gallery has been instrumental in promoting new artists and introducing them to a wider audience.

In conclusion, Charles Saatchi's contribution to the advertising and art worlds has been significant, and his innovative approach to both fields has been groundbreaking. His ability to identify and promote talent has made him one of the most influential business minds of all time. Whether in advertising or art, Saatchi's approach has always been to challenge the status quo and to push boundaries. His legacy will undoubtedly continue to inspire future generations of entrepreneurs and artists.

Charles Saatchi is known for his unconventional business tactics and work ethic, which have contributed to his success in both the advertising and art industries.

One of Saatchi's key business tactics is his ability to identify and nurture talent. In advertising, he was known for hiring creatives who were not necessarily experienced in the industry but had the potential to be great. He believed that having a diverse team with different backgrounds and perspectives was essential in creating innovative and successful campaigns.

Similarly, in the art world, Saatchi was known for discovering unknown artists and promoting their work. He had a keen eye for talent and was willing to take risks on emerging artists who had not yet been established in the art world. His willingness to take chances on these artists often paid off, with many of them going on to achieve great success.

Saatchi's work ethic was also notable. He was known for being a hard worker who was always willing to put in the time and effort required to achieve success. He was also known for being very hands-on in his work, whether it was in advertising or art. In advertising, he would often personally review and edit ad copy and creative concepts, while in the art world, he would personally curate his exhibitions.

Another aspect of Saatchi's business ethic was his willingness to take risks and try new things. He was not afraid to challenge the status quo and push boundaries, which led to some of his most successful campaigns and exhibitions. For example, the Sensation exhibition, which he curated in 1997, was highly controversial and received criticism for featuring provocative and explicit works. However, Saatchi stood by his decision to showcase the works, believing that they were important in challenging traditional ideas about art.

Overall, Charles Saatchi's unconventional tactics,

willingness to take risks, and strong work ethic have contributed to his success in both advertising and the art world. His ability to identify and nurture talent, combined with his willingness to challenge the status quo, has made him one of the most influential business minds of all time.

The one thing that he did, that an entrepreneur should follow to be great today

There are many things that entrepreneurs can learn from Charles Saatchi's business career. However, one thing that stands out is his ability to identify and promote talent.

In both advertising and the art world, Saatchi had a knack for identifying individuals who had the potential to be successful and providing them with the support and platform they needed to achieve their goals. This approach helped him build successful businesses and cultivate a reputation as one of the most influential business minds of all time.

To follow in Saatchi's footsteps, entrepreneurs today should focus on identifying and promoting talent within their organizations. This could involve hiring individuals who may not have traditional qualifications but show potential for success, as well as providing opportunities for growth and development within the company. By doing so, entrepreneurs can build a strong team that is capable of driving innovation and achieving success.

Additionally, entrepreneurs should be willing to take risks and challenge the status quo, as Saatchi did throughout his career. This may involve pushing boundaries and trying new things, even if they are controversial or unconventional. By doing so, entrepreneurs can differentiate themselves from their competitors and create a unique brand identity that resonates with consumers.

Ultimately, Charles Saatchi's success can be attributed to his ability to identify and promote talent, as well as his willingness to take risks and challenge traditional ideas. By following in his footsteps and embracing these principles, entrepreneurs can increase their chances of achieving success in today's competitive business landscape.

Some additional interesting facts about Charles Saatchi:

Saatchi co-founded the advertising agency Saatchi & Saatchi with his brother, Maurice, in 1970. The agency went on to become one of the largest and most successful in the world, creating campaigns for major brands such as Procter & Gamble and British Airways.

In 1985, Saatchi & Saatchi acquired the U.S. agency Ted Bates Worldwide, making it the largest advertising agency in the world at the time.

Saatchi is known for his extensive collection of contemporary art, which includes works by Damien Hirst, Tracey Emin, and Jeff Koons. He has been a major influence on the contemporary art world, both through his collection and his exhibitions.

Saatchi is also known for his work as a publisher, having founded the publishing house Quadrille Publishing in 1994. The company has published a wide range of books, including cookbooks, art books, and lifestyle books.

Saatchi has been a controversial figure throughout his career, particularly in the art world. His Sensation exhibition, which showcased works by the Young British Artists, was criticized for featuring provocative and explicit works. He has also been involved in numerous legal disputes over the ownership and authenticity of artworks.

In 2013, Saatchi and his then-wife, Nigella Lawson, made headlines when he was photographed with his hands around her neck at a restaurant. The incident led to their divorce and a public backlash against Saatchi.

Despite his controversial reputation, Saatchi remains a respected figure in the art and business worlds, and his influence can still be seen today. His innovative approach to advertising and his ability to identify and promote talent have made him one of the most influential business minds of all time.

HOWARD SCHULTZ

is an American businessman and entrepreneur who is widely recognized for his transformative work as the CEO of Starbucks Corporation, a global coffeehouse chain. He was born in Brooklyn, New York, on July 19, 1953, and grew up in a working-class family in the Canarsie neighborhood. Schultz's family struggled financially, and he learned the value of hard work and determination from a young age.

Schultz attended Northern Michigan University on a football scholarship, where he earned a degree in Communications. After graduation, he began his career in sales at Xerox Corporation, where he quickly rose through the ranks and became one of the top salespeople in the company. However, Schultz's passion for coffee and his desire to create a new kind of coffee experience led him to leave Xerox and join Starbucks in 1982.

At the time, Starbucks was a small coffee roaster and retailer based in Seattle, Washington. Schultz was immediately struck by the quality of the coffee and the company's commitment to creating a unique customer experience. However, he also saw room for improvement and innovation. Schultz was particularly interested in the Italian espresso bars he had seen during a business trip to Milan, where coffee was not just a drink, but a social and cultural experience.

Schultz convinced Starbucks' founders to start serving espresso drinks, and he quickly became the company's top marketing executive. However, in 1985, Schultz left Starbucks to start his own coffee business, Il Giornale. Il Giornale was a success, and in 1987, Schultz purchased Starbucks from its founders and merged the two companies.

Under Schultz's leadership, Starbucks grew rapidly, opening new stores across the United States and around the world. Schultz's innovative approach to coffee retailing, which included creating a warm and welcoming atmosphere, offering high-quality coffee and snacks, and providing excellent customer service, quickly made Starbucks a household name.

One of Schultz's most significant innovations was his approach to employee training and development. Schultz believed that the key to creating a successful and sustainable business was to invest in his employees and create a positive work environment. To this end, he instituted comprehensive training programs, offered health benefits and stock options to all employees, and created a company culture that valued diversity, inclusivity, and innovation.

Schultz's focus on social responsibility and sustainability also set Starbucks apart from its competitors. He implemented programs to reduce the company's environmental impact, such as using recycled materials and investing in renewable energy sources. Schultz also created partnerships with fair-trade coffee growers to ensure that Starbucks' coffee was ethically sourced and produced.

In addition to his innovative approach to coffee retailing and employee development, Schultz is also known for his bold and strategic business tactics. In the early 2000s, Starbucks faced significant competition from other coffee retailers, and Schultz recognized the need to expand the company's offerings beyond coffee. He introduced new food items, such as pastries and sandwiches, and acquired other brands, such as Tazo Tea and Ethos Water.

Schultz's leadership and innovative approach to business have earned him numerous accolades and awards, including being named one of Time magazine's 100 most influential people in the world in 2011. He has also been recognized for his philanthropic work, particularly his support of veterans and his advocacy for social and environmental causes.

Overall, Howard Schultz is considered one of the most influential business minds of all time due to his innovative approach to coffee retailing, his commitment to employee development and social responsibility, and his bold and strategic business tactics. His leadership at Starbucks transformed the coffee industry and set a new standard for corporate responsibility and sustainability.

Howard Schultz was known for his innovative work tactics and strong business ethics, which helped him to build a highly successful and socially responsible business.

One of Schultz's most important tactics was his emphasis on building a strong company culture. He believed that creating a positive work environment and investing in employee development was crucial to building a sustainable and successful business. To this end, he instituted comprehensive training programs, offered health benefits and stock options to all employees, and created a company culture that valued diversity, inclusivity, and innovation.

Schultz also believed in the importance of listening to customers and adapting the business model to meet their needs. He would regularly visit Starbucks stores to observe customer behavior and gather feedback, and he encouraged employees at all levels to share their ideas and suggestions for improving the business.

Another important tactic that Schultz employed was his

focus on creating a premium brand. He believed that Starbucks should be more than just a coffee shop, but a lifestyle brand that represented quality and sophistication. To achieve this, he invested heavily in store design, packaging, and advertising, and introduced premium products such as single-origin coffees and handcrafted espresso drinks.

Schultz was also known for his strategic business decisions and willingness to take risks. In the early 2000s, Starbucks faced significant competition from other coffee retailers, and Schultz recognized the need to expand the company's offerings beyond coffee. He introduced new food items, such as pastries and sandwiches, and acquired other brands, such as Tazo Tea and Ethos Water. These acquisitions helped to diversify the company's offerings and expand its customer base.

In terms of business ethics, Schultz was committed to social responsibility and sustainability. He implemented programs to reduce the company's environmental impact, such as using recycled materials and investing in renewable energy sources. Schultz also created partnerships with fair-trade coffee growers to ensure that Starbucks' coffee was ethically sourced and produced. He was also an advocate for social causes such as gun control and LGBTQ rights.

Overall, Howard Schultz's work tactics and business ethics were focused on building a strong company culture, listening to customers, creating a premium brand, taking strategic risks, and prioritizing social responsibility and sustainability. These values helped him to build a highly successful and socially responsible business that set a new standard for corporate responsibility and sustainability.

The one thing that he did, that an entrepreneur should

follow to be great today

One thing that entrepreneurs can learn from Howard Schultz is the importance of creating a strong company culture. Schultz believed that the success of Starbucks was largely due to the company's culture, which valued employee development, innovation, and customer service.

To create a strong company culture, entrepreneurs should prioritize investing in their employees' training and development, and foster a work environment that encourages open communication, feedback, and collaboration. This can help to build a team that is motivated, engaged, and committed to achieving the company's goals.

Entrepreneurs should also prioritize building a brand that resonates with customers and represents quality and innovation. This can involve investing in branding and marketing efforts, developing premium products and services, and consistently delivering a high-quality customer experience.

Additionally, entrepreneurs can learn from Schultz's willingness to take strategic risks and adapt to changing market conditions. This may involve diversifying the company's offerings, acquiring other businesses, or expanding into new markets.

Overall, the key lesson that entrepreneurs can take from Howard Schultz is the importance of building a strong company culture, developing a brand that resonates with customers, and being willing to take strategic risks and adapt to changing market conditions.

Some additional interesting facts about Howard Schultz:

Schultz was born in Brooklyn, New York, in 1953. He grew up in public housing and was the first person in his family to attend college.

After graduating from Northern Michigan University,

Schultz worked for Xerox and then joined a Swedish company called Hammarplast, which made housewares and kitchen gadgets. He became the company's U.S. sales manager before leaving to start his own business.

In 1981, Schultz joined Starbucks as the director of retail operations and marketing. At the time, Starbucks was a small Seattle-based coffee roaster with just a few stores.

Schultz left Starbucks in 1985 to start his own coffee company, Il Giornale, which he named after an Italian newspaper. Il Giornale was successful and Schultz used the profits to purchase Starbucks in 1987, merging the two companies and becoming CEO.

Under Schultz's leadership, Starbucks grew rapidly and became a global brand with thousands of stores in more than 70 countries. The company also diversified its offerings to include food, tea, and other products.

Schultz has been a vocal advocate for social causes, including gun control, LGBTQ rights, and supporting veterans. In 2018, he launched a nonprofit called "From the Ground Up" to create jobs and provide training for young people in distressed communities.

Schultz has written two books: "Pour Your Heart Into It: How Starbucks Built a Company One Cup at a Time" (1997) and "Onward: How Starbucks Fought for Its Life without Losing Its Soul" (2011).

JAMES SINEGAL

is a name that may not be immediately familiar to many, but his impact on the business world is undeniable. Born in 1936 in Pittsburgh, Pennsylvania, Sinegal grew up in a working-class family and started working at the age of 14 to help support his family. He eventually went on to become one of the most successful and innovative businessmen of his generation.

Sinegal's career began in the retail industry when he was hired as a bagger at a FedMart store in San Diego, California. He quickly rose through the ranks, and by the age of 25, he was the executive vice president of merchandising at the company. In 1983, Sinegal co-founded Costco Wholesale Corporation, a membership-based warehouse club that has become one of the largest and most successful retailers in the world.

One of Sinegal's most significant contributions to the business world is his commitment to employee satisfaction and retention. He is a strong advocate for paying employees a living wage, providing them with excellent benefits, and promoting from within the company. This philosophy has helped Costco become known for its loyal and dedicated workforce, which, in turn, has helped drive the company's success.

Sinegal's commitment to employee satisfaction has also

led him to make some unconventional business decisions. For example, while many companies try to cut costs by outsourcing jobs, Sinegal has taken the opposite approach, investing in his employees' training and development to ensure they have the skills they need to succeed. He has also been known to visit stores and warehouses regularly to talk to employees and get feedback on how the company can improve.

Another area in which Sinegal has shown innovation is in the way he has structured Costco's business model. Unlike traditional retailers, Costco operates on a membership-based model, where customers pay an annual fee to shop at the store. This model has allowed Costco to keep its prices low and its profit margins high, which has been a key factor in the company's success.

Sinegal has also been a vocal advocate for ethical business practices. He has spoken out against the practice of outsourcing jobs to countries with lower labor standards, arguing that it is not only morally wrong but also bad for business in the long run. He has also been a strong supporter of sustainability initiatives, such as reducing waste and energy consumption, which has helped Costco become known as one of the most environmentally conscious retailers in the world.

Despite his many achievements, Sinegal has remained humble and committed to his employees and customers. He has been known to work long hours and to lead by example, showing his employees that he is willing to do whatever it takes to help the company succeed. He has also been a strong advocate for corporate social responsibility, using his position to give back to the community and to promote philanthropic causes.

In conclusion, James Sinegal is undoubtedly one of the most influential business minds of all time. His commitment to employee satisfaction, innovative business tactics, and ethical practices have set the standard for other companies to follow. His philosophy of investing in employees and promoting from within has helped Costco become one of the most successful and beloved retailers in the world, and his leadership style has inspired countless other business leaders to follow in his footsteps. For all these reasons and more, Sinegal deserves a place on any list of the most influential entrepreneurs and businessmen of all time.

One of Sinegal's most notable work tactics was his focus on cost control. Sinegal believed that by keeping costs low, Costco could pass on the savings to customers in the form of low prices. This philosophy is reflected in many of Costco's business practices, such as their minimal advertising budget and their focus on bulk purchases. By buying products in large quantities, Costco is able to negotiate lower prices from suppliers, which allows them to offer products to customers at lower prices than their competitors.

Another key work tactic of Sinegal's was his commitment to simplicity. Sinegal believed that by keeping things simple, Costco could reduce costs and improve efficiency. For example, Costco has a limited product selection compared to other retailers, which allows them to keep their inventory costs low. Additionally, Costco's warehouses are designed to be simple and easy to navigate, which helps customers find what they need quickly and efficiently.

Sinegal's business ethics were also a significant factor in his success. He believed in treating employees with respect and providing them with good wages and benefits. This commitment to employees was reflected in many of Costco's policies, such as their practice of promoting from within and their generous benefits packages. Sinegal believed that by treating employees well, they would be more productive and loyal, which would ultimately benefit the company.

Another key aspect of Sinegal's business ethics was his commitment to sustainability. Sinegal was a strong advocate for reducing waste and energy consumption, and he worked to make Costco one of the most environmentally friendly retailers in the world. For example, Costco has invested in solar panels and other renewable energy sources, and they have implemented recycling and waste reduction programs in their stores and warehouses.

In addition to his commitment to cost control, simplicity, employee satisfaction, and sustainability, Sinegal was also known for his ethical leadership style. He led by example and was willing to roll up his sleeves and work alongside his employees to get the job done. He was transparent and open with his employees, regularly communicating with them about the company's goals and challenges. He also believed in giving back to the community and supported philanthropic causes, such as education and healthcare.

Overall, James Sinegal's work tactics and business ethics were focused on keeping costs low, simplifying operations, treating employees well, and promoting sustainability. These values helped him build a successful and respected company, and they continue to influence business leaders around the world.

The one thing that he did, that an entrepreneur should follow to be great today

There are many things that James Sinegal did throughout his career that could serve as valuable lessons for entrepreneurs today. However, if I had to pick just one thing that entrepreneurs should follow to be great today, it would be Sinegal's emphasis on putting customers first.

Sinegal understood that customers are the lifeblood of

any business, and he made it a priority to provide them with high-quality products at low prices. He also believed in creating a positive shopping experience for customers, which included keeping stores clean and well-organized, and providing excellent customer service.

By putting customers first, Sinegal was able to build a loyal customer base that valued Costco's products and shopping experience. This customer loyalty helped to fuel the company's growth and success over the years.

Today, in an age where customers have more choices than ever before, it's more important than ever for entrepreneurs to prioritize the customer experience. This means understanding your customers' needs and preferences, providing high-quality products and services, and offering a seamless and enjoyable shopping experience.

In short, if entrepreneurs want to be great today, they should follow Sinegal's lead and make customer satisfaction their top priority. By doing so, they can build a loyal customer base and create a strong foundation for long-term success.

Some more things about James Sinegal:

James Sinegal was born on January 1, 1936, in Pittsburgh, Pennsylvania. His father worked as a coal miner, and his mother was a homemaker.

Sinegal started working at a young age, delivering newspapers and working in his uncle's grocery store. After graduating from high school, he worked for the retail giant FedMart, where he learned the basics of the retail industry.

In 1983, Sinegal co-founded Costco Wholesale Corporation with his business partner Jeffrey H. Brotman. The first Costco warehouse opened in Seattle, Washington, and the company quickly expanded across the United States and around the world.

Sinegal served as CEO of Costco from 1983 until his

retirement in 2012. During his tenure, he helped to build Costco into one of the world's largest retailers, with over 800 warehouses in 12 countries.

Despite his success, Sinegal remained humble and down-to-earth. He was known for his frugal lifestyle, and he famously drove an old Volvo instead of a luxury car.

Sinegal was a strong advocate for education and served on the boards of several universities, including the University of San Diego and the University of Washington.

In addition to his work at Costco, Sinegal was also involved in philanthropy. He and his wife donated millions of dollars to charitable causes, including education, healthcare, and the arts. Sinegal received numerous awards and accolades throughout his career, including being named one of the "100 Best CEOs in the World" by Barron's magazine and being inducted into the Retail Hall of Fame.

Overall, James Sinegal was a highly respected and influential business leader who built a successful company based on a commitment to cost control, simplicity, employee satisfaction, sustainability, and customer service. His legacy continues to inspire entrepreneurs and business leaders around the world.

CARLOS SLIM HELU

Is one of the most influential businessmen of all time. Born in Mexico City in 1940, he is the son of Lebanese immigrants who had a successful dry goods business. Slim grew up surrounded by commerce and developed an interest in business from an early age.

Slim's path to success was not a straight line. He studied engineering at the National Autonomous University of Mexico but dropped out before completing his degree. Instead, he started working in his father's business and quickly learned the ins and outs of the retail industry. Slim's entrepreneurial spirit led him to start his own business, a stock brokerage firm called Inversora Bursátil, which he founded in 1965.

In the 1970s, Slim began expanding his business interests into a variety of industries, including real estate, mining, and telecommunications. He acquired a number of companies, often turning them around and making them more profitable. By the 1980s, Slim had become one of the richest men in Mexico.

One of Slim's key strengths as a businessman is his ability to see opportunity where others do not. For example, in the 1990s, when Mexico was going through a financial crisis, Slim bought up a number of struggling companies at bargain prices. He also saw the potential for growth in the telecommunications industry and acquired a number of companies, including Telmex, which he turned into one of the largest telecommunications companies in Latin America.

Slim is also known for his innovative approach to business. He is a strong believer in using technology to increase efficiency and cut costs. In the 1990s, he invested heavily in fiber-optic networks, which allowed him to offer high-speed internet and other digital services. He also implemented a number of cost-cutting measures, such as reducing the number of employees and streamlining operations.

Another key aspect of Slim's success is his focus on long-term goals. He is known for taking a patient approach to business, investing for the long-term and not being swayed by short-term trends or market fluctuations. This approach has allowed him to weather economic storms and emerge stronger than ever.

Slim's success has not gone unnoticed. He has been recognized as one of the most influential business leaders in the world, appearing on Forbes' list of the world's richest people for many years. He has also been honored with numerous awards and accolades, including the Order of the Aztec Eagle, the highest honor awarded to a non-Mexican citizen by the Mexican government.

In conclusion, Carlos Slim Helu is an influential businessman who has made a significant impact on a variety of industries. His innovative approach to business, focus on long-term goals, and ability to see opportunity where others do not have made him one of the most successful businessmen of all time. His achievements serve as a reminder of what can be accomplished with hard work, innovation, and a strong entrepreneurial spirit.

One of the key tactics that Slim employs is his ability to focus on the fundamentals of business. He believes that success in business is not about being flashy or trendy, but rather about being disciplined and focused on the basics. For example, when he acquired Telmex, he focused on improving the company's customer service and investing in infrastructure to improve the quality of its services. This strategy helped him to grow Telmex into a major player in the telecommunications industry.

Another tactic that Slim uses is his ability to negotiate effectively. He is known for being a tough negotiator, but he also believes in creating mutually beneficial partnerships. He has formed alliances with other companies and governments, and has been able to leverage his network of relationships to create new opportunities for his businesses.

In addition, Slim is known for his frugal approach to business. He believes in keeping costs low and using resources efficiently. For example, he famously works out of a modest office and drives a modest car, despite being one of the richest men in the world. This approach to business has allowed him to maximize profits and achieve success even in challenging economic environments.

Finally, Slim is known for his philanthropic efforts. He has used his wealth to support a variety of causes, including education, healthcare, and the arts. He believes that business leaders have a responsibility to give back to their communities and to use their resources to help those in need.

In terms of business ethics, Slim is known for his integrity and honesty. He has built his businesses on a foundation of trust and transparency, and he expects the same from his partners and employees. He is committed to following ethical business practices and has been recognized for his commitment to corporate social responsibility.

In conclusion, Carlos Slim Helu is a successful businessman who has achieved his success through a combination of innovative thinking, discipline, and a commitment to ethical business practices. His work tactics include a focus on the fundamentals of business, effective negotiation skills, a frugal approach to business, and a commitment to philanthropy. His business ethic is characterized by integrity, honesty, and a commitment to corporate social responsibility. These qualities have made him one of the most influential and respected business leaders of all time.

The one thing that he did, that an entrepreneur should follow to be great today

It is difficult to point to just one thing that Carlos Slim Helu did that entrepreneurs should follow to be great today, as his success can be attributed to a combination of factors. However, if I had to choose one key takeaway from his success, it would be his ability to see opportunity where others do not.

Slim has a knack for identifying undervalued companies or industries and investing in them at the right time. For example, when he acquired Telmex, the telecommunications industry was still in its early stages in Latin America, and many people did not see the potential for growth in the industry. Slim saw an opportunity where others did not, and he invested heavily in Telmex, turning it into one of the largest telecommunications companies in Latin America.

In today's fast-paced and competitive business environment, entrepreneurs must be able to identify and capitalize on opportunities quickly in order to succeed. This requires a combination of vision, intuition, and a willingness to take calculated risks.

Entrepreneurs can learn from Slim's approach by keeping an eye out for emerging trends and industries, and by being willing to take bold steps to pursue new opportunities. This may involve taking risks that others are not willing to take, or investing in new technologies or business models that are unproven but have the potential for significant growth.

Ultimately, the key to success as an entrepreneur is to have a clear vision, a willingness to take risks, and the ability to see opportunities where others do not. By following in Carlos Slim Helu's footsteps and cultivating these qualities, entrepreneurs can increase their chances of achieving great success in today's dynamic and ever-changing business world.

Some additional details about Carlos Slim Helu:

Born in Mexico City in 1940, Slim comes from a family of Lebanese immigrants who made their fortune in commerce.

He received a degree in civil engineering from the National Autonomous University of Mexico, and later went on to study economics at the same university.

He began his career in business in the 1960s, when he founded a stock brokerage firm called Inversora Bursátil.

In the 1980s, Slim began acquiring companies in a variety of industries, including construction, mining, and retail.

He made his biggest acquisition in 1990, when he bought a controlling stake in Telmex, Mexico's national telecommunications company.

Slim is known for his disciplined approach to business and his focus on the fundamentals of finance, such as generating cash flow and reducing debt.

He is also known for his frugal lifestyle, and is often seen wearing a simple suit and driving an older model car.

In addition to his business interests, Slim is involved in a variety of philanthropic causes. His foundation, the Carlos Slim Foundation, supports initiatives in education, health, and the arts.

According to Forbes, Slim was the richest person in the world from 2010 to 2013, with a net worth of over $70 billion.

Despite his enormous wealth, Slim is known for his humility and his commitment to giving back to his community. He has said that he believes that wealth should be used for the betterment of society, and that true success comes from making a positive impact on the world.

ALFRED P. SLOAN

Was a prominent American businessman who is widely regarded as one of the most influential figures in the history of modern business. He was the president and CEO of General Motors (GM) from 1923 to 1946 and is credited with transforming the company into one of the largest and most successful corporations in the world.

Early Life and Education:

Alfred Pritchard Sloan Jr. was born on May 23, 1875, in New Haven, Connecticut. He was the son of an affluent businessman and grew up in a privileged and intellectually stimulating environment. Sloan attended the prestigious Phillips Exeter Academy and then went on to study electrical engineering at the Massachusetts Institute of Technology (MIT). After completing his studies, he started his career as a draftsman at a small machine shop in New York City.

Early Career:

Sloan's career took a major turn when he was recruited by the Hyatt Roller Bearing Company in 1899. Hyatt was a small but growing company that produced bearings for the automotive industry, and Sloan quickly rose through the ranks to become the company's president in 1916. Under his leadership, Hyatt expanded its product line and developed innovative new bearings that were more durable and efficient than those of its competitors.

Sloan's success at Hyatt caught the attention of General Motors, and in 1916, he was invited to join the company's board of directors. Two years later, he was named the head of GM's newly-formed overseas operations. In this role, he oversaw the company's expansion into Europe and other markets, and he played a key role in establishing GM as a global leader in the automotive industry.

Transformation of General Motors:

In 1923, Sloan was named the president and CEO of General Motors, a position he held for over two decades. During this time, he oversaw a period of rapid growth and expansion for the company. One of Sloan's most significant innovations was the development of the concept of "brand management." Sloan realized that GM could appeal to a wider range of consumers by offering a variety of different car models, each targeted at a specific market segment. He created a separate division for each brand, such as Chevrolet, Buick, and Cadillac, and each division was responsible for developing and marketing its own unique product line.

Sloan also introduced a number of other important innovations at GM. He established a system of annual model changes, which encouraged consumers to trade in their old cars for new ones more frequently. He also pioneered the use of installment credit, making it easier for people to finance the purchase of a car. Additionally, Sloan implemented a system of decentralized management, giving each division of GM greater autonomy and accountability.

Legacy:

Alfred P. Sloan's innovations and strategies had a profound impact on the automotive industry and on modern business practices in general. Under his leadership, General Motors became one of the largest and most successful corporations in the world, and his ideas about brand management, model changes, and decentralized management have become standard practices in many industries.

Sloan was also a prominent philanthropist, donating millions of dollars to support education and scientific research. He established the Sloan Foundation, which has provided funding for a wide range of scientific and educational projects.

In conclusion, Alfred P. Sloan was a visionary businessman whose innovative ideas and strategies transformed the automotive industry and had a lasting impact on modern business practices. His commitment to brand management, model changes, and decentralized management revolutionized the way companies operate, and his philanthropic efforts continue to support important scientific and educational initiatives.

In addition to his work at General Motors, Sloan was also a philanthropist, and donated significant amounts of money to institutions like the Massachusetts Institute of Technology (MIT) and the University of Chicago. He also established the Alfred P. Sloan Foundation, which provides funding for scientific research, education, and economic performance.

Sloan was known for his emphasis on teamwork and collaboration within General Motors. He believed that success was best achieved through the collective effort of talented individuals working together, rather than the work of one or a few exceptional individuals.

Sloan was also a proponent of market research and consumer feedback, and implemented methods of market research within General Motors to better understand the needs and desires of consumers. This led to the development of new products, such as the Chevrolet, which was designed to be an affordable, mass-market car that could compete with Ford's Model T.

Sloan was a strong believer in decentralization and delegation of authority, and implemented a system of divisionalized management within General Motors, with each division responsible for its own profits and losses. This allowed for greater flexibility and responsiveness to changing market conditions.

In addition to his work at General Motors, Sloan also served as chairman of the Business Advisory Council for the Department of Commerce under President Herbert Hoover, and was appointed by President Franklin D. Roosevelt to serve on the National Defense Advisory Commission during World War II.

Sloan was a prolific author, and wrote several books on management and business strategy, including "My Years with General Motors," which is still widely read and studied by business students and professionals today.

Overall, Sloan's impact on the business world can be seen through his emphasis on teamwork, market research, decentralization, and management strategy. His legacy is still felt today in the principles and practices used by many successful businesses.

The one thing that Sloan did, that an entrepreneur should follow to be great

If there's one thing that entrepreneurs can learn from Alfred P. Sloan, it's the importance of teamwork and collaboration in achieving business success. Sloan understood that no individual, no matter how talented, can single-handedly drive the success of an organization. Instead, he believed in the power of a team of talented individuals working together towards a common goal.

To apply this lesson in modern business, entrepreneurs

should focus on building a strong, collaborative team with diverse skills and perspectives. This means hiring people who bring different experiences and ideas to the table, and fostering an environment where open communication and collaboration are encouraged.

Entrepreneurs can also follow Sloan's lead by implementing a system of divisionalized management, which allows for greater flexibility and responsiveness to changing market conditions. By delegating authority to each division, entrepreneurs can ensure that decisions are made quickly and efficiently, and that each team member has a clear sense of their responsibilities and goals.

Finally, entrepreneurs can also follow Sloan's lead by emphasizing the importance of market research and customer feedback. By gathering data on customer needs and preferences, entrepreneurs can make informed decisions about product development and marketing strategy, and ensure that their business stays relevant and competitive in a constantly evolving market.

Some additional details about Alfred P. Sloan:

Sloan was a lifelong learner: Even though Sloan was a successful businessman, he never stopped learning. He was an avid reader and believed in the importance of education. He also attended business school while he was running GM to gain more knowledge and insights into management and strategy.

Sloan was a proponent of planned obsolescence: Sloan is often credited with inventing the concept of planned obsolescence, which involves designing products that are meant to be replaced after a certain period of time. While some criticize this approach for being wasteful and environmentally damaging, Sloan believed it was necessary to keep the economy growing and to keep consumers interested in buying new products.

Sloan was a philanthropist: After he retired from GM, Sloan became a philanthropist and donated millions of dollars to various causes. He established the Alfred P. Sloan Foundation, which supports research and education in science, technology, and economics. He also supported the arts and contributed to the Metropolitan Museum of Art in New York City.

Sloan was a believer in data-driven decision making: Sloan was a pioneer in using data and analytics to make business decisions. He implemented a system of accounting that allowed for greater visibility into the financial performance of each division of GM. He also emphasized the importance of market research and customer feedback in developing new products and marketing strategies.

Sloan was a leader in corporate social responsibility: Sloan believed that businesses had a responsibility to the communities in which they operated. He implemented a number of social programs at GM, including providing employees with health insurance and pension benefits, and creating programs to support education and job training. He also advocated for responsible corporate citizenship and was involved in various philanthropic efforts throughout his life.

GEORGE SOROS

is undoubtedly one of the most influential businessmen and entrepreneurs of all time. Born in Budapest, Hungary in 1930, Soros has had a long and successful career as an investor, philanthropist, and entrepreneur. Throughout his life, he has demonstrated an exceptional ability to innovate, create new business models, and adapt to changing market conditions.

Soros's early years were marked by the turbulence of World War II and the subsequent communist takeover of Hungary. He fled to England in 1947 and attended the London School of Economics, where he studied under the economist Karl Popper. After graduation, Soros worked as a stock trader in London, eventually moving to New York City in 1956 to work on Wall Street.

In the 1960s, Soros founded his own investment firm, Soros Fund Management. He quickly established a reputation as a skilled and innovative investor, using techniques such as short selling and currency speculation to generate substantial profits. Soros's early success was driven by his ability to spot market inefficiencies and take advantage of them before others did. For example, in the 1970s, he was one of the first investors to recognize the potential of the Japanese yen and began investing heavily in it, reaping enormous profits.

Soros's success as an investor allowed him to expand his business interests into other areas. In the 1980s, he founded the Open Society Foundations, a network of philanthropic organizations that promote democracy, human rights, and economic development around the world. He has also been a vocal advocate for social justice and has used his wealth and influence to support causes such as marriage equality, criminal justice reform, and the fight against climate change.

In addition to his philanthropic work, Soros has continued to be an influential figure in the financial world. He has been an active participant in debates about economic policy and has written extensively on topics such as globalization, capitalism, and financial markets. He has also continued to be a successful investor, with his net worth estimated at over $8 billion as of 2023.

What sets Soros apart from other successful businessmen is his willingness to take risks and his ability to think creatively about business opportunities. He is not afraid to challenge conventional wisdom and is always looking for ways to innovate and create value. For example, in the 1990s, Soros recognized the potential of the internet and invested heavily in tech companies such as Amazon and Google, long before they became household names.

Soros's success as an entrepreneur and businessman is also due in part to his ability to adapt to changing market conditions. He has shown a remarkable ability to anticipate and respond to shifts in the global economy, such as the rise of emerging markets and the growing importance of the internet. This has allowed him to stay ahead of the curve and remain a major player in the financial world.

In conclusion, George Soros is one of the most influential entrepreneurs and businessmen of all time. His innovative mind, willingness to take risks, and ability to adapt to changing market conditions have made him a successful investor, philanthropist, and advocate for social justice. He has demonstrated an exceptional ability to create value and has been a driving force behind many important initiatives aimed at promoting democracy, human rights, and economic development around the world. For all these reasons and more, Soros deserves to be considered one of the most influential business minds of all time.

George Soros's work tactics and business ethics have been shaped by his experiences as an investor, entrepreneur, and philanthropist. One of the key aspects of his business approach is his willingness to take risks and think creatively about investment opportunities.

Soros has often talked about his concept of "reflexivity," which he defines as the interplay between the beliefs of investors and the underlying realities of the markets. According to Soros, investors' beliefs about the markets can influence the direction of those markets, creating feedback loops that can lead to self-fulfilling prophecies. Soros has used this concept to develop his investment strategies, which are based on identifying trends in the markets and anticipating their potential impact.

Another important aspect of Soros's work tactics is his use of leverage. Soros has often used borrowed money to make his investments, which allows him to magnify his returns when his bets pay off. This approach has allowed him to generate substantial profits, but it also carries risks, as losses can be magnified in the same way.

Soros has also been known for his willingness to challenge conventional wisdom and think outside the box. He has been a vocal critic of what he sees as the flaws in traditional economic theory, particularly the idea that markets are always efficient and self-correcting. Instead, he has advocated for a more nuanced approach that takes into account the role of human psychology and market dynamics in shaping economic outcomes.

In terms of business ethics, Soros has been a strong advocate for transparency and accountability. He has often criticized the lack of transparency in financial markets, particularly in the realm of hedge funds and private equity, and has called for greater regulation and oversight to ensure that investors are protected. He has also been a vocal opponent of corruption and authoritarianism in all its forms, and has used his philanthropic work to support democratic movements and human rights initiatives around the world.

One of the hallmarks of Soros's business ethic is his commitment to giving back to society. He has used his wealth and influence to support a wide range of philanthropic initiatives, including efforts to promote democracy, human rights, and economic development in disadvantaged communities around the world. He has also been a strong advocate for social justice, supporting causes such as marriage equality and criminal justice reform.

In summary, George Soros's work tactics and business ethic have been shaped by his experience as an investor, entrepreneur, and philanthropist. He is known for his willingness to take risks and think creatively about investment opportunities, as well as his use of leverage and his advocacy for transparency and accountability in financial markets. He is also committed to giving back to society and using his wealth and influence to promote democracy, human rights, and social justice.

The one thing that he did, that an entrepreneur should follow to be great today

One thing that entrepreneurs today can learn from George Soros is his willingness to think independently and challenge conventional wisdom. Soros has always been a critical thinker who is not afraid to challenge established beliefs or take unpopular positions. He has also been willing to take risks and pursue investments that others might consider too risky or unconventional.

As an entrepreneur, it can be tempting to follow the herd and stick with established practices or popular trends. However, Soros's success shows that there is value in thinking independently and pursuing your own ideas, even if they run counter to prevailing wisdom. By doing so, you may be able to identify opportunities that others overlook and create a competitive advantage for yourself and your business.

Of course, it's important to balance independent thinking with careful analysis and risk management. Soros is a successful investor and businessman not just because he thinks differently, but because he combines that thinking with rigorous analysis and disciplined risk management.

Overall, entrepreneurs can learn from Soros's willingness to challenge conventional wisdom and pursue his own ideas, while also recognizing the importance of careful analysis and risk management.

Some additional interesting facts about George Soros:

George Soros was born in Budapest, Hungary, in 1930. He survived the Nazi occupation of Hungary during World War II and emigrated to England in 1947, where he attended the London School of Economics.

Soros is widely regarded as one of the most successful investors of all time. He made his fortune primarily through his hedge fund, Soros Fund Management, which he founded in 1969.

In addition to his success as an investor, Soros is also a noted philanthropist. He has donated billions of dollars to support various causes, including human rights, democracy, and education.

Soros is a well-known advocate for liberal political causes and has been involved in various political campaigns and organizations over the years. He has also been a vocal critic of authoritarian regimes and has supported various efforts to promote democracy and human rights around the world.

Soros has authored numerous books and articles on a wide range of topics, including finance, politics, and philosophy. His most famous work is probably "The Alchemy of Finance," which explores his investment philosophy and approach to financial markets.

Soros has received numerous honors and awards over the years, including the Presidential Medal of Freedom, the highest civilian honor in the United States. He has also been awarded honorary degrees from numerous universities around the world.

Soros has faced significant criticism and controversy over the years, particularly from conservative and nationalist groups who view him as a symbol of globalism and liberal politics. He has been the target of various conspiracy theories, many of which are unfounded and based on anti-Semitic stereotypes.

MARTHA STEWART

is a name synonymous with entrepreneurship and innovation. Known as the "Queen of Domesticity," she has made a name for herself in the world of business, media, and lifestyle. Throughout her career, Martha Stewart has been a force to be reckoned with, and her impact on the business world cannot be overstated.

Born in 1941 in Jersey City, New Jersey, Martha Stewart grew up in a family that valued education and hard work. Her father was a pharmaceutical salesman, and her mother was a teacher. Stewart attended Barnard College, where she studied art history and architecture, and later went on to work as a stockbroker on Wall Street.

Stewart's entrepreneurial journey began in the 1970s, when she started a catering business out of her basement. Her attention to detail and impeccable taste quickly made her a hit with clients, and before long, she was catering events for the likes of Ralph Lauren and the New York Stock Exchange.

But it wasn't until the 1980s that Martha Stewart truly became a household name. In 1982, she published her first book, "Entertaining," which was a guide to hosting elegant and sophisticated parties. The book was a huge success, and Stewart followed it up with several more books on cooking, decorating, and entertaining.

But it was her media empire that truly set Martha Stewart

apart. In 1990, she launched "Martha Stewart Living," a magazine that focused on cooking, decorating, and lifestyle. The magazine was an instant hit, and within a few years, Martha Stewart Living Omnimedia had become a multimillion-dollar company.

One of the keys to Martha Stewart's success was her ability to innovate and stay ahead of the curve. In the 1990s, she was one of the first entrepreneurs to recognize the potential of the internet, and she launched a website that offered recipes, decorating tips, and other lifestyle content.

Stewart also recognized the power of branding, and she worked tirelessly to build her personal brand. She appeared on numerous television shows, including her own daytime talk show, and she even had a line of products at Kmart.

But perhaps what truly sets Martha Stewart apart is her work ethic and attention to detail. She is known for her perfectionism and her ability to turn even the most mundane tasks into works of art. Whether she is arranging flowers, decorating a cake, or folding a napkin, Stewart approaches every task with the same level of care and precision.

All of these factors combine to make Martha Stewart one of the most influential business minds of all time. Her ability to innovate, her dedication to her personal brand, and her tireless work ethic have made her a true icon of entrepreneurship. And her impact on the business world continues to be felt to this day.

Martha Stewart's legacy is not without controversy, however. In 2004, she was convicted of conspiracy and obstruction of justice in connection with a stock trading scandal. She served five months in prison and has since worked to rebuild her reputation.

Despite this setback, Martha Stewart remains an inspiration to entrepreneurs and businesspeople around the world. Her creativity, innovation, and attention to detail are a testament to the power of hard work and dedication. And her legacy as one of the most influential business minds of all time is secure.

Martha Stewart's work tactics and business ethics are a key reason why she is considered one of the most influential business minds of all time. Here are some more details on her approach:

Attention to detail: One of Martha Stewart's defining characteristics is her attention to detail. From the way she arranges flowers to the way she folds a napkin, she approaches every task with a meticulous eye. This attention to detail has been a key factor in her success, as it has allowed her to create products and content that are of the highest quality.

Innovation: Martha Stewart has always been ahead of the curve when it comes to innovation. She was one of the first entrepreneurs to recognize the potential of the internet, and she launched a website that offered lifestyle content long before most people had even heard of the world wide web. She has also been quick to embrace new technologies and trends, always looking for ways to stay relevant and engaging.

Branding: Martha Stewart is a master of personal branding. She has carefully crafted an image of herself as a domestic goddess, and everything she does is designed to reinforce that image. From her cookbooks to her TV shows to her line of products, everything Martha Stewart touches is stamped with her personal brand.

Hard work: Martha Stewart is famous for her tireless work ethic. She is known for working long hours and approaching every task with the same level of enthusiasm and dedication. Her work ethic has been a key factor in her success, as it has allowed her to produce a vast amount of content and products over the years.

Perfectionism: Martha Stewart is a perfectionist, and she expects nothing less than perfection from herself and those around her. This has been both a blessing and a curse in her career, as it has led to some truly exceptional work but has also caused friction with colleagues and employees.

Creative problem-solving: Martha Stewart is a master of creative problem-solving. She has a knack for finding elegant solutions to complex problems, whether it's how to decorate a cake or how to launch a new product line. Her ability to think outside the box has been a key factor in her success.

Strong leadership: Martha Stewart is a strong leader who inspires those around her to do their best work. She has a clear vision of what she wants to achieve, and she is not afraid to make tough decisions to get there. Her leadership has been a key factor in the success of her media empire.

Overall, Martha Stewart's work tactics and business ethics are characterized by attention to detail, innovation, branding, hard work, perfectionism, creative problem-solving, and strong leadership. It is these traits that have made her one of the most influential business minds of all time.

The one thing that she did, that an entrepreneur should follow to be great today

There are many things that an entrepreneur can learn from Martha Stewart's career and business tactics, but one key takeaway is her emphasis on quality and attention to detail.

Martha Stewart's success can be attributed in large part to her unwavering commitment to excellence. Whether she was creating a recipe, designing a product, or producing a TV show, she always put in the time and effort to ensure that every detail was just right. This commitment to quality has been a hallmark of her career and is something that any entrepreneur can learn from.

In today's fast-paced business environment, it can be tempting to cut corners and sacrifice quality in the pursuit of short-term gains. However, Martha Stewart's success serves as a reminder that taking the time to do things right can pay off in the long run. By focusing on quality and attention to detail, entrepreneurs can differentiate themselves from their competitors and build a loyal customer base that values excellence.

So, the one thing that an entrepreneur can follow to be great today, inspired by Martha Stewart, is to make quality and attention to detail a top priority in everything they do. By doing so, they can create products and services that stand out from the crowd and build a reputation for excellence that will drive long-term success.

PENNY STREETER

Is a renowned entrepreneur who has made a name for herself in the business world due to her innovative thinking, hard work, and effective business tactics. Her accomplishments speak volumes about her abilities and it is no surprise that she is considered to be one of the most influential business minds of all time.

Penny was born in South Africa in 1957 and spent the majority of her early years in Zimbabwe. She moved to the UK in 1980 and started her first business venture in 1987, selling flowers from a market stall in London. This venture quickly grew and within a year, she had opened her first florist shop in London.

Penny's drive and determination to succeed was evident from the outset. She worked long hours, often seven days a week, and her focus on delivering exceptional customer service was the key to her success. She quickly established a reputation for quality and reliability, and her business grew rapidly.

In the early 1990s, Penny recognized the potential of the UK's healthcare industry and decided to diversify her business. She started a healthcare staffing agency that provided temporary staff to hospitals and nursing homes. This business, called Ambition 24Hours, grew rapidly and soon became one of the largest healthcare staffing agencies in the

UK.

Penny's innovative approach to business was a key factor in the success of Ambition 24Hours. She recognized that the traditional approach to healthcare staffing was inefficient and expensive, and she developed a new model that focused on providing temporary staff quickly and cost-effectively. This approach proved highly successful and the business quickly expanded to other areas of the UK.

In 2001, Penny launched a new venture, A24 Group, which specialized in providing healthcare staffing solutions to clients across the globe. A24 Group went from strength to strength, and by 2010, the company had offices in over ten countries and was providing staffing solutions to clients in over 50 countries. Penny's focus on innovation, quality, and customer service was key to the success of A24 Group.

Penny's entrepreneurial success did not come without its challenges, however. In 2007, the global financial crisis hit, and the healthcare industry was severely impacted. A24 Group suffered significant losses, and Penny was forced to sell her home and personal assets to keep the business afloat. However, her determination and hard work paid off, and by 2012, the business had recovered and was profitable once again.

Throughout her career, Penny has been recognized for her innovative approach to business and her commitment to quality and customer service. In 2006, she was awarded an OBE (Order of the British Empire) for her services to business, and in 2014, she was named as one of the top 100 most influential businesswomen in the UK.

Penny's success as a businesswoman can be attributed to her innovative thinking, hard work, and effective business tactics. Her focus on delivering exceptional customer service and her commitment to quality have been key factors in the success of her businesses. She has also demonstrated an ability to adapt to changing market conditions and to develop new business models that are both efficient and effective.

In conclusion, Penny Streeter is one of the most influential business minds of all time. Her innovative thinking, hard work, and effective business tactics have made her a success in the highly competitive world of business. Her commitment to quality and customer service has been key to the success of her businesses, and her ability to adapt to changing market conditions has enabled her to thrive in an ever-changing business environment. It is clear that Penny Streeter's legacy will continue to inspire entrepreneurs for generations to come.

Penny Streeter's work tactics and business ethic have been key to her success. Her commitment to quality, customer service, and innovation are evident in the way she conducts business. Here are some specific details about her work tactics and business ethic:

Customer Service: Penny has always placed a strong emphasis on providing exceptional customer service. She believes that customers are the lifeblood of any business, and that their satisfaction is crucial to the success of a business. This philosophy is evident in the way she runs her businesses, where customer service is always a top priority.

Quality: Penny is a firm believer in quality, and she believes that it should be at the heart of any business. She has always strived to deliver high-quality products and services, and her businesses have become synonymous with quality. Her focus on quality has earned her a reputation for reliability and dependability.

Innovation: Penny is a natural innovator and has a gift for identifying opportunities and developing new business models. Her ability to innovate has been a key factor in the success of her businesses. She has always been willing to try new things and to take calculated risks, which has allowed her to stay ahead of the competition.

Hard Work: Penny is known for her work ethic, which is based on hard work, dedication, and perseverance. She is not afraid to put in the long hours and hard work required to make her businesses successful. Her determination and hard work have been crucial to her success as an entrepreneur.

Adaptability: Penny has always been able to adapt to changing market conditions and to develop new business models when required. This has enabled her to stay ahead of the competition and to continue to grow her businesses over time. She is not afraid to make changes and to take risks when necessary, which has helped her to remain successful in a constantly changing business environment.

Ethical Business Practices: Penny is committed to ethical business practices and has always conducted her businesses with integrity and honesty. She believes that business should be conducted with transparency and that honesty is the best policy. This philosophy has earned her the trust and respect of her customers and employees alike.

Overall, Penny Streeter's work tactics and business ethic are centered around quality, innovation, customer service, hard work, adaptability, and ethical business practices. These factors have been key to her success as an entrepreneur and have helped her to establish a reputation as one of the most influential business minds of all time.

The one thing that she did, that an entrepreneur should follow to be great today

There are many things that Penny Streeter did that entrepreneurs could learn from to be successful today. However, one of the most important things that she did, which any entrepreneur can follow, is to focus on the needs of the customer.

Penny recognized early on that the success of any business is ultimately determined by the satisfaction of its customers. She made it her priority to understand her customers' needs, preferences, and pain points, and to design her products and services to meet those needs. She also emphasized the importance of providing exceptional customer service, which helped her to build a loyal customer base.

Today, with the rise of e-commerce and social media, it is easier than ever for entrepreneurs to connect directly with their customers and to understand their needs. By taking the time to listen to customer feedback, responding to their concerns, and delivering products and services that meet their needs, entrepreneurs can build a strong and loyal customer base.

In short, to be great today, entrepreneurs should follow Penny Streeter's lead and focus on providing exceptional customer service, understanding their customers' needs, and designing their products and services accordingly. This approach will help entrepreneurs to build a strong foundation for their business, and to establish themselves as leaders in their industry.

Some additional details about Penny Streeter:

Early Life and Career: Penny Streeter was born in South Africa in 1957, and grew up in Zambia. She moved to the UK in the early 1980s, and started her career as a recruitment consultant. In 1986, she founded her first business, Ambition 24 Hours, a medical recruitment agency that provided staffing solutions for the National Health Service (NHS).

Entrepreneurial Success: Penny's success as an entrepreneur began with Ambition 24 Hours, which quickly became one of the UK's leading medical recruitment agencies. She later founded a second recruitment agency, The Care Bureau, which provided healthcare staffing solutions for the private sector. In 1997, she founded her third business, A24 Group, which provided staffing solutions for a variety of industries, including healthcare, aviation, and hospitality.

International Expansion: Under Penny's leadership, A24 Group expanded rapidly, and by 2017, it had operations in the UK, South Africa, Australia, and the United Arab Emirates. Today, the company is one of the world's largest healthcare staffing agencies, with over 20,000 employees.

Awards and Recognition: Penny Streeter's achievements as an entrepreneur have been recognized with numerous awards and honors. In 2009, she was awarded the Queen's Award for Enterprise, in recognition of her company's international growth. She was also named the UK's Ernst & Young Entrepreneur of the Year in 2012.

Philanthropy: Penny Streeter is also known for her philanthropic work, and has been involved in a number of charitable initiatives. She established the Penny Streeter Charitable Trust in 2005, which supports a variety of causes, including education, healthcare, and poverty alleviation.

Overall, Penny Streeter is a highly successful entrepreneur who has built a reputation for innovation, hard work, and exceptional customer service. Her achievements in the healthcare staffing industry, both in the UK and internationally, have earned her numerous awards and honors, and she continues to be a leading figure in the business world today.

GERARD SWOPE

Was an American businessman who is widely regarded as one of the most influential business minds of the early 20th century. He was born in 1872 in St. Louis, Missouri, and attended MIT, where he earned a degree in electrical engineering. After graduating, he began his career with General Electric (GE), where he quickly rose through the ranks to become the company's president in 1922.

Swope was a visionary leader who was known for his innovative approach to business. One of his most significant contributions was the development of the "Swope Plan," which was a blueprint for a national system of collective bargaining. The plan was introduced in 1933 and became a cornerstone of the New Deal, helping to establish labor rights and improve working conditions for millions of American workers.

However, Swope's impact on American business was much broader than just his work on collective bargaining. Throughout his career, he was a champion of innovation and a firm believer in the power of technology to transform industries. He was instrumental in bringing about several technological advancements that revolutionized the way businesses operate.

One of Swope's most notable innovations was the creation of

the first research and development (R&D) department at GE. Under his leadership, the company invested heavily in R&D, which led to the development of several groundbreaking products, including the electric refrigerator and the electric range. These products not only transformed the home appliance industry but also helped to improve the standard of living for millions of people around the world.

Swope was also a pioneer in the field of industrial design. He recognized that the aesthetic appeal of products was just as important as their functionality, and he pushed GE to invest in design and aesthetics. This led to the creation of some of the most iconic products of the 20th century, including the GE Monitor Top refrigerator, which is now considered a design classic.

In addition to his work at GE, Swope was also a key figure in the establishment of the National Recovery Administration (NRA) during the New Deal. The NRA was a federal agency that was charged with regulating industry and promoting fair competition. Swope was instrumental in its creation and served as its first administrator. He worked tirelessly to help American businesses recover from the Great Depression, and his efforts were widely praised for their effectiveness.

Overall, Gerard Swope's life and work as a businessman were marked by innovation, vision, and a commitment to social responsibility. He was a trailblazer who believed that business could be a force for good in the world and that technology could be harnessed to create a better future for all. His legacy continues to inspire business leaders today, and he remains one of the most influential and respected figures in the history of American business.

In addition to his work at GE and the National Recovery Administration, Swope was also a pioneer in the field of management theory. He recognized the importance of creating a strong corporate culture and developing effective leadership, and he was known for his ability to inspire and motivate his employees. Under his leadership, GE became known as one of the most innovative and successful companies in the world.

Swope was also a proponent of the social responsibilities of business. He believed that companies had a duty to give back to society and to use their resources for the greater good. He was a philanthropist who supported a wide range of causes, including education, healthcare, and the arts.

Another area where Swope made significant contributions was in the development of international business. He recognized the importance of global markets and worked to expand GE's presence overseas. He helped to establish the company's first foreign subsidiary in the United Kingdom and played a key role in the formation of the American Chamber of Commerce in Paris.

Swope's contributions to American business were recognized with numerous honors and awards. He was inducted into the National Business Hall of Fame in 1976, and the Swope School of Business at the University of Missouri was named in his honor. His legacy continues to inspire business leaders around the world, and his ideas about innovation, leadership, and social responsibility remain relevant today.

In conclusion, Gerard Swope was a remarkable businessman and innovator who made significant contributions to American business during the early 20th century. His work in areas such as collective bargaining, research and development, industrial design, and international business helped to transform industries and improve the lives of people around the world. His commitment to social responsibility and his belief in the power of technology to create a better future continue to inspire business leaders today, and his legacy is a testament to the enduring importance of innovation, leadership, and vision in business.

The one thing that Swope did, that an entrepreneur should follow to be great

Gerard Swope's legacy as a businessman offers many lessons and insights for entrepreneurs today. However, if there is one thing that stands out as particularly relevant and valuable, it would be his emphasis on innovation.

Swope was a pioneer in the field of innovation, and he recognized the importance of staying ahead of the curve and constantly pushing the boundaries of what was possible. He understood that innovation was the key to success in business, and he invested heavily in research and development to bring new products and technologies to market.

For entrepreneurs today, this emphasis on innovation is more important than ever. In today's fast-paced and constantly evolving business landscape, the ability to innovate is essential to staying competitive and achieving long-term success. Entrepreneurs who are able to identify new opportunities, challenge established norms, and embrace emerging technologies are more likely to thrive and grow.

Innovation doesn't just mean creating new products or services. It can also involve finding new and better ways to solve problems, streamlining operations, improving customer experiences, and more. The key is to always be looking for ways to improve and evolve, and to never become complacent or stagnant.

So, the one thing that an entrepreneur can learn from Gerard Swope is the importance of innovation. By embracing innovation and making it a central part of their business strategy, entrepreneurs can position themselves for success in today's rapidly changing and highly competitive business environment.

A few more key points about Gerard Swope's life and business career:

Swope was a skilled engineer and inventor who held several patents related to electrical engineering and manufacturing processes. He was known for his ability to innovate and improve upon existing technologies, as well as his talent for designing new products from scratch.

Swope was also an effective manager who was skilled at motivating his employees and fostering a positive work environment. He was a strong believer in the value of employee engagement and empowerment, and he was known for his efforts to create a sense of teamwork and collaboration within his companies.

In addition to his work in the electrical and manufacturing industries, Swope was also involved in politics and public policy. He served as a key advisor to President Franklin D. Roosevelt during the New Deal era, and he was instrumental in the development of several major pieces of legislation, including the National Labor Relations Act.

Swope was a strong advocate for corporate social responsibility, and he believed that companies had a responsibility to serve not just their shareholders, but also their employees, customers, and communities. He was a supporter of progressive social policies, including labor rights and environmental protection, and he worked to implement these values within his own companies.

Swope was a key player in the development of the modern consumer goods industry. He recognized the importance of creating products that were not only functional but also appealing to consumers on an emotional level. This led him to focus on design and marketing, as well as product development.

One of Swope's most significant contributions to business was his role in the development of the modern corporate structure. He believed that large corporations needed to be organized more efficiently and that workers needed to be treated fairly and given a voice in decision-making. His ideas influenced the development of labor relations, employee benefits, and corporate governance.

Swope was a strong advocate for government-business partnerships, arguing that the two sectors needed to work together to promote economic growth and social welfare. He was instrumental in the development of the National Recovery Administration, which was aimed at stimulating economic recovery during the Great Depression.

In addition to his business career, Swope was also a noted philanthropist and supporter of the arts. He donated significant sums of money to a variety of causes, including education, medical research, and the arts.

Finally, Swope was a visionary leader who was always looking to the future. He understood the importance of innovation and the need to stay ahead of the competition, and he was not afraid to take risks and invest in new ideas and technologies.

Overall, Gerard Swope was a visionary businessman and leader who left a lasting impact on the electrical and manufacturing industries. By studying his life and career, entrepreneurs can learn valuable lessons about innovation, leadership, corporate social responsibility, and more.

SAKICHI TOYODA

Was a Japanese inventor and industrialist who founded the Toyota Industries Corporation and the Toyota Motor Corporation. He is considered one of the most influential business minds of the 20th century, and his innovations and ideas have had a profound impact on the automotive industry and beyond.

Toyoda was born in 1867 in Kosai, a town in what is now Shizuoka Prefecture, Japan. He grew up in a family of poor farmers, but he had a natural curiosity and an aptitude for mechanics and engineering. As a young man, he began to experiment with machines and tools, and he developed a number of innovative devices that would lay the foundation for his future success.

One of Toyoda's earliest inventions was a textile loom that could automatically stop when a thread broke, preventing errors and improving efficiency. This invention was a major breakthrough in the textile industry, and it earned Toyoda international recognition and awards.

In the years that followed, Toyoda continued to experiment with new technologies and inventions. He developed a number of devices that would later be used in the automotive industry, including a power loom, a spinning machine, and an automatic shuttle-changing mechanism for textile machines.

But perhaps Toyoda's most significant contribution to the world of business was his philosophy of continuous improvement, which he called "kaizen". This philosophy emphasized the importance of constantly seeking to improve processes and systems, and it laid the foundation for the Toyota Production System, which revolutionized the manufacturing industry.

The Toyota Production System, which is based on the principles of "just-in-time" production and "lean manufacturing", is now widely used in industries around the world. It emphasizes the importance of eliminating waste, reducing inventory, and optimizing production processes to improve efficiency and quality.

Under Toyoda's leadership, Toyota became known for its innovative approach to manufacturing and its commitment to quality and customer satisfaction. The company introduced a number of groundbreaking models, including the Toyota Corolla and the Toyota Prius, which helped establish Toyota as a leader in the automotive industry.

Toyoda's contributions to business and industry were recognized with a number of awards and honors, including the Order of the Sacred Treasure, one of the highest honors awarded by the Japanese government.

Today, Toyoda's legacy continues to inspire entrepreneurs and business leaders around the world. His philosophy of kaizen has become a guiding principle for businesses of all kinds, and his commitment to innovation and continuous improvement has helped transform industries and improve the lives of people around the world.

After developing the automatic loom, Toyoda founded the Toyoda Spinning and Weaving Company in 1918 to manufacture and sell his machines. However, he soon realized that the company was not profitable and that he needed to find a way to improve his manufacturing processes to reduce costs and increase efficiency. This led him to develop the concept of "jidoka", or automation with a human touch, which he applied to his looms and later to his automotive production.

Toyoda's son, Kiichiro Toyoda, also played a significant role in the development of Toyota as a major automotive company. Kiichiro shared his father's passion for engineering and innovation, and he was instrumental in expanding Toyota's product line and global reach.

In addition to his contributions to business and industry, Toyoda was also a philanthropist who donated generously to charitable causes. He established a number of schools and hospitals in Japan, and he supported efforts to promote education and healthcare around the world.

Despite his success and influence, Toyoda remained humble and committed to his work throughout his life. He once said, "There is no such thing as an end to kaizen. You must continue to improve or you will be overtaken by competitors." This commitment to continuous improvement and innovation remains a core value of Toyota and has helped the company maintain its position as a leader in the automotive industry.

Toyoda passed away in 1930 at the age of 63, but his legacy lives on through Toyota and the many businesses and industries that have been influenced by his ideas and innovations.

The one thing that Toyoda did, that an entrepreneur should follow to be great

One of the most important things that entrepreneurs can learn from Sakichi Toyoda is his emphasis on continuous improvement and innovation. Toyoda believed that there was always room for improvement, and he was constantly seeking ways to make his machines and processes better.

This commitment to kaizen, or continuous improvement, is a key component of Toyota's business philosophy, and it has helped the company stay competitive and successful for decades. Entrepreneurs can apply this same mindset to their own businesses by always seeking ways to improve their products, services, and processes.

Another important lesson from Toyoda is the concept of jidoka, or automation with a human touch. This means using automation to improve efficiency and reduce costs, but also ensuring that human workers are still involved in the process and can detect and correct any errors or problems that arise. This approach has been instrumental in Toyota's success and can be applied to many different industries and businesses.

Overall, entrepreneurs can learn from Toyoda's dedication to innovation, continuous improvement, and balancing automation with human involvement. By adopting these principles and applying them to their own businesses, entrepreneurs can increase their chances of success and stay ahead of the competition.

some additional things to know about Sakichi Toyoda:

In addition to his work in manufacturing and automation, Toyoda was also an inventor and held numerous patents for his inventions throughout his career.

One of Toyoda's most significant inventions was the "Type G" automatic loom, which revolutionized the textile industry by automating the process of weaving cloth. This invention helped Toyoda establish his reputation as an innovative engineer and entrepreneur.

Toyoda was a strong believer in the power of teamwork and collaboration. He often worked closely with his son, Kiichiro Toyoda, as well as other engineers and designers, to develop and refine his inventions.

Despite his success, Toyoda was known for his frugality and simplicity. He lived a modest lifestyle and was always looking for ways to reduce waste and improve efficiency, both in his personal life and in his business.

Toyoda's legacy continues to be felt today through the Toyota Production System, which he helped develop. This system emphasizes efficiency, quality, and continuous improvement, and has been adopted by many other businesses and industries around the world.

Toyoda was also a philanthropist and donated generously to educational and charitable causes throughout his life. He believed in using his success to help others and was dedicated to improving the lives of people in his community and beyond.

One of Toyoda's most significant contributions to the automotive industry was the development of the "Just-in-Time" manufacturing process. This system is based on the idea of producing goods only when they are needed, rather than keeping large inventories of finished products on hand. This approach helps to reduce waste and improve efficiency, and it has been widely adopted in many different industries around the world.

Another key innovation from Toyoda was the development of the Type G automatic loom. This machine was capable of stopping automatically when a thread broke or the shuttle ran out of thread, reducing the need for human intervention and increasing productivity. The Type G loom became very popular in the textile industry and helped to establish Toyoda's reputation as a leading inventor and innovator.

In addition to his work in business and industry, Toyoda was also a devoted family man and a strong supporter of education. He believed that education was essential to the success of any society, and he established several schools and scholarship programs in Japan. He also supported efforts to improve education in other countries, and he believed that education was the key to achieving a more peaceful and prosperous world.

Despite his many accomplishments, Toyoda remained humble and focused on his work throughout his life. He once said, "If you have a dream, don't just sit there. Gather courage to believe that you can succeed and leave no stone unturned to make it a reality." This commitment to hard work and determination is a key aspect of Toyoda's legacy and has inspired countless entrepreneurs and innovators around the world.

Overall, Sakichi Toyoda was a visionary entrepreneur and inventor who revolutionized the textile industry and helped lay the foundation for modern manufacturing and automation. His commitment to innovation, teamwork, and continuous improvement continue to inspire entrepreneurs and business leaders around the world.

DONALD TRUMP

is widely known as a successful businessman and entrepreneur, having made his fortune in real estate and other industries, and after making a big name for himself throughout his life as a media persona, he achieved becoming the President of the United States. His innovative mind, work ethic, and business tactics have been admired by many, and he is often considered one of the most influential business minds of all time.

Born in 1946 in Queens, New York, Trump grew up in a wealthy family with a strong entrepreneurial spirit. His father, Fred Trump, was a successful real estate developer who instilled in Donald a passion for business and entrepreneurship from an early age.

After graduating from college in 1968, Trump joined his father's real estate business and began working on a variety of development projects. He quickly made a name for himself as a skilled negotiator and deal-maker, and he soon began to pursue his own real estate ventures.

In the early 1980s, Trump began to focus on developing high-end properties in Manhattan, including luxury condominiums, office buildings, and hotels. He became known for his bold, flamboyant style, and his willingness to take risks and make big bets on high-profile projects.

One of Trump's most famous projects was the development

of the Trump Tower, a 58-story skyscraper in Midtown Manhattan. The building, which opened in 1983, was one of the most expensive and luxurious in the city, and it helped to cement Trump's reputation as a major player in the real estate industry.

Trump's success as a businessman and real estate developer was due in large part to his innovative mind and his willingness to take risks. He was always on the lookout for new opportunities and was not afraid to pursue unconventional strategies to achieve his goals.

For example, Trump was one of the first developers to use television advertising to promote his properties. He also pioneered the use of tax abatements and other government incentives to help finance his projects.

In addition to his innovative tactics, Trump was also known for his hard work and dedication. He was known to work long hours and was always striving to find ways to improve his businesses and increase his wealth.

However, Trump's business career has not been without controversy. He has been involved in numerous legal battles and has faced accusations of fraud and unethical behavior. Some have criticized his business practices as ruthless and cutthroat, and others have accused him of exploiting workers and engaging in unethical business practices.

Despite these criticisms, it is clear that Donald Trump has had a major impact on the business world and has been one of the most influential entrepreneurs and businessmen of all time. His innovative mind, work ethic, and business tactics have been emulated by countless others, and his name has become synonymous with success and wealth.

In conclusion, Donald Trump's life as a businessman has been marked by innovation, hard work, and a willingness to take risks. While his business practices have not been without controversy, there is no denying his impact on the business world and his status as one of the most influential business minds of all time.

One of the most notable aspects of Trump's work tactics was his ability to negotiate deals and make bold business moves. He was always looking for opportunities to expand his empire and was not afraid to take risks to achieve his goals. Trump was known for being a skilled negotiator who could drive a hard bargain and get the best possible deal for himself and his businesses.

Another important aspect of Trump's work tactics was his focus on marketing and branding. He understood the importance of building a strong brand and was always looking for ways to promote his businesses and increase their visibility. Trump was one of the first developers to use television advertising to promote his properties, and he was also a master of self-promotion, often appearing in the media to talk about his projects and his business success.

In addition to his focus on marketing and branding, Trump was also known for his attention to detail and his insistence on quality. He was committed to building the best possible properties and was not willing to cut corners or compromise on quality. Trump was also a hands-on manager who was deeply involved in all aspects of his businesses, from design and construction to marketing and sales.

When it comes to his business ethics, opinions on Trump's practices are somewhat divided. Some view him as a ruthless businessman who was willing to do whatever it took to get ahead, including engaging in questionable practices like tax evasion and bankruptcy fraud. Others see him as a savvy entrepreneur who simply played by the rules of the game and used his skills and resources to achieve his goals.

Regardless of one's perspective on Trump's business ethics, it is clear that he operated in a highly competitive and often cutthroat industry. Real estate development is a notoriously challenging business, and success often requires a willingness to take risks and push the boundaries of what is considered acceptable.

In conclusion, Trump's work tactics and business ethics were characterized by a focus on negotiation, branding, quality, and a willingness to take risks. While opinions may differ on his practices and ethics, there is no denying his impact on the business world and his status as one of the most influential entrepreneurs and businessmen of all time.

The one thing that he did, that an entrepreneur should follow to be great today

While there are certainly many things that an entrepreneur can learn from Donald Trump's success, one of the most important lessons is the value of perseverance.

Throughout his career, Trump faced numerous setbacks, failures, and obstacles, but he never gave up. Instead, he persisted through difficult times, kept his focus on his goals, and continued to work tirelessly to achieve success.

For example, Trump faced numerous setbacks and bankruptcies in the 1990s, but he was able to bounce back and rebuild his businesses. He also faced significant opposition and criticism during his 2016 presidential campaign, but he continued to campaign tirelessly and ultimately emerged victorious.

In the business world, perseverance is a crucial trait that can make the difference between success and failure. Entrepreneurs who are able to persevere through difficult times, adapt to changing market conditions, and remain focused on their goals are more likely to achieve success than those who give up at the first sign of adversity.

Ultimately, the key to success as an entrepreneur is

not just about having innovative ideas or cutting-edge business tactics, but also about having the resilience and determination to push through difficult times and overcome obstacles. By following Trump's example of perseverance, entrepreneurs can increase their chances of success and achieve their goals, no matter what challenges they may face along the way.

Some additional facts about Donald Trump as a businessman:

Real estate development was his main focus: While Trump has had business interests in many industries, including casinos, golf courses, and beauty pageants, his primary focus throughout his career has been on real estate development. He has been involved in the development of numerous high-profile properties, including the Trump Tower in New York City and the Trump International Hotel and Tower in Chicago.

He has authored several books: In addition to his business pursuits, Trump has also authored several books on business and personal success, including "The Art of the Deal," "The Art of the Comeback," and "Think Like a Billionaire." These books provide insights into Trump's strategies for success and offer advice to aspiring entrepreneurs.

He has a history of controversy: While Trump's success as a businessman is undeniable, he has also been the subject of numerous controversies throughout his career. These controversies have included allegations of sexual assault, lawsuits related to his business practices, and criticism of his political views and statements.

He is a self-made billionaire: Despite coming from a wealthy family, Trump is considered a self-made billionaire because he built his fortune through his own business ventures rather than inheriting it from his family. According to Forbes, Trump's net worth was estimated at $3.1 billion as of

2023.

Branding: Trump was also known for his branding expertise. He attached his name to everything from hotels and golf courses to bottled water and steaks, and his name became synonymous with luxury and wealth. While some criticized his approach as being more about self-promotion than business success, there is no doubt that his branding strategy was effective and contributed to his success.

The Apprentice: In addition to his business ventures, Trump is also well-known for his time as the host of the reality TV show "The Apprentice." The show, which ran from 2004 to 2017, featured aspiring entrepreneurs competing for a job with Trump's organization. The show was a massive success and helped to cement Trump's image as a savvy businessman and tough negotiator.

Politics: Trump's foray into politics began in the late 1980s, when he briefly considered a run for president as a third-party candidate. He also flirted with the idea of running for governor of New York in 2006. However, it was his successful 2016 campaign for president that thrust him into the political spotlight.

TED TURNER

is widely considered one of the most influential businesspeople in history. He was a visionary entrepreneur who was a pioneer in multiple industries, including television and media, and his impact can still be felt today.

Turner was born in Cincinnati, Ohio, in 1938, and was the son of a wealthy businessman. After his father's suicide in 1963, he inherited his father's struggling billboard company and began to turn it around with his innovative marketing tactics. Turner was known for his willingness to take risks and try new things, even if they seemed unconventional.

One of Turner's most significant contributions to the business world was his creation of the first 24-hour news network, CNN. In 1980, he launched the Cable News Network, which revolutionized the way people consumed news. Before CNN, news programs were only aired a few times a day, but Turner saw the potential in providing constant updates, and it paid off. CNN was an immediate success, and it paved the way for other 24-hour news networks to follow.

Turner's innovation didn't stop there, though. He was also one of the first businesspeople to recognize the potential of satellite technology, which allowed him to broadcast his programming to a global audience. In 1983, he launched the first satellite news gathering system, which allowed CNN to cover breaking news events from anywhere in the world. This technology was quickly adopted by other news organizations and is now an essential part of modern news reporting.

Turner's entrepreneurial spirit didn't just benefit the media industry, though. He also saw potential in the hospitality industry and bought the Atlanta Braves baseball team in 1976. He was a hands-on owner and was known for his passion for the sport, often making decisions based on his gut instinct rather than purely financial calculations. Under his ownership, the Braves became one of the most successful teams in the league, winning multiple division titles and even a World Series championship in 1995.

Turner's business success wasn't just about innovation, though. He was also a skilled negotiator and knew how to make deals that benefited both parties. One of his most famous negotiations was the acquisition of MGM's film library, which gave Turner access to a vast collection of classic movies. He was able to acquire the library for a fraction of its value, and it became a cornerstone of his media empire.

Perhaps one of the most impressive things about Turner's business career was his ability to rebound from setbacks. In the late 1980s, he found himself in financial trouble after a series of bad investments and a hostile takeover attempt by Rupert Murdoch. But Turner didn't give up. He sold off some of his assets, including the Atlanta Hawks basketball team, and focused on rebuilding his media empire. Within a few years, he had bounced back, and his company was stronger than ever.

In conclusion, Ted Turner was an influential businessman who revolutionized multiple industries through his innovative ideas, risk-taking mentality, and negotiation skills. His creation of CNN and his use of satellite technology changed the way people consume news, and his acquisition of the MGM film library and ownership of the Atlanta Braves helped cement his place in history as one of the most influential business minds of all time. His ability to rebound from setbacks is a testament to his resilience and determination, and his impact on the business world will be felt for years to come.

Ted Turner was known for his unconventional work tactics and his commitment to ethical business practices. Here are some more details about his work tactics and business ethic:

Risk-taking mentality: Turner was not afraid to take risks and try new things. He often went against conventional wisdom and trusted his gut instincts. For example, he launched CNN at a time when many people thought that 24-hour news programming would not be successful. This willingness to take risks paid off for him in many ways, including the success of CNN and his other business ventures.

Hands-on management style: Turner was known for being very involved in the day-to-day operations of his companies. He was a hands-on owner and liked to be involved in all aspects of his businesses. He would often make decisions based on his personal experiences rather than just looking at financial data.

Ethical business practices: Turner was committed to ethical business practices throughout his career. He believed in treating his employees fairly and paying them well. He also believed in giving back to the community and was known for his philanthropic efforts. In 1997, he donated $1 billion to the United Nations, which was the largest single donation ever made to the organization.

Negotiation skills: Turner was a skilled negotiator and knew how to make deals that benefited both parties. For example, when he acquired the MGM film library, he was able to negotiate a deal that allowed him to acquire the library for a fraction of its value. He was also able to negotiate a merger with Time Warner in the 1990s that created one of the largest media companies in the world.

Long-term vision: Turner was known for having a long-term vision for his companies. He was not focused on short-term profits but instead focused on building sustainable businesses that would be successful for years to come. For example, he invested heavily in CNN in the early years, even though it was not profitable at first, because he believed in its potential for long-term success.

Passion and drive: Finally, Turner was driven by his passion for his businesses. He was known for working long hours and being fully committed to his companies. His passion and drive were infectious, and they helped to motivate his employees and drive the success of his businesses.

In conclusion, Ted Turner was a unique businessman who had a risk-taking mentality, a hands-on management style, a commitment to ethical business practices, excellent negotiation skills, a long-term vision, and a passion for his businesses. These traits helped him to build successful companies and revolutionize multiple industries.

The one thing that he did, that an entrepreneur should follow to be great today

It's difficult to single out one thing that Ted Turner did that entrepreneurs should follow to be great today, as his success was the result of a combination of various factors such as his unique personality, innovative mindset, and specific circumstances. However, if I had to choose one thing, I would say that Turner's willingness to take risks and try new things is a trait that entrepreneurs should follow.

In today's rapidly changing business landscape, the ability to take calculated risks and adapt to new situations is crucial for success. By taking risks and trying new things, entrepreneurs can innovate, differentiate themselves from competitors, and uncover new opportunities. Of course, taking risks does not mean blindly jumping into new ventures without considering the potential downsides. Instead, it involves carefully weighing the risks and rewards and being willing to pivot or change course if necessary.

Turner's success with CNN is a great example of the power of taking risks. At a time when 24-hour news programming was considered unprofitable, Turner had the vision to see its potential and launched CNN. Despite initial skepticism and financial struggles, CNN eventually became a leading news network, and Turner's risk-taking paid off.

Therefore, if there is one thing entrepreneurs can learn from Ted Turner's life as a businessman, it is to have the courage to take calculated risks and try new things. This mindset can help entrepreneurs to innovate, adapt, and succeed in today's fast-paced business world.

A few more interesting facts about Ted Turner:

Turner was a pioneer in cable television: Turner started his career in the 1970s with a small UHF television station in Atlanta. He later purchased a satellite transmission system, which allowed him to broadcast his station's programming to cable systems across the country. This led to the creation of the first "superstation," which was called WTBS (now known as TBS).

He revolutionized the media industry: In addition to creating the first superstation, Turner is also credited with revolutionizing the media industry with the launch of CNN. CNN was the first 24-hour news network, and it changed the way people consumed news. Turner's innovations helped to shape the modern media landscape, and his influence is still felt today.

He is a philanthropist: Turner is also known for his philanthropic efforts. In addition to his $1 billion donation to the United Nations, he has also donated millions of dollars to various causes such as wildlife conservation, childhood education, and nuclear disarmament. He has also pledged to give away 80% of his wealth to charity.

He is a competitive sailor: Turner is an avid sailor and has competed in many high-profile sailing races, including the America's Cup. He has won several races and is known for his competitive spirit.

He is a conservationist: Turner is passionate about conservation and has purchased large tracts of land in the United States and South America to protect them from development. He has also created several conservation organizations, including the Turner Foundation and the Captain Planet Foundation, which focus on environmental issues.

He has faced personal challenges: Despite his many successes, Turner has also faced personal challenges in his life. He has been married and divorced three times, and he has struggled with bipolar disorder. However, he has been open about his struggles and has used his platform to raise awareness about mental health issues.

These are just a few of the many interesting aspects of Ted Turner's life and career as a businessman, innovator, and philanthropist.

CORNELIUS VANDERBILT

Was a 19th-century American industrialist and entrepreneur who made a name for himself in the shipping and railroad industries. He was born on May 27, 1794, on Staten Island, New York, and grew up in a family of modest means. Despite his humble beginnings, Vanderbilt would eventually become one of the wealthiest men in America, earning the nickname "Commodore" for his success in the shipping industry.

Vanderbilt's first foray into business was as a ferry operator, running a ferry service between Staten Island and Manhattan. He quickly realized that he could make more money by owning the boats himself rather than simply operating them, so he began investing in steamships. This proved to be a shrewd move, as steam-powered vessels were faster and more efficient than traditional sailing ships, and Vanderbilt was able to outcompete his rivals by offering faster and more reliable service.

Vanderbilt was also a pioneer in the railroad industry, investing heavily in the development of railroads and helping to build the New York and Harlem Railroad. He was a firm believer in the power of rail transportation, recognizing its potential to revolutionize the way goods and people were moved across the country. He was known for his aggressive business tactics, often engaging in cutthroat competition with his rivals and using his wealth and influence to gain an edge.

One of Vanderbilt's most famous business tactics was his use of rebates, or discounts offered to large customers in exchange for their exclusive business. This allowed him to dominate the shipping industry by offering lower prices than his competitors and undercutting their profits. He was also known for his ability to negotiate favorable rates with suppliers and vendors, using his vast wealth and influence to secure the best deals possible.

Another key to Vanderbilt's success was his focus on efficiency and innovation. He was always looking for ways to streamline his operations and reduce costs, whether by using steam power instead of sail power, investing in faster and more reliable engines, or developing new business models that allowed him to operate more efficiently. He was also an early adopter of telegraph technology, which allowed him to communicate quickly and efficiently with his business partners and stay ahead of his competitors.

Despite his reputation as a ruthless businessman, Vanderbilt was also known for his philanthropy, donating millions of dollars to charity during his lifetime. He funded the construction of Vanderbilt University in Nashville, Tennessee, and was a major benefactor of the New York and Brooklyn Bridge, which was named in his honor after his death in 1877.

In conclusion, Cornelius Vanderbilt was one of the most influential business minds of the 19th century, thanks to his innovative approach to transportation, aggressive business tactics, and unwavering focus on efficiency and innovation. His use of steam-powered ships and railroads helped revolutionize the way goods and people were moved across the country, while his aggressive business tactics and focus on efficiency allowed him to dominate his competitors and build a vast business empire. Despite his reputation as a ruthless businessman, Vanderbilt was also a philanthropist who used his wealth and influence to make a positive impact on society, leaving behind a legacy that continues to inspire entrepreneurs and businessmen today.

Vanderbilt was known for his aggressive business tactics and cutthroat competition with his rivals. He was not afraid to use his wealth and influence to gain an advantage over his competitors, and he often engaged in fierce price wars and undercutting of profits. However, he also believed in fair competition and was known to offer better services and lower prices to customers as a way of outcompeting his rivals.

One of Vanderbilt's key business tactics was his use of rebates, which he used to attract large customers and gain an edge over his competitors. He would offer large discounts to customers who agreed to exclusive contracts with his shipping lines, thereby locking in their business and preventing them from doing business with his rivals. This allowed him to dominate the shipping industry and set the standard for pricing and service quality.

Another tactic that Vanderbilt employed was his focus on efficiency and innovation. He was always looking for ways to reduce costs and streamline his operations, whether by using faster and more reliable steam engines, developing new business models that allowed him to operate more efficiently, or investing in telegraph technology to improve communication with his business partners. By focusing on efficiency, Vanderbilt was able to keep his costs low and maintain a competitive advantage over his rivals.

Vanderbilt was also known for his negotiation skills, which he used to secure favorable rates with suppliers and vendors.

He was not afraid to bargain hard and play hardball with his business partners, using his wealth and influence to get the best deals possible. This allowed him to keep his costs low and maintain his competitive edge, even in the face of stiff competition.

Finally, it's worth noting that Vanderbilt was not just focused on making money for himself. He was also a philanthropist who used his wealth and influence to make a positive impact on society. He donated millions of dollars to charity during his lifetime, funding projects like Vanderbilt University and the New York and Brooklyn Bridge. He believed that wealth came with a responsibility to give back to the community, and he set an example for future generations of business leaders to follow.

In summary, Vanderbilt's work tactics and business ethic were focused on aggressive competition, innovation, efficiency, and negotiation. He was not afraid to use his wealth and influence to gain an advantage over his rivals, but he also believed in fair competition and offered better services and lower prices to customers as a way of outcompeting his rivals. He was a shrewd negotiator and focused on reducing costs and streamlining operations to maintain his competitive edge. Above all, he believed in using his wealth for the greater good, setting an example for future generations of business leaders to follow.

The one thing that he did, that an entrepreneur should follow to be great today

One thing that modern entrepreneurs can learn from Vanderbilt's success is his unwavering focus on innovation and efficiency. Throughout his career, Vanderbilt was always looking for ways to improve his business and stay ahead of the competition. He invested in new technologies, developed new business models, and streamlined his operations to reduce costs and increase profits.

Today's entrepreneurs can apply this same mindset by constantly seeking out new opportunities to innovate and improve their business. They should always be looking for ways to streamline their operations, reduce costs, and improve the quality of their products or services. By adopting a relentless focus on innovation and efficiency, entrepreneurs can stay ahead of the competition and build successful, sustainable businesses.

Another lesson from Vanderbilt's career is the importance of negotiating hard and playing hardball with business partners. In today's fast-paced business environment, entrepreneurs need to be able to negotiate effectively and secure favorable deals with suppliers, vendors, and other partners. They should be willing to bargain hard and use their leverage to get the best possible terms.

Finally, Vanderbilt's philanthropic legacy is another important lesson for modern entrepreneurs. While building wealth and creating successful businesses is important, entrepreneurs should also recognize the importance of giving back to the community. By using their resources to support charitable causes and make a positive impact on society, entrepreneurs can build a legacy that extends beyond their business success.

Some additional facts about Cornelius Vanderbilt:

Vanderbilt was born in 1794 in Staten Island, New York. He grew up in a poor family and left school at the age of 11 to work on his father's ferry. He quickly proved himself to be a savvy businessman, and by the age of 16, he had saved up enough money to start his own ferry service.

Vanderbilt went on to build a shipping empire that dominated the East Coast trade routes. He invested in faster and more reliable steam engines, which allowed his ships to travel more quickly and efficiently than his competitors.

In the 1850s, Vanderbilt turned his attention to the nascent railroad industry, investing heavily in railroad companies and helping to establish the New York and Harlem Railroad. He eventually became one of the wealthiest men in America.

Vanderbilt was known for his tough business tactics and cutthroat competition with his rivals. He was not afraid to use his wealth and influence to gain an advantage, and he often engaged in fierce price wars and undercutting of profits.

Vanderbilt was a controversial figure, and many of his competitors and contemporaries saw him as ruthless and unscrupulous. However, he was also respected for his business acumen and his ability to build successful businesses from the ground up.

In addition to his business pursuits, Vanderbilt was also a philanthropist who donated millions of dollars to charitable causes during his lifetime. He helped to fund the establishment of Vanderbilt University and donated to other educational institutions and charitable organizations.

Vanderbilt died in 1877 at the age of 82. At the time of his death, he was one of the wealthiest men in the world, with an estimated net worth of $100 million.

GARY VAYNERCHUK,

born in 1975 in Babruysk, Belarus, is an entrepreneur, investor, and internet personality who is widely regarded as one of the most innovative and influential business minds of our time. Gary has successfully built and grown several companies, including Wine Library, VaynerMedia, and VaynerX, which have collectively generated billions of dollars in revenue.

Gary's journey as an entrepreneur began when he was just a teenager. His father owned a liquor store, and at the age of 14, Gary started working there. It was during this time that he developed a deep passion for wine and started learning as much as he could about it. In 1998, Gary took over the family business and renamed it Wine Library. He then began to apply his innovative mind and work ethic to grow the company, which resulted in a massive increase in revenue.

One of Gary's most significant contributions to the business world is his innovative use of social media marketing. He recognized early on that social media was the future of marketing and began using platforms such as Twitter, Facebook, and Instagram to promote his company and build his personal brand. His success in this area led to him founding VaynerMedia in 2009, a social media-focused digital agency that has worked with some of the world's largest brands.

Gary's approach to business is centered around hard work and hustle. He believes that success comes from putting in the work and grinding every day. He has famously said that "There's no substitute for hard work" and "The market doesn't care about your excuses; it only cares about your results." This attitude has helped him build several successful companies and has inspired countless entrepreneurs to follow in his footsteps.

Another key aspect of Gary's success is his willingness to take risks. He has a keen eye for spotting trends and is not afraid to pivot his business in a new direction if necessary. For example, when he saw the potential of social media marketing, he shifted his focus from wine to digital marketing. This willingness to take risks has allowed him to stay ahead of the curve and continue to grow and evolve as a businessman.

Gary is also known for his unique leadership style. He believes in leading by example and puts a lot of emphasis on company culture. He has created a work environment that encourages creativity, innovation, and a strong work ethic. He has also emphasized the importance of empathy and emotional intelligence in business, which has helped him build strong relationships with clients and employees alike.

Finally, Gary's impact on the business world can be seen in the countless entrepreneurs he has inspired. His books, speeches, and social media content have encouraged millions of people to pursue their dreams and start their own businesses. He has become a mentor and role model to many young entrepreneurs, who look up to him for his innovative mind and work ethic.

In conclusion, Gary Vaynerchuk is an incredibly innovative and influential businessman whose impact on the business world is impossible to ignore. His unique approach to marketing, emphasis on hard work and hustle, willingness to take risks, and focus on company culture have made him a true visionary and role model. His influence can be seen in the countless entrepreneurs he has inspired and the companies he has built, making him a worthy addition to any list of the most influential business minds of all time.

Gary Vaynerchuk is known for his unique work tactics and business ethics, which have played a significant role in his success as an entrepreneur.

One of Gary's primary work tactics is his ability to stay ahead of the curve. He is constantly studying trends and looking for new opportunities. For example, when he saw the potential of social media marketing, he shifted his focus from traditional marketing to digital marketing. He also recognizes the importance of emerging technologies, such as blockchain and cryptocurrency, and is always exploring new ways to integrate them into his businesses.

Gary is also known for his work ethic, which can only be described as relentless. He often works 12 to 18 hours a day, seven days a week. He believes that success requires hard work and that there are no shortcuts to success. He also stresses the importance of focusing on the right things and not wasting time on activities that do not contribute to achieving one's goals.

Another important aspect of Gary's work tactics is his emphasis on building relationships. He places a high value on networking and building strong connections with clients, partners, and employees. He often speaks about the importance of empathy and emotional intelligence in business, stressing that people are the foundation of any successful company.

Gary is also a big believer in the power of branding. He understands that a strong brand is essential for building a successful business and has built several successful brands throughout his career. He often speaks about the importance of consistency and authenticity in branding, stressing that a brand must be true to itself to succeed.

When it comes to business ethics, Gary is known for his transparency and honesty. He believes in being upfront and honest with clients and partners, even if it means delivering bad news. He also stresses the importance of delivering on promises and doing what is right, even if it is not the easiest or most profitable thing to do.

Another important aspect of Gary's business ethics is his focus on giving back. He is a big believer in using his success to help others and is involved in several philanthropic initiatives. He has also launched several programs aimed at helping entrepreneurs and small businesses succeed, including the Vayner Mentors program and the VaynerX Small Business Relief program.

In summary, Gary Vaynerchuk's work tactics and business ethics are characterized by his ability to stay ahead of the curve, his relentless work ethic, his emphasis on building relationships and branding, his transparency and honesty, and his focus on giving back. These traits have helped him build several successful businesses and have made him a role model for entrepreneurs around the world.

The one thing that he did, that an entrepreneur should follow to be great today

It's difficult to pinpoint just one thing that Gary Vaynerchuk did that entrepreneurs should follow to be great today, as his success is the result of a combination of various factors. However, one aspect of his work tactics that stands out is his ability to identify and capitalize on emerging trends.

Gary has a keen eye for emerging technologies, social media trends, and other cultural shifts that could potentially impact the business world. He has consistently demonstrated his ability to stay ahead of the curve and identify opportunities before they become mainstream.

For example, he recognized the potential of social media marketing early on and was able to build a successful agency around it. He also saw the potential of video content and launched the YouTube channel Wine Library TV, which helped him gain a large following and establish himself as an authority in the wine industry.

Today, entrepreneurs should follow in Gary's footsteps by staying abreast of emerging trends and technologies in their industry. They should be open to new ideas and willing to experiment with new approaches to marketing, branding, and customer engagement.

By being able to identify emerging trends and technologies early on, entrepreneurs can position themselves to take advantage of new opportunities and gain a competitive advantage over their peers. This requires a willingness to take risks and be proactive in exploring new ideas and approaches, just as Gary Vaynerchuk has done throughout his career.

A few more things about Gary Vaynerchuk:

Gary Vaynerchuk was born in Belarus in 1975 and moved to the United States with his family when he was just 3 years old. His parents worked long hours in their liquor store, which is where Gary developed his interest in wine.

In 1997, Gary joined his family's business, Wine Library, and helped grow it from a local liquor store to a $60 million wine retailer. He achieved this by launching Wine Library TV, a video blog where he shared his knowledge and passion for wine with his audience.

In 2009, Gary launched VaynerMedia, a digital marketing agency that has worked with clients such as PepsiCo, General

Electric, and Anheuser-Busch. VaynerMedia has grown rapidly over the years and now has offices in New York, Los Angeles, London, and Singapore.

In addition to his work at VaynerMedia, Gary has launched several other successful businesses, including a sports agency called VaynerSports and a cannabis-focused marketing agency called Green Street.

Gary is a prolific author and has written several best-selling books, including "Crush It!: Why Now Is the Time to Cash in on Your Passion" and "Jab, Jab, Jab, Right Hook: How to Tell Your Story in a Noisy Social World." He is also a sought-after public speaker and has given keynote speeches at events such as SXSW, the Web 2.0 Summit, and the Inc. 500|5000 Conference.

Gary is known for his strong personality and no-nonsense approach to business. He is not afraid to speak his mind and is known for delivering tough love to his clients, employees, and even his own family members.

Despite his success, Gary remains humble and grounded. He often speaks about his gratitude for his upbringing and the opportunities he has been given, and he is committed to using his success to help others. He is involved in several philanthropic initiatives, including the Vayner Foundation, which supports education and entrepreneurship programs for underprivileged youth.

Overall, Gary Vaynerchuk is a multi-faceted entrepreneur and business leader who has made a significant impact on the worlds of marketing, branding, and entrepreneurship. His success is a testament to his relentless work ethic, innovative thinking, and commitment to building strong relationships and brands.

MADAM CJ WALKER

born Sarah Breedlove, was an African-American entrepreneur and philanthropist who revolutionized the hair care industry for black women in the early 20th century. She was born on December 23, 1867, in Delta, Louisiana, and was the daughter of formerly enslaved parents. Despite facing poverty, discrimination, and multiple setbacks throughout her life, Madam CJ Walker's innovative mind, hard work, and business tactics propelled her to become one of the most successful and influential business minds of all time.

Madam CJ Walker's journey towards entrepreneurship began in 1904, when she began experiencing hair loss due to a scalp condition. At the time, black women had limited access to hair care products, and the available options were often harmful and ineffective. Recognizing this gap in the market, Madam CJ Walker started experimenting with different hair care ingredients and eventually developed a line of hair care products specifically designed for black women.

To promote her products, Madam CJ Walker used a combination of innovative marketing tactics that were ahead of their time. She traveled extensively, giving lectures and demonstrations on hair care, and often partnered with local churches and community organizations to reach a wider audience. She also placed ads in black-owned newspapers and printed testimonials from satisfied customers on her product labels, which helped build trust and credibility with potential buyers.

Another key factor in Madam CJ Walker's success was her ability to build a strong team of sales agents, which she called "Walker Agents." She provided her agents with training, support, and incentives, and in doing so, created a network of empowered and financially independent black women. This network not only helped sell her products but also served as a platform for advocacy and social change.

Madam CJ Walker's business success was not without its challenges. She faced fierce competition from other hair care entrepreneurs, many of whom tried to imitate her products and marketing strategies. She also faced criticism from some in the black community who felt that her focus on beauty and personal grooming perpetuated negative stereotypes. Despite these challenges, Madam CJ Walker remained committed to her vision and worked tirelessly to expand her business.

In addition to her business success, Madam CJ Walker was also a philanthropist and advocate for social change. She used her wealth and influence to support causes such as education, healthcare, and civil rights. She donated generously to black colleges and universities and was a vocal supporter of the NAACP and other civil rights organizations.

Madam CJ Walker's legacy as an entrepreneur and business innovator is undeniable. Her pioneering work in the hair care industry helped pave the way for future generations of black entrepreneurs and empowered countless black women. Her innovative marketing tactics, emphasis on team building, and commitment to social change continue to inspire business leaders today.

In conclusion, Madam CJ Walker's life as a businessman was defined by her innovative mind, hard work, and business tactics. Her focus on creating a product that addressed the needs of an underserved market, combined with her marketing and sales strategies, allowed her to become one of the most successful and influential business minds of all time. Her philanthropic work and advocacy for social change further cemented her legacy as a leader and trailblazer. Madam CJ Walker is a true inspiration and role model for aspiring entrepreneurs and business leaders around the world.

Madam CJ Walker's success as an entrepreneur can be attributed to several key work tactics and business ethics. Here are some examples:

Innovation: Madam CJ Walker's success in the beauty industry was largely due to her innovative approach. She developed a line of hair care products specifically for black women, who had previously been underserved by the beauty industry. Her products were unique and catered to the specific needs of her customers. She also developed a line of cosmetics for black women, which was groundbreaking at the time.

Marketing and Promotion: Madam CJ Walker was a master of marketing and promotion. She traveled extensively, giving demonstrations of her hair products and distributing literature about hair care to black women. She also established a network of sales agents, who she called "beauty culturists," to sell her products across the country. She trained her sales agents in her methods and techniques, which included offering personalized hair consultations to her customers. Her promotional efforts helped to spread the word about her products and build a loyal customer base.

Customer Service: Madam CJ Walker believed in providing excellent customer service. She offered personalized consultations to her customers, helping them to select the products that were best suited to their individual needs. She also provided training to her sales agents, so they could offer the same level of personalized service to their customers. By focusing on the needs of her customers, Madam CJ Walker was able to build a loyal following and establish a reputation for quality and reliability.

Entrepreneurial Spirit: Madam CJ Walker had a strong entrepreneurial spirit. She was always looking for new opportunities and ways to expand her business. She established a factory to manufacture her products, which allowed her to increase production and lower costs. She also opened a beauty school to train her sales agents, which helped to build a skilled workforce for her growing business. By constantly seeking out new opportunities and taking risks, Madam CJ Walker was able to grow her business and establish herself as a leader in the industry.

Social Responsibility: Madam CJ Walker was committed to using her wealth and influence for the betterment of her community. She donated money to support black causes and organizations, including the NAACP and the National Association of Colored Women. She also funded scholarships for black students and donated money to support the construction of a YMCA in Indianapolis. By giving back to her community, Madam CJ Walker demonstrated her commitment to social responsibility and the importance of using one's success to make a positive impact on the world.

In summary, Madam CJ Walker's work tactics and business ethics included innovation, marketing and promotion, customer service, entrepreneurial spirit, and social responsibility. Her approach to business was focused on providing high-quality products and services to her customers, while also giving back to her community. These values helped her to build a successful and sustainable business, and her legacy continues to inspire entrepreneurs and business leaders today.

The one thing that she did, that an entrepreneur should follow to be great

It is difficult to single out just one thing that Madam CJ Walker did that an entrepreneur should follow to be great today, as her success was the result of a combination of many factors, such as innovation, marketing, customer service, and social responsibility. However, if I had to choose one thing, it would be her unwavering determination and persistence in the face of obstacles.

Madam CJ Walker faced many challenges in her life, including poverty, discrimination, and illness. Despite these obstacles, she persevered and continued to work towards her goals. She had a strong vision for her business and was determined to make it a success. She worked tirelessly to develop her products, promote her brand, and build a network of sales agents.

Her determination and persistence paid off, and she eventually became one of the most successful and influential entrepreneurs of her time. Her story is a testament to the power of hard work, perseverance, and a never-give-up attitude.

In today's fast-paced and competitive business world, entrepreneurs face many challenges and obstacles. To be successful, it is important to have a clear vision for your business, and to be determined and persistent in pursuing that vision. You will likely face setbacks and failures along the way, but it is important to learn from these experiences and keep pushing forward.

So, the one thing that an entrepreneur can learn from Madam CJ Walker is to never give up, and to keep working towards your goals, no matter how difficult the journey may be. With determination and persistence, anything is possible.

Here are some additional details about Madam CJ Walker's life and work:

Early Life: Madam CJ Walker was born Sarah Breedlove on December 23, 1867, on a plantation in Delta, Louisiana. Her parents and older siblings were all born into slavery, and her mother died when Sarah was just six years old. She married at the age of 14 and became a widow at 20, with a young daughter to support. She moved to St. Louis, Missouri, where she worked as a washerwoman and cook.

Hair Care Products: Madam CJ Walker's hair care products were based on a formula she developed in 1904 to treat her own hair loss. She named her company the Madam C.J. Walker Manufacturing Company, and her products quickly gained popularity among black women. She marketed her products as a way for black women to achieve healthy, beautiful hair, which was a radical idea at the time. Her products were sold through a network of sales agents, who she trained and mentored.

Philanthropy: In addition to her business success, Madam CJ Walker was a philanthropist who donated generously to black causes and organizations. She was a strong supporter of the NAACP, the National Association of Colored Women, and the YMCA. She also funded scholarships for black students and donated money to support the construction of a new high school for black students in Indianapolis.

Legacy: Madam CJ Walker's legacy extends far beyond her success as a businesswoman. She was a trailblazer who broke barriers and paved the way for other black entrepreneurs and businesspeople. She was a symbol of empowerment for black women, who had been largely excluded from the mainstream beauty industry. Her entrepreneurial spirit, determination, and philanthropy continue to inspire and motivate people today.

Honors and Recognition: Madam CJ Walker was widely recognized for her business and philanthropic accomplishments during her lifetime. She was the first female self-made millionaire in the United States, and one of the wealthiest African Americans of her time. She was honored with numerous awards and accolades, including an invitation to the White House by President Woodrow Wilson in 1917. In 2020, Netflix released a limited series about her life, titled "Self Made: Inspired by the Life of Madam C.J. Walker," which brought her story to a wider audience.

SAM WALTON

born on March 29, 1918, in Kingfisher, Oklahoma, is widely recognized as one of the most influential business minds of the 20th century. He was the founder of Walmart, which is now one of the largest retail corporations in the world. His innovative approach to business and relentless focus on customer satisfaction has made him a legend in the business world.

Walton grew up during the Great Depression, which instilled in him a strong work ethic and an entrepreneurial spirit. After serving in World War II, Walton purchased a Ben Franklin variety store in Newport, Arkansas, in 1945, which was the start of his retail career. He opened his first Walmart store in Rogers, Arkansas, in 1962, and from there, his business empire grew.

One of Walton's greatest strengths was his ability to innovate. He was always looking for new and better ways to do things, and he was not afraid to take risks. For example, in the early days of Walmart, he introduced the concept of high-volume, low-margin retailing. This approach involved selling products at a lower price than his competitors, but making up for it with the volume of sales. It was a strategy that proved to be extremely successful, as it allowed Walmart to offer customers lower prices than anyone else, while still making a profit.

Another of Walton's innovations was the use of technology to improve operations. He was an early adopter of computer systems in his stores, which allowed him to track inventory, analyze sales data, and make better business decisions. He also pioneered the use of satellite communication to coordinate the logistics of his supply chain, which was a major contributor to Walmart's success.

In addition to his innovative mind, Walton was known for his tireless work ethic. He was always looking for ways to improve his business, and he was willing to put in the long hours and hard work necessary to achieve his goals. He was also a hands-on manager, frequently visiting stores and talking to employees and customers to get a better understanding of their needs.

Walton was also known for his tactical approach to business. He was a master of the art of negotiation, and he was not afraid to use his bargaining power to get the best possible deals from his suppliers. He also had a keen eye for real estate, and he was able to secure prime locations for his stores at a fraction of the cost that his competitors were paying.

Perhaps most importantly, Walton was a firm believer in putting the customer first. He once said, "The goal as a company is to have customer service that is not just the best but legendary." He understood that by putting the customer first, he would be able to build a loyal customer base that would keep coming back to Walmart for years to come.

Today, Walmart is a retail giant with over 11,000 stores worldwide and more than 2.2 million employees. It is a testament to the vision and determination of Sam Walton, who passed away in 1992. His innovative mind, tireless work ethic, tactical approach to business, and commitment to customer satisfaction have made him one of the most influential business minds of all time.

Early Life: Sam Walton was the oldest of four children born to Thomas Gibson Walton and Nancy Lee Walton. His father was a banker and his mother was a homemaker. He grew up in rural Missouri during the Great Depression.

Education: Walton graduated from the University of Missouri in 1940 with a degree in Economics. During his time at university, he was a member of the Beta Theta Pi fraternity and was elected president of the student body.

Military Service: After college, Walton joined the Army and served in World War II. He rose to the rank of captain and was awarded the Bronze Star for his service in the Army Intelligence Corps.

Early Career: After his military service, Walton began his retail career with J.C. Penney. He eventually left to start his own variety store in Newport, Arkansas.

Walmart: In 1962, Walton opened the first Walmart store in Rogers, Arkansas. Over the years, he expanded the company through a combination of opening new stores and acquiring existing ones.

Family: Walton was married to Helen Robson Walton, who he met while they were both working at J.C. Penney. They had four children together.

Philanthropy: Walton was a firm believer in giving back to the community. He established the Walton Family Foundation, which has donated billions of dollars to various charitable causes.

Personal Traits: Walton was known for his frugality and his down-to-earth personality. Despite his immense wealth, he drove an old pickup truck and frequently shopped at Walmart stores himself.

Honors and Awards: Walton was inducted into the Retail Hall of Fame in 1989 and was posthumously awarded the Presidential Medal of Freedom by President George H.W.

Bush in 1992.

Legacy: Walton's legacy lives on through Walmart, which remains one of the largest and most successful retailers in the world. He is also remembered for his innovative approach to business, his commitment to customer satisfaction, and his philanthropic work.

The one thing that Walton did, that an entrepreneur should follow to be great

There are many things that an entrepreneur can learn from Sam Walton's approach to business, but if I had to choose just one, it would be his relentless focus on customer satisfaction.

Walton believed that the customer was the most important part of his business, and he was always looking for ways to improve their experience. He was known for visiting his stores and talking to customers and employees to get a better understanding of their needs. He also encouraged his employees to take ownership of the customer experience, empowering them to make decisions and take action to ensure that customers were satisfied.

This customer-centric approach is just as important today as it was when Walton was building Walmart. In today's competitive business landscape, it is critical to put the customer first and to continually look for ways to improve their experience. By doing so, entrepreneurs can build a loyal customer base that will keep coming back and will also recommend their products or services to others.

In short, entrepreneurs should strive to adopt Sam Walton's customer-centric approach to business, by always putting the customer first and seeking ways to improve their experience. This will help them build a strong brand, a loyal customer base, and ultimately, a successful business.

Certainly, here are a few more things about Sam Walton:

Innovation: Sam Walton was an innovative thinker who was always looking for new ways to improve his business. He pioneered several retail practices that are now commonplace, such as using computers to track inventory and using satellite technology to communicate with stores.

Low Prices: Walton was famous for his commitment to offering low prices to customers. He believed that by keeping prices low, he could attract more customers and sell more products, which would ultimately lead to higher profits.

Frugality: Despite his immense wealth, Walton was known for his frugal lifestyle. He would frequently fly coach and would often stay in cheap motels when traveling for business. This frugal mindset helped him keep costs low and allowed him to reinvest more money in his business.

Employee Relations: Walton was a strong believer in treating employees well. He believed that happy employees would be more productive and would provide better service to customers. He implemented several policies to help achieve this, such as profit-sharing plans and stock purchase programs.

Community Involvement: Walton was deeply involved in the communities where his stores were located. He believed that businesses had a responsibility to give back to their communities and was known for his philanthropic work.

Growth: Under Walton's leadership, Walmart grew from a single store to a global retail giant. He was always looking for new opportunities to expand and was willing to take risks to achieve his goals.

Leadership: Walton was a charismatic leader who was loved by his employees. He had a hands-on

PIERS M. WOLF

AARON MONTGOMERY WARD

Was an American businessman and the founder of the world's first mail-order catalog company. He is considered one of the most influential business minds in history due to his innovative approach to retail and his pioneering role in the development of modern marketing and advertising.

Born on February 17, 1844, in Chatham, New Jersey, Ward was the youngest of five children. His family moved to Niles, Michigan when he was nine years old. His father was a farmer and a traveling salesman, and young Ward quickly developed a love of business and entrepreneurship.

At the age of 14, Ward became a traveling salesman himself, selling goods door-to-door in rural Michigan. He quickly realized that many of his customers lived in isolated areas and had limited access to quality goods. This sparked an idea in his mind, which would later become the foundation of his business.

In 1865, at the age of 21, Ward moved to Chicago and took a job as a clerk in a dry goods store. He worked his way up to become a partner in the business, but he soon realized that the traditional retail model was not meeting the needs of his customers.

In 1872, Ward launched his own business, the world's first mail-order catalog company. He sent out a single sheet of paper with a list of goods and prices to customers in rural areas, who could then order by mail. This was a revolutionary idea at the time, and it allowed Ward to reach a much larger customer base than traditional brick-and-mortar stores.

Over the years, Ward's business grew rapidly. He expanded his product line to include everything from clothing and housewares to farm equipment and musical instruments. He also developed a sophisticated marketing and advertising strategy, using newspaper ads and other promotional materials to attract new customers.

Ward was a true innovator, constantly looking for ways to improve his business and better serve his customers. In the 1880s, he began offering a money-back guarantee on all of his products, a radical idea at the time that helped to build trust with his customers. He also introduced installment payments, allowing customers to pay for their purchases over time.

Ward's business continued to grow throughout the 20th century, even as new competitors entered the market. He remained at the helm of the company until his death in 1913, at the age of 69.

Today, Ward's legacy lives on. His mail-order catalog model paved the way for the rise of e-commerce and online shopping, and his innovative marketing and advertising strategies continue to influence businesses around the world. He is remembered as one of the most important figures in the history of American retail, a true pioneer whose ideas and innovations transformed the way we shop.

In conclusion, Aaron Montgomery Ward was a true business visionary who revolutionized the retail industry with his innovative mail-order catalog company. His relentless focus on customer service, combined with his innovative marketing and advertising strategies, helped him build one of the most successful businesses of his time. Today, he is remembered as one of the most influential business minds in history, a true trailblazer who paved the way for the modern retail industry.

Early Life and Education: Before becoming a businessman, Ward received a basic education and also worked as a farmer, teacher, and traveling salesman in Michigan.

The Birth of the Catalog: Ward's initial catalog was a single sheet of paper with a list of products and prices, but it soon grew to a full-fledged catalog with hundreds of pages. The catalog was so popular that by the 1880s, Ward was printing millions of copies each year.

Innovations in Shipping: Ward was not just a pioneer in the mail-order industry, but also in shipping and delivery. He developed a system for shipping products that allowed him to send goods quickly and cheaply to customers all over the country.

Social Activism: Ward was a strong advocate for workers' rights and social justice. He believed that all Americans, regardless of their social class, deserved access to high-quality goods at reasonable prices. He also spoke out against monopolies and supported laws that would break up large corporations.

Philanthropy: Ward was also a generous philanthropist, donating money to various causes and charities throughout his life. He believed that businesses had a responsibility to give back to their communities and to improve the lives of those around them.

Legacy: Today, Aaron Montgomery Ward is remembered as a

true visionary whose ideas and innovations transformed the retail industry. His mail-order catalog company paved the way for the rise of e-commerce and online shopping, and his commitment to customer service and social responsibility continue to inspire businesses around the world.

> *The one thing that Ward did, that an entrepreneur should follow to be great*

One of the most important lessons that entrepreneurs can learn from Aaron Montgomery Ward is the importance of putting the customer first. Ward's success was largely due to his relentless focus on providing high-quality products and excellent customer service.

In today's business world, it's easy to get caught up in the latest technology or trend, but at the end of the day, it's the customer who matters most. Entrepreneurs who prioritize the customer experience and work to build strong relationships with their customers are much more likely to succeed than those who don't.

In addition to putting the customer first, entrepreneurs can also learn from Ward's innovative approach to marketing and advertising. Ward was not afraid to try new things and was always looking for ways to reach new customers and grow his business. Entrepreneurs who are willing to take risks, experiment with new marketing strategies, and embrace innovation are more likely to succeed in today's fast-paced and competitive business environment.

Finally, entrepreneurs can learn from Ward's commitment to social responsibility and philanthropy. Today's consumers are increasingly interested in doing business with companies that have a positive impact on the world, and entrepreneurs who prioritize social responsibility and give back to their communities are more likely to build strong, loyal customer bases and earn the trust and respect of their peers.

Here are some additional details about Aaron Montgomery Ward's life and work:

Early Struggles: After leaving school at the age of 14, Ward worked a series of odd jobs before becoming a traveling salesman in Michigan. He struggled financially for many years and was constantly looking for new opportunities to improve his situation.

Mail-Order Innovation: Ward's idea for a mail-order business was initially met with skepticism, as many people believed that customers would be hesitant to buy products sight unseen. However, Ward was confident in his idea and was able to convince customers of the value of his products through detailed descriptions and high-quality images in his catalog.

Business Ethics: Ward was a firm believer in the importance of business ethics, and he was known for his fair and honest business practices. He treated his employees well and was committed to providing high-quality products at fair prices. He also spoke out against monopolies and believed that businesses had a responsibility to contribute to the communities they served.

Entrepreneurial Spirit: Ward was a true entrepreneur at heart and was constantly looking for new opportunities to grow his business. He was not afraid to take risks or try new things, and he was always on the lookout for innovative ways to market and sell his products.

Legacy: Today, Aaron Montgomery Ward is remembered as a pioneer of the mail-order industry and a true visionary in the world of business. His ideas and innovations paved the way for the rise of e-commerce and online shopping, and his commitment to customer service, fair business practices, and social responsibility continue to inspire entrepreneurs around the world.

JACK WARNER

Was a pioneering American businessman who made significant contributions to the entertainment industry in the 20th century. He is most well-known for his role as the co-founder and driving force behind Warner Bros. Studios, one of the most successful film studios in Hollywood history. Jack Warner's life was defined by his tireless work ethic, his innovative mindset, and his unique approach to business, all of which contributed to his status as one of the most influential business minds of all time.

Born in London, Ontario in 1892, Jack Warner was the youngest of twelve children. His family moved to Youngstown, Ohio when he was a child, and it was there that he first became interested in the entertainment industry. After dropping out of school at age 15, he began working at a local theater, where he learned about projection and sound systems. In 1909, he and his brothers Sam, Harry, and Albert founded the Duquesne Amusement Company, which operated theaters in Pennsylvania and Ohio.

The Warner brothers soon expanded their operations, opening theaters in New York City and Los Angeles. In 1923, they founded Warner Bros. Studios in Hollywood, which quickly became one of the most successful film studios in the world. Jack Warner was instrumental in the studio's success, using his innovative mind and business tactics to help it grow and prosper.

One of Jack Warner's key innovations was his use of sound in films. In 1926, Warner Bros. released the first feature-length "talkie," The Jazz Singer, which revolutionized the film industry and helped cement the studio's reputation as a leader in the field. Warner also introduced other technological advances, such as synchronized sound effects and music, which helped make his films more immersive and entertaining for audiences.

Another aspect of Jack Warner's business acumen was his ability to identify and promote talent. He was known for discovering and nurturing some of the most famous actors and actresses of the time, including James Cagney, Humphrey Bogart, and Bette Davis. He also had a keen eye for successful film projects, and was responsible for many of the studio's most iconic films, such as Casablanca, The Maltese Falcon, and Gone with the Wind.

In addition to his innovative approach to filmmaking, Jack Warner was also known for his shrewd business tactics. He was a tough negotiator who was not afraid to take risks and make bold moves in order to secure a better deal for his studio. He famously fought against unionization in Hollywood, and was involved in several high-profile legal battles with actors and other studios.

Despite his controversial tactics, Jack Warner's influence on the entertainment industry cannot be denied. He helped to transform Hollywood into a major cultural force, and his legacy continues to be felt today. His contributions to film technology and talent scouting have become standard practices in the industry, and his commitment to innovation and hard work have inspired generations of entrepreneurs and business leaders.

In conclusion, Jack Warner's life as a businessman was

defined by his innovative mindset, tireless work ethic, and shrewd business tactics. He was responsible for some of the most important technological advances in the film industry, and was a key figure in the rise of Hollywood as a cultural force. His ability to identify and promote talent, as well as his willingness to take risks and fight for what he believed in, make him one of the most influential business minds of all time.

Jack Warner's work tactics and business ethics were shaped by his early experiences in the entertainment industry and his drive to succeed. He was known for his determination, his willingness to take risks, and his shrewd negotiating skills, all of which played a role in his success as a businessman.

One of Warner's key tactics was his use of vertical integration. He recognized early on that owning the entire process of film production, from creation to distribution, would give his studio a significant advantage over competitors. To this end, he acquired numerous theaters around the country, as well as a film processing plant and a music publishing company. By controlling every aspect of the film production and distribution process, he was able to maximize profits and exert greater control over the industry.

Another tactic that Warner used was his willingness to take risks on unconventional projects. He was known for his ability to recognize potential in films and actors that others might have overlooked. For example, he gave Humphrey Bogart his big break in the film High Sierra, despite resistance from other studio executives who felt that Bogart was not leading man material. Similarly, he took a chance on a relatively unknown actress named Bette Davis, who went on to become one of Hollywood's biggest stars.

In addition to his business tactics, Warner was known for his strong work ethic and attention to detail. He was famous for working long hours and being heavily involved in every aspect of his studio's operations, from casting to editing to marketing. He was also a perfectionist who demanded the highest standards from his employees and collaborators.

However, Warner's business ethics were not always admired by his peers or the public. He was known for being a tough negotiator who sometimes used strong-arm tactics to get what he wanted. For example, he famously feuded with actor James Cagney over contract negotiations, and was sued by numerous actors and other studios over issues related to contracts and intellectual property.

Despite these controversies, Warner's impact on the entertainment industry was undeniable. His innovations in film technology, talent scouting, and business practices helped to shape Hollywood into the cultural powerhouse that it is today. His legacy continues to be felt in the countless films and actors that he championed, and his influence on the business world can be seen in the many entrepreneurs and business leaders who have been inspired by his example.

The one thing that he did, that an entrepreneur should follow to be great today

One thing that entrepreneurs today can learn from Jack Warner is the importance of taking calculated risks in business. Warner was known for his willingness to take chances on unconventional projects and ideas, even when others were skeptical or resistant.

Today's business landscape is constantly evolving, and entrepreneurs must be able to adapt and innovate in order to succeed. This often requires taking risks and pursuing new ideas that may not be immediately accepted or understood by others.

Of course, it's important to note that taking risks does not mean being reckless or careless with one's resources. Warner's success was built on a foundation of careful planning, hard work, and shrewd negotiation. Entrepreneurs should strive to follow these same principles as they navigate the challenges of the modern business world.

Ultimately, the key takeaway from Jack Warner's life and work is that success in business requires a combination of vision, determination, and willingness to take calculated risks. By following in Warner's footsteps and embracing these qualities, entrepreneurs can help to ensure their own success and make a lasting impact on their industries.

A few more interesting facts about Jack Warner:

He was one of the four founding members of Warner Bros. Pictures, along with his brothers Harry, Albert, and Sam. The studio was originally named "Warner Brothers," but the space was later dropped to make the name more memorable.

Warner was a pioneer in the use of synchronized sound in film. In 1927, Warner Bros. released the film "The Jazz Singer," which featured a few sequences with sound. The film was a huge commercial success, and it helped to usher in a new era of "talkies" in Hollywood.

Warner was also known for his talent scouting abilities. He had a knack for recognizing potential in actors and actresses that others might have overlooked. In addition to giving Bogart and Davis their big breaks, he also discovered stars like Errol Flynn and Olivia de Havilland.

Despite his reputation as a shrewd businessman, Warner was also known for his philanthropic efforts. He was a supporter of numerous charitable causes, including the Motion Picture Relief Fund and the American Red Cross.

Warner's legacy continues to be felt in the entertainment industry today. Warner Bros. Pictures is still one of the most successful studios in Hollywood, and its films and television shows continue to be popular around the world. In addition, the Warner family's contributions to the film industry have been recognized with numerous awards and honors, including a star on the Hollywood Walk of Fame.

THOMAS WATSON JR.

is widely recognized as one of the most influential and innovative businessmen of the 20th century. He was the second CEO of IBM, and under his leadership, the company became one of the most successful and powerful corporations in the world. Watson Jr.'s innovative mind, unique work ethic, and tactical approach to business have made him an icon in the history of entrepreneurship.

Early Life and Education

Thomas Watson Jr. was born in Dayton, Ohio in 1914. His father, Thomas Watson Sr., was the founder and CEO of IBM, and he was deeply involved in the company from a young age. Watson Jr. attended private schools in New York and Connecticut and then went on to attend Brown University, where he studied economics.

Watson Jr. was a bright student, but he struggled with dyslexia and did not excel in traditional academic settings. He was much more interested in hands-on learning and practical experience, and he was always looking for new ways to innovate and create.

Early Career

After graduating from Brown University in 1937, Watson

Jr. began working for IBM as a salesman. He quickly rose through the ranks of the company, and by the early 1950s, he was serving as the vice president of IBM's international operations.

In 1952, Watson Jr. was appointed as the president of IBM, and he set about implementing a series of major changes and innovations that would transform the company and the entire computer industry.

Innovations and Contributions

One of Watson Jr.'s most important contributions to IBM was his emphasis on research and development. He believed that the key to success in the computer industry was constant innovation and the development of new technologies, and he invested heavily in R&D throughout his career.

Thomas Watson Jr. (1914-1993) was an American businessman who served as the CEO of IBM from 1956 to 1971. He was the eldest son of IBM's founder, Thomas J. Watson Sr. Under his leadership, IBM transformed from a primarily mechanical equipment company into one of the world's largest and most successful computer companies.

Here are some of Thomas Watson Jr.'s key contributions to IBM and the business world:

Emphasizing customer service: Watson Jr. believed that IBM's success was directly tied to its ability to serve its customers. He encouraged his employees to focus on understanding and meeting customer needs, and he personally met with clients to learn about their businesses and how IBM could help them.

Investing in research and development: Watson Jr. recognized the importance of innovation in a rapidly changing industry. He increased IBM's investment in research and development, leading to groundbreaking advances in computer technology.

Promoting diversity and social responsibility: Watson Jr. was a strong advocate for diversity and social responsibility. He was one of the first business leaders to publicly support civil rights, and he established IBM's Equal Opportunity Policy in 1953, which prohibited discrimination based on race, religion, or gender. He also promoted the hiring and advancement of women and minorities within IBM.

Building a strong corporate culture: Watson Jr. believed that a company's success depended on its culture. He established IBM's famous "Think" motto and encouraged his employees to think creatively and take risks. He also fostered a collaborative and supportive work environment, which helped IBM attract and retain top talent.

Expanding globally: Watson Jr. recognized the importance of expanding IBM's reach beyond the United States. Under his leadership, IBM established operations in Europe, Asia, and Latin America, becoming a truly global company.

Overall, Thomas Watson Jr.'s leadership transformed IBM into a technology powerhouse and set a standard for corporate responsibility and innovation in the business world.

The one thing that Watson did, that an entrepreneur should follow to be great

One thing that Thomas Watson Jr. did that entrepreneurs today can follow to be great is to prioritize customer service.

Watson Jr. recognized that a company's success is directly tied to its ability to serve its customers. He emphasized the importance of understanding and meeting customer needs, and he personally met with clients to learn about their businesses and how IBM could help them. This focus on customer service helped IBM build strong, long-term relationships with its customers and establish itself as a trusted partner in the technology industry.

In today's business world, customers have more choices than ever before, and their expectations are higher than ever. By prioritizing customer service, entrepreneurs can differentiate themselves from their competitors and build loyal customer bases. This means not only understanding what customers want and need, but also providing exceptional support throughout the customer journey.

Entrepreneurs who prioritize customer service are more likely to build strong, sustainable businesses that deliver value to their customers and drive long-term growth.

Some additional things about Thomas Watson Jr.:

He served in the U.S. military: During World War II, Watson Jr. served as a pilot in the U.S. Army Air Forces. He received the Distinguished Flying Cross for his service.

He was a philanthropist: In addition to his work at IBM, Watson Jr. was also involved in philanthropic efforts. He served as chairman of the board of the Memorial Sloan-Kettering Cancer Center and supported other charitable causes throughout his life.

He was a pioneer in the computer industry: Watson Jr. played a key role in IBM's development of the System/360, a groundbreaking computer system that was introduced in 1964. The System/360 was the first computer system that allowed customers to upgrade their machines without having to replace all of their software.

He wrote a book: In 1990, Watson Jr. published a memoir called "Father, Son & Co.: My Life at IBM and Beyond." The book chronicles his life and career, as well as his relationship with his father and the history of IBM.

He received numerous awards and honors: Watson Jr. was awarded the Presidential Medal of Freedom in 1964, and he received honorary degrees from several universities. He was also inducted into the Junior Achievement U.S. Business Hall of Fame in 1979 and the National Business Hall of Fame in 1990.

Overall, Thomas Watson Jr. was a visionary leader who transformed IBM and helped shape the computer industry as we know it today. His legacy continues to inspire entrepreneurs and business leaders around the world.

JAMES WATT

Was a Scottish inventor, mechanical engineer, and businessman who played a crucial role in the development of the Industrial Revolution. His invention of the steam engine, which was much more efficient than previous designs, revolutionized transportation and manufacturing, making him one of the most influential business minds in history.

Watt was born in Greenock, Scotland, and showed an early aptitude for mechanics and engineering. After serving as an apprentice to a London instrument maker, he returned to Glasgow and opened his own workshop. In 1763, he was asked to repair a model of Thomas Newcomen's steam engine, which was used to pump water out of coal mines. Watt quickly realized that the engine was inefficient and that there was an opportunity to improve its design.

Over the next several years, Watt worked tirelessly to develop a new type of steam engine that was more efficient and powerful than Newcomen's. He invented a separate condenser that allowed the engine to reuse steam instead of wasting it, and he also introduced a new type of rotary engine that could be used in a variety of industrial applications.

Watt's innovations were not immediately embraced by the business community, however. In order to gain acceptance for his steam engine, he had to partner with Matthew Boulton, a wealthy businessman and fellow innovator. Together, they formed the firm Boulton & Watt, which produced and sold steam engines to customers throughout Britain and abroad.

One of the keys to Boulton & Watt's success was their approach to business. They were among the first companies to offer leasing options for their machines, allowing customers to pay for them over time rather than upfront. They also developed a reputation for quality and reliability, and their engines were in high demand from industries ranging from mining and textile production to transportation and agriculture.

Beyond his work on the steam engine, Watt was also a prolific inventor and entrepreneur in other fields. He developed a copying machine, which was used by businesses to make duplicates of documents, and he also worked on new methods of bleaching and dyeing textiles. In addition, he was an early advocate for the metric system, and he helped to popularize its use in Britain.

Watt's legacy as a businessman and innovator is difficult to overstate. His work on the steam engine helped to power the Industrial Revolution, and his approach to business set the standard for modern manufacturing and entrepreneurship. By partnering with Boulton, he was able to bridge the gap between technical innovation and commercial success, and his commitment to quality and reliability helped to build a loyal customer base. Today, entrepreneurs can still learn valuable lessons from Watt's approach to innovation, business strategy, and customer service.

Early Life and Education

James Watt was born on January 19, 1736, in Greenock, Scotland. His father was a shipwright, and his mother came from a family of skilled craftsmen. Watt showed an early aptitude for mathematics and engineering, but his parents could not afford to send him to university. Instead, he became an apprentice to a local instrument maker, where he learned the skills that would later prove essential to his inventions.

In 1757, Watt moved to Glasgow to set up his own business as a maker of scientific instruments. He quickly established a reputation for quality workmanship and innovative designs, and his instruments were highly sought after by scientists and universities throughout Scotland.

The Steam Engine

In 1764, Watt was asked to repair a model of a Newcomen steam engine, which was used to pump water out of coal mines. He quickly realized that the design was highly inefficient, wasting a great deal of energy in the process of heating and cooling the steam. Watt set out to improve on the design, and after several years of experimentation, he came up with a much more efficient engine that used a separate condenser to cool the steam, greatly reducing the amount of energy wasted.

Watt's new steam engine was not only more efficient than previous designs, but it was also much more versatile. It could be used to power a wide variety of machines, including textile mills, ironworks, and transportation systems. This made it a game-changer for the Industrial Revolution, which was just beginning to gain momentum.

Business Success

With his new invention, Watt became a successful businessman almost overnight. He formed a partnership with Matthew Boulton, a wealthy manufacturer in Birmingham, and together they set up a factory to produce steam engines. The partnership was highly successful, and they soon became the leading manufacturers of steam engines in Britain.

Watt's success was due in large part to his innovative mind and his willingness to experiment with new ideas. He was constantly looking for ways to improve his designs and to make his engines more efficient and reliable. He was also a savvy businessman, who understood the importance of marketing and customer service. He made sure that his engines were not only the best on the market, but that they were also backed by excellent customer support.

Legacy

James Watt's legacy as a businessman is twofold. First, he was an innovator who developed one of the most important technologies of the Industrial Revolution. His steam engine made it possible to power machines on a large scale, which led to the mass production of goods and the growth of industrial capitalism.

Second, Watt was a successful businessman who understood the importance of quality, innovation, and customer service. He was not content to rest on his laurels, but was always looking for ways to improve his products and to stay ahead of the competition. This made him a model for other entrepreneurs, who saw in him a blueprint for success.

In conclusion, James Watt was one of the most influential business minds in history. His innovation mind and work led to the development of the steam engine, which revolutionized transportation and manufacturing, making him a crucial figure in the Industrial Revolution. His success as a businessman was due to his willingness to experiment with new ideas and his commitment to quality, innovation, and customer service. His legacy continues to inspire entrepreneurs today, and he remains a symbol of what can be achieved through hard work, perseverance, and innovation.

The one thing that James

Watt did, that an entrepreneur should follow to be great

One of the key things that an entrepreneur today can learn from James Watt is the importance of perseverance.

When Watt began working on improving the steam engine, he faced many setbacks and challenges. He had to overcome technical problems, financial difficulties, and even legal obstacles, as his inventions were often met with skepticism and resistance. Despite all of these challenges, Watt remained persistent in his pursuit of success.

He continued to experiment, refine his designs, and seek out new opportunities, eventually succeeding in creating a more efficient and reliable steam engine that transformed the world. His perseverance and determination were instrumental in his success, and his example serves as a reminder to entrepreneurs today that they must be willing to face challenges and setbacks, and to persist in their pursuit of their goals.

So, to be great today, entrepreneurs should follow James Watt's example and cultivate a mindset of perseverance and determination. They should be willing to learn from their mistakes, adapt to changing circumstances, and never give up on their vision for success. By doing so, they can overcome obstacles and achieve their goals, just as James Watt did with his steam engine.

While James Watt is primarily known as an inventor and engineer, his contributions to the development of the steam engine and his impact on industry and transportation have also made him one of the most influential businessmen of all time.

One of the reasons why Watt is considered such an influential businessman is that his improvements to the steam engine enabled the industrial revolution to take off.

The steam engine was a key technology that powered many of the factories and machines of the time, leading to a significant increase in productivity and output. This, in turn, helped to create new markets, stimulate economic growth, and transform society as a whole.

Watt was also an astute businessman in his own right. He recognized the commercial potential of his invention and entered into partnerships with other entrepreneurs, including Matthew Boulton, to manufacture and market steam engines. These partnerships allowed Watt to secure patents, protect his intellectual property, and generate significant revenues from his inventions.

In addition, Watt's work on the steam engine had a profound impact on transportation, making it possible to power steamships and locomotives, which revolutionized travel and trade around the world. This also created new opportunities for entrepreneurs, as new markets and industries emerged around transportation.

Overall, James Watt's innovations and business acumen helped to shape the modern world and laid the foundation for many of the technologies and industries that we take for granted today. His impact on industry and business has been profound and enduring, making him one of the most influential businessmen of all time.

Some interesting facts and accomplishments about James Watt:

Watt was born in Greenock, Scotland, in 1736. He initially trained as a instrument maker, and later became interested in the steam engine after being asked to repair a model of Thomas Newcomen's steam engine. One of Watt's most important contributions to the steam engine was the invention of the separate condenser, which improved efficiency and made the engine more practical for industrial use. Watt worked closely with entrepreneur Matthew

Boulton to manufacture and market his steam engines. The partnership between Watt and Boulton was highly successful, and the two men became good friends.

In addition to his work on the steam engine, Watt also made important contributions to other fields, such as chemistry, optics, and mathematics. He invented a number of instruments and devices, including a copying press, a micrometer, and a photometer. Watt was a highly respected figure in his lifetime, and was awarded numerous honors and accolades, including being elected a fellow of the Royal Society of London in 1785.

The unit of power known as the watt, which is used to measure the rate of energy transfer, is named after James Watt in recognition of his contributions to the field of mechanical engineering. Watt died in 1819 at the age of 83. Today, he is remembered as one of the most important inventors and engineers of the Industrial Revolution, and his work continues to have an impact on modern technology and industry.

JOSIAH WEDGWOOD

Was an English potter who is widely regarded as one of the most innovative and influential businessmen of the 18th century. He was born in Staffordshire, England, into a family of potters, and he began his career in the family business at a young age.

Wedgwood was known for his entrepreneurial spirit and his innovative approach to business. He was a pioneer in many areas, including marketing, design, and manufacturing. He was a master craftsman who developed many new techniques and processes for creating high-quality pottery, and he was also a shrewd businessman who understood the importance of branding and marketing.

One of Wedgwood's most significant contributions to the world of business was his development of the "division of labor" concept in manufacturing. He recognized that by breaking down the production process into smaller, specialized tasks, he could increase efficiency and reduce costs. This concept became known as the "factory system," and it revolutionized manufacturing in the 18th century.

Wedgwood was also a master of marketing and branding. He was one of the first businessmen to use his products as a means of social signaling, using high-quality design and craftsmanship to appeal to the upper classes. He also used clever marketing techniques, such as offering free samples and using celebrity endorsements, to promote his products.

Perhaps Wedgwood's greatest legacy, however, was his contribution to the field of design. He was a master craftsman who created many iconic pottery designs, including the famous "Jasperware" line of ceramics. He was also a patron of the arts and worked with some of the most talented designers and artists of his time, including the renowned sculptor John Flaxman.

Wedgwood's innovations and contributions to business were widely recognized during his lifetime. He was a member of the Royal Society, and he was awarded the prestigious Copley Medal for his work in the field of ceramics. He was also a noted abolitionist and philanthropist who supported many charitable causes.

In conclusion, Josiah Wedgwood was a remarkable businessman and innovator who made significant contributions to business during the 18th century. His emphasis on innovation, marketing, and design helped to transform the world of business and set the stage for many of the technological and cultural advancements of the modern era. His legacy continues to inspire businessmen and entrepreneurs today, and his ideas about innovation, marketing, and design remain relevant and valuable in the 21st century.

One of Wedgwood's most significant innovations was his development of "transfer printing" for ceramics. This technique allowed for the mass-production of decorative designs, which was a major breakthrough in the field of ceramics. It allowed Wedgwood to produce high-quality pottery at a lower cost, making it more accessible to a wider range of consumers.

Wedgwood was also a pioneer in the field of social responsibility. He was an advocate for workers' rights and fair labor practices, and he implemented many progressive policies in his factories, including education programs and healthcare benefits. He was also a vocal supporter of the abolitionist movement, and he used his business to promote anti-slavery causes.

In addition to his work as a potter and businessman, Wedgwood was also an important member of the cultural and intellectual community of his time. He was a close friend of the writer and philosopher Erasmus Darwin, as well as the politician and social reformer Thomas Day. He was also a patron of the arts, supporting many talented designers and artists, including John Flaxman, who worked with him on many of his most iconic pottery designs.

Wedgwood's innovations and contributions to business were not only recognized during his lifetime, but they continue to be celebrated today. His name has become synonymous with high-quality pottery and innovative design, and his legacy as a businessman and social reformer has inspired generations of entrepreneurs and business leaders.

The one thing that Wedgwood did, that an entrepreneur should follow to be great

One thing that entrepreneurs can learn from Josiah Wedgwood's success is the importance of innovation and continuous improvement. Wedgwood was constantly experimenting with new techniques and materials, and he was always looking for ways to refine and improve his products.

Wedgwood also understood the importance of branding and marketing. He created a strong brand identity and marketed his products to a wide range of customers, both in Britain and abroad. By creating a reputation for quality and innovation, he was able to build a loyal customer base and command premium prices for his products.

Another key lesson from Wedgwood is his ability to adapt to changing market conditions. He was quick to recognize trends and respond to changing consumer preferences, and he was always looking for new opportunities to expand his business.

Finally, Wedgwood's commitment to craftsmanship and quality is also a lesson that entrepreneurs can learn from. He believed that his success was due to the quality of his products, and he was willing to invest in the time and resources needed to create the very best.

Overall, by following Wedgwood's example of innovation, branding, adaptability, and commitment to quality, entrepreneurs can build successful businesses that stand the test of time.

Here are a few more key points about Josiah Wedgwood's life and business career:

Wedgwood was a pioneer in the development of mass production techniques, which allowed him to produce high-quality pottery at a lower cost than his competitors. He used innovations such as division of labor, standardized production processes, and mechanization to improve efficiency and reduce waste.

Wedgwood was also a master marketer who understood the importance of branding and advertising. He created a distinctive logo for his products (the famous Wedgwood medallion), and he used his connections with aristocratic and royal circles to build a reputation for his brand.

Wedgwood was a social reformer who believed in the power of education to improve people's lives. He was a supporter of the Enlightenment philosophy and believed in the importance of reason and knowledge. He also supported the abolition of slavery and was a member of the Society for the Abolition of the Slave Trade.

In addition to his business career, Wedgwood was also a noted scientist and inventor. He made important contributions to the fields of geology and chemistry, and he invented several new materials and processes that were used in pottery production.

Wedgwood was a pioneer of modern marketing techniques, using innovative advertising and branding strategies to promote his products. He created catalogs, used testimonials from satisfied customers, and employed celebrities of the day to endorse his products.

Wedgwood was an early adopter of industrialization and automation, developing new techniques for mass production that enabled him to increase efficiency and reduce costs. He was known for his focus on quality, investing heavily in research and development to improve his products.

Wedgwood was also a social and political reformer, using his wealth and influence to advocate for a variety of causes. He was a supporter of the abolition of slavery, and he also worked to improve the living and working conditions of his employees.

In addition to his work in ceramics, Wedgwood was also a noted collector and patron of the arts. He was particularly interested in the work of neoclassical sculptors, and he commissioned a number of pieces for his personal collection.

Overall, Josiah Wedgwood was a visionary leader who helped to shape the modern business landscape. By studying his life and career, entrepreneurs can learn valuable lessons about marketing, industrialization, social responsibility, and the importance of arts and culture in business

PIERS M. WOLF

CHARLES KEMMONS WILSON

is widely regarded as one of the most influential businessmen of the 20th century, having founded the Holiday Inn hotel chain and revolutionizing the hotel industry. He was a true innovator, a shrewd businessman, and a visionary leader whose ideas and tactics continue to influence the hospitality industry to this day.

Early Life and Career

Wilson was born on January 5, 1913, in Osceola, Arkansas. He grew up during the Great Depression and dropped out of school at the age of 16 to work and support his family. He started his career as a small-time businessman, selling popcorn and soft drinks at a movie theater in Memphis, Tennessee.

After serving in the U.S. Army during World War II, Wilson returned to Memphis and started a home building company with his brother. The company was successful, and by the early 1950s, Wilson had become a millionaire.

Founding of Holiday Inn

In 1951, Wilson embarked on his most significant business venture when he founded the Holiday Inn hotel chain. At the time, most hotels were luxury establishments that catered to wealthy travelers. Wilson saw an opportunity to create a chain of affordable, family-friendly hotels that would appeal to the average American traveler.

He was a firm believer in the power of brand recognition and invested heavily in advertising and marketing to promote the Holiday Inn name. He also implemented several innovative ideas to make his hotels stand out from the competition, including:

Standardization: Wilson insisted on standardizing all Holiday Inn hotels to ensure consistency and quality across the chain. This included everything from the color scheme and furniture to the size of the rooms and the amenities provided.

Franchising: Wilson was one of the first entrepreneurs to adopt the franchising model, which allowed him to expand his chain rapidly and with minimal capital investment. By 1958, there were more than 100 Holiday Inn hotels across the United States.

Reservation System: Wilson introduced a centralized reservation system that made it easy for travelers to book a room at any Holiday Inn hotel. This was a major innovation at the time and helped to establish the Holiday Inn brand as a reliable and convenient option for travelers.

Legacy

Wilson's innovations and tactics revolutionized the hotel industry, and the Holiday Inn chain became one of the most successful and recognizable brands in the world. By the time Wilson retired in 1979, there were over 1,400 Holiday Inn hotels in more than 40 countries.

In addition to his contributions to the hospitality industry, Wilson was also known for his philanthropic work. He was a strong supporter of St. Jude Children's Research Hospital, which was founded by his friend, Danny Thomas. Wilson donated millions of dollars to the hospital and served on its board of directors for many years.

Conclusion

Charles Kemmons Wilson was a true pioneer in the business world, and his ideas and tactics continue to influence entrepreneurs and business leaders to this day. His innovative approach to franchising, standardization, and branding set a new standard for the hotel industry and made the Holiday Inn chain a household name. Wilson's legacy is a testament to the power of hard work, innovation, and a visionary mind. He will undoubtedly be remembered as one of the most influential business minds of all time.

Wilson was known for his innovative business tactics and his strong work ethic, both of which played a crucial role in his success.

Work Tactics

One of Wilson's key work tactics was his focus on standardization. He believed that in order to ensure quality and consistency across his hotels, every detail needed to be standardized, from the room sizes and furniture to the color schemes and amenities. This helped to create a consistent and reliable experience for guests, which in turn helped to build brand loyalty.

Wilson was also a firm believer in the power of advertising and marketing. He invested heavily in promoting the Holiday Inn brand, using catchy slogans and memorable jingles to capture the attention of potential customers. He also pioneered the use of television advertising in the hotel industry, recognizing that the medium was a powerful way to reach a broad audience.

Another key aspect of Wilson's work tactics was his embrace of the franchising model. He saw franchising as a way to rapidly expand the Holiday Inn chain without the need for significant capital investment. By offering franchisees a proven business model and a recognizable brand, Wilson was able to attract entrepreneurs from all walks of life and build a vast network of hotels around the world.

Business Ethics

In addition to his innovative work tactics, Wilson was also known for his strong business ethics. He believed in treating his employees fairly and providing them with opportunities for growth and advancement. He also believed in giving back to the community and was a strong supporter of various charitable causes.

Wilson's commitment to ethical business practices was evident in his approach to franchising. Unlike some franchisors, who were known to exploit their franchisees for profit, Wilson saw franchisees as partners in his business. He offered them extensive training and support, and was known for being accessible and approachable to franchisees who had questions or concerns.

Wilson also had a strong sense of personal integrity. He was known for his honesty and transparency in his business dealings, and he held himself and his employees to high ethical standards. This helped to build trust and credibility with customers, franchisees, and other stakeholders, and helped to establish the Holiday Inn brand as a trustworthy and reliable option in the hospitality industry.

Overall, Wilson's work tactics and business ethics were key factors in his success as an entrepreneur. His focus on standardization, franchising, and marketing helped to revolutionize the hotel industry, while his commitment to ethical business practices helped to build a strong and enduring brand. Wilson's legacy continues to inspire entrepreneurs and business leaders today, and serves as a testament to the power of innovation and integrity in business.

The one thing that he did, that an entrepreneur should follow to be great today

One of the most important things that Wilson did, and one that entrepreneurs can still learn from today, was his focus on standardization.

Wilson recognized that in order to build a successful and sustainable business, he needed to provide his customers with a consistent and reliable experience every time they stayed at a Holiday Inn hotel. This meant standardizing every aspect of the hotel experience, from the room layouts and furnishings to the amenities and services offered.

This focus on standardization allowed Wilson to create a brand that customers could trust and rely on, which in turn helped to build brand loyalty and drive repeat business. It also enabled him to rapidly expand the Holiday Inn chain through franchising, since franchisees could easily replicate the standard Holiday Inn model in their own hotels.

For entrepreneurs today, the lesson is clear: in order to build a successful business, you need to focus on providing a consistent and reliable experience for your customers. Whether you're selling a product or a service, your customers should know what to expect every time they interact with your business. This means standardizing your processes and procedures, and ensuring that every member of your team is trained to deliver a consistent experience.

By focusing on standardization, you can build a brand that customers trust and rely on, which will help to drive customer loyalty and repeat business. And if you choose to franchise your business, standardization will be even more important, since it will enable you to replicate your business model in new markets and with new franchisees.

A few more things about Charles Kemmons Wilson:

He was a self-made millionaire: Wilson grew up in poverty and had to drop out of school in the eighth grade to support his family. Despite these challenges, he was able to start several successful businesses before founding Holiday Inn.

He was a risk-taker: Wilson was not afraid to take risks in order to grow his business. For example, he invested heavily in advertising and marketing when other hotel chains were cutting back, and he launched the first-ever hotel franchising program when franchising was still a relatively new concept.

He was a philanthropist: Wilson was a generous philanthropist who donated millions of dollars to various charitable causes throughout his life. He also established the Kemmons Wilson Family Foundation to support education and entrepreneurship.

He was a family man: Wilson was married to his wife, Dorothy, for over 60 years, and they had five children together. Despite his busy schedule, he always made time for his family and was known for being a devoted husband and father.

He was a visionary: Wilson's vision for Holiday Inn was to create a chain of hotels that would provide a consistent and reliable experience for travelers, no matter where they were in the world. His focus on standardization and franchising helped to turn this vision into a reality, and his innovative business tactics and strong work ethic helped to make Holiday Inn one of the most successful hotel chains in history.

Overall, Wilson was a remarkable entrepreneur and businessman who overcame incredible odds to achieve success. His legacy continues to inspire entrepreneurs and business leaders today, and his focus on standardization, risk-taking, philanthropy, family, and vision are all lessons that can be applied to any business or industry.

OPRAH WINFREY

is a name that has become synonymous with success and inspiration, both in the entertainment industry and as a businesswoman. She is a self-made billionaire, media mogul, philanthropist, and actress. Her innovative mind, work ethics, and tactics have set her apart from others, making her one of the most influential business minds of all time.

Early Life and Career

Born on January 29, 1954, in Kosciusko, Mississippi, Oprah Winfrey faced several challenges during her childhood. She was raised in poverty, and her parents were not always able to provide for her. However, she was an exceptional student and was offered a scholarship to Tennessee State University, where she studied communication.

After college, Oprah began her career in media as a news anchor in Nashville, Tennessee. She then moved to Baltimore, Maryland, where she co-anchored the evening news. In 1976, she moved to Chicago to host a morning talk show called "AM Chicago." The show's popularity skyrocketed, and it was soon renamed "The Oprah Winfrey Show."

Innovative Mind and Work Ethics

Oprah Winfrey's innovative mind and work ethics are what

have made her one of the most successful businesswomen in the world. She has always been a forward-thinker and has always been willing to take risks. She saw the potential in her morning talk show, and she worked tirelessly to make it a success.

One of the key factors that set her show apart from others was the way she connected with her audience. She was able to relate to people from all walks of life, and her show tackled topics that were not typically discussed on television. She also used her platform to bring attention to important social issues, such as child abuse and domestic violence.

Another aspect of Oprah's innovative mind was her ability to diversify her business ventures. She launched her own production company, Harpo Productions, which produced several successful television shows and movies. She also started her own book club, which became a huge success and helped to boost the sales of several books.

Tactics

Oprah Winfrey's tactics have also contributed to her success as a businesswoman. She is a master at branding, and her name has become a brand in itself. She has been able to use her name and reputation to launch successful products and initiatives.

One of her most successful tactics was the "Favorite Things" episode of her show. Each year, she would dedicate an episode to showcasing her favorite products and gifts. The products would be a mix of high-end luxury items and affordable, everyday items. This episode was so popular that it became an annual event, and the products featured on the show would often sell out within hours.

Another tactic that Oprah has used to great effect is the power of partnerships. She has partnered with several companies over the years to launch successful products and initiatives. For example, she partnered with Starbucks to launch the Oprah Chai Tea, which was a huge success. She also partnered with Weight Watchers and became a spokesperson for the company. Her endorsement helped to boost the company's stock by 20%.

Philanthropy

Oprah Winfrey's philanthropy work has also contributed to her status as one of the most influential business minds of all time. She has donated millions of dollars to various charities and causes over the years, including education, health, and the arts. She has also established her own foundation, the Oprah Winfrey Foundation, which supports education and empowerment programs for women and children.

Conclusion

In conclusion, Oprah Winfrey's innovative mind, work ethics, and tactics have set her apart from others and have made her one of the most influential business minds of all time. She has shown that it is possible to succeed in business while also making a positive role model and impact on society.

Oprah Winfrey's work tactics and business ethics.

Empathy and Connection with her Audience:

One of the tactics that Oprah used to make her show successful was her ability to connect with her audience on a personal level. She was known for her ability to empathize with people and to create a safe space for them to share their stories. Her show was not just about entertainment, but it also tackled important issues and helped to create a community of people who felt seen and heard.

Leveraging her Personal Brand:

Oprah Winfrey's name has become a brand in itself, and she has been able to leverage her personal brand to launch successful products and initiatives. She has also been able to use her brand to attract partnerships and collaborations with other businesses.

Diversifying Business Ventures:

Oprah Winfrey is known for her ability to diversify her business ventures. She has launched several successful businesses, including Harpo Productions, O, The Oprah Magazine, and the Oprah Winfrey Network. By diversifying her business ventures, she has been able to create multiple streams of income and to reach a wider audience.

Investing in Personal Development:

Oprah Winfrey is a firm believer in the power of personal development. She has invested in her own personal development over the years, and she encourages others to do the same. She has also used her platform to promote personal development and to share her own experiences and insights.

Giving Back to the Community:

Oprah Winfrey is a philanthropist at heart, and she has used her wealth and influence to give back to the community. She has donated millions of dollars to various charities and causes, including education, health, and the arts. She has also established her own foundation, the Oprah Winfrey Foundation, which supports education and empowerment programs for women and children.

Using the Power of Partnerships:

Oprah Winfrey has been able to leverage the power of partnerships to launch successful products and initiatives. She has partnered with several companies over the years, including Weight Watchers, Starbucks, and Apple. Her partnerships have helped to boost her brand and to reach a wider audience.

Taking Calculated Risks:

Oprah Winfrey is not afraid to take calculated risks in her business ventures. She saw the potential in her morning talk show, and she worked tirelessly to make it a success. She has also taken risks in launching new businesses and initiatives, but she always does her due diligence and makes informed decisions.

In summary, Oprah Winfrey's work tactics and business ethics include empathy and connection with her audience, leveraging her personal brand, diversifying her business ventures, investing in personal development, giving back to the community, using the power of partnerships, and taking calculated risks. These tactics have set her apart from others and have contributed to her success as a businesswoman.

The one thing that she did, that an entrepreneur should follow to be great today

One thing that entrepreneurs can learn from Oprah Winfrey is the importance of authenticity in building a brand and connecting with customers.

Throughout her career, Oprah has always been true to herself and her values, which has helped her to build a strong personal brand and to connect with her audience on a deep level. She has been honest about her struggles and vulnerabilities, and she has used her platform to promote causes that she is passionate about.

In today's world, customers are looking for authenticity in the brands they support. They want to know that the companies they buy from share their values and are making a positive impact in the world. By being true to yourself and your values, you can build a brand that resonates with your customers and creates a loyal following.

So, the one thing that entrepreneurs can learn from Oprah Winfrey is to stay true to themselves and their values. By doing so, they can build a brand that connects with customers and makes a positive impact in the world.

Some additional things about Oprah Winfrey:

Early Life and Career:

Oprah Winfrey was born on January 29, 1954, in Kosciusko, Mississippi. She grew up in poverty and was raised by her grandmother in rural Mississippi until the age of six. She later moved to Milwaukee, Wisconsin, to live with her mother, where she faced significant challenges, including abuse and neglect.

Despite her difficult upbringing, Oprah excelled academically and won a full scholarship to Tennessee State University, where she studied communication. She began her career in media as a news anchor and talk show host in Nashville, Tennessee, before moving to Chicago in 1983 to host her own talk show, The Oprah Winfrey Show.

The Oprah Winfrey Show:

The Oprah Winfrey Show was a groundbreaking talk show that aired from 1986 to 2011. It became the highest-rated talk show in the United States and was syndicated in 145 countries around the world. The show tackled a wide range of topics, including self-improvement, health, relationships, and social issues.

Oprah's interviewing style was unique and authentic, and she was known for her ability to connect with her guests and her audience. She used her platform to promote important causes, including literacy and education, and to give a voice to people who had been marginalized or overlooked.

Business Ventures:

Oprah Winfrey has launched several successful business ventures over the years. In addition to The Oprah Winfrey Show, she founded Harpo Productions, which produced several popular shows, including Dr. Phil and The Dr. Oz Show.

She also launched O, The Oprah Magazine, which became one of the most successful magazines in the United States, and the Oprah Winfrey Network (OWN), a cable channel that features programming focused on self-improvement and personal growth.

Philanthropy:

Oprah Winfrey is a generous philanthropist who has donated millions of dollars to various charities and causes over the years. She has established several foundations, including the Oprah Winfrey Foundation, which supports education and empowerment programs for women and children.

In addition to her financial contributions, Oprah has used her platform to raise awareness about important issues and to promote causes that are close to her heart. She has been a vocal advocate for education, health, and social justice, and she has used her personal experiences to inspire and empower others.

Overall, Oprah Winfrey is a remarkable figure who has achieved great success through hard work, determination, and a commitment to authenticity and values. Her life and career are an inspiration to many, and her legacy will continue to inspire future generations of entrepreneurs and business leaders.

MARK ZUCKERBERG

is widely known as the co-founder of Facebook, a social networking platform that has become one of the most dominant forces in the tech industry. Born in 1984 in New York, Zuckerberg showed a keen interest in computer programming from a young age, creating games and other software programs in his spare time. It was this passion for technology that would eventually lead him to start Facebook and become one of the most influential business minds of his time.

Zuckerberg's entrepreneurial journey began in his sophomore year at Harvard University, where he created a website called Facemash. The website allowed students to compare and rate the attractiveness of their peers, using photos pulled from the university's database. Though the website was quickly shut down by the university, it demonstrated Zuckerberg's ability to create something innovative and engaging.

A few months later, Zuckerberg began working on what would eventually become Facebook. Along with a few classmates, he created a social networking platform that allowed students to connect with one another, share photos and other content, and join interest-based groups. The site quickly grew in popularity, and Zuckerberg dropped out of Harvard to focus on Facebook full-time.

One of the key factors that set Zuckerberg apart as a business leader was his focus on innovation. From the beginning, he saw Facebook as a platform that could be constantly evolving and improving, and he was always looking for ways to stay ahead of the competition. He famously declared that "move fast and break things" was the motto of Facebook, indicating his willingness to take risks and push boundaries.

This approach to innovation was evident in many of the features that Facebook introduced over the years. For example, the company was one of the first to introduce the "like" button, which allowed users to quickly show approval or support for a particular post or comment. This feature has since become a standard part of many social media platforms, demonstrating Zuckerberg's ability to anticipate and shape industry trends.

Another key aspect of Zuckerberg's approach to business was his focus on user engagement. He recognized early on that the success of Facebook would depend on the platform's ability to keep users coming back and spending time on the site. To this end, he invested heavily in features that would encourage social interaction and create a sense of community among users.

For example, Facebook introduced the concept of a news feed, which allowed users to see updates and posts from their friends and other people they were connected to. This feature proved to be incredibly popular, and helped to solidify Facebook's position as the leading social networking platform. Other innovations that helped to increase user engagement included the introduction of live video streaming, the ability to create groups and events, and the integration of chat and messaging features.

Zuckerberg's tactics as a businessman have not always been without controversy. In particular, the company has faced criticism over issues related to user privacy and data protection. However, it is clear that Zuckerberg's approach to business has had a significant impact on the tech industry as a whole.

Today, Facebook is one of the largest and most successful companies in the world, with over 2 billion active users and a market capitalization of over $800 billion. The platform has become an integral part of modern communication and social interaction, and has fundamentally changed the way that people connect with one another.

In conclusion, Mark Zuckerberg's approach to business has been marked by a relentless focus on innovation, user engagement, and staying ahead of the competition. He has demonstrated an exceptional ability to anticipate industry trends and shape the future of social media, and has played a major role in the growth and success of Facebook. Despite some controversy, there is no denying that Zuckerberg is one of the most influential business minds of his generation, and his impact on the tech industry is likely to be felt for many years to come.

In addition to his focus on innovation and user engagement, Mark Zuckerberg's work tactics and business ethics have also played a significant role in his success as a business leader.

One of the key aspects of Zuckerberg's work tactics is his emphasis on collaboration and teamwork. He has consistently emphasized the importance of working together and fostering a culture of openness and communication within the company. This approach has helped to ensure that Facebook is able to move quickly and effectively in response to changes in the industry and user needs.

Zuckerberg has also been known for his hands-on approach to management. Despite his position as CEO, he has continued to be actively involved in the day-to-day operations of the company, including attending product meetings and working closely with engineers and other key team members. This approach has helped to ensure that Facebook remains agile and responsive to the needs of its users.

In addition to his work tactics, Zuckerberg's business ethics have also been a significant factor in his success. He has consistently emphasized the importance of transparency and accountability, both within the company and with external stakeholders such as advertisers and regulators. This approach has helped to build trust and credibility for Facebook, which has been critical in its ability to maintain its position as a leader in the tech industry.

Another key aspect of Zuckerberg's business ethics has been his commitment to giving back. He and his wife, Priscilla Chan, have pledged to give away 99% of their wealth over their lifetimes through the Chan Zuckerberg Initiative, a philanthropic organization that aims to promote education, health, and scientific research. This commitment to social responsibility has helped to build goodwill for Facebook and has demonstrated Zuckerberg's belief in using his platform and resources for the greater good.

However, as mentioned earlier, Zuckerberg's business tactics and ethics have also faced some criticism. Facebook has faced scrutiny over issues such as privacy, data protection, and the spread of misinformation on the platform. In response, Zuckerberg has emphasized the need for the company to take responsibility for its actions and to work to address these issues. He has also been willing to testify before Congress and other regulatory bodies in order to address these concerns and demonstrate the company's commitment to transparency and accountability.

Overall, Mark Zuckerberg's work tactics and business ethics have played a critical role in his success as a business leader. His focus on collaboration, transparency, and social responsibility has helped to build trust and credibility for Facebook, while his hands-on approach to management has helped to ensure that the company remains agile and responsive to the needs of its users. Despite some controversy, it is clear that Zuckerberg's impact on the tech industry and his contributions to innovation and social responsibility are likely to be felt for many years to come.

The one thing that he did, that an entrepreneur should follow to be great

There are many things that Mark Zuckerberg has done throughout his career that have contributed to his success as an entrepreneur and businessman. However, if I had to highlight one key thing that other entrepreneurs could follow to be great today, it would be his emphasis on innovation and user-centricity.

From the early days of Facebook, Zuckerberg has been laser-focused on understanding and meeting the needs of his users. He has consistently emphasized the importance of building products that people actually want to use, rather than just trying to push out the latest technology or feature. This approach has helped Facebook to remain relevant and valuable to its users, even as the tech industry has undergone significant changes over the years.

Moreover, Zuckerberg has demonstrated a willingness to take risks and try new things in pursuit of innovation. This has led to the development of new products and features that have helped to solidify Facebook's position as a leader in the tech industry. For example, Facebook's acquisition of Instagram and WhatsApp allowed the company to expand its user base and diversify its offerings, while initiatives such as Facebook Live and Oculus VR have helped to keep the platform fresh and engaging.

In short, if you want to be a great entrepreneur today, you should focus on understanding and meeting the needs of your users, and be willing to take risks in pursuit of innovation. This approach can help you to build products that truly resonate with your target audience, and can help you to stay ahead of the curve in a constantly evolving industry.

Some additional things about Mark Zuckerberg:

Mark Zuckerberg was born on May 14, 1984, in New York. He was raised in a Jewish family and had a passion for computers and programming from a young age.

Zuckerberg attended Harvard University, where he initially pursued a degree in psychology but ultimately dropped out to focus on building Facebook full-time.

Facebook was initially launched in 2004 as a social networking site for Harvard students. It quickly expanded to other universities and eventually became available to the general public in 2006.

Zuckerberg is known for his frugal lifestyle, despite being one of the richest people in the world. He famously wears the same gray t-shirt every day and drives a modest car.

In addition to his work at Facebook, Zuckerberg has also been involved in several other philanthropic and business ventures. He and his wife Priscilla Chan founded the Chan Zuckerberg Initiative, which aims to promote social equality and improve the lives of people around the world through education, healthcare, and scientific research.

Zuckerberg has faced significant criticism over the years, particularly related to issues such as privacy, data protection, and the spread of misinformation on Facebook. He has testified before Congress and other regulatory bodies multiple times to address these concerns and has pledged to do more to protect user data and address these issues going forward.

Despite the controversies, Zuckerberg remains one of the most influential business leaders of our time. He has been recognized by numerous organizations and publications for his contributions to the tech industry and his philanthropic work.

EPILOGUE

As I bring this book to a close, I am struck by the incredible range of stories and experiences that it has contained. From ancient merchants and traders to modern-day tech giants and innovators, the individuals we have explored in these pages have left an indelible mark on the world of business and beyond.

But what strikes me most about these individuals is not their wealth or their power, but rather their resilience, their perseverance, and their willingness to take risks and pursue their dreams. Whether they were starting a small business from scratch or building a global empire, they all faced challenges and setbacks, but they never gave up.

And while each of these individuals had their own unique strengths and weaknesses, there are a few common threads that run through all of their stories. They were all driven by a sense of purpose, a desire to make a difference in the world, and a willingness to work hard and take risks in pursuit of their goals.

As we look to the future, it is clear that entrepreneurship and business will continue to play a vital role in shaping our world. The challenges we face today, from climate change to social inequality to technological disruption, will require new ideas, new approaches, and new leaders to tackle them. And I have no doubt that the entrepreneurs and businessmen of tomorrow will rise to the occasion, just as their predecessors did.

So as we close the book on these 100 remarkable individuals, let us remember their stories, their achievements, and their legacies. Let us learn from their successes and their failures, their strengths and their weaknesses, and let us use those lessons to shape a better future for ourselves and for generations to come.

GOOD LUCK

Made in the USA
Columbia, SC
03 May 2023